PARK, RECREATION & LEISURE FACILITIES SITE PLANNING GUIDELINES

by:

GEORGE E. FOGG, FASLA

Published by
National Recreation & Park Association

ISBN 0-9758926-5-7
First Printing 2005

CREDITS AND THANKS

Much of *Park, Recreation and Leisure Facilities Site Planning Guidelines* is based on the various editions of *Park Planning Guidelines*, which, in turn, was based on a manual written by this author entitled *State Park Planning Guidelines*. It was a manual for the various professionals planning Pennsylvania's State Parks. The material in the earliest versions of *Park Planning Guidelines* was contributed to by members of Pennsylvania's former Department of Forests and Waters, Bureau of State Parks, Division of Planning and Development.

Data for this book has been secured from the several sources listed in the bibliography, as well as the continued observations and designs of the author and the contributing authors. The National Recreation and Park Association, through its continuous support, has helped make this book possible. Without the continued interest of the users in the author's various books, however, the writing and publishing of this book would not have been undertaken.

The author wishes to expressly thank the following for their efforts and participation in the development of *Park, Recreation and Leisure Facilities Site Planning Guidelines:* Doug Eckmann, PE (utilities and engineering), Wayne Hook, ASLA (golf courses), Michael W. Fogg (whitewater boating, canoeing, biking, and skiing), Dennis Pagen for his preparation of the material on hang gliding and paragliding, Ben Johnson for his input on skate/bike park design, and the National Off-Highway Vehicle Conservation Council for its considerable assistance on Chapter 10, Off-Highway Vehicles. Photographs were contributed by my family and friends, including the Fethke family, Mark Anderson, Michael Fogg, Stanley Fogg, the Parrish family, Thomas Brooks, and Louise Rowland.

As you can see, Thomas Brooks has done a great job in laying out the book and producing over 285 computer-generated drawings. Thanks also to Christian Andrea of Architectural Land Design, his boss, for allowing Thomas to work on the book with me.

Finally, I would like to thank my family and friends for their support and help in providing that one more photo or one more needed piece of information. To my wife Rebecca goes very special thanks for her help, encouragement, translation of my handwriting, and her untold hours of typing, proofing, and editing.

Rebecca, Thomas, and I hope that we have provided you with a useful book.

TABLE OF CONTENTS

INTRODUCTION

Parks, recreation, and leisure time facilities are provided by various public, quasi-public, and private agencies and companies for use during people's leisure time. It is important to understand, when contemplating the development of a leisure facility, that each individual's leisure time is currently being used for something (fishing, going to parties, watching TV, surfing the net, computer game playing, bicycling, art classes, doing crossword puzzles, tourism, going to cultural events, etc.).

The primary potential patrons for any new or expanded leisure time facilities and programs are a result of increases in population in the service area and/or increases in the amount of leisure time held by the existing population. Population increases in most developed, industrialized countries or portions thereof are generally due to immigration from other countries and migration from other in-country areas. In the U.S. this is generally not increased numbers of children. Any migration of people, of course, has a corresponding opposite effect on the area being left.

Leisure time for most segments of the population is not, and probably will not be, increasing in the foreseeable future. Areas with increasing numbers of older people, however, are the exception. Most older people have significantly more leisure time than other segments of the population. People in most developed countries have increasing life spans due to better health. The rapidly increasing percentage of the population over-55 segment of any society will have a significantly, greater impact on the numbers and kinds of leisure facilities than other population groups. This increase in older participants will have a corresponding impact on the kinds of leisure facilities and programs needed.

If an existing park is to be rebuilt or expanded, or if a new park facility is being proposed, careful consideration should be given to who is going to use the facilities and where are these users coming from. Are you competing with other already established leisure time patterns in the facilities' service area. *A Site Design and Management Process* by this author and published by the National Recreation and Park Association will be useful when approaching this aspect of preparing a development program and the subsequent design of the proposed park, recreation or leisure time facility.

Park, Recreation and Leisure Facilities Site Planning Guidelines is intended to provide information on the physical aspects of planning, primarily on medium- to large-scale facilities and, especially, resource-oriented projects. This book, which replaces *Park Planning Guidelines 3rd Edition*, includes new information gathered since 1990, and includes information useful for smaller and more recreation-oriented facilities. New chapters have been added on Off-Highway Vehicle Recreation Facilities, Major Tourism Facilities, Minor Tourism Facilities, and Site Management Planning. New sections have been added to previous chapters on Retention Areas, Reduced Chemical Use Through Design, Motorized/OHV Trails and Facilities, Street Biking, Paragliding, Skateboarding, Rollerblading, Trick Biking, Disc Golf, Snorkeling, Dog Parks, Equestrian Campgrounds, OHV Campgrounds, Accessibility, Water Play Areas, Water Skiing, "Audubon" -type Golf Courses, Ski Boarding, Noise Control, and Sub or Secondary Service Areas. Personal observations, new research, and available reference information have been incorporated into this text. A special emphasis has been placed on accessibility, sustainability, and environmental aspects of projects throughout the book. The text has been expanded by 30± percent, and 50± new drawings have been added to bring the total to over 300. All previous drawings have been updated, computerized, and had color added. All of the photographs have been replaced and are now in color.

The sources from which data were gathered are footnoted and shown in the bibliography. Unfortunately, there is still little research and documentation available on the physical aspects of leisure facility planning. Data developed by a number of agencies and organizations, plus the Commonwealth of Pennsylvania's Department of Environmental Resources' Bureau of State Parks, is used at the beginning of each applicable chapter. There are other activities that could have been included, but there was insufficient information or too little use at this time to consider them, i.e., paint ball, hot air ballooning, etc.

This resource book cannot assure good design or plans. It does present, however, practical information on many of the components necessary to plan leisure facilities for people. To make full use of the material, it is necessary to conduct a thorough, in-depth study of the facility site and its setting in the surrounding region. Such a study must include, among other items, information and analysis of soils, geology, hydrology, climatology, ecology, cultural features, history, vegetation, archaeology, utilities, and site access. Please refer to the Summary of the *Site Design and Management Process* that has been included at the end of this introduction.

Planners and managers should consider several alternatives to achieving the goals set for the resource use. They should question the end results and the side effects of the proposed project. In particular, they must look at the requirements for operating and maintaining the facility. New approaches, ideas, and concepts, which might solve problems not adequately handled through existing and/or conventional techniques, should be investigated, not only for the development phase but, more importantly, for reducing ongoing operations and maintenance costs, including vandalism.

If it is concluded that a specific activity is necessary, the question should be asked, "Is it necessary within this project or the project boundaries?" If the development is necessary, it should not exceed the capacity of the land's resources to sustain use without deterioration. Basically, the greater the number of users, the greater the management effort that will be needed (staff and dollars) to maintain a quality facility. It should be clearly understood that these planning guidelines are just that – guidelines. The information presented should not be used as final answers to a project's development, but rather as a point of departure for innovative and imaginative design solutions.

There are many steps to be taken in the design and development and ongoing site management of a park, recreation, or leisure facility. The following is a summary of these steps, which are explained in detail in *A Site Design and Management Process.*

SUMMARY OF THE SITE DESIGN AND MANAGEMENT PROCESS

STEP

1 **RESEARCH**
This is one of the primary areas where *Park, Recreation and Leisure Facilities Site Planning Guidelines* information is most useful.
- Activities and their needed space
- Citizen Participation

2 **REGIONAL ANALYSIS**
Data on off-site surroundings that may affect the site and/or program.

3 **SITE ANALYSIS**
Site specific information – this guides where, what and how much development can take place.
- Built Facilities
  - Archaeological
  - Historical
  - Cultural
- Natural Environment
- Climatic Conditions (including both macro and micro climate)

4 **PROGRAMMING & RELATIONSHIPS**
Shown in graphic and/or in written form:
- What is to be built,
- Who will be served,
- How many people will be served,
- What are the space requirements, and what are the relationships between elements.

5 FUNCTIONAL ANALYSIS – SHOWN IN WRITTEN AND GRAPHIC FORM

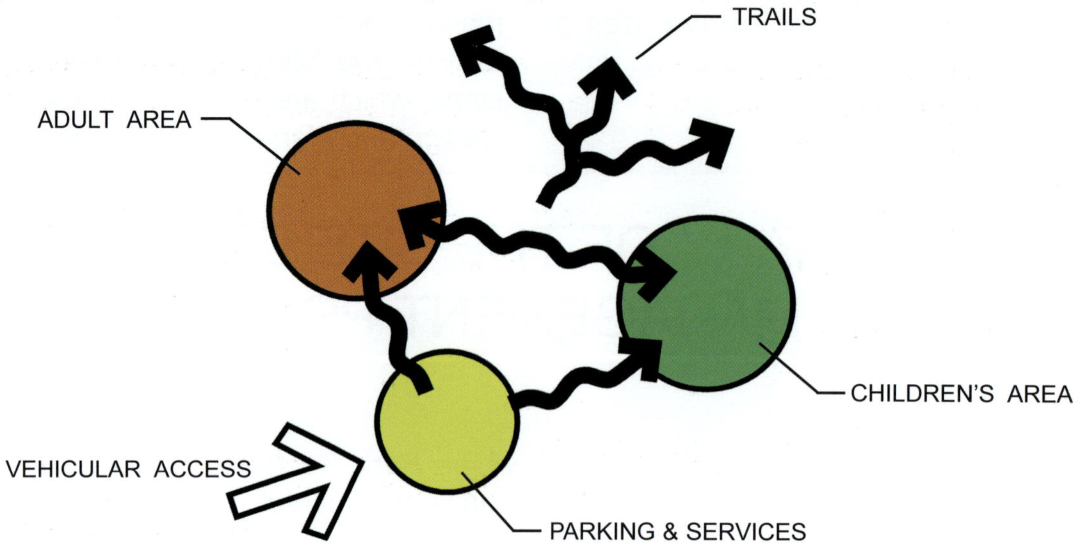

Fig. 1.1 – A typical bubble diagram

6 COMBINE SITE AND FUNCTION

The combining of Functional Analysis with the Site Analysis and participant input.

7 LAND USE

Develop a conceptual land use plan.

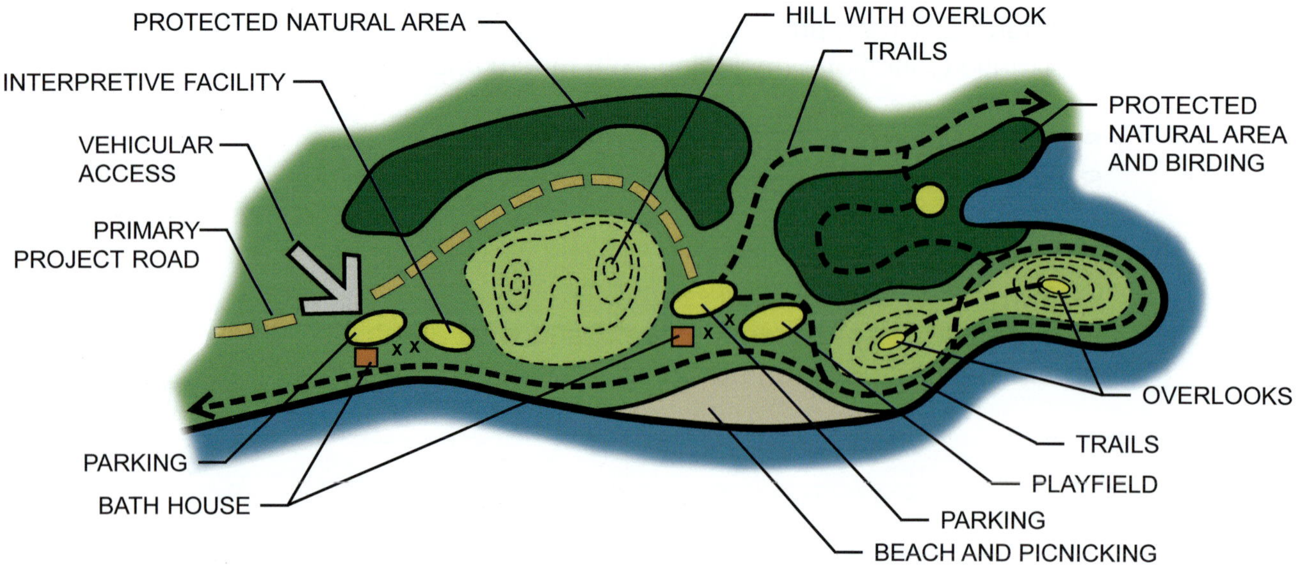

Fig. 1.2 – Schematic land use concept

8 **SITE PLAN/OVERALL DESIGN**
This is the second area where the contents of this book can be very helpful.

Concentrates on the translation of the land use concept into the desired design style concept or effect within the capabilities and constraints of the site. Participant input needed.

9 **CONSTRUCTION DOCUMENTS AND THE BIDDING PROCESS**
Contract Plans, Specifications, Bidding, and Award of Contracts.

10 **CONSTRUCTION**
Building the facility.

11 **REVIEW AND FEEDBACK** (Post Construction Evaluation)
After the park has been opened and in use, see if the project does what it is suppose to do. Include in your review analysis of both the visitor satisfaction and the site's physical aspects, both built and natural

12 **PREPARATION OF A MANAGEMENT PLAN**
This document is perhaps the most important in the site design process. It describes, in written and graphic form, how the park, recreation and leisure facilities are to be operated and maintained.

Chapter 1

METHODS FOR DETERMINING VISITOR DEMAND

One of the first steps in planning facilities for any park, recreation or leisure project is determining the visitor demand. That is, who the projected visitors are and what do they want, how many are likely to use the facility, and when they will come. From this starting point, the data must be refined to provide the design load (the actual numbers) and their characteristics for the present and projected for future years to permit the proper kind of facilities and phasing of the development.

Crowds of people at the International Jazz Festival – Molde, Norway

A low-use time at Audubon's Corkscrew Sanctuary – Collier County, Florida

The following are two of the best methods for the estimation of recreation demand, which have been successfully used by this author on many projects. The success of each method depends, of course, on the relative accuracy of the input data.

MAXIMUM CARRYING CAPACITY METHOD

When a project is to be located in an area of probable heavy use, the capacity of the land to sustain the proposed use without deterioration of the resource should be determined. This method assumes a thorough and comprehensive site analysis by knowledgeable professionals. (See *A Site Design and Management Process*, Chapter 4.)

The maximum carrying capacity method should be considered for all parks in urban areas. Effective utilization of this approach is dependent on a corresponding analysis of the potential park users and an inventory of the regional leisure time services currently available and the level of their use. This is necessary in order to be able to develop a realistic program of the kinds of facilities needed. Without the knowledge and understanding of what people need/want in a park, even new urban parks may be underused.

COMPARABLE DEMAND METHOD

This methodology is particularly useful if there are similar projects available for comparison.

One or more existing recreation resources are selected to be, as close as possible, comparable to the resource under consideration. Expected recreation use at the proposed resource is computed by analogy with the existing, comparable project(s)

The process of analogy involves several steps.

1. Determine the population of the travel time zones around the proposed park and the existing park(s) being used for comparison.

    For smaller scale projects, the service area may only have one service "zone," which may be defined by walking distance and/or biking distance. This may result in a more homogeneous user group and can lead to a very clear, focused development program.

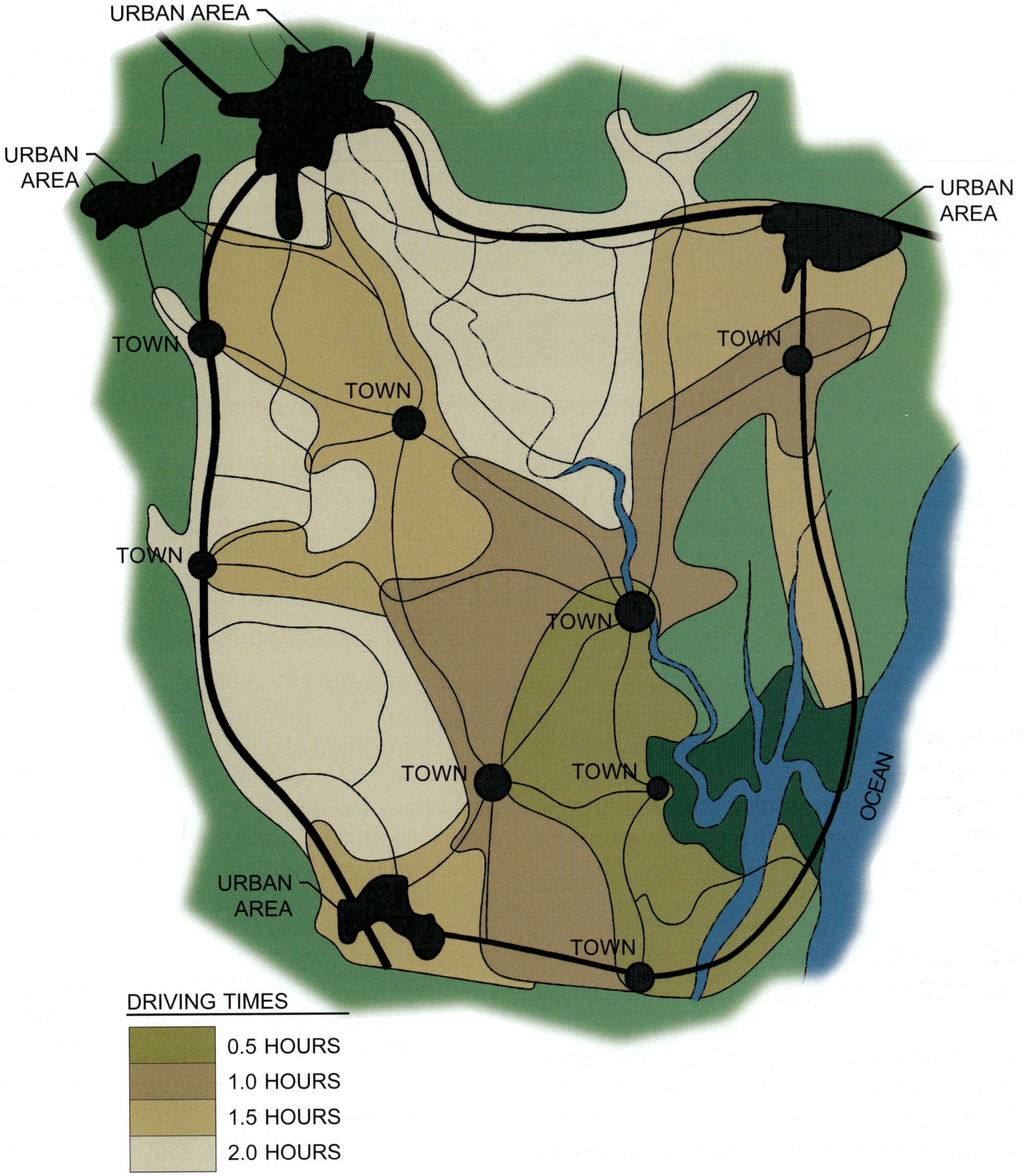

FIG. 1.1 – SERVICE AREA – LARGE-SCALE PARK
Maps from A Site Design and Management Process by George E. Fogg. Please refer to this book for further details on "service area."

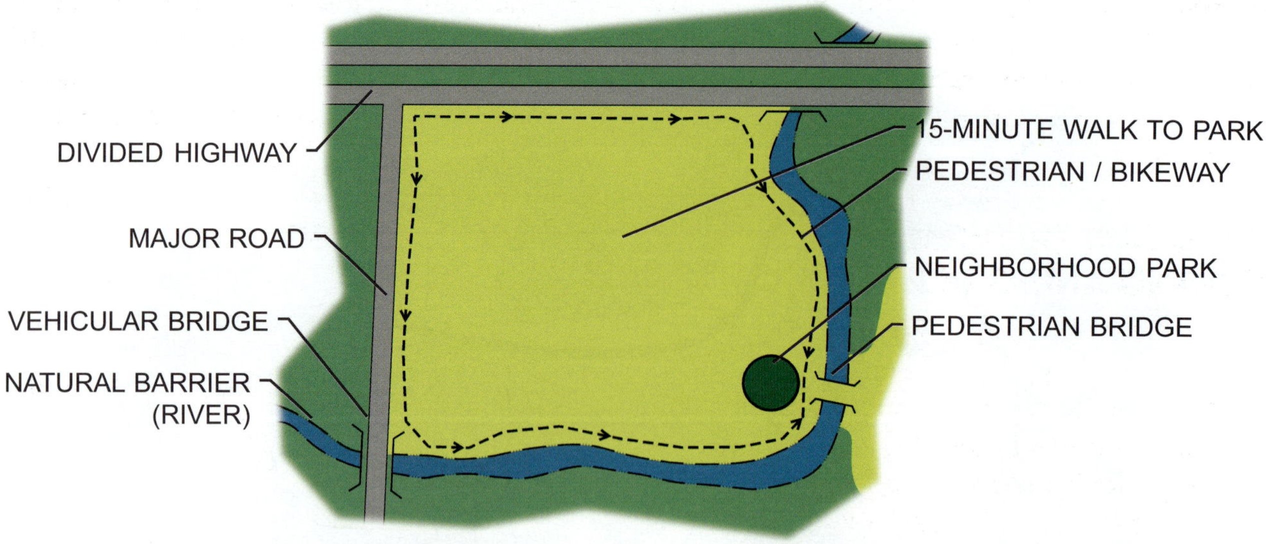

FIG. 1.2 SERVICE AREA – NEIGHBORHOOD PARK FOR CHILDREN AND SPECIAL USER GROUPS

2. Determine the per capita use at the existing comparable project(s) area from the total population served and attendance figures from the comparison park(s).

Check attendance trends in the park(s) and population trends in the proposed service area and, if possible, the various time zones. If specific activity use figures are available, an even more accurate projection tailored to the specific proposed program would be possible.

Example

150,000 population within one-half hour's driving time of the facility (the area served by the neighborhood park) and 10,000 within 10 minute's walk – number of users is 1,500 on a maximum day or a per day, per capita use of 0.01 within the ½ hour's drive and as high as 0.15 within walking distance of, say, 3/4± mile.

3. After establishing a ratio using the population and attendance of the existing park(s), apply this to the proposed park, which will give a projected attendance for the new facility.

Example

If the population in the proposed park's one-half hour service area is 100,000, then the number of users would be 100,000 x 0.01, or 1,000, plus the additional walk-in users 1,500 x 0.15 or 225. This brings the total to 1,225± likely users

4. Adjust the figures to account for the influence of existing and proposed recreation developments in the zone of influence. Also, the figures would be adjusted, possibly significantly, if the access is improved, e.g., new bridge across a river or a new safe pedestrian crossing over a major highway, etc.

$$\frac{\text{Actual Use (in surrounding comparable facilities)}}{\text{Population in the various service areas}} = \text{per capita use}$$

The reliability of this method depends largely upon the degree of comparability between the two resources, both as to intrinsic recreation potential and as to distribution and type(s) of population.

FACILITIES DETERMINE DEMAND AND/OR LEADERS DETERMINE DEMAND

It is believed by some resource researchers, planners, and this author that the provision of recreation facilities themselves and/or, more probably, recreation leaders themselves, can create visitor demand. Another mitigating factor is the quality of the facilities and their maintenance. This is particularly true for organized sports and other supervised activities. There is no way of effectively calculating the increased or, in some cases, decreased number.

DETERMINATION OF VISITOR DAY CAPACITIES

Most large parks can be reached only by car. Therefore, the daily capacity of these parks can generally be determined by multiplying the number of cars the project can accommodate times the average turnover rate times the number of people per car. It should be clearly understood that a visitor day usually consists of more than one activity day. A typical visitor to a picnic area will also participate in other activities, such as playing ball, throwing a Frisbee, going on a hike, going fishing, etc. In Pennsylvania in the 1970s, the average was 2.2 activity days/visitor days. In other words, the visitor did, on average, over two activities for each visit, i.e., picnicking and swimming or swimming and shelling, etc. There is no available information on how this number has changed over the years.

Formula

Number of cars + turnover x's number of people/car = daily capacity.

Example

1000 cars + 0.05 turnover =
50 cars would use the facility or 1050 cars

1050 x 1.8 (number of people per car) =
1,890 people per day

It should be noted that if space permitted and use (people turned away) indicated, capacity could be increased by increasing the number of parking spaces. This may also necessitate increasing other site facilities.

In neighborhood parks, play areas, etc., the number of walk- and bike-ins would be a significant additional number of users.

Type of Activity	No. of People per Car (Summer)*	Average Turnover Rate**
Sightseeing	2.5	Variable 1 – 10 or more
Family Picnic	2.5	1.0 to 1.5
Family Camping	2.5	1.0
Group Picnic	3.0	1.0
Group Camping	3.0	1.0
Boat Ramp	1.8	1.0 to 20
Freshwater Beach/Pool Access	2.5	2.0 (for pool or beach only – not for multi-use beach/ picnic, etc. areas)
Coastal Beach Areas	1.8	1.3 to 15
Boat Concession	1.5	2.0
Overlook	2.5	Variable 1 - 10 or more
Golf (During main use season)	1.5	1.3 Private 2.0 Public – max
Restaurant	2.5	4.0
Stables	1.2	2.0 to 3.0
Equestrian Area	1.2	1.0
Fishing	1.2	1.0
Hiking	1.5	1.0 to 1.5 (depending on the trail length)

FIG. 1.3 – AVERAGE NUMBER OF PEOPLE PER CAR

* The average number of people/car used here was determined by limited sample counts conducted by the author. The number of people in a vehicle entering a park or special-use facility were counted and divided by the number of vehicles. This figure has decreased from 3.5 in the 1960s to 1.8± in 2000-2003, and probably will continue to vary with changes due to cost of travel, car size and type, and family composition. The number of people per party is frequently much larger than the number of people/car indicating that there is more than one car per party.

** Judgment should be used in applying turnover factors since little data is available to substantiate these turnover rates. These numbers still have not been accurately verified but are the best available.

ANNUAL CAPACITY

The annual capacity of a park can be determined by multiplying the daily capacity by the number of capacity days per year. Each area of the country has a different number of capacity days per year per facility. In Central Atlantic States, a typical park might enjoy fifty capacity days of use determined as follows: three days of use per week (40 percent during the week, 20 to 25 percent on Saturday, and 35 to 40 percent on Sunday) x 13 weeks summer season + 30 percent off-season use (3 x 13 + 30 percent = 51). In milder areas there might be as many as 100 capacity days, while in colder climates only 40 days. These figures must be adjusted to take into consideration differences in traveling time, variety and kinds of facilities and local weather.

Example

(People / day x number of capacity day/year) + off-season use = Annual use

(2,940 x 50) + 30% =
147,000 + 44,100 =
191,000 People / year would use the park

Float trip at the put-in point on the Colorado River – Grand Canyon National Park

Chapter 2

VISITOR DATA TRENDS

The number and type of activities at a given leisure area vary over the year. Cool weather (for much of the northern hemisphere in spring) is high in sightseeing, bird watching and bird migrations, hiking, and fishing; fall is high in hunting and fall foliage viewing. Warmer (summer) weather is high in picnicking, water skiing, boating and swimming-related activities; and, colder weather (winter) is the time for skiing, ice fishing, skating, and snowmobiling, etc. In warmer climates, such as southeastern Texas, Florida, southern California, and Arizona, the winter tourist season becomes the heavy use time.

• Outdoor Recreation in America stated in its 2001 survey that there were increasing participation rates in some activities; in particular, wildlife viewing, hiking, running, and power boating but, overall, there was a decrease in participation frequency. This could mean a change in some leisure areas facilities and programs and, possibly, a reduction in the number of users. (31)

• Cost-sensitive activities are skiing, golfing, OHV riding, and bicycling. (34)

Seasonal use varies

"Off-season" use (fall) – Naples, FL

"In-season" use (winter) – Naples, FL

• Length of stay in day-use areas averages approximately 3 to 5 hours. With facilities that are closer to peoples' homes, the visitors may stay a shorter length of time, three to four hours. A typical resource user may experience a five- to six-hour stay; sightseeing would only be about 3 hours. Sundays average one-half hour longer than the remainder of the week.

• Length of stay for camping is three days and two nights. [11] This activity usually occurs on weekends – Friday p.m. through Sunday p.m.

• Numbers of day-use visitors per car will vary between Sunday and all others – spring, fall, summer, and winter. These numbers are trending downward with peak use now averaging below 2 people per car.

• The average day-use party size has been declining steadily over the last several years from 6.7 in 1971 to 4.35 in 1977 (4.06 on week days and 4.80 on weekends). This is higher than the average car capacity, 1.8±. [11] There has been a steady decline in the number of people per car from a high of 4.0 in 1965 to 2.82 in 1979, and 1.8 in 2004. It is projected that this figure will or has been leveled off at approximately 1.8 people per car.

• Park satisfaction increases with age. [11]

• Transportation is a significant limitation to non drivers' attending parks, recreation, and leisure facilities at greater than walking/biking distance from their home or starting point. [11]

• The major reason people do not attend parks is the availability of a person's leisure time. Over 90 percent of all people who say they would like to attend parks more often do not do so because, according to them, they do not have the time. [12]

• Wildlife viewing is a year-round activity, which usually peaks when the desired objects to be viewed are present in their greatest numbers (the migratory season for each species). Bird watching continues to increase in popularity. [29]

There are ten to twelve activities that account for most recreation time for non-organized recreation type users: camping, hiking, picnicking, relaxing, sightseeing/pleasure driving, historic and archaeological viewing, swimming, sunbathing, and wildlife viewing (birds, animals, plants). Wildlife-related viewing and learning is one of the growth areas, both as primary and secondary activities, and may surpass, in some areas, other more traditional leisure activities.

In the teenage bracket, the activities rank in this order: sunbathing, swimming and water play, biking, picnicking, hiking, sightseeing/pleasure driving, tourism, camping, relaxing, fishing, and nature study. [11, 12]

In the 20-29 age bracket, the activities rank in this order: sunbathing, nature walk/study, camping, sightseeing/pleasure driving, tourism, biking, swimming/water-related sports, picnicking, relaxing, walking/hiking, and fishing. [11, 12]

In the 30-44 age bracket, the activities rank in this order: camping, fishing, relaxing, hiking/walking, swimming/water-related sports, picnicking, sightseeing/pleasure driving, tourism, nature study walk, biking, and sunbathing. [11, 12]

In the 45-64 age bracket, the activities rank in this order: fishing, biking, relaxing, walking/hiking, picnicking, nature study, sightseeing/pleasure driving, tourism, swimming and water-related activities, sunbathing, and camping. [11, 12]

In the 65+ age bracket, the activities rank in this order: nature study, sightseeing/pleasure driving, tourism, fishing, walking/hiking, relaxing, picnicking, camping, biking, sunbathing, swimming and water-related activities. [11, 12]

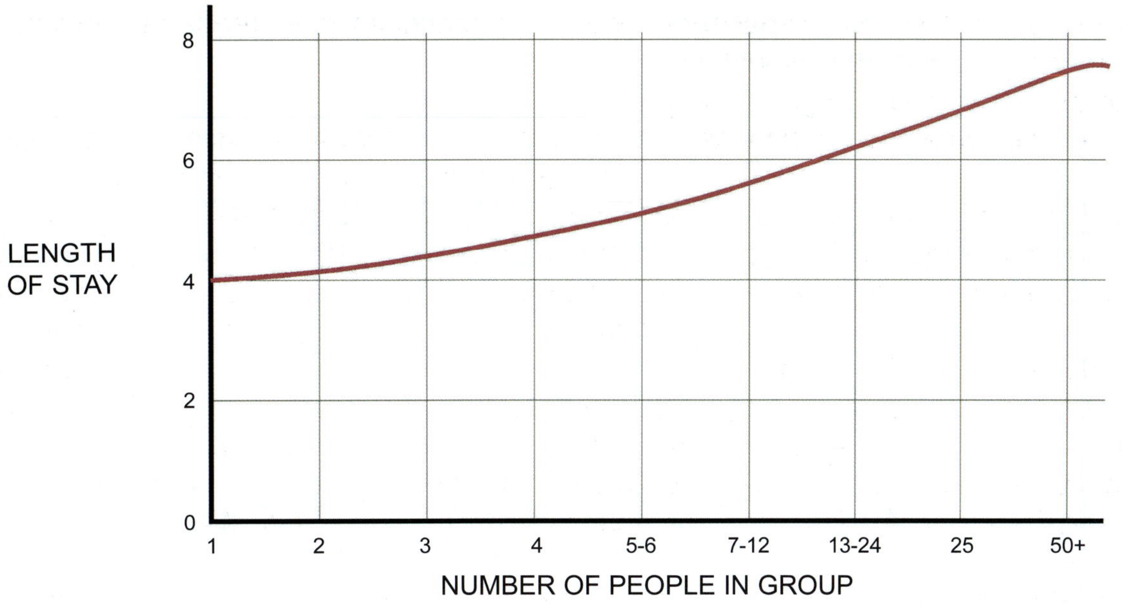

FIG. 2.1 – GROUP SIZE AND LENGTH OF STAY (GENERALIZED PATTERN)

Picnicking parties tend to be the largest – fishing and non-rental boating parties the smallest. [8]

In leisure areas with facilities designed for large group activities, longer stays and lower turnover of visitors can be expected. [8]

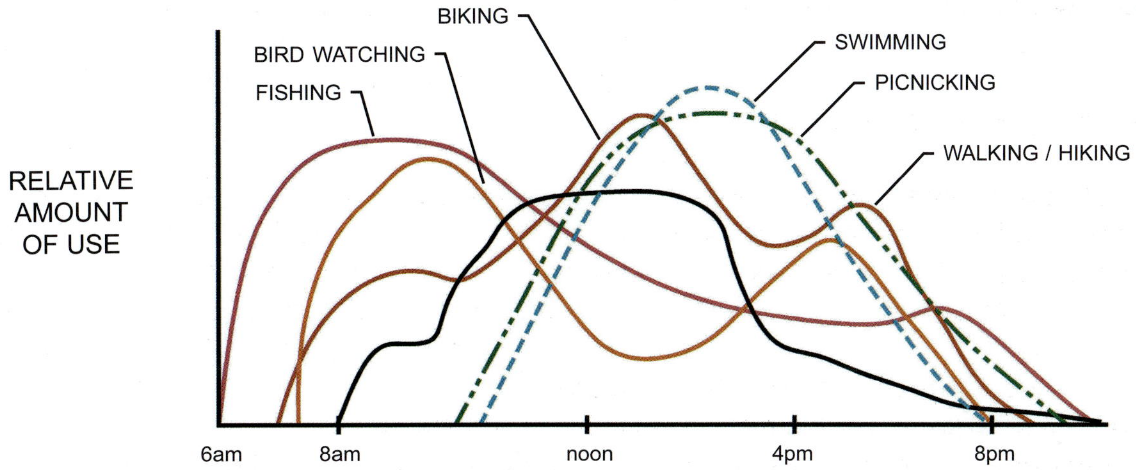

FIG. 2.2 – ACTIVITY AND TIME OF DAY (GENERALIZED PATTERN)

Swimming is strongly dependent on weather (warm and sunny), usually peaks from noon to 4:00 p.m., has the severest peaking in activity, and in a sense, the most excess capacity during the remainder of the day. Fishing, in contrast, is a relatively early-in-the-day activity and relatively unaffected by weather temperature conditions, but, in coastal areas, is dependent on tidal conditions. [8, 11] Bird watching is primarily a very early-in-the-day type of activity; dawn is frequently the best time.

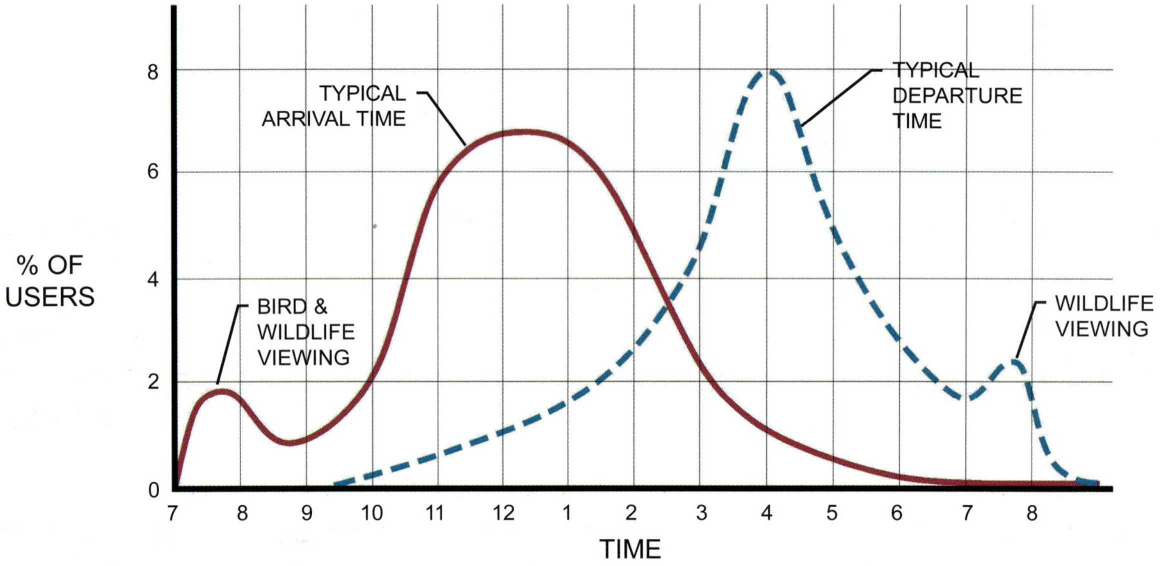

FIG. 2.3 – ARRIVAL/DEPARTURE TIMES FOR A TYPICAL RESOURCE-ORIENTED PARK ARRIVAL/DEPARTURE TIMES ARE GREATLY DEPENDENT ON THE KIND(S) OF ACTIVITY(IES) AT THE PARK

Chapter 3

PARKSCAPE

A leisure visitor experiences with all his senses. Therefore, leisure planning should enhance desirable attributes, i.e. good views, pleasant aromas, intriguing sounds, and eliminate or minimize obtrusive elements, such as views of junkyards, sewage plant odors, highway noise, etc.

ENHANCEMENT OF DESIRABLE ATTRIBUTES

The visual environment is of major importance to most leisure facility users. Coordinating all aspects of the project development can enhance this visual experience. All elements, both natural and project-related, should enhance the resource either by blending with it or improving it. Some areas to be considered are:

1. Planned sequences of visual experiences for all roads and trails that are used by the visitors.

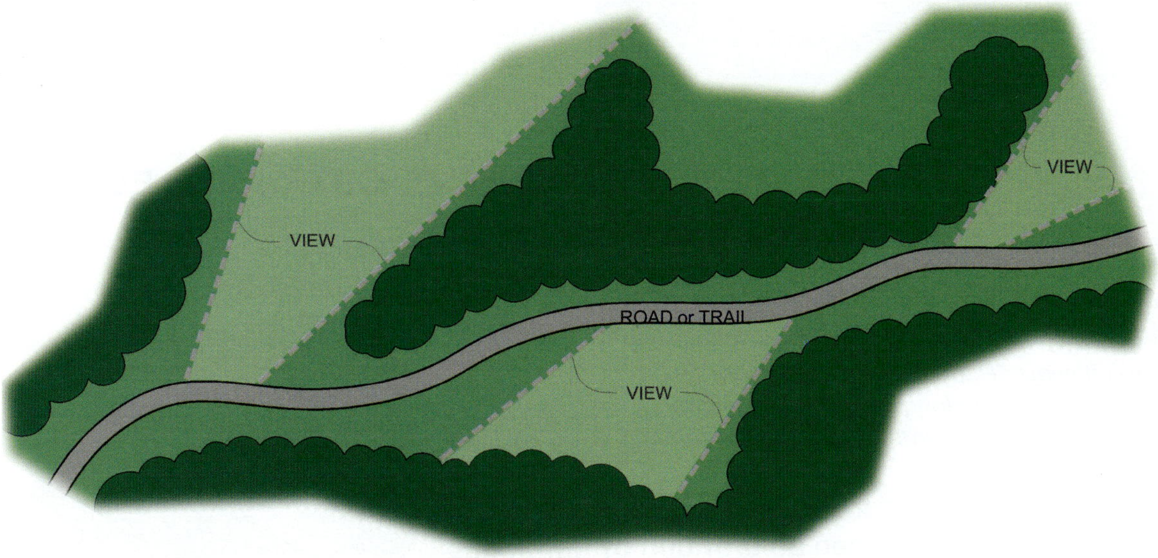

FIG. 3.1 – A PLANNED SEQUENCE OF VIEWS
(See Chapter 11 "Roads and Parking")

2. Plantings that will harmonize with existing vegetation. Wherever possible, native plant material should be used in rural and natural-type facilities. A proper balance of wooded and open spaces is one of the prime requisites in the overall planning of resource-related leisure facilities. The desirable amount of open space varies greatly between areas.

Photo of Tamiami Trail - Collier County, FL

3. Lands formerly used for farming and other man-controlled activities generally have straight lines of plant materials and frequently have large, unforested fields. An early planning/management decision should be made in regard to revegetation of old farm fields due to the long time needed to get effective results. In many areas of the country, open fields will, within ten years, be well on the way to reverting to forested spaces. It is, therefore, necessary to make an early decision to keep fields open or the decision will have been taken out of your hands by the natural successional growth.

Photo of Tamiami Trail - Collier County, FL

Spring flowers (Poppies) – These flower fields will remain only as long as grazing continues. No grazing, fewer flowers – Southern California

4. Odors are also important in leisure facility planning. Pleasing odors can be provided by planting (pine, other evergreens, flowering plants, etc.), and by taking advantage of existing natural elements.

5. One aspect of scenic highways is roadside vegetation. Young growth may quickly obscure views or, in reality, eliminate desirable views completely. Selective roadside pruning or grooming of roadways is often required to keep or enhance the leisure facility's positive attributes.

MINIMIZE OBTRUSIVE ELEMENTS

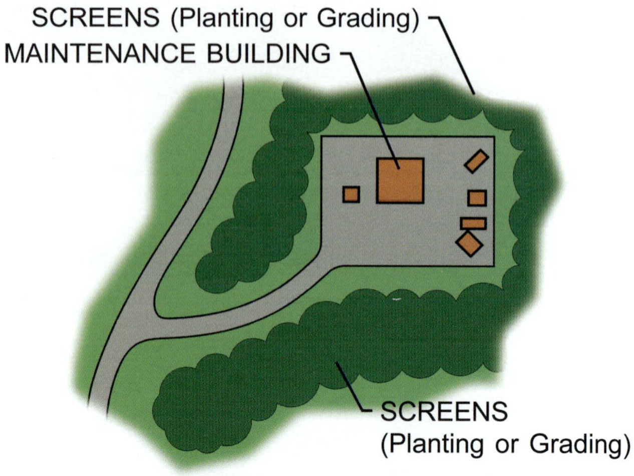

FIG. 3.2 – SCREENING

CONSIDERATION FOR NOISE ABATEMENT

Sound waves travel in a straight line.

The basic methods for noise abatement are land use planning and sound barriers.

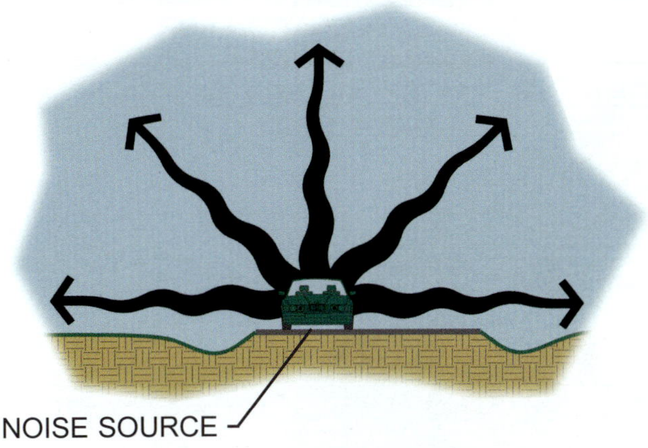

FIG. 3.3 – SOUND TRAVELS IN A STRAIGHT DIRECTION

• Land Use –

1. Noise-sensitive developments shouldbe located as distant from sources of noise as possible.

2. Noise-compatible uses, such as entrance stations, interior development roads, parking lots, the project's office and/or maintenance area, and utility lines, etc., can be placed in project areas subject to excessive noise.

3. Use buildings as sound barriers.

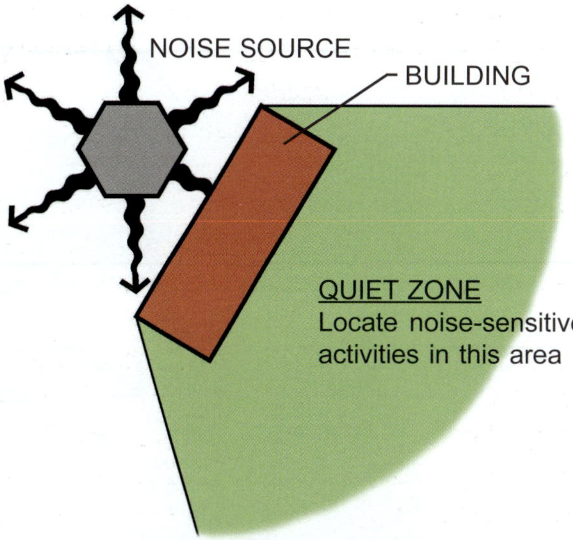

FIG. 3.4 – BUILDINGS MAKE GOOD NOISE BARRIERS

"Noise barriers can be erected between noise sources and noise-sensitive areas." Any sound abatement barriers must be solid and should be easy to maintain and aesthetically pleasing. They can be made of earth (earth berms would be typically used in a large-scale development) or constructed from concrete, wood, or other solid building materials where space is limited

Solid barriers are necessary to effectively block undesirable noises, i.e., traffic, firing ranges, and industrial areas.

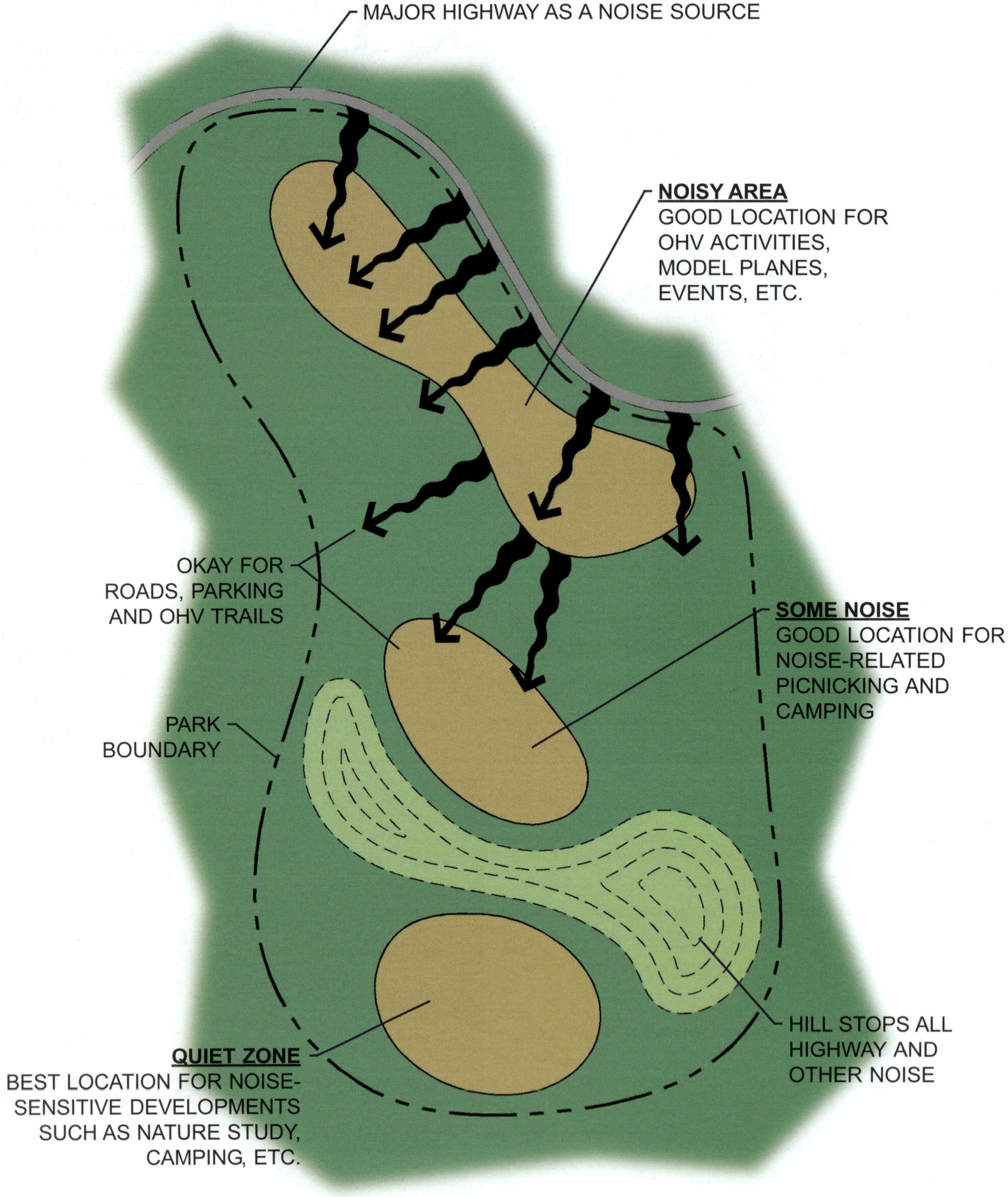

FIG. 3.5 – LOCATION OF ACTIVITIES IN RELATIONSHIP TO NOISE SOURCE(S)

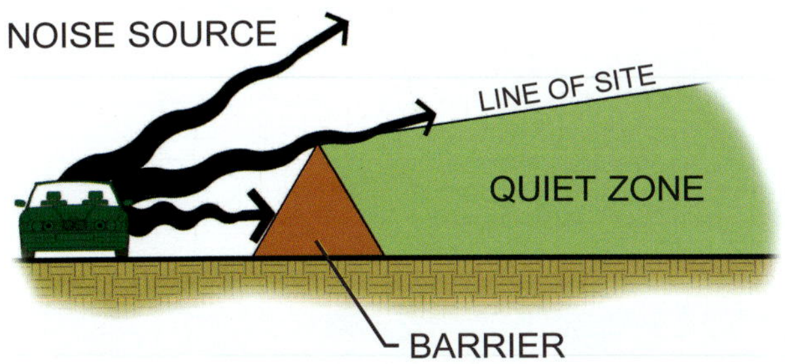

FIG. 3.6 – SECTION THROUGH A NOISE BARRIER

To be effective, a noise barrier must block the line of site. The closer the barrier to the noise source, the greater the area it will protect. [23]

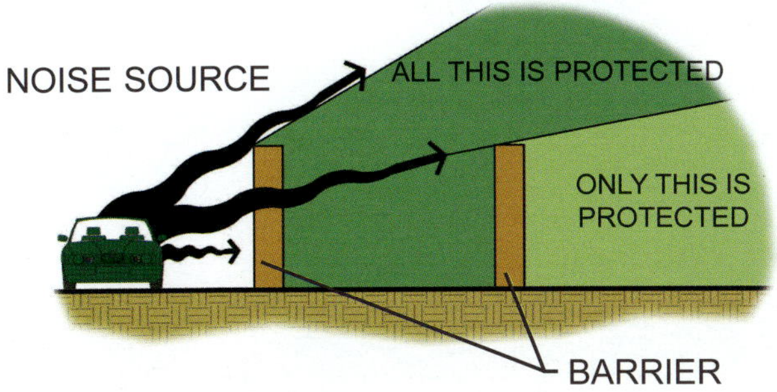

FIG. 3.7 – SECTION OF LOCATION FOR NOISE BARRIER

The use of plant material for sound reduction is of limited value with only an additional 3 to 5 dBA reduction per 100' feet (30 m) of width of dense planting likely. The main effect of planting is psychological. Basically, if you can't see the source of noise, it doesn't bother some people as much. Plant material, when used for sound abatement, is useful in conjunction only with other sound abatement techniques and, then, primarily and importantly from an aesthetic standpoint.

ODORS

Care should be taken to minimize offensive noises and odors through proper site selection, the provision of buffers, and the zoning of leisure facility uses, i.e., campgrounds should be located away from noise and offensive odors; sewage treatment plants should be downwind from all development areas, etc.

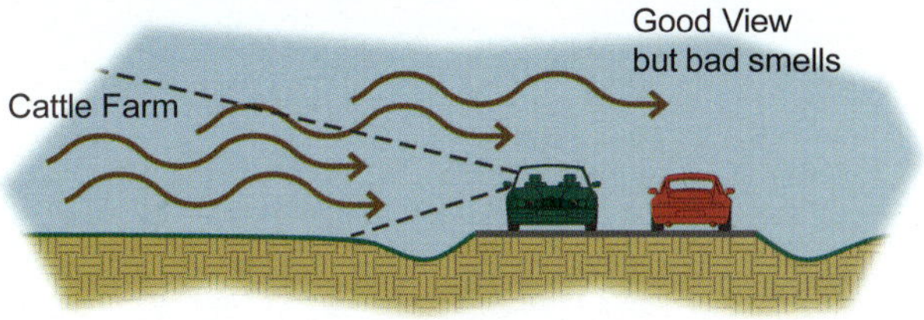

FIG. 3.8 – OFFENSIVE ODORS

Cattle grazing can be a bucolic scene or result in bad odor.

FIG. 3.9 – GOOD ODORS

Chapter 4

ENVIRONMENTALLY SENSITIVE DESIGN

The designed environment is composed of two basic interactive parts – living (plants and animals) and non-living (rocks, water, climate) – providing spaces for people.

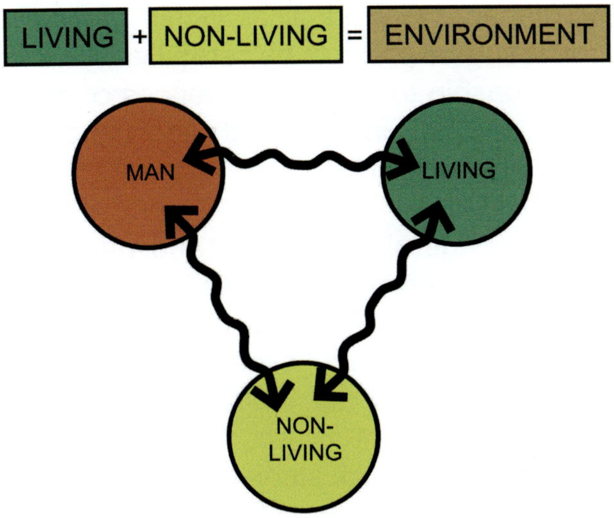

FIG. 4.1 – MAN AND THE ENVIRONMENT

Grey Heron – Scandanavia

Man is an integral part of the environment. Everything that we as people do has an impact, either positively or negatively, on the environment.

If we choose to ignore this fact, we do so at our own peril. The development of barrier islands and coastal wetlands and the removal of mangrove forests are examples of man's actions in coastal areas that have led to major natural systems problems. Every year throughout the world billions of dollars of damage and hundreds and sometimes thousands of lives are lost due to storm damage in inappropriately developed coastal areas. On the opposite end of the environmental spectrum are the destruction of vegetation in arid environments through overgrazing and the use of its vegetation for fuel. This has resulted, and continues to result, in desertification (the increase of desert lands) around the world, including the United States.

Grand Canyon

In addition to these well known natural calamities due to man's actions, there are many almost unnoticed examples of well meaning actions, which have occurred due to little things people have done that have had major impacts on the environment. One example of such actions is the importation of African bees into Brazil for experimental purposes. Since their escape in South America, they have multiplied and taken over the more docile European bees used throughout Europe and the Americas for crop pollination and the making of honey. The resulting losses in crop pollination and honey production have been substantial. A second example is the use of the Australian pine (Casuarina sp.) for windbreaks in Florida. Unfortunately, the Pine was a very successful adaptation, which has naturalized throughout the southern part of the State of Florida and is forcing out, together with two other imports (Melaleuca and Brazilian Pepper), much of the native vegetation in some areas of the state. This invasion of non-native plant material is profoundly affecting the ecology of this Southern state while similar biological invasions affect other areas of the country, i.e., gypsy moth in the Northeast, tumbleweed throughout the Western U.S., Dutch Elm disease throughout much of America, and starlings to name only a few.

Melaleuca – Lee County, FL

Parks are generally places where man and nature co-exist in harmony. They are, because of this fact, one of the prime resources for teaching the public, by example, about the man/environment interrelationship. It is, therefore, imperative that ALL development and management practices within parks and other resource projects be carefully evaluated in relationship to the consequences of man's actions for their impact, both good and bad, on the environment.

The U.S. Federal government and many state and local governmental jurisdictions have laws or rules governing the preparation of Environmental Impact Assessments (EIA) and Environmental Impact Studies (EIS) for any major development project. Some also have requirements for such studies for management actions.

An EIA is simply an analysis of the impact of a proposed action by man on the affected and surrounding environments. An EIS is a proposed course of action to be taken with the alternatives considered that must include the alternative of "no action."

Utilization of proper site planning procedures will automatically provide the necessary data with which to know the environment, the

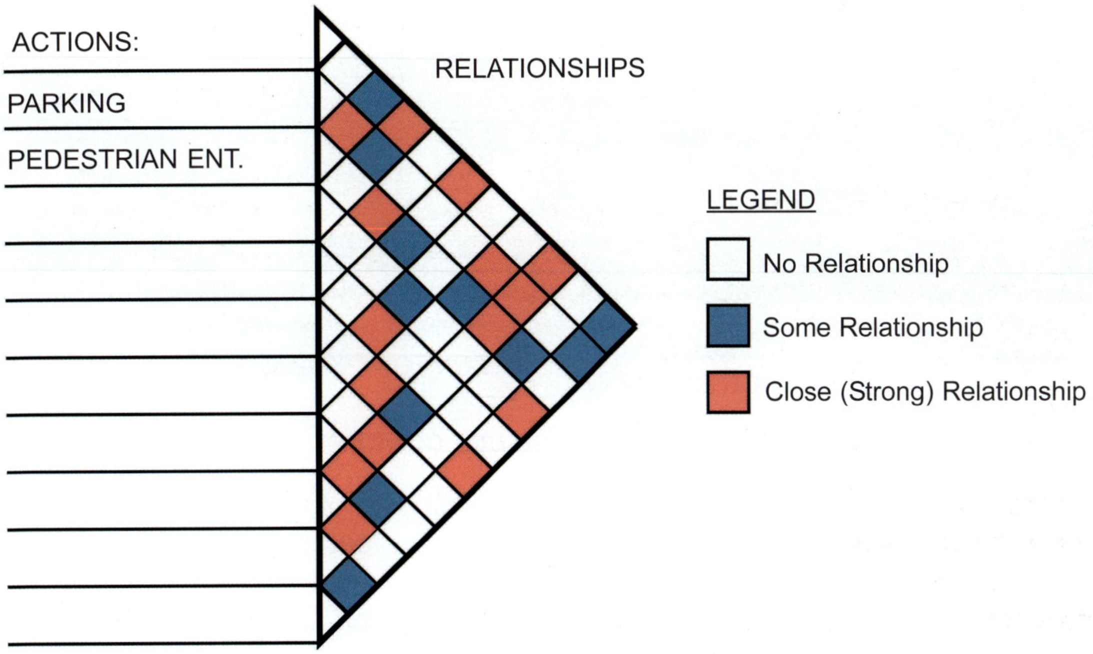

FIG. 4.2 – RELATIONSHIP DIAGRAM

use(s), and the users. (See *A Site Design and Management Process* by this author and published by the National Recreation and Park Association.) These steps are:

1. **Research** into the needs of the users and their proposed activities.

2. **Regional Analysis** – Data on off-site surrounding areas that may affect or be affected by the site.

3. **Site Analysis**, including existing manmade features (both historical and cultural), natural features (living and non-living), and climatic factors.

4. **Programming and Relationships** – What is to be built? Who is to be served? How many people? How much space do they need? The relationship between the various proposed elements should be in both written and graphic form.

5. **Functional Analysis**

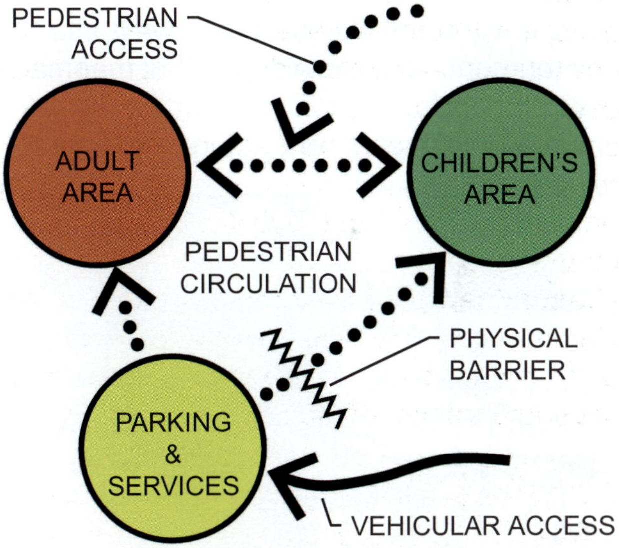

FIG. 4.3 – FUNCTIONAL ANALYSIS

6. **Land Use** – The critical step where the synthesis of the site information and user needs occurs. All too frequently, the site analysis and/or programming are disregarded, and a non workable development, either for the project's various users or the site, is the result.

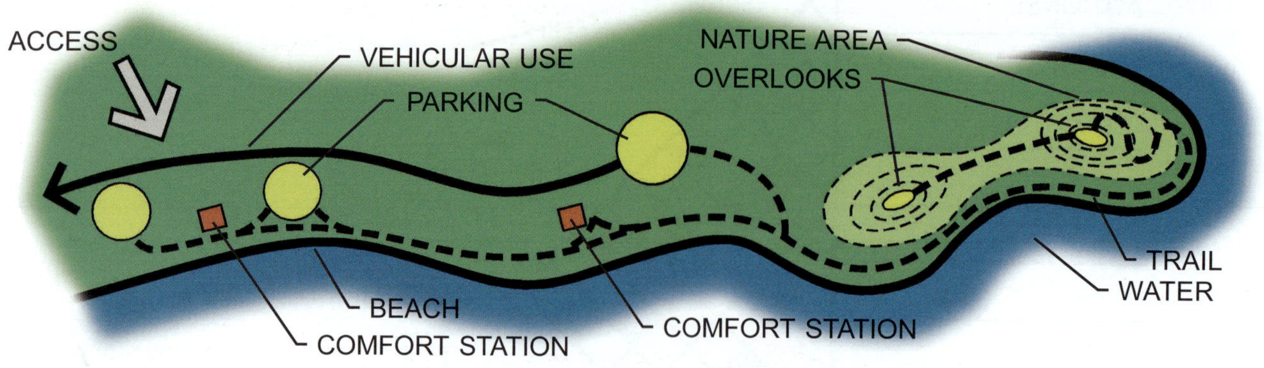

FIG. 4.4 – LAND USE CONCEPT

For more detailed information on the site planning process, please refer to *A Site Design and Management Process* as previously referenced.

The Environmentally-Sensitive Design title of this chapter infers that design and development of manmade features should fit, in an environmentally-sensitive way, into the environment. It acknowledges that manmade development is necessary, but further indicates that man must work with nature, not fight it.

Large regional park - Eastern England

Some factors that must be considered in all projects and, especially, in environmentally-sensitive developments, are:

- Disposal of sewage
  - can it be treated and reused?
  - on-site
  - off-site

- Protection of environmentally sensitive areas, such as primary andsecondary dunes at beach areas.

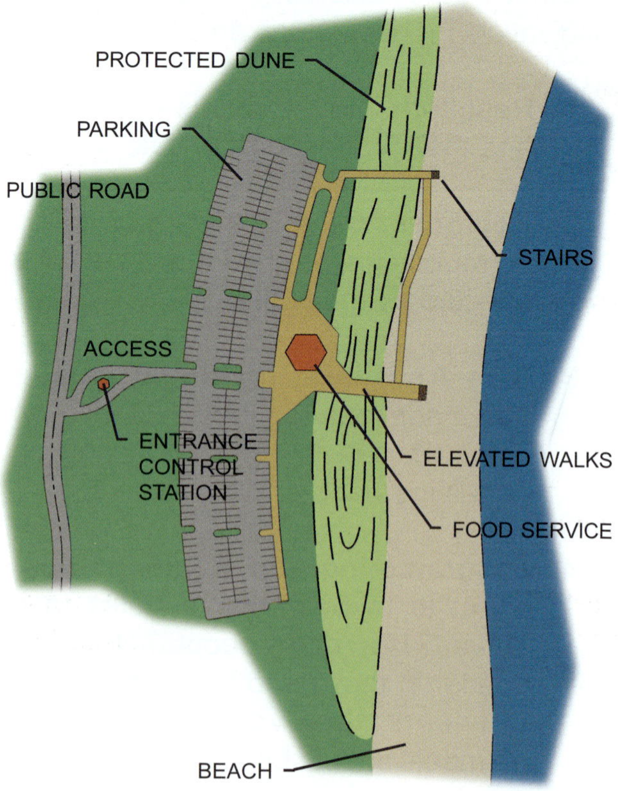

FIG. 4.5 – COASTAL DEVELOPMENT

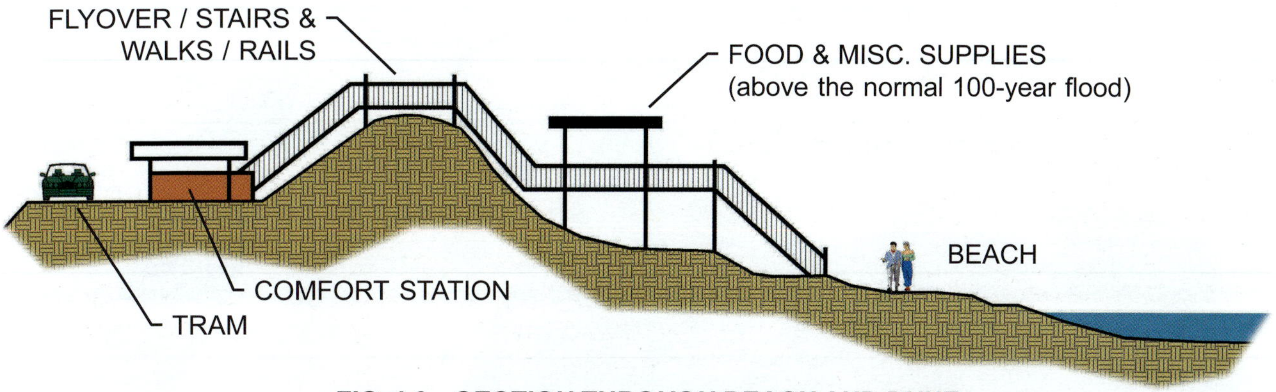

FIG. 4.6 – SECTION THROUGH BEACH AND DUNE

• Use of elevated boardwalks in wet areas and swamps. See Chapter 8, Trails and Pathways for additional information.

Boardwalk – Audubon Sanctuary
Collier County, FL

• Securing detailed topographic information so that parking lots, buildings, and other physical developments will fit the land, not change it.

• Retention on site, generally in informal basins, of surface water run-off generated by the development.

Retention Area – Conner Park
Collier County, FL

Porous Pavement – Sugden Park
Collier County, FL

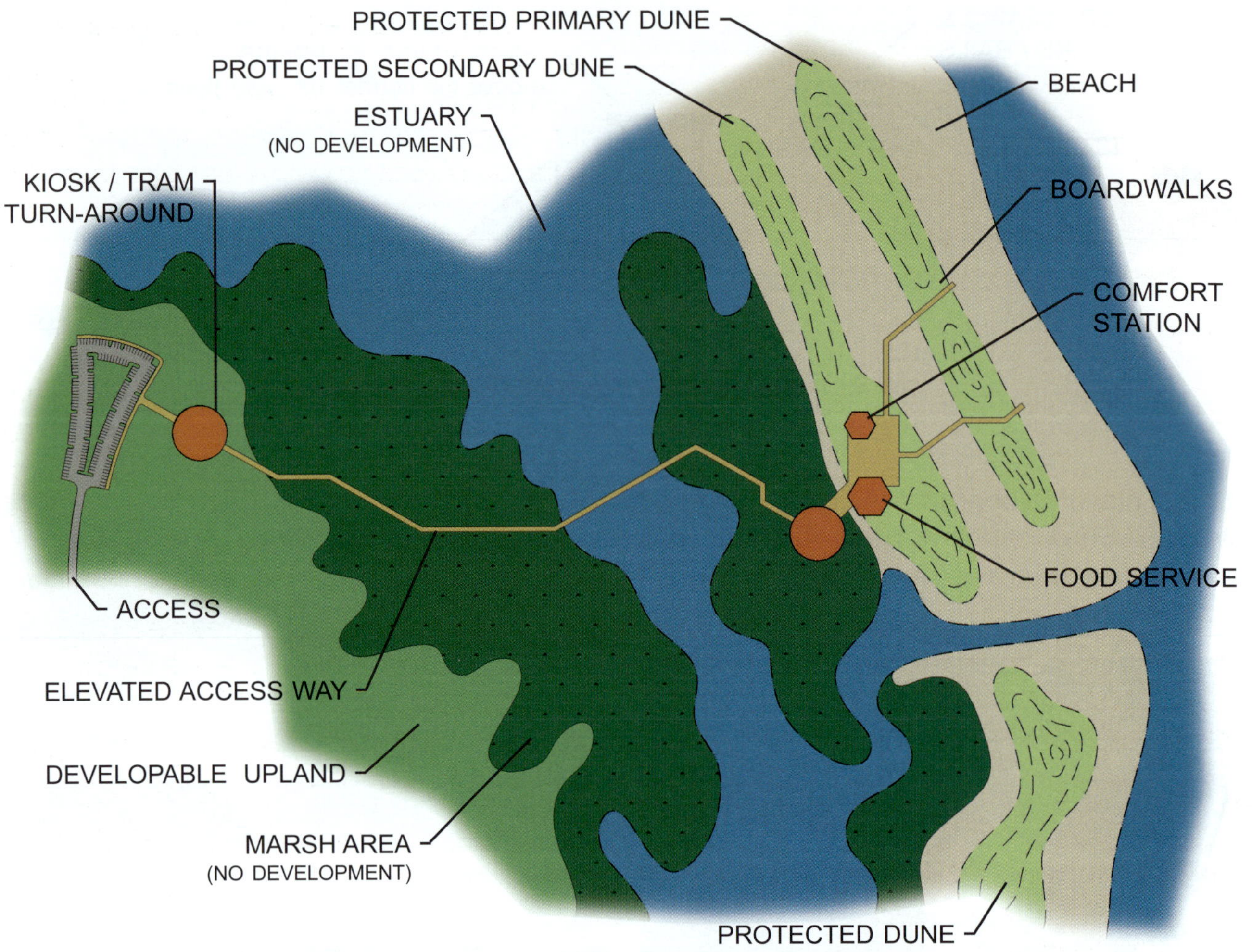

FIG. 4-7 – SCHEMATIC ENVIRONMENTALLY-SENSITIVE BEACH DEVELOPMENT

• Use of porous pavements, where possible, to permit water to penetrate to the aquifer. See Chapter 10, Roads and Parking for additional details.

• Use of xeriscape practices, i.e., grouping of plants with like cultural and, in particular, water requirements. This is especially important in the desert, arid, and semi-arid environments, and those areas where supplemental watering is commonly done. Wherever possible, material that will grow in the selected environment without additional water being required for their maintenance should be used. This usually means minimizing the use of turf where irrigation will almost always, to some extent, be required.

Native grasses along walkway at birding site – Eastern England. No care needed.

• Provision of educational displays and exhibits to help people understand their environment and how man affects the environment by his actions. (See Chapter 7, Interpretive Facilities.)

• Birding/wildlife/nature viewing areas continue to expand in popularity. Every effort should be made to enhance access to viewing areas without diminishing their numbers and amount of biological diversity.

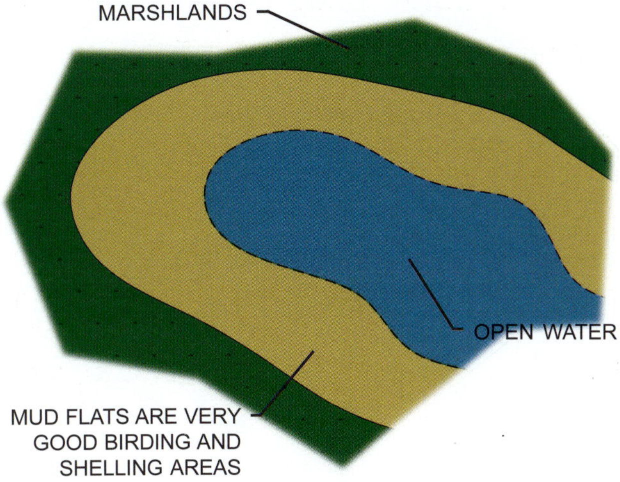

FIG. 4-8 – MARSH/MUDFLATS/OPEN WATER

• Preparation of an environmentally-sensitive management plan to accompany any development. See Chapter 31, Management and Management Planning for Park and Recreation Areas as previously referenced for detailed information on what a management plan is and how to prepare it. [27]

• Provide, where possible, for a diverse habitat, which will encourage a wide variety of life, both animals and plants. This would put an emphasis on the biological edges and transition zones in developments, i.e., fields/ forests, swamps, open water, river and estuarine tidal flats, and ocean water.

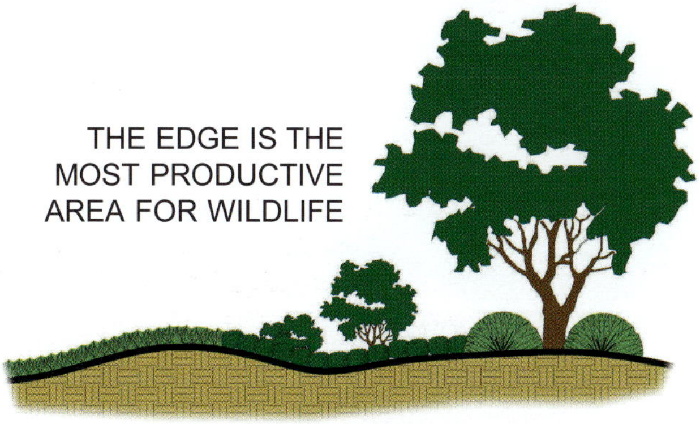

FIG. 4-9 – VARIETY AND DIVERSITY OF LIFE IS GREATEST AT EDGES, **i.e.,** ***WOODS/FIELD EDGE***

Chapter 5

PARK ARCHITECTURE

Most park developments require structural element(s). All park structures must relate in an appropriate manner to their functions. They should reflect a meaningful and logical concept based upon the environment of the specific area involved. Buildings should also relate to the topography and "feeling" of the land and should be designed as an integral part of the setting; not forced upon it.

Recreation building at beach area – Paris Mountain State Park, South Carolina

The buildings must show concern for the scale of particular sites; relationships to existing and proposed facilities reflected by the master plan; and a design continuity throughout the park, including such elements as benches, fountains, play areas and other park features.

Design considerations should include:

- Need or use the building is to serve. (Can those functions be better served elsewhere?)
- The existing topography and its future planned development.
- Subsurface conditions.
- Wind direction(s).
- Orientation to the sun.
- Drainage conditions (air as well as water).
- Availability of utilities.
- Means of access.
- Locations of trees that should be preserved. Other natural features, such as rock formations or overlook areas, that, likewise, should be preserved or made an integral part of the design.

• Necessary off-season "mothballing" for facilities of such use as bathhouses, pools and picnic areas, comfort stations that are not used during the winter, ski areas, etc.

• Materials – maintenance, durability, economy.

• Aesthetics – all structures should look like they belong together.

• Acccessibility (no longer referred to as handicapped accessible) must be provided. It is only fair, and it is the law.

• Energy self-sufficiency, where possible. This must include such items as wind/air movement or lack thereof.

Sod roof – Norway

BUILDING CONSTRUCTION IN FLOOD PLAIN AREAS

Many park, recreation, and leisure facilities are located within the 100-year flood plain. The ideal design for any buildings to be located in areas subject to flooding would be such that all portions of the structure are above the maximum flood level ("C" curve).

In order to minimize construction, operations and maintenance costs yet provide recreation facilities at a desirable location, the following should be considered:

1. All major permanent buildings, especially restaurants and habitable structures, should be located above the "C" curve flood level.

2. Minor-type concession buildings in which limited food and/or novelties are sold, and bathhouses that can be subject to occasional flooding, should be placed at or above the 100-year flood level.

3. Buildings such as boat houses, pavilions and comfort stations, and other non-inhabited structures may be considered for levels where flooding occurs at greater frequency than 100 years.

In all cases, structures constructed below "C" curve flood level should be anchored to prevent flotation and should be constructed of materials that can withstand submergence and can be easily cleaned, usually by hosing them down.

An alternate approach to constructing permanent structures within flood plains is to use portable buildings and, in unusual conditions, even floating buildings.

Factors to consider in this flooding condition would include:

1. Aesthetics (of course).

2. Modular construction for both the movable buildings and any expansion of existing, non-movable buildings.

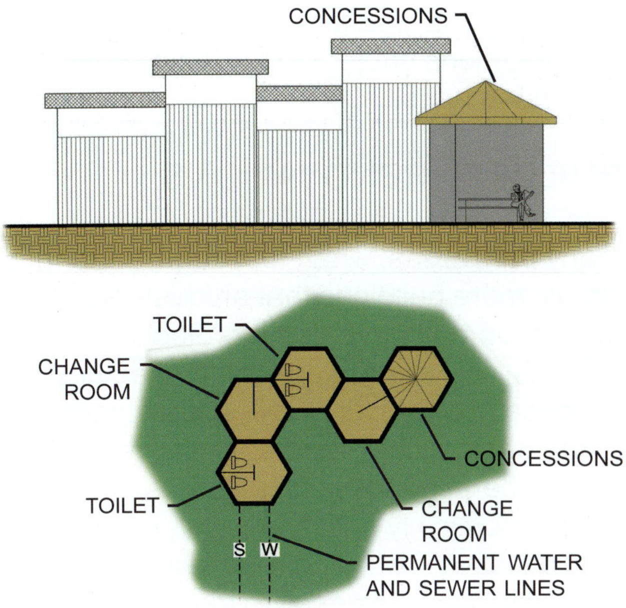

FIG. 5.1 – PORTABLE STRUCTURES

3. Anchorage of floating or portable structures where water currents are not likely to cause damage or wash them away.

Windscreen - Eastern England coastal beach

HURRICANE AND STRONG WIND PRONE AREAS

Most coastal areas on the East and Gulf coasts are subject to occasional and, sometimes, even frequent hurricanes. Many areas in the Middle Western plains experience frequent strong winds and, sometimes, severe tornadic activity. Any buildings to be constructed in these and similar adverse environments must, in addition to designing for flooding covered in previous sections, consider the following:

1. Wind protection -

• Building orientation for protection of user areas from strong winds.

• Storm shutters on window openings to prevent window breakage from the wind and wind-driven debris.

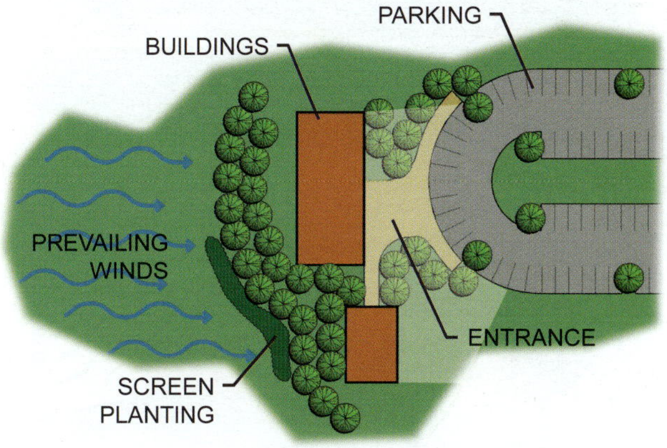

FIG. 5.2 – BUILDINGS AS A WINDSCREEN

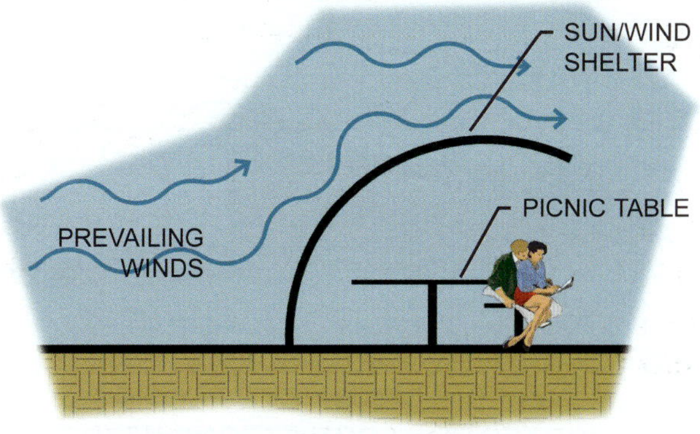

FIG. 5.3 – SUN/WINDSCREEN

• Planting of storm-resistant screening material (must be in a location to interrupt wind during storms).

• Grading to direct wind flows.

• Planting of wind-tolerant species.

2. Electrical failure -

• Provision of emergency generators are desirable. This is critically important for sewage and water lift and pump stations.

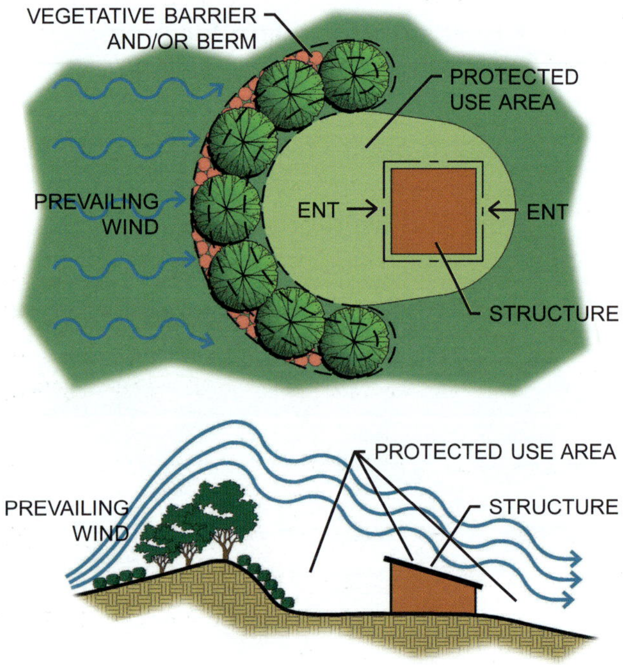

FIG. 5.4 – WINDSCREENS

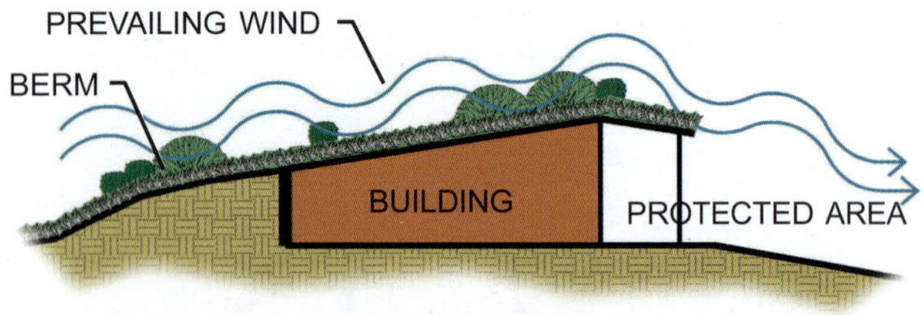

FIG. 5.5 – GRADING AND/OR PLANTING AND/OR BUILDING DESIGN CAN PROVIDE PROTECTION FROM STRONG WINDS

3. Storm shelters must be provided in locations subject to tornadic activity and hurricanes.

BUILDING RENOVATIONS

Many park areas, when first acquired, contain one or more buildings that are historically significant or may have some project use potential. Unless a structure is architecturally or historically significant or it adds significantly to the aesthetics/character of the resource, it should be used for facility purposes only if it will economically satisfy a need, i.e., will it be cost effective? Building renovation and repair for public use is expensive, frequently costing more than a new, similar square footage structure. Please note that almost all remodeling is time consuming and generally has many unexpected and usually expensive repairs to be made.

Historic residence in Greenville, South Carolina – now used by garden club and others

Factors to consider:

1. Complete evaluation of existing building and site conditions and a determination of the most cost effective and site correct solution.

2. Intended use(s).

3. Changes needed to meet current building code requirements, especially in relationship to ADA access, plumbing, structural, and electrical requirements.

4. Changes required to make building operationally cost effective, i.e., insulation, water, lighting, heat, etc.

ENERGY REDUCTION IDEAS

All architectural elements, both new and rehabilitated, must consider every feasible means to minimize the use of energy. On rehabilitation of the building, this effort can be quite expensive.

1. Orientation is critical. Factors to consider:

• Orientation to sun - maximum heat gathering and retention during the winter, and minimum summer heat absorption with maximum heat dissipation.

• Wind direction by seasons. Protection from strong winter winds and storms is necessary if the facilities are to be utilized during that time of year. Advantage of summer breezes enhances visitor comfort and enjoyment while reducing mechanical cooling requirements and energy costs.

2. Building design

• In northern climates with winter use, have windowless facades facing north and into the most frequent storm winds.

• Adequate non-mechanical ventilation during warm seasons.

• Adequate insulation, the "R" factor. Important for buildings used during all seasons of inclement weather.

• Consider low profile and depressed buildings to take advantage of the insulating qualities of earth.

3. Heat sources

• Solar

- active
- passive - preferable.

Show the energy-conserving systems off through integration with the interpretive program(s).

• Consider a variety of types of heating - solar, firewood, electrical, fuel oil, gas. Choose the most non-pollutive and life cycle cost effective method of heating.

4. Landscaping

• Screen planting (evergreen) for reducing strong winter winds. These would be the most beneficial plants in northern climates.

• Deciduous plantings on south sides of buildings for summer shade and winter sun. This will provide maximum benefits.

• Grading to divert winds and eliminate cold pockets. This is most effective in northern locations.

Chapter 6

ACCESSIBILITY REQUIREMENTS

ADA COMPLIANCE

FIG. 6.1 – INTERNATIONAL SYMBOL FOR ACCESSIBILITY

By law, public facilities in the United States and many other countries, including park, recreation, and leisure (tourism) areas, must be made accessible to those with handicaps. Approximately 12 percent of Americans have some type of limitation that may, in some manner, require physical modifications in typical site developments. Less than 1 percent of the population is confined to wheelchairs, the single disabled group most likely to have a full range of accessibility features provided. Eleven percent, therefore, of the U.S. population's needs are probably not fully met. Making physical modifications to leisure sites not only will make the facilities accessible to a wider range of people, they will make them much more usable by the elderly, most of which have little or no handicaps other than age. This is particularly important since those fifty-five and over make up the most rapidly expanding segment of the population in almost all developed countries. Although reference is made throughout this book to making facilities accessible for all people, this chapter is intended to focus attention on the subject, with particular attention to the aging population.

Visitor overlook accessible to all – Shark Valley at Everglades National Park – South Florida

GENERAL

The handicapped/disabled and aging do not desire to be segregated from the mainstream of society. Therefore, do not provide separate special facilities for them for this only draws attention to their age or limitation, frequently causing negative attitudes by them and the rest of society about their disabilities. In addition, most people with limitations arrive at the facility accompanied by friends and/or family who frequently have no handicaps. Details for each activity are included in the appropriate section.

Prior to determining the type, location and extent of the facilities to be made accessible, work closely with those individuals and organizations who are disabled and who would be the likely users. In addition, consult:

- American National Standard Specifications for Making Building and Facilities Accessible to and Usable by Physically Handicapped People A.N.S.I. A117.1 – the latest revision.

- The Uniform and Federal Accessibility Standards distributed by the National Recreation and Park Association.

Not all activities and facilities (e.g., backpack camping accessible to wheelchairs) need to be made accessible to all handicapped, but at least some of each kind of activity or facility must be made accessible (e.g., typical family campsite). Even though it may not be legally necessary, it is a good policy, morally and politically, to exceed ADA requirements.

PARKING

A reasonable number of surfaced parking spaces must be made available at all sites. At least one space located as close to and on an accessible route to the desired facility/activity as possible must be available. The following number of handicapped parking is required to meet federal accessibility standards.

Total Parking	Minimum Spaces
1 to 25	1
26 to 50	2
51 to 75	3
76 to 100	4
101 to 150	5
151 to 200	6
201 to 300	7
301 to 400	8
401 to 500	9
501 to 1000	2% of Total
1001 & over	20 + 1 for each 100 over 1000

FIG. 6.2 – HANDICAPPED SPACES NEEDED IN PARKING AREAS.

Parking overhang shall not reduce the accessibility route to less than the 36-inch (91.5 cm) minimum.

A curb break or ramp must be provided to the accessibility route. It may be desirable to design parking lots without curbing, thus eliminating the need for curb breaks and making it easier for older people to access the walk system.

Slopes shall be 2 percent or less in the accessible parking section of the parking lot.

The accessible parking can be distributed throughout the lot to provide the best accessibility to the site and facilities.

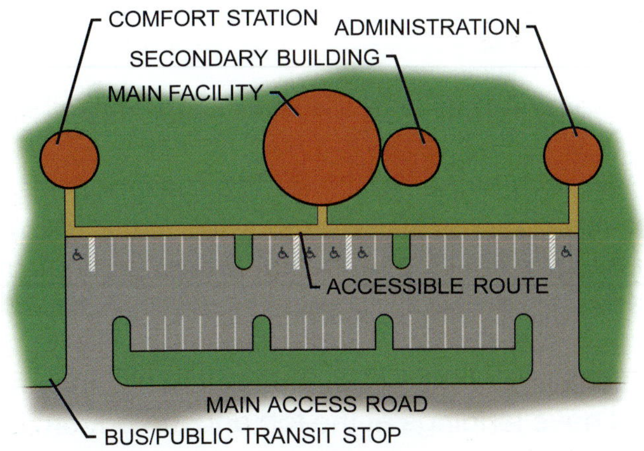

FIG. 6.3 – ACCESSIBLE PARKING CAN BE DISTRIBUTED THROUGHOUT THE SITE

All accessible parking spaces shall be signed with the international symbol of accessibility as reserved for the handicapped and visible when the space is filled.

FIG. 6.4 – ACCESSIBLE SIGN

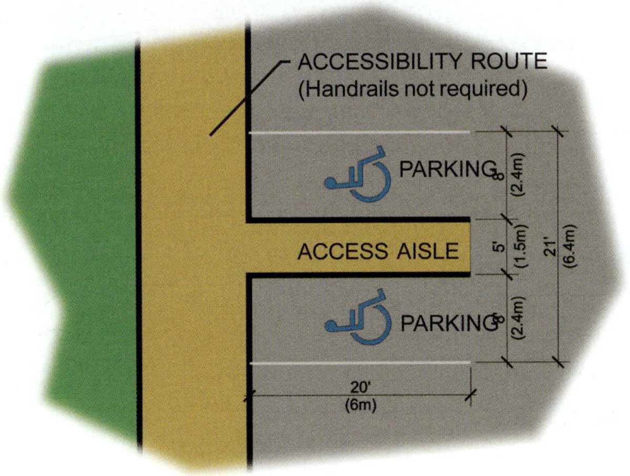

FIG. 6.5 – PARKING

ACCESSIBLE ROUTE

There shall be at least one accessible route within the boundary of the site from the point(s) of access to the site to the accessible facility(ies).

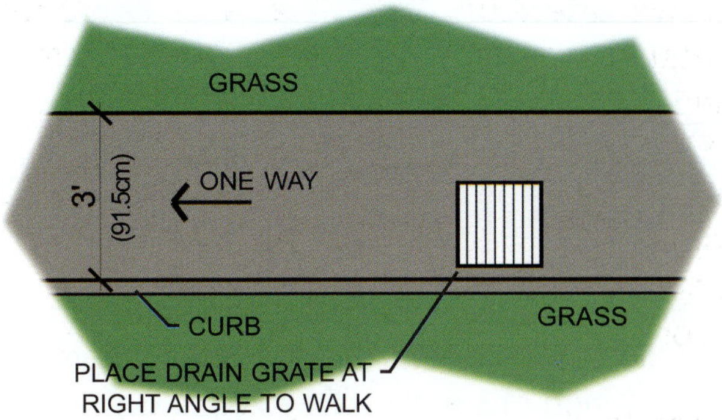

FIG. 6.6 – ACCESSIBLE ONE-WAY WALK (NOT NORMALLY RECOMMENDED)

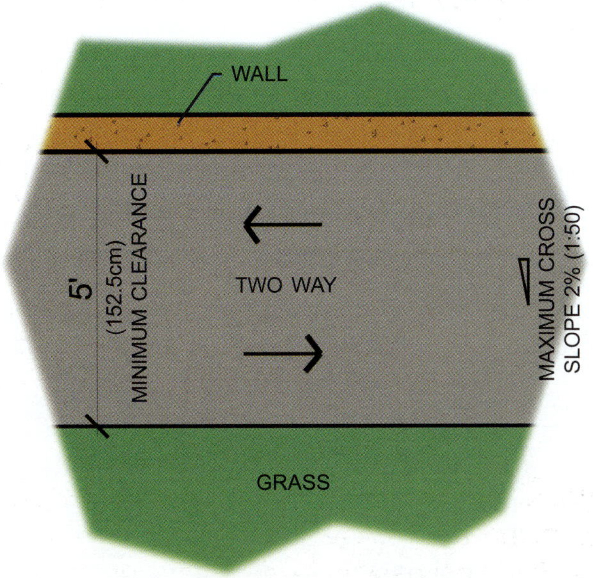

FIG. 6.7 – ACCESSIBLE TWO-WAY WALK (NORMALLY RECOMMENDED)

No objects shall protrude more than 4 inches (10 cm) into an accessible route if they are mounted between 27 inches and 80 inches high (68 to 200 cm). If objects are built, they shall not, however, reduce the clear space to less than the required 36 inches (91.5 cm) minimum. [22]

Ground surfaces along accessible routes (including floors, walks, ramps, stairs, and curb breaks, etc.) shall be stable, firm and slip-resistant and shall not exceed 5 percent (1:20). Soft, loose surfaces (sand, clay, etc.) and irregular surfaces (cobbles, rough stone, etc.) should be avoided.

Changes in level up to ¼ inch (6 mm) are acceptable; ¼ to ½ inch (6 to 13 mm) can be handled with a 1:2 slope, and anything greater will be treated as a ramp.

Drainage grates – Place perpendicular to the direction of travel with the openings no greater than ½ inch (13 mm). (See Fig. 6.6.)

Emergency egress – Where fire codes require more than one emergency exit, then more than one exit shall be provided for the handicapped. (22)

Stairs on accessible routes must have a minimum of tread of 11 inches (28 cm); no open risers shall be permitted; and handrails shall be provided on both sides of the stairway.

Access is critical at all facilities for the very young as well as those with handicaps.

Elevators or other lifting devices may be provided for elevation changes in lieu of ramps and stairs.

RAMPS

Make all ramps with the least slope possible.

Maximum slope 1:12 with the maximum rise of 30 inches (760 cm) per run. Basically, a resting place is needed for every 30 feet of ramp.

Ramps with a rise of over 30 inches (760 cm) will have landings at the top and the bottom of each run.

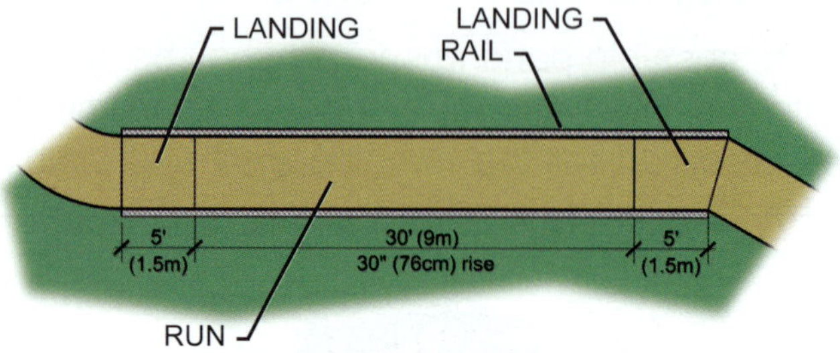

FIG. 6.8 – RAMP/HANDRAILS

Combination stairway and ramp – Hopewell Iron Furnace National Park – Southeastern Pennsylvania

Handrails are required on both sides of all ramps (except curb ramps) of greater than six inches (150 cm) or six feet (1.8 m) in length.

DOORWAYS

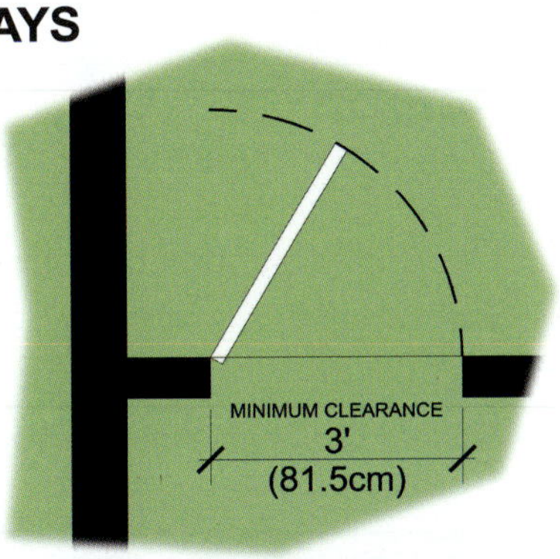

FIG. 6.9 – DOORWAYS

TOILET FACILITIES

Each public or common use toilet building shall have toilet facilities for the handicapped. Reference Federal Accessibility Standards for required details. Also see Chapter 11, Utilities.

DRINKING FOUNTAINS

Accessible drinking fountains must be provided with a clear paved space in front of 48 inches (120 cm) wide and 30 inches (76 cm) deep, and the fountain shall be no higher than 36 inches (91.5 cm) with a clearance under the fountain of at least 27 inches (68.5 cm) and a minimum depth of 17 inches (43 cm).

Braille informational display – Cambridge University, England

INFORMATION

Sometimes it is possible to make places more interesting for people with vision problems, i.e., Braille floor symbols in elevators or to scale, non-destructible models at points of interest.

BEACH/LAKE ACCESS

Provide standard ramps down to the beach.

Coastal beaches will require a surfaced way to the low water depth or the provision of beach-usable wheelchairs (large tires).

Water access demonstration at Florida Gulf Coast University – Southwest Florida

Baby carriages can use the same access way as wheelchairs – Clam Pass – Naples, FL

Chapter 7

INTERPRETIVE FACILITIES

The purpose of an interpretive program is to relate and explain to people the archaeological, natural, historic and/or cultural values of the resources of the project and the surrounding lands and waters through various means so that the site values will be made more meaningful and enjoyable to the visitor.

Docents (interpretive people) dressed in period costumes explaining how charcoal is made – the fuel for firing the iron furnaces at Hopewell Furnace National Historic Site – Pennsylvania

Before including interpretive programs and facilities in a development or management plan, an inventory of interpretive opportunities should be made and a program concept developed. It should be clearly understood that it takes a great deal of research and time to prepare a good interpretive program, plus it may require significant staff and operating funds to keep it in operation.

OBJECTIVES OF THE INTERPRETIVE PROGRAM (1)

- To help the visitor enjoy the facility through better understanding and appreciation of its purposes and resources.

- To promote intelligent use of the resources and facilities through educational programs and activities.

- To help the visitor develop a sense of responsibility concerning the conservation and use of our natural resources.

- To instill in the visitor a sense of appreciation for the natural and manmade resources of the facilities in order to reduce willful destruction and vandalism of irreplaceable facility resource property.

- To help the visitors increase their knowledge and understanding of their role in the natural and/or historic environment.

- To help the visitors understand, enjoy, appreciate, and develop respect for their environment.

- To develop a knowledge and understanding of ecology, especially as it relates to the facility being visited.

- To help the visitor develop an interest in the site's past, both historic and archaeological.

CONSIDERATIONS

- Effective access to the interpretive facilities is a prerequisite for use.

- Heavily used interpretive areas may require substantial parking and often need sanitary and other support facilities.

- Accessibility for all is necessary for interpretive facilities and must be provided. (See Chapter 6, Accessibility Requirements.)

FACILITIES

Nature Centers – should be used, where necessary, for the purpose of displaying materials associated with flora, fauna, and other phases of the site's natural resources relative to its resources-related facility's environment. They should only be considered where adequate staff is available to operate them. Usually only the very largest projects can afford a separate nature area(s). Generally, a nature center is combined in a limited form with a visitor center or project's office.

Historic and Archaeological Facilities – should be used to explain the past activities of a site. They generally are most effective when located where the past activities took place.

Protection from rain – Archaeological site – Guatemala

Museums – should be constructed at significant sites within the project's facilities. They combine the features of a nature center with other exhibits explaining the history of a site. These exhibits are even more expensive than a nature center to build and usually equally or more expensive, dollar-wise and in manpower, to operate and maintain.

Interpretive center and park office – Hopewell Furnace National Historic Site – Pennsylvania

GUIDED AND SELF-GUIDED TRAILS

This is the heart of most facility interpretive programs and should be studied for inclusion in all visitor facilities design.

Guided nature walk
Asa Wright Nature Preserve – Trinidad

REQUIREMENTS:

• Trailside information displays and/or, where appropriate, self-guiding brochures coordinated with trail markers are a necessity for visitor enjoyment of educational trails. They permit use during all seasons and do not require the services of a trained staff person on a regular basis.

Information display – Pisa, Italy

• Width – adequate to provide for anticipated use with wider areas at interest points along the trail. The trail(s) must normally be accessible. When accessible trails are provided, the trail surface must be hard, firm and smooth (no sand, clay or cobbles), which could cause falling or slipping.

• Make the trail interesting, but do not fake what is not there.

Wheelchair use of Hershey Botanical Garden
– Hershey, Pennsylvania

• Nature trails should be kept as inconspicuous as possible to keep the effect of the natural surroundings.

• Do not connect areas of heavy use in parks with a nature trail; it will become a thoroughfare and lose its natural character.

• Consider rest areas along the way on longer trails. These can be effectively combined with exhibits.

• Surfacing depends on amount of use – varies from wood chips to blacktop or concrete.

• Trails should be loop types, ending at the point of beginning and generally one-half to two miles (.8 to 3.2 km) long, a distance that can be readily negotiated by most people.

GUIDED AND SELF-GUIDED VEHICLE TOURS OR TRAILS

These types of trails can be effectively used to interpret the scene in areas where this form of locomotion is the most effective means of seeing the features. Self-guiding vehicular trails are frequently used in large parks, both along major through roads, and in specially designed vehicular interpretive trails. See Chapter 25, Non-Consumptive Wildlife, for a typical vehicular trail. The only addition to such a trail layout would be interpretive signs or markers at appropriate locations.

Bicycle, boat and bridle trails – can be constructed in appropriate situations. The design criteria would basically match vehicle trails.

Interpretive shelters (kiosks) and wayside exhibits – should be installed where on-site interpretation can be effectively utilized. Keep them simple and vandal resistant. They will require maintenance.

Wayside exhibit – stabilized iron furnace structure
Hopewell Furnace National Historic Site
– Pennsylvania

SCENIC OVERLOOKS AND OBSERVATION TOWERS

Consider incorporating in other required park structures, including water towers.

EVENING CAMPFIRE PROGRAMS – can be effectively utilized in any area of 150+ units for overnight park use. Campfire facilities should be so located as to minimize disturbance of those not desiring to participate. They can vary in size and complexity from a simple campfire circle to formal amphitheaters. This space may also serve for church services. (See Chapter 14, Overnight Use.)

AMPHITHEATER

Amphitheater – City Park
– South Central Pennsylvania

• LOCATION

1. They should be located within 500 feet (150 m) of adequate parking. One good solution is to combine parking with concession use or day use, thus making effective, non-conflicting dual use of this necessary resource.

2. Within walking distance of the overnight accommodations unless it is not possible – 1000 feet (300 m).

3. Must have adequate visual and sound separation from campsites.

4. Can sometimes utilize visitor center parking facilities.

5. Must be accessible to handicapped.

Amphitheater in a campground
French Creek State Park – Pennsylvania

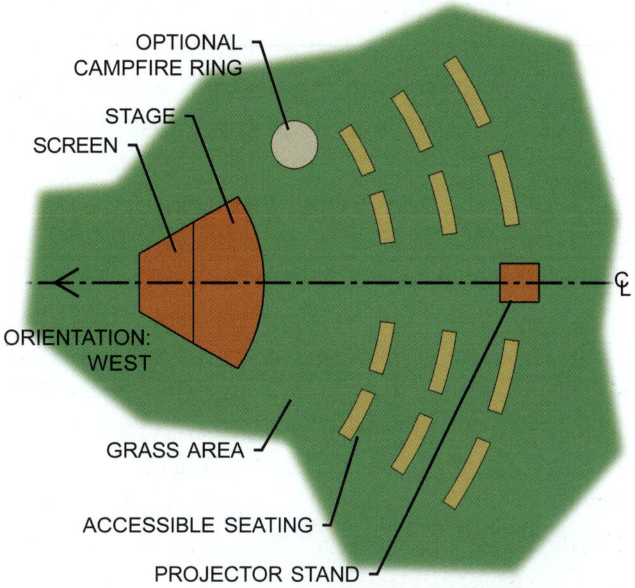

FIG. 7.1 – AMPHITHEATER LAYOUT

- **DESIGN**

1. The size is determined by the planned type(s) of program(s), potential day-use audiences, and proximity to the overnight accommodations. Approximately one-quarter to one-half of the overnight-use capacity (varies with quality of the evening program and distance from the campground) will participate.

2. Orientation – screen must be in evening shade, facing east.

3. Projector stand – 40 feet (12 m) from screen for most areas, greater distance for larger audiences.

4. Accessible sitting space must be provided – suggest appropriately 10 percent of total sitting area.

5. Sloping site is desirable, or major earth work will be necessary on larger projects to get proper visual exposure.

6. Facilities needed:

a. Benches for a normal capacity audience.

b. Level space for handicapped on the handicapped-accessible route(s).

c. Stage – ground level acceptable for small (50± persons) facilities; raised is better for larger facilities.

d. Screen (rear projection is best but not required) with projector stand.

7. Facilities desirable:

   a. Lighting – along walks, flood lighting in seating area;

   b. Drinking fountain(s).

8. Utilities:

   a. Electricity – needed.

   b. Water – desirable.

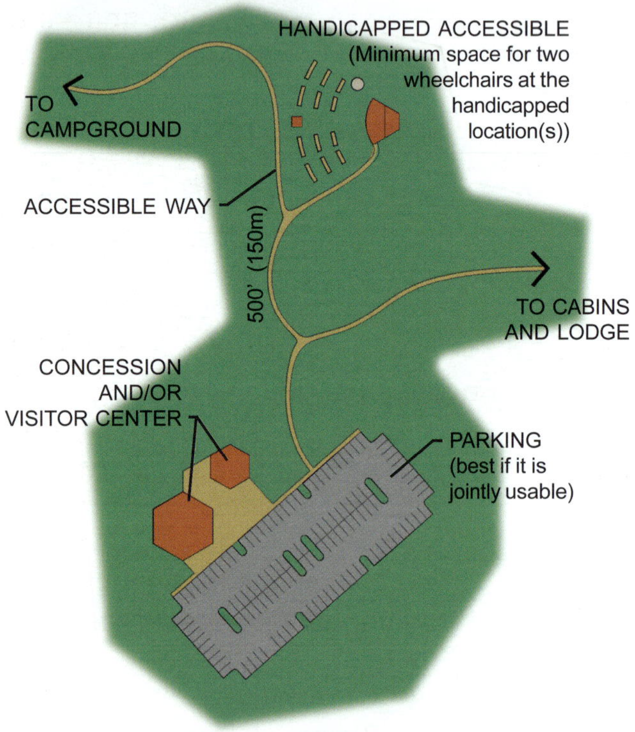

FIG. 7.2 – AMPHITHEATER LOCATION

ENVIRONMENTAL EDUCATION CENTERS

Some governmental agencies and private non-profit organizations have developed facilities that will supplement school education programs in environmental education. These facilities are for in-depth training of young people. Another major function is to educate the teachers in the potential of using the total environment in their teaching process. They exist to provide a way for society to become aware of the potential for both good and bad that man can experience within his environment. They are usually very costly to build, maintain, and operate.

Environmental teaching station – Birding preserve – Eastern England

VISITOR CENTERS

Most large park, recreation, and tourist facilities require some type of visitor contact point where information about the site, its facilities, and its programs can be secured. A simple counter in the main office may suffice; however, major leisure projects may benefit from a more elaborate visitor center with displays covering the site's natural resources and cultural heritage. In most instances, the educational facilities should be combined with the facility's administrative activities permitting the administrative/clerical staff to provide a dual educational/administrative function during low-user periods. The visitor center should be located on the major access road and as close to the project entrance as possible.

DEMONSTRATION FARMS

Major park systems, especially those serving urban populations, should consider developing a demonstration farm. They are of great interest to adults as well as children. Children from three to ten years of age, together with their parents and teachers, constitute the major clientele during the week, with families and older people the major users on the weekends. Main use occurs during the good weather seasons, generally April to November in the northern half of the country and winter in the south. No school periods will see a significant reduction in use during the weekdays. A demonstration farm can only be effective when adequately interpreted. Visitors and farming activities do not readily mix, and careful planning in conjunction with the farm staff and the interpretive personnel is a necessity. Some factors to consider in addition to the interpretive ones are the need for adequate staffing, including maintenance and interpretive personnel, availability of existing land and building, parking (both car and bus), sanitary facilities, food, and other concession operations, such as souvenirs and animal feed.

Period farm at Hopewell Furnace National Historic Site – Pennsylvania

Chapter 8

TRAILS AND PATHWAYS

There are several commonly identified trail and pathway types: hiking, biking, equestrian, cross-country skiing, water (canoe, raft, boats), off-highway vehicles, motorcycles, and snowmobiles. They have been divided into motorized and non-motorized categories. This chapter will cover only hiking, biking, equestrian, and water trails. Water (blue trails) are covered in Chapter 18, Boating; cross-country skiing and snowmobiles are covered in Chapter 21, Winter Use Areas; and motorcycles and off-highway vehicles are covered in Chapter 10, Off-Highway Vehicle Facilities.

NON-MOTORIZED TRAILS

GENERAL

Trails and pathways should be provided where they enhance public health, enjoyment of the environment, and utilization of fish and wildlife resources. Trails and pathways can provide enjoyable, safe, and environmentally-sensitive passage for foot travelers, equestrians, bicyclists, boaters, and for off-highway vehicle use. There is no better way to convey the true spirit of the out-of-doors to the users than to provide an opportunity to see the facility by trail.

There are two kinds of trails and pathways. One is primarily for trail/pathway activities themselves - the experience of being on the trail/pathway - and the other is to provide effective and economical access to and between areas of development and/or points of interest.

Heavily used park pathway – Central England

Important factors to consider when designing either type of trail/pathway are alignment, terrain, topography, cover, aesthetic value, points of interest, road crossings or other potential dangers, and destination(s).

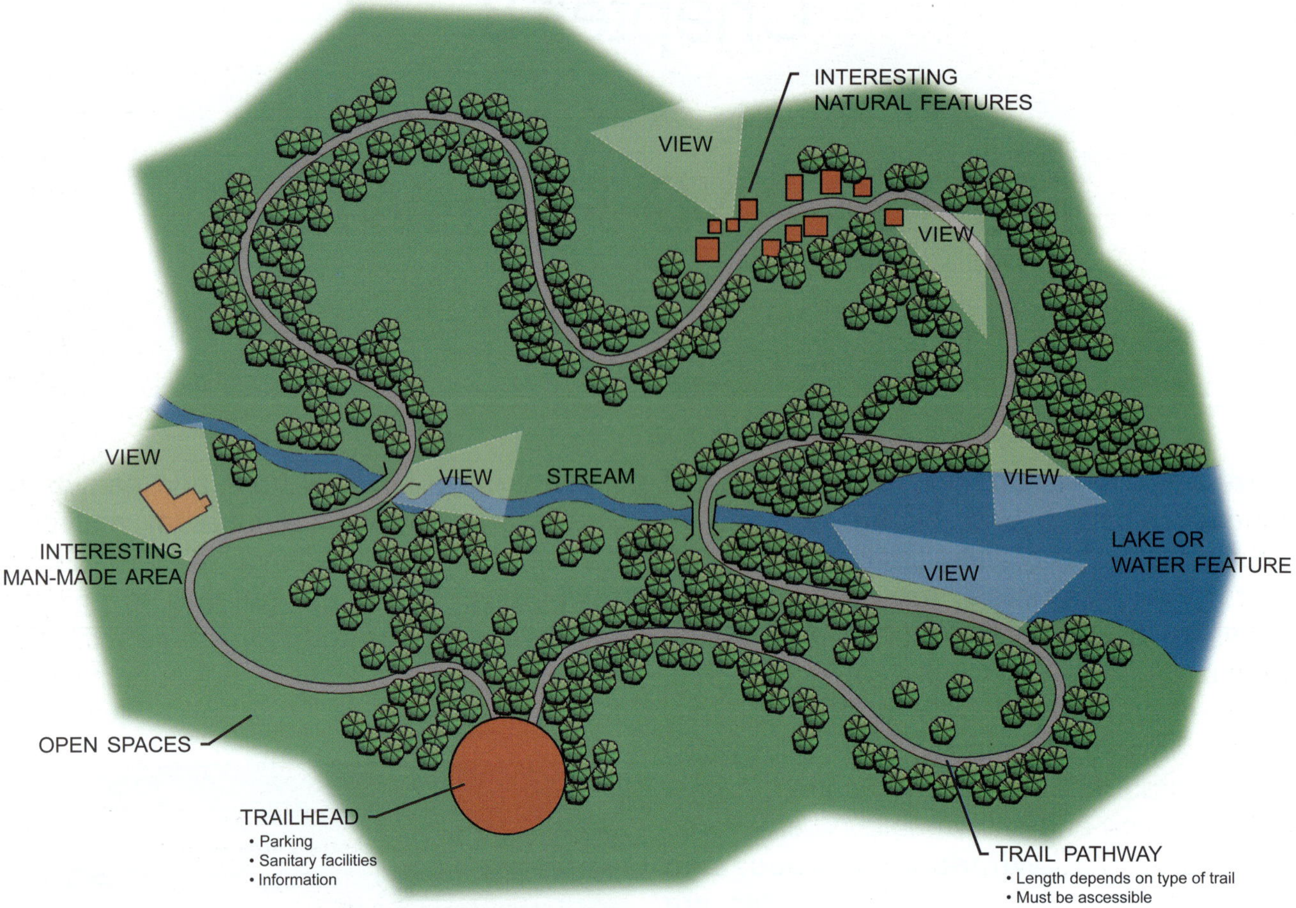

FIG. 8.1 – CONCEPTUAL TRAIL/PATHWAY LAYOUT

Zoning of trails and pathways for the types of use intended is necessary, i.e., motorized vehicles are not compatible in primitive areas, snowmobiles conflict with skiers, and inline skaters can cause conflicts with walkers.

Low use access from Colorado River in a primitive area at Grand Canyon National Park, Arizona

Parks and/or recreation areas can serve ideally as trailheads (terminus points) for comprehensive trails systems; such trail systems are complemented by the park or other leisure facilities. A park/recreation-administered trailhead can also provide for user safety, control of use, and trail information.

Trail use is subject to a continuous series of seasonal changes, which must be considered in any trail/pathway planning.

Spring floral display – Southern California

Whenever possible, hikers and horseback riders should be kept separate for sanitary as well as safety reasons. Consideration should be given to developing trails with adequate width – minimum of eight feet (2.4 m) – for service and emergency vehicles. Trails can serve as fire trails, but must then have a minimum width of greater than eight feet (2.4 m) or greater for emergency fire equipment access. Also, whenever possible, OHVs should also be kept separate from all non-OHV trails.

Multipurpose trail and service access – Sugden Regional Park – Collier County, Florida

LAYOUT

Trails should have a variety of experiences taking advantage of views (vistas and intimate), traversing ridges and valleys, open spaces and forested areas, and, where possible, water bodies.

Heavily used pathway – Europe

- Vary trail alignments.
  - Avoid "sameness."

The Mall – Washington, DC

- Take advantage of natural and manmade features.
- Vary vegetative cover.
- Changes in grade.
- OHV trails must be carefully studied for all sound basins, and avoid those that adversely affect other facility users and adjacent resource users, especially those requiring quietness. (See Chapter 10, Off-Highway Vehicle Facilities, for information on these types of trails.)

• Trails should fit the land. Do not fight contours unless there is no other choice. All construction should be visually inconspicuous.

Hiking trail

• Consider all of the senses: sight, touch, hearing (both pleasing sounds and annoying sounds), and, where possible, smell.

• Avoid straight lines (monotonous).

• Avoid poor soil conditions (wet areas, erosion-prone areas, etc.).

• Avoid over use.

Over use of trail
Asa Wright Nature Preserve – Trinidad

• Utility lines.

- Avoid, where possible. In urban and suburban areas, however, utility R/W may be the only relatively undeveloped space where trails can be constructed.

- Cross as quickly as possible and screen from view with topography or vegetation unless they are a trail component.

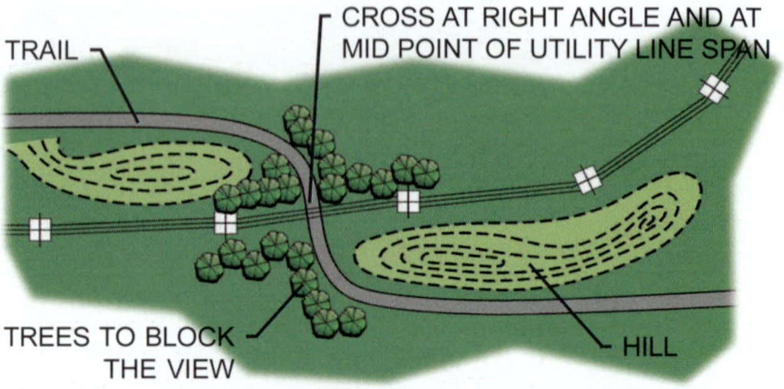

FIG. 8.2 – BEST TYPE OF TRAIL CROSSING OF A UTILITY LINE

PATHWAY DRAINAGE

Drainage is one of the most important items in trail/pathway construction and is often the most neglected. Like roads, pathways and trails will fail if not properly drained.

The volume of water on a trail must be kept within manageable limits to prevent trail damage from erosion and to keep it usable during the travel season.

- Sheet water drainage, which occurs where water drains from a short uphill slope and is drained across the trail in a sheet, is the least objectionable type of drainage.

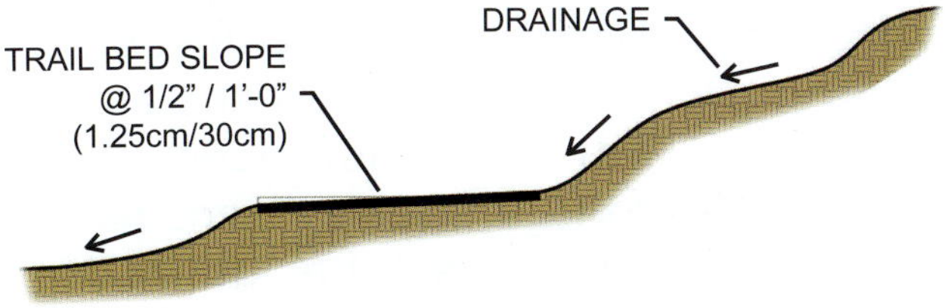

FIG. 8.3 – TRAIL BED
(ALL LOW-USE DENSITY TRAILS)

- Water stops and gutters (made from natural materials) are necessary on many trails that traverse steep hills.

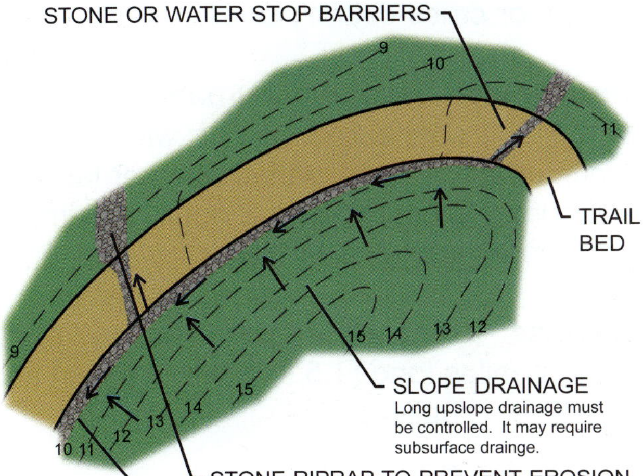

FIG. 8.4 – TRAIL SURFACE DRAINAGE

- Wet areas should be avoided if at all possible; if you must cross such areas, it takes care. Trails and pathways across wet areas are expensive to build and maintain. If wet areas are not avoidable, foot trails can be made of large flat rocks 18 inches (45 cm) o.c. or elevated wood walkways can be provided.

- All natural drainage normally must be considered for a 100-year flood. Drainage structures must be kept inconspicuous and all end sections should be tapered and, if possible, finished in native materials.

- Make sure that trails do not become drainage channels.

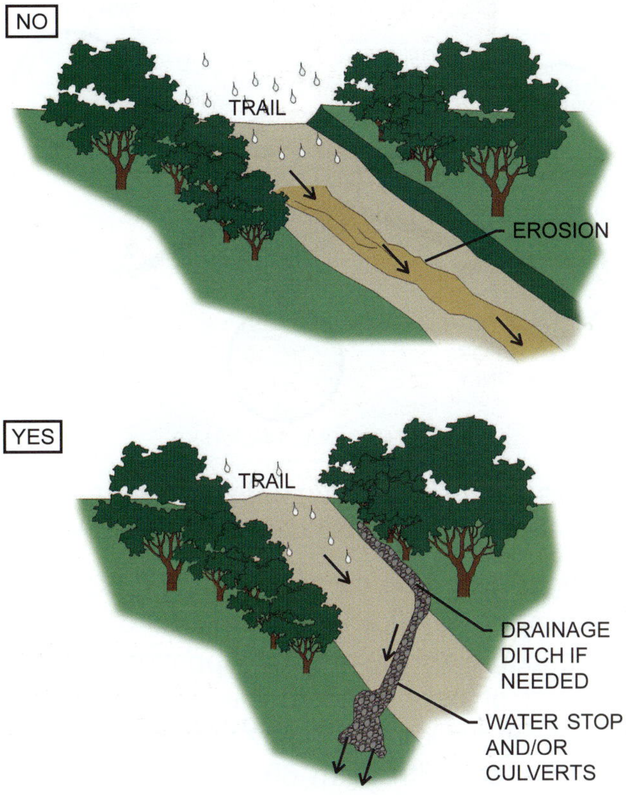

FIG. 8.5 – STEEP TRAILS NEED SPECIAL ATTENTION TO DRAINAGE TO PREVENT EROSION

STREAM CROSSINGS

Trail users, as almost all recreationists, like to see bodies of water. Where trails come in contact with water, special care must be taken, especially at crossings. The preferred crossing will minimize the visual and physical intrusion on the stream environment; use fords for horses and inconspicuous bridges for all others, especially OHVs.

HIKING TRAILS

USER CHARACTERISTICS

Short hikes or nature walks seem to appeal to all age groups. However, longer hikes and backpacking tend to be the domain of the younger and the more educated recreationists.

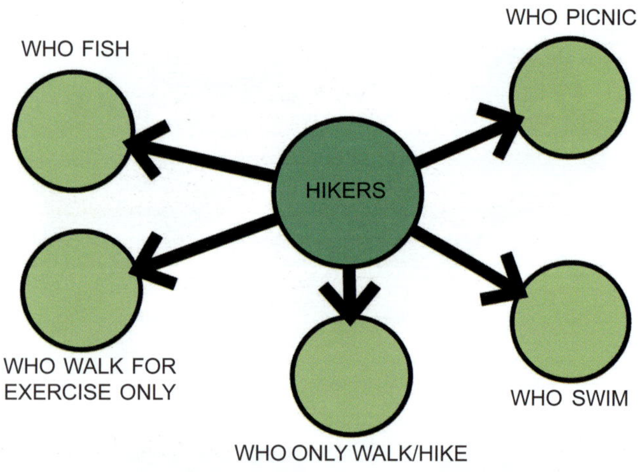

FIG. 8.6 – THE ACTIVITY MIX FOR HIKERS IS AS VARIED AS THE USERS THEMSELVES

Trail/pathway use as an activity by itself has become one of the few areas of major recreation/exercise growth. Approximately 80 percent of people up to the age of 55 are hiking or walking to some extent. This is rounded out with even 65 percent of people over 65 still participating. [42] Of all these recreational walkers, only a few stay overnight. (See later in this chapter for long trail and overnight planning details.)

ATTITUDES

Hikers feel that trails should be designed to provide:

1. maximum scenic beauty.

2. large rock outcrops where hikers can observe the surrounding landscape.

3. natural openings in forest stands where there is variety in lighting, color, temperature, and view distances.

GENERAL

Hiking trails, where possible, should be for hiking only. Under most circumstances, motorized vehicles and equestrians are not compatible with non-motorized uses. Barriers, such as logs, stairways, and narrow stream crossings can be utilized to discourage non-pedestrian users.

LENGTH

Trails are generally classified as short (pleasure walking), exercise, long loop, and cross-country. They should, if possible, be loop-type returning to the point of beginning, except for cross-country ones.

Short trails: Frequently urban/suburban in nature and connecting homes with schools, parks, urban centers, parks, or other facilities – generally 30 minutes to 2 hours maximum, 1 to 3 miles long (1.1 to 5 km).

Exercise: Generally a fixed distance (1 to 2 or more miles long (1.5 to 3 km or more) and attractive visually.

Long loop: 7 to 14 miles (10 to 20 km), a one-day hike.

Cross-country: 20 miles (30 km) or longer with as few road crossings as possible and one or more overnight stops.

TRAILSIDE CAMPING

Cross-country trails should have overnight stopping points every 7 to 10 miles (10 to 15 km). These areas require a source of potable water, sanitary facilities, and rubbish containers. They should be located off the main trail far enough away to give the camper privacy from the trail users and sufficiently far away or screened from any noise source to provide the desired solitude. They also should be at least one mile (1.5 km) from the nearest parking area to discourage their use as a "hike-in"-type campground. Access for service vehicles is also desirable. (See Chapter 14, Overnight Use – Camping - Primitive.)

Trail shelters are particularly desirable in areas having frequent precipitation during the use seasons. Shelters should blend into the countryside.

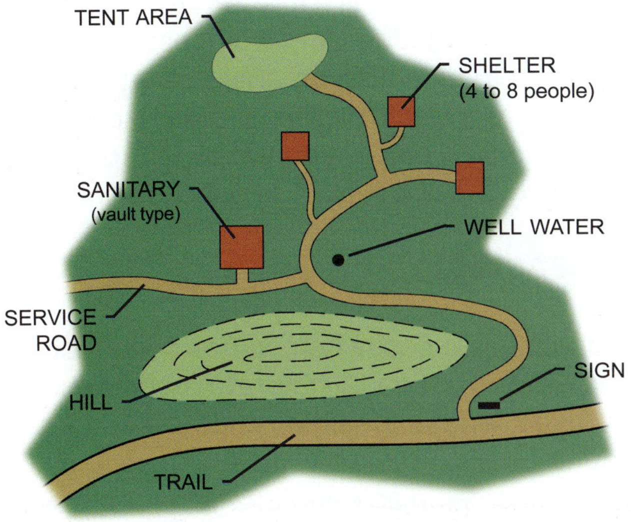

FIG. 8.7 – TRAILSIDE CAMPING

Open rain shelters in the warmer southern climates

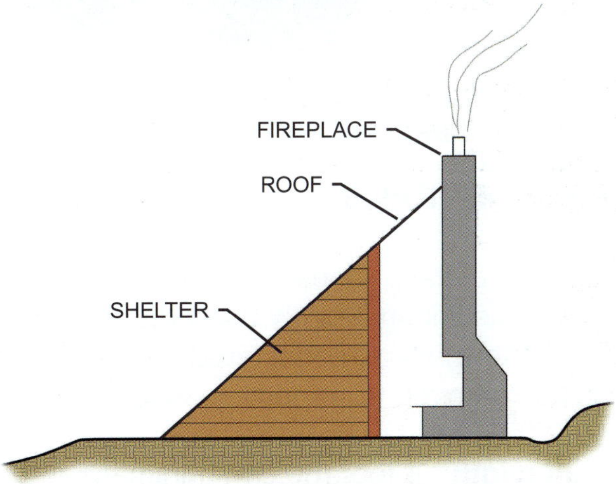

FIG. 8.8 – TRAILSIDE SHELTER

GRADIENTS

Trail gradients that are satisfactory from the standpoint of erosion prevention and control will ordinarily be suitable for hiking use. Maximum sustained gradient should not exceed ten percent. When pitches in excess of ten percent must be used, the length and steepness of these should be governed by sound engineering judgment and cannot be defined by formula or arbitrary limitations. The extent of such pitches should be broken at short intervals by gently sloping sections of trail, and the number of these sharp pitches should be kept to a minimum. To avoid steep gradients, considerable trail distance can be side hill construction with variable side slopes. Avoid switchbacks wherever possible since this leads to shortcutting and quickly to erosion problems.

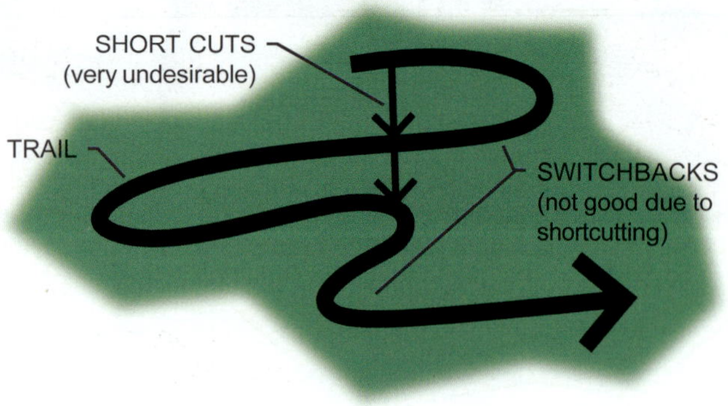

FIG. 8.9 – SWITCHBACKS CAN BECOME SHORTCUTS

WIDTH OF TRAILS

The width of trails varies according to their use. Short trails within heavily used recreation areas will normally be considered wider than the trail far removed from heavily used areas.

Tread width: 1 foot (60 cm) minimum; 6 to 8 feet (1.8 to 2.4 m) for pleasure walking or in areas with steep drop-offs, and 8 to 10 feet (2.4 to 3.0 m) or greater for exercise walking and service access.

Clearing width: 1 foot (0.3 m) minimum on each side of pathway.

Height of clearing: 7 feet (2.1 m) minimum.

Clearing for trails should be kept to a minimum. All vegetation removed should be cut flush with the ground. Remove all hazardous material. Some obstructions, such as fallen logs and large rocks, at trailheads are desirable to discourage vehicular or equestrian use.

Trails for winter use should have a correspondingly higher clearing line depending on snow depth. (See Chapter 21, Winter Use Areas - Trails).

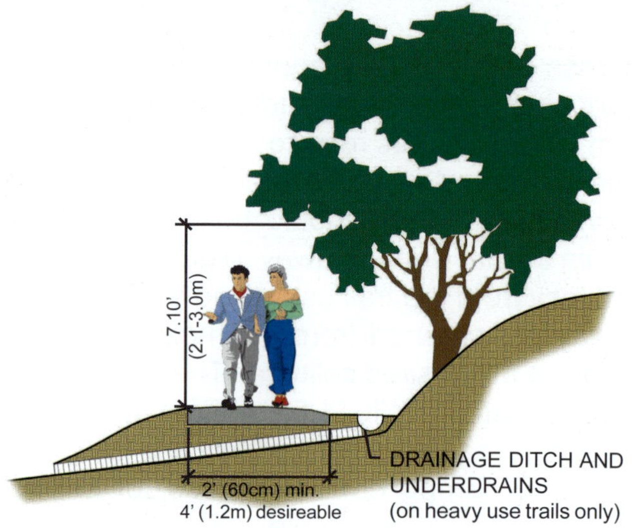

FIG. 8.10 – SECTION – HIKING TRAIL

CUT/FILL SLOPES

The cut slopes may be as steep as the hillside material will stand without serious erosion. Most soils will stand with a ½:1 or ¾:1 cut slope; however, 1:1 is a maximum unless there is a sufficient ledge. In fill slopes, care must be taken to establish an angle or repose that will ensure a stable slope condition indefinitely and which will permit vegetation to grow. This is usually 2:1 or even 3:1 in gentle rolling hills.

SURFACING

Surfacing is a costly item in trail construction, and existing or nearby natural materials should be used where feasible, especially in back country trails. Basically, the finish should discourage erosion and encourage natural cover. Compacted stone, concrete, bituminous, or other materials will probably be needed on trails in highly used recreation areas or at points of concentrated use.

Multipurpose hiking/biking pathway – Norway

SIGNING

Adequate signing is essential at trailheads, intersections, and at locations on the trail where the trail direction is not readily discernible. Trail signs should include mileage to various points of interest along the way, as well as with the total trail mileage. Frequent mileage markers along the longer trails are helpful to the hiker and useful in the operations and maintenance of the facility.

VIEWS

Selective clearing to enhance views is frequently desirable, especially in areas of dense understory vegetation.

EXERCISE PATHWAYS

These types of pathways have undergone a recent resurgence in popularity, especially with play equipment manufacturers. This is particularly being promoted for trails and pathways serving older people. The exercise stations can be spaced out along the pathway or alternatively clustered. Accessibility will be a major factor in the planning and design of these exercise pathways.

BICYCLE TRAILS

Combination rollerblading, pedestrian, and bicycle pathway – Southern California

Bicycling as a recreation activity has remained at a relatively high level of participation for the last thirty years with approximately ten million new bicycles of all types being sold per year. The only significant trend appears to be a substantial increase in all-terrain bikes, which appears to have crested in the last few years. With the continuation of high energy costs and physical fitness awareness, walking and bicycling will undoubtedly continue as the most popular recreation activities, with approximately 40 percent of 16 to 24 year-olds and 26 percent of those 45 years old, but only 9 percent of those over age 65 involved.[42]

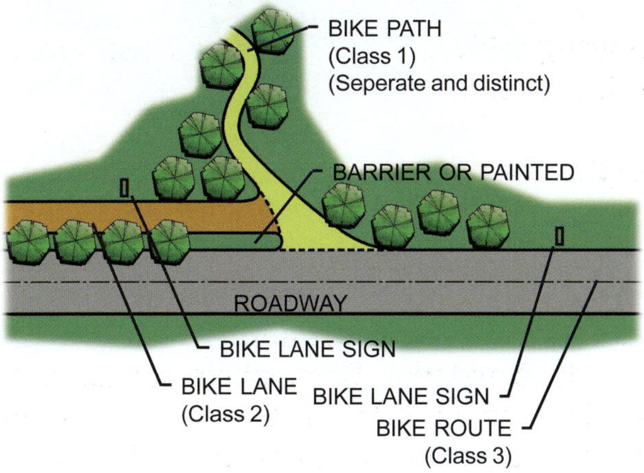

FIG. 8.11 – USE CLASSIFICATION OF BIKEWAYS

USE CLASSIFICATION

Bikeways encompass a wide range of development options from shared right-of-way with other vehicles to trails reserved exclusively for bicyclists. The following are nationally accepted classifications:

BIKE PATH (Class 1): The safest system of bicycle use completely separated from motor vehicle traffic and where conflicts with pedestrians, equestrians, and motor vehicles are limited. The bike path is often located within parks and neighborhoods and is often used to connect shopping centers, schools, and areas of scenic interest, especially within residential areas. Approximately 50 to 80 bikers per mile of trail per day can be accommodated on such a trail.

Class 1 bike and pedestrian path – Southern California coast

BIKE LANE (Class 2): A restricted segment of a shared street or roadway for use by bicycles where, at least, a stripe serves as a separation between the two users – vehicles and bicycles. The stripe provides psychological rather than physical protection. The barrier may also be physical, such as the placement of plant materials, guardrails, or a type of low curbing.

BIKE ROUTE (Class 3): A shared right-of-way located on lightly traveled streets and roadways designated solely by "bike route" signs. These signs help encourage use and warn motorists that bicyclists may be using the road. This is the least expensive route, but it is dangerous, especially for bicyclists, on narrow back country roads where it is most frequently used.

Both the bike lane and the bike route are dependent upon existing roadways for their alignments as they either share or closely follow these vehicular corridors. They should be developed in conjunction with new or reconstructed roadways and, therefore, would be used mainly as transportation routes. Close coordination with the appropriate transportation department is a necessity to make Class 2 and 3 bikeways a reality.

GENERAL

Multipurpose hiking/biking trail – Norway

Trails should be so designed that the rider can have many interesting and exciting visual experiences. In addition, consideration should be given to adding interpretive information along the trail. Finally, the trail/pathway should be physically challenging if the facility is to be primarily an exercise way.

LOCATION

When determining the location of Class 1 bike paths, consideration should be given to utilizing abandoned canal towpaths, abandoned railroads, utility R/W, and utility corridors. Close coordination of planning efforts with transportation and utility officials in the various jurisdictions traversed by the trail is a necessity.

LENGTH

The average cyclist can easily sustain speeds of 10 mph (16 kph) on level terrain. Sports cyclists and exercise riders can travel at 17 mph (27 kph) and cover, at an average speed of 22 mph (55 kph), 20 to 50 miles (30 to 80 km) in a vigorous workout. Trails should be designed with varying lengths and, preferably, with a loop system. Three to five miles (5 to 8 km) would be a minimum length with trails of 20 to 50 miles (30 to 80 km) desirable. Touring trails can be much longer and can tie into youth hostels and campgrounds for overnight stopovers.

GRADIENT

Bicycle trails should follow the contour wherever possible. Bicycle gradients should not exceed 10 percent and pitches from 4 to 8 percent should occur for short intervals only. Basically, make it like a road. When long grades are unavoidable, provide frequent, wide, level areas where the less-than-average cyclist can dismount without difficulty and rest and not endanger the more experienced riders. On the steeper grades, it is desirable to provide sufficient space to push the bike to the top of the grade.

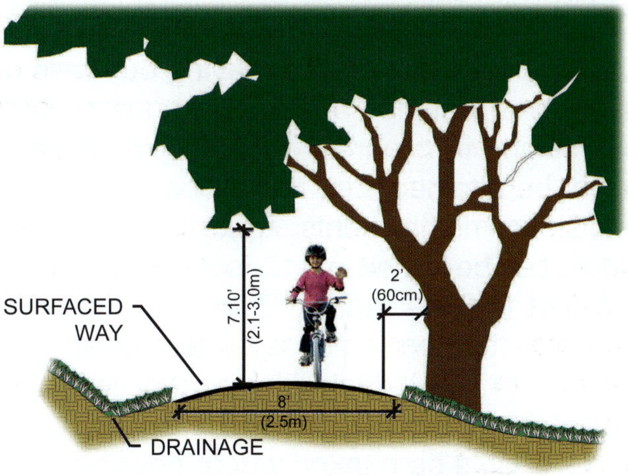

FIG. 8.12 – PATHWAY SECTION TWO-WAY BICYCLE TRAIL (The 8-foot (2.4 m) paved way can also serve for maintenance and patrol vehicles.)

WIDTH OF TRAILS

A desirable width for a two-way trail is 9 feet (2.7 m) with a minimum recommended width of 5 feet (1.5 m) and then only on trails with low use. Curves should be widened by 4 feet (1.2 m) if not banked. To add variety, divided trails could be used to bypass boulders, trees, a descriptive marker, etc. Trails less than 8 feet (2.4 m) are not usable by most service staff vehicles.

CLEARING

Vertical: Removal of all obstructions under 7 feet (2.1 m) is necessary. It is desirable to remove everything under 10 feet (3 m). Vegetation should be removed on a regular (monthly) basis.

Horizontal: Remove all obstructions beyond the trail edge for a minimum of 2 feet (60 cm) with additional clearing to 4 feet (1.2 m) on the inside curves to improve site distance and driving safety.

TURNING RADIUS

Care must be taken when laying out trails to avoid sharp angles and short radius curves, particularly in an area where higher speeds might be attained, i.e., recreation riding trails or distance riding events. A bicycle going quite slowly can be turned in a 12-foot (3.6 m) space; a 6-foot (1.8 m) radius. The recommended minimum turning radius is 10 feet (3 m) with 15 feet (4.5 m) desirable, except in areas where high bicycle speeds are expected. Turns should be banked where possible.

DRAINAGE

A paved bicycle trail is very similar to a properly constructed road, and the same general conditions and solutions for drainage would apply as for road construction. In essence, the better the drainage, the longer lasting the bikeway.

SURFACING

The design cross-sections of the bicycle trail are generally the same as sidewalk design sections. The recommended surfacing material is bituminous paving or concrete. Other acceptable choices are soil, cement and compacted gravel. A widely used trail section is 4 inches (10 cm) or more of crushed stone choked and rolled with fines (quarry dust).

SIGNING

Utilize standard highway department bikeway markers and signs.

SAFETY MEASURES

Safety measures must be taken to protect the bicyclists. These measures would, as a minimum, include, wherever physically possible, realigning drainage grates at right angles to the bike paths, and widening curves, etc.

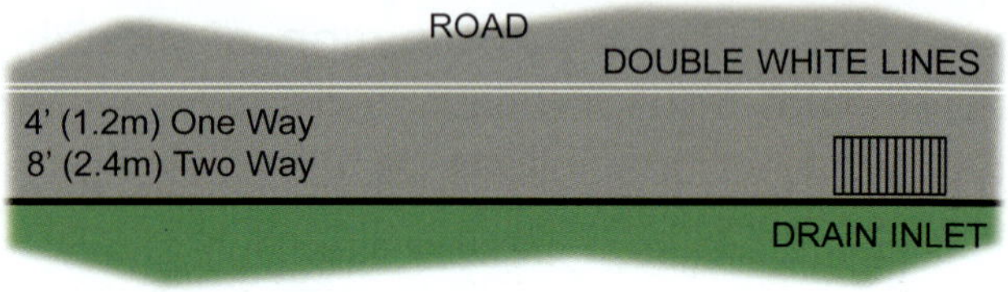

FIG. 8.13 – BICYCLE TRAIL SAFETY MEASURES

BICYCLE RENTAL

Facility trails with heavy use by non-local people should probably include bicycle rental as an option. These can be developed in conjunction with other concession operations in the facility (boat rental and food services) for more economical operation. Bicycle rental facilities should be located only when and where there is sufficient pedestrian traffic or vehicular parking to ensure adequate customers for a viable financial operation.

EQUESTRIAN TRAILS AND FACILITIES

EQUESTRIAN USER CHARACTERISTICS

Riding is normally a short-time activity. "A few available hours" account for about half of all rides, while slightly over one-quarter of all rides are one-day outings.

Most riding is done close to home, but where opportunities exist for overnight horse camping, it has been popular. The riders are primarily women, with a ratio of 7 to 8 women per man. The sanitary facilities for equestrian areas should be designed to be predominantly skewed to women.

TRAIL DESIGN

See Hiking Trails for general alignment criteria. Remember 8-foot (2.4 m) or wider trails are better from a maintenance and operation standpoint.

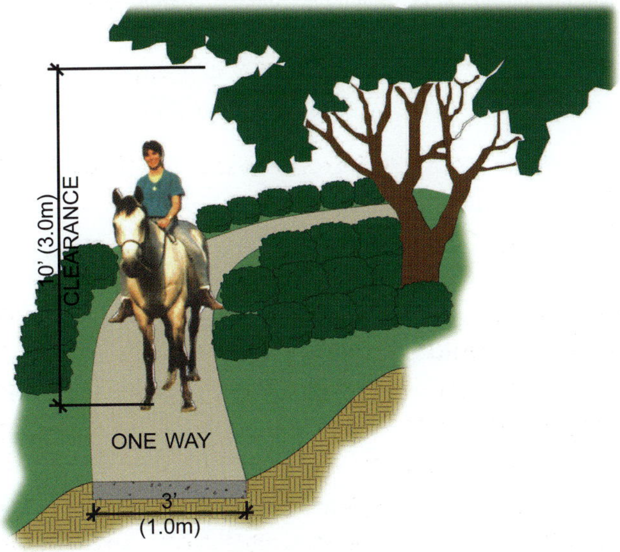

FIG. 8.14 – SECTION – SINGLE-PURPOSE EQUESTRIAN TRAIL

SPECIAL EQUESTRIAN CONSIDERATIONS

- Loop trails are best – 7 to 10 miles (10 to 15 km), ½ day; 10 to 20 miles (15 to 30 km), one day.
- Trips of two or more days are usually destination trips. Vehicular access points near overnight stops are frequently necessary so that food and water can be provided for the horses. If adequate water and grazing are available, vehicular access is not mandatory, but it can be useful for small maintenance vehicles. Riders can bring sufficient feed to their horses for a few days. A shuttle arrangement for cars and trailers is required if it is a destination-type trip.
- Adequate car/trailer parking facilities are required at all trailheads.
- Short stretches (½ mile (1 km)) of straight alignment are useful to provide for running the horses. An adjoining open field of ½ mile or longer is also a desirable feature and can serve the same function as straight trail segments. It must be regularly checked for any unseen holes or depressions for safety purposes.
- Switchbacks must be gentler than pedestrian trails.
- Trail grades to 15 percent are permissible.
- Trail surfacing should be of native material. Where heavy use occurs, a mixture of sand, sawdust, and oil can be utilized, but it must be environmentally friendly and not pollute the surrounding lands and waters. There are also chemical trail stabilizers on the market.

MULTIPLE USE

Multiple use of equestrian trails for hiking is recommended only for low volume use facilities. Horses and hikers do not mix well due to horse excrement, desired trail finishes, accelerated trail erosion, spooking of horses by walkers, the frightening of people by horses, and different lengths of required trails between walkers and equestrians.

Winter use of equestrian trails for ski touring or snowshoeing is compatible and, where snow conditions permit, desirable. Snowmobiling can also be compatible physically, but careful consideration must be given to sound basins and noise conflicts with cross-country skiers and snowshoers.

EQUESTRIAN FACILITIES

Most successful stables depend on boarding horses as their main source of income. Boarded horses need a place to be ridden, preferably on trails. This activity can be combined with a rental (hack) operation. Rental of horses is difficult by itself to make financially self-sustaining due to high insurance costs.

For any equestrian facility to be truly successful, it must be associated with an equestrian trail system. The more comprehensive and varied the trails, the better the opportunity for equestrian center success.

Chapter 9

SPECIAL USE FACILITIES

There are a number of leisure time activities that do not fit the traditional concept of "parks, recreation, and tourism." This chapter will cover some of them, including hang gliding and paragliding, both quiet, non-polluting uses. It will cover skateboarding, trick biking, rollerblading, disc golf, mountain climbing, scuba diving, snorkeling, dog parks, and motorized vehicle models of all kinds (all of which are noisy and many of which can cause severe site erosion problems). They will be covered in several groups, both full-sized and remote-controlled models.

HANG GLIDING

Hang gliding is a recreation activity that uses non-powered, fixed-wing flying vehicles. There are currently three or more types of vehicles available. This chapter only covers the traditional fixed-wing types of crafts.

GENERAL

Where suitable conditions exist, hang gliding can be an attractive addition to the traditional leisure facility uses, both for the flyers and for many of the resource's other users who become spectators.

Traditional hang gliding in its modern form is a far cry from the popular conception of a dare-devil activity. In its purest form, it requires the participant to be a rated pilot under the close scrutiny of the United States Hang Gliding Association (USHGA). The association's equipment certification program and its standard operating procedures are a large part of the current good safety record of hang gliding. Sites are rated I, II, III, and IV (similar to boating waters), with IV being for advanced pilots.

SITE REQUIREMENTS

There are two areas required for hang gliders – the take-off (launching area) and landing space. They do not, and frequently are not, directly physically connected.

Take-Off Area:

Consider using overlooks, ski slopes, and ledding areas for launching sites. Choice of site is directly related to wind direction and velocity.

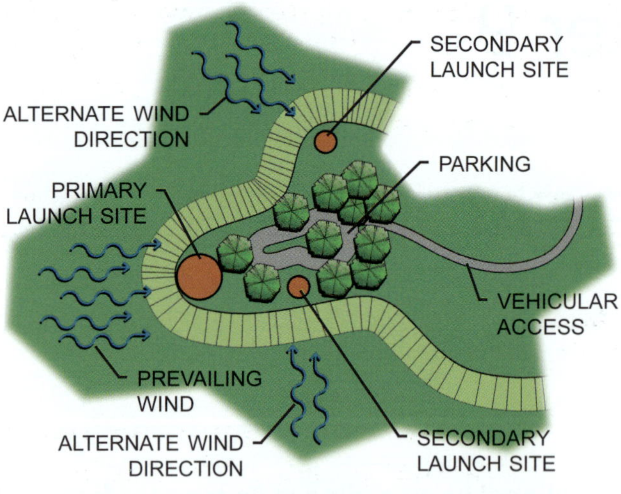

FIG. 9.1 – HANG GLIDER LAUNCH SITE

Hang gliders normally require an elevated launch site facing the wind. This will be best satisfied by having multiple launch points oriented in different directions to increase the number of days when flying can occur. The largest and most developed one would be facing into the prevailing wind. An alternative launching site would be a flat area with little used roads on which would provide a way to get sufficient launching wind speed by driving rapidly down the open fields or roads.

Minimum unassisted launching area requires a slope of 20 percent with a 50-foot (15 m) wide cleared area extending down slope approximately 200 feet (60 m).

Maximum slope for launching is a vertical drop with a 50-foot (15 m) wide cleared area extending down slope approximately 100 feet (30 m).

Minimum height 100 feet (30 m) – sites below 300 feet (90 m) are normally considered training slopes.

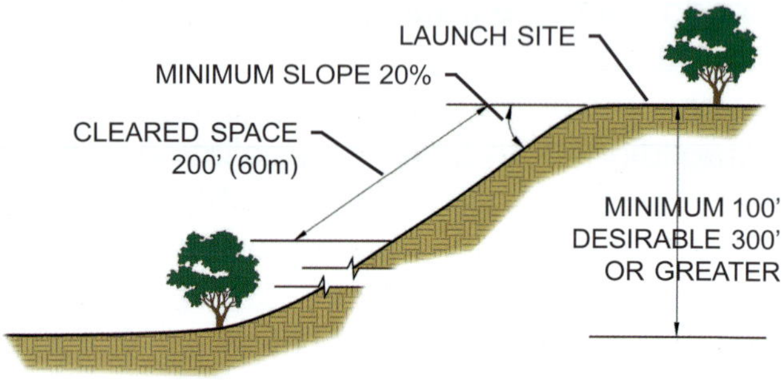

FIG. 9.3 – SLOPING SITE

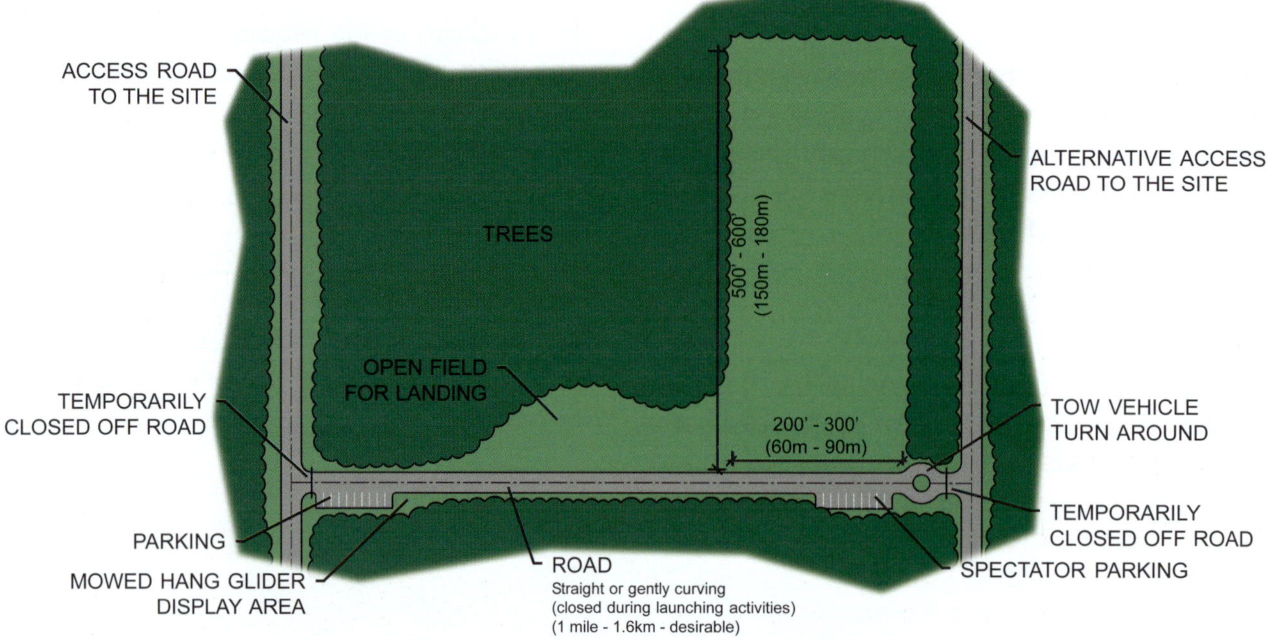

FIG. 9.2 – ROADWAY LAUNCHING

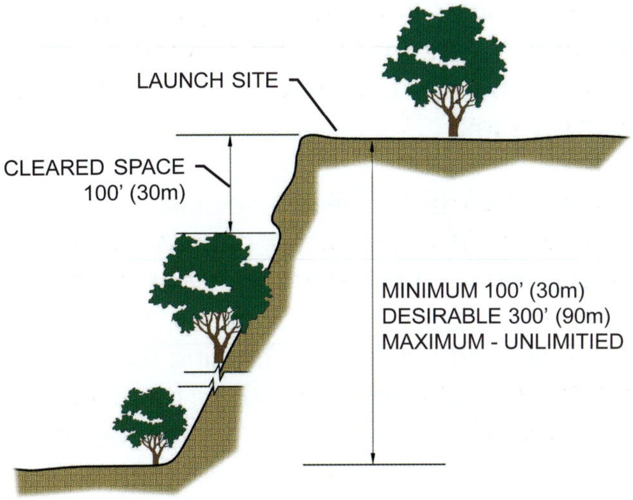

FIG. 9.4 – VERTICAL SITE

Air movement over and around solid objects causes turbulence, which leads to accidents. It is necessary, therefore, to have a relatively clear area from abrupt objects, including other hills or mountains for approximately one mile (1.6 km) in front (up wind) of the hang glider flying area. This can be readily achieved by launching from vehicle-driven launching on flat or relatively flat sites.

Access and parking for at least one car/truck is needed within 300 feet (90 m) of the launch site. One car per participant is necessary. Parking for a shuttle service between the launch site and landing area is needed. The provision of a shuttle vehicle is a desirable operating feature for any heavily used site(s).

A small sanitary facility is needed at the launch site (unisex vault or composting toilets are acceptable) and would be desirable at any major landing site.

Landing Site:

A flat site easily seen from the launch area and free of obstructions is needed. It must be free of surrounding power lines, buildings, and tall trees. Desired: approximately 200 feet (60 m) x approximately 500 feet (150 m) minimum. Advanced level IV landing areas can be as small as 150 feet (45 m) x 300 feet (90 m).

Space for spectator viewing is desirable. If a road passes nearby, it might cause people to pull off and watch the activity. This spectator space must be taken into consideration during facility planning.

Parking for one car per flyer at the take-off area and one car per 2.5 flyers at the landing areas should be provided. In addition, there should be at least one vehicle space at the landing or soaring areas per each 2.5 anticipated spectators.

Sanitary facilities are necessary (flush toilets desirable). Use picnic area standards for determining the number of fixture units.

PARAGLIDING

This sport is very popular and is growing in the U.S. Because of various reasons (liability being a major one), it may have reached its maximum use. It consists of foot launching

Paragliding – Key West, Florida

from a high point (or more likely being towed – see Boating) of an inflatable canopy that can be steered to find lift and maneuver to a landing area. It is lightweight and can be taken along when hiking or mountain climbing.

Paragliding in the U.S. is regulated by the American Paragliding Association (APA). It has become significantly popular in beach communities and is usually operated by a concession (for a fee) facility.

SITE REQUIREMENTS

Basically, the same as for hang gliding. The two activities are compatible and paragliding can use the same facilities as hang gliding.

Launching:

For pulled launching, an open space where a pulling vehicle can continue to proceed at speed for several minutes is needed – usually boats are chosen. Land still-launched paragliders require an elevated launch site facing the wind as in hang gliding.

For still-launched, gliders a minimum slope of 30 percent with approximately a 50-foot (15 m) x 250-foot (75 m) cleared space is needed. Maximum slope vertical with a 50-foot (15 m) x 150-foot (45 m) cleared space. Minimum height 100 feet (30 m) for training slopes to unlimited height for experts. Access to the launching area can be by trail due to the light weight (10 to 15 pounds (4 to 6 kg)) of the equipment.

Landing Area:

For pulled paragliders, a flat, unobstructed area free of obstacles is needed. Approximate size for shore-pulled paragliders is 100 feet x one-half mile. For high, still launching, 50 feet (15 m) x 50 feet (15 m) cleared space, free of nearby power lines and tall obstructions is needed. Ski lifts can be utilized to move people and equipment between launch and landing sites.

Safety has become of special concern, especially in concession or non-controlled operations. Of particular concern are electrical storms (electrocution), equipment that fails, and inadequate training (both of the staff and the participants). These are all factors that can cause the termination of the activity.

SKATEBOARD/ROLLERBLADE/ TRICK BIKE

CONCEPT

Skateboarding – Eastern England

Skateboarding (including in-line skating and trick biking) has emerged from its early bad-boy image. Skateboarding has rapidly been taken on as a mainstream recreation activity. Many sites and some states have incorporated it as a dedicated facility in their park and recreation districts. The City of Phoenix in Arizona has three parks with skatepark components and is actively pursuing the development of more. Throughout the U.S.,

Rollerblading at in-ground skatepark – Washington State Photo by Linda Parrish

the provision of skatepark facilities seems to have come of age. Generally, facilities being reasonably equal, 50 percent of participants are skateboarders, 30 percent are in-line skaters, and 20 percent are bicyclists.

These percentages are based on equipment cost per activity and will vary by region. Currently, most of the participants are 8 to 16 years of age and male, with only 2 to 5 percent of participants being female, but the female percentage seems to be increasing. By high school, participation is dropping off. Only a handful of people skateboard or trick bike after high school and later into life.

Trick biking has a relatively small number of usually teenage practitioners – Bonita Springs, Florida

There are two commonly accepted approaches to providing these much wanted skateboard, rollerblade, and trick bike facilities. They are above ground (usually the ramps are partially movable) and below ground (poured or sprayed in place concrete with the ramps generally not movable). For the most part, the eastern portion of the U.S. is choosing the above ground facilities, while the west has tried both fixed below grade and above grade.

Above ground skatepark – Hudson River Park, Manhattan, NY Photo by Mike Bozlin

WHAT TYPE OF FACILITIES ARE NEEDED?

Skateparks consist of obstacles commonly called ramps. Other features in a skatepark usually include rails, stairs and platforms, gaps, and flat ground space. The three most common types of skateparks are:

1. **Wood-framed:** Generally, the lowest initial cost alternative and usually on a flat, well-drained surface. They are very flexible in design, easiest to modify or renovate, and require some maintenance, especially keeping the ramp surfacings tight and the ramp supports free of rotting.

Wood-framed ramps
– Bonita Springs Skatepark – Florida

2. **Steel-framed:** Slightly more expensive than wood-framed. Can be stronger frame than wood, but more limited in modification (basically the same as wood-framed parks), but more limited in modification. They require the same or more maintenance as wood framed ramps, especially the painting/ preservation of the metal framing and the keeping of the wood decking tight.

3. **Cement:** The most expensive type of construction, and usually set below grade and fluid in form. Good drainage is essential. The structures are permanent and cannot be readily modified to meet changing interests. Maintenance is limited until the concrete surface begins to deteriorate and/or breaks up.

In-ground skatepark – Washington State
Photo by Linda Parrish

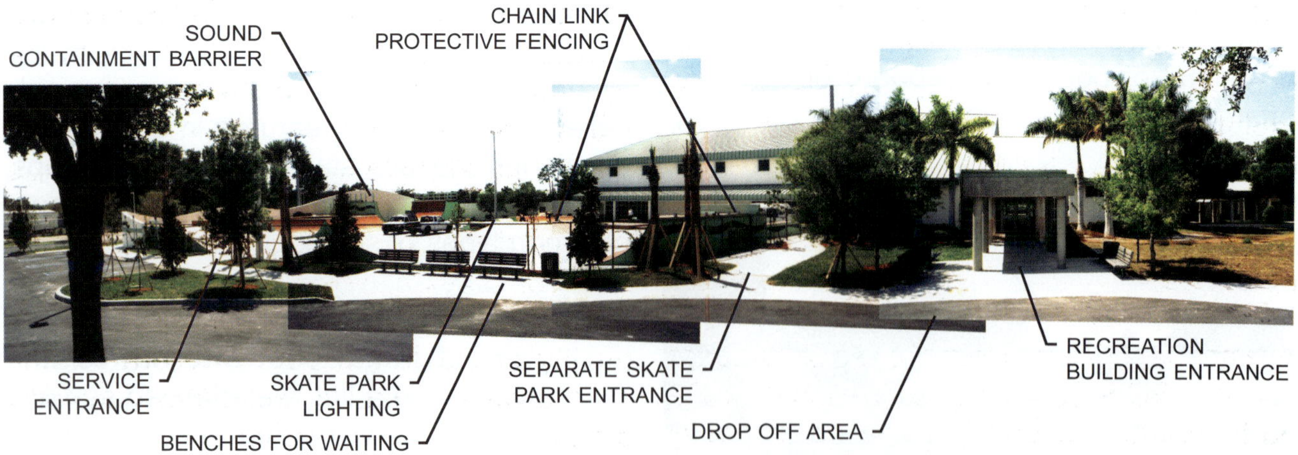

Bonita Springs Skatepark – Florida

CONTROL

• Fencing may be necessary to limit accessibility on all three types of skateparks to deter theft of obstacles and provide control of use. A controlled, fenced area also makes it easily possible to collect user fees.

• Skateparks should have a recognizable main entrance and a separate maintenance entrance. Emergency exits are desirable and frequently required for fire code enforcement.

• Sound containment from the skaters and adjacent use areas is sometimes necessary, and can be a very significant design and cost factor.

DESIGN AND LAYOUT

Given the three types of parks described previously, the design and layout of the skatepark is the most important factor in determining the success of the park. An experienced skatepark designer or builder should be familiar with the latest, most popular structures. It is good, as in any "park" facility, to poll the opinions of the local participants on what structures are desirable to them.

LOCATION

An important factor in regards to a skatepark's success is its location. Since most of the participants are under 18, a safe, easily accessible location for the skatepark is essential. This will provide parents and care providers with a sense of security when dropping off the participants.

PROTECTIVE GEAR

The issue of protective gear is important and should not be overlooked. Participants strongly prefer to be able to choose the use of protective gear under their own discretion.

A type of pad that is useful for one participant may be a hindrance for another. The best policy from a participant standpoint to have at a skatepark is an "open pad" policy. The safest operator's procedure requirement of full pads has been known to deter participants, especially trick bikers.

LIGHTING

Adequate lighting is necessary to eliminate shadows for safe usage of all ramps during non-daylight periods.

WEATHER CONDITIONS

A skatepark facility in a given location should be designed to withstand the normal adverse weather conditions occurring at the site, i.e., snow in the northeast or hurricanes on the Gulf coast and Atlantic Coast, etc. The experienced skatepark builder should be familiar with the most suitable materials in the region to meet these conditions. Some areas in the country, due to an abundance of extreme adverse weather, may require an indoor facility, e.g., Alaska. Drainage is necessary for all three types of skateparks previously listed. Also, the drainage should not compromise the quality of the skatepark; therefore, drains should be avoided in the primary skating areas.

STAFFING

Staffing of skateparks is expensive. If the skatepark is in connection with other facilities, staffing may be necessary. If staffing is chosen, it is helpful to include at least one staff member who is knowledgeable about the sport.

Hudson River Park Skatepark
Credit: Mike Bozlin, Hudson River Park

SPECTATOR AND PARTICIPANT ACCOMMODATIONS

• Vending machines are very cost effective and necessary. They must be regularly stocked. They can significantly help finance the operations and maintenance of the skatepark. (See photo - Vending machine area)

• Trash receptacles near beverage dispensers and other vending machines are a necessity.

• Shaded tables and benches positioned away from the flow of skatepark traffic for rest and visiting by participants. It is desirable to have some picnic tables near vending machines.

• Shaded areas for spectator and participant comfort, including a waterproof covered area for rain retreat.

Vending machine area
Bonita Springs Skatepark – Florida
(Note location of trash receptacle in foreground and picnic table in background.)

• Toilets – men's and women's restrooms with greater numbers of men's facilities should be designed so that rollerbladers can use facilities without removing their blades.

• Outdoor lockers for temporary storage are desirable.

SKATEPARK ACCESS

• Sidewalks or pathway leading to recognizable entrance.

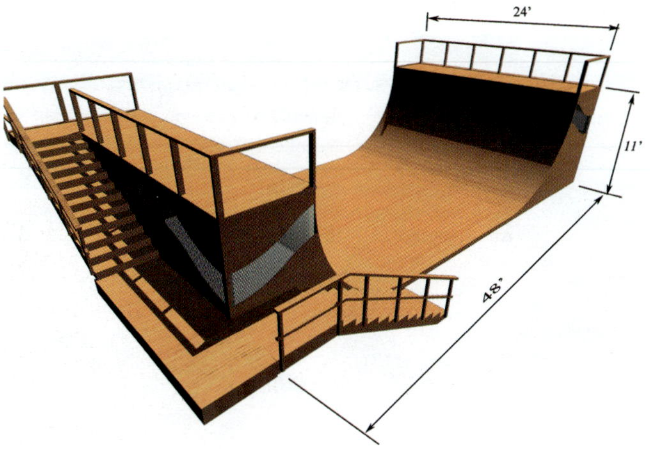

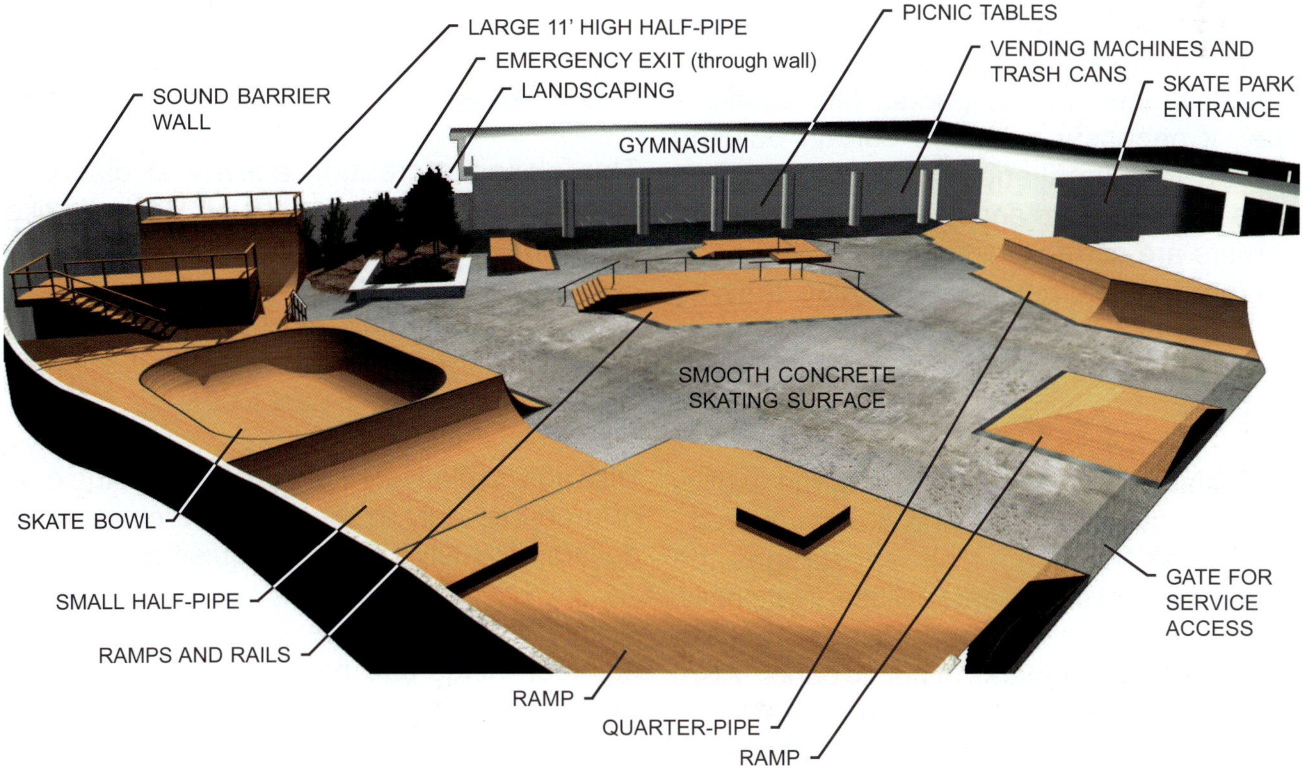

FIG. 9.5 – SCHEMATIC SKATEPARK DESIGN LAYOUT – BONITA SPRINGS SKATEPARK – FLORIDA
(Ramp design by: Ben Johnson)
(Images courtesy of Mark Smith)

• Vehicle pick-up and drop-off area with sitting and trash receptacles set back slightly from the driveway.

• Bicycle, scooter, and motorcycle parking. They should be easily seen from inside the park to help deter theft.

• Vehicle parking with particular emphasis on shaded areas for drivers and others waiting in cars. A good view of skate facilities is very desirable.

SKATEPARK FACILITY SPECIFICS

Standards

There are no current national skatepark construction standards or guidelines other than current national ASTM standards for various materials used in skateparks. Municipalities may, if necessary, impose certain building criteria for compliance with local/regional codes. Skateparks and their jump ramps and barriers are currently commonly classified as playground equipment. This also may be reviewed by the CPSC.

Liability

Most states have statutes limiting the liability of municipalities who provide skateparks, e.g., FL Statute 316.0085. This encourages the construction of skatepark facilities. Nationally, most insurance companies now include coverage for skateparks at public parks. Also, the CPSC has information on the safety of skatepark sports in relationship to that of other sports.

Revenue

Generally, skateparks can be a break-even venture if you compare the revenue generated to the facilities' operational and maintenance costs.

½ Pipe even on the island of Spitzbergen off the Norwegian coast far above the Artic Circle

DISC GOLF

This skilled recreation activity of disc golf started probably in the 1970s.[43] Recently, like skateboarding, it has become much more popular with several hundred courses, most on public lands, now available. The largest concentration of courses is in the north central section of the East Coast.

Disc golf is relatively inexpensive, with the cost of a course only in the tens of thousands of dollars, exclusive of land acquisition.

A disc golf course like its parent, golf, has eighteen holes and needs parking and toilet facilities. A course requires15 to 18 acres± (6 to 7.3 ha) with the average of 250 feet (75 m) per hole. The course should be one way on the front nine (clockwise) and the opposite direction (counter clockwise) on the back nine.

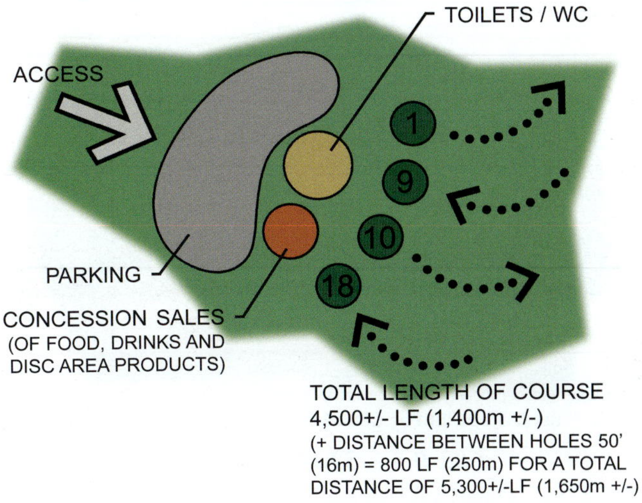

FIG. 9.6 – CONCEPTUAL DISC GOLF COURSE

GENERAL

Required:

- Keep the course away from conflicting activities, i.e., children's play, picnic tables, sports fields, parking lots, etc. (44)
- Tees to be surfaced preferably with concrete, asphalt, compacted crushed stone, etc.
- Course playing surface (the fairway) should be grass-covered or, where wooded, mulched.
- Trash receptacles and a means of trash pick-up.
- Toilets.
- Parking – vehicles and bicycles.

Desirable:

- Walkway around entire course.
- A shaded drop-off area with sitting can be useful where there is significant use by people who are not driving.

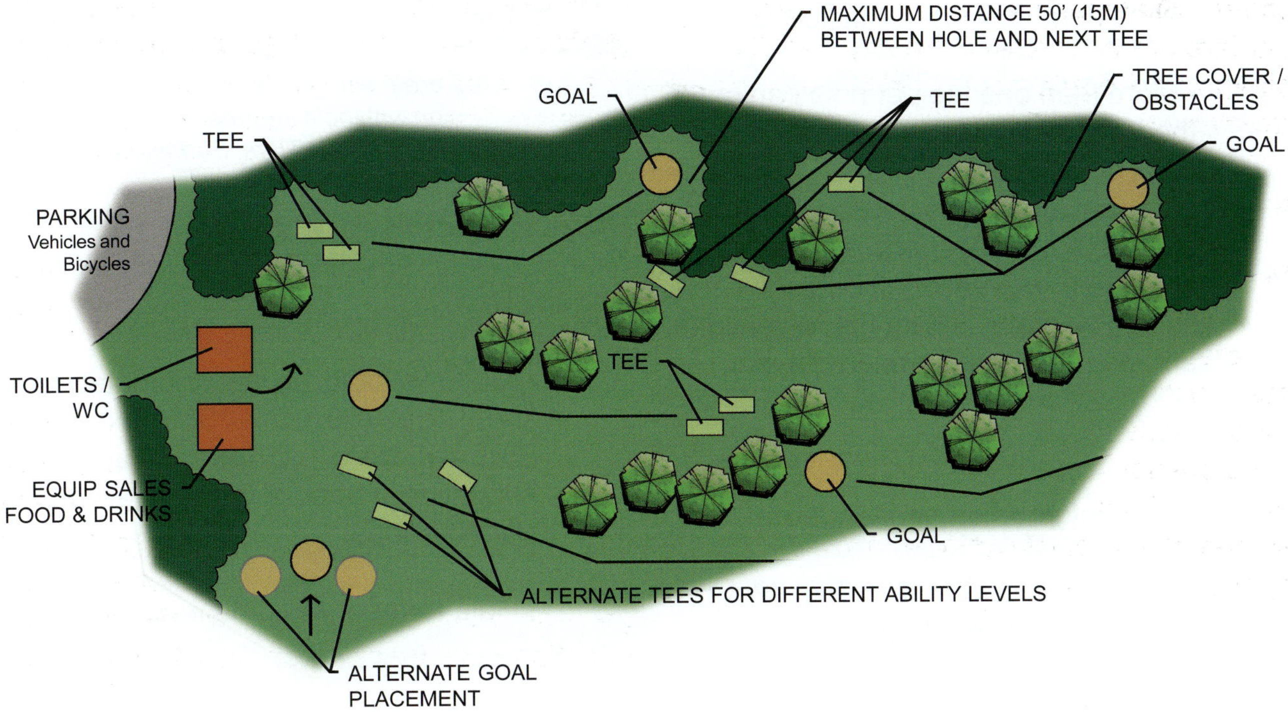

FIG. 9.7 – PARTIAL LAYOUT OF THE BEGINNING/ END OF AN 18-HOLE COURSE

Fairway on #1 hole (normally grassed, but surface has been mulched in this wooded area) – French Creek State Park, Pennsylvania

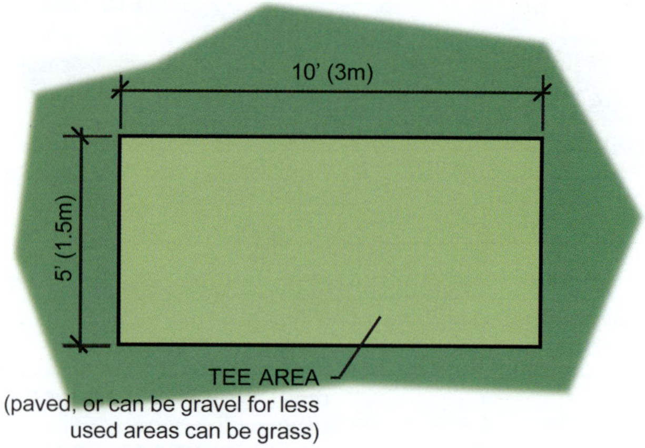

FIG. 9.8 – STANDARD TEE

TEE

Required:

- Tees should be approximately five feet (1.5 m) x 10 feet (3.0 m) and surfaced with concrete, asphalt, or possibly gravel.

- Hole number must be included.

- More than one tee per hole can make the hole and course usable by a wider range of abilities and increase participation and satisfaction. Three are suggested. Give them a name, e.g., advanced, recreational, beginner. Par should be about 20± for the recreational and 55± for the advanced players.

Desirable:

- Hole information at each tee.

- A shaded, benched (6 feet (2.8 m)) waiting area at each tee.

- Trash receptacle.

Tee area with gravel base and sign with hole information – French Creek State Park, Pennsylvania

GOAL/HOLE/PIN (44)

Required:

- Goals should be approximately 200 lineal feet (60 m) to 350 lineal feet (105 m) from the tees. Each hole should be located at different distances from the tees.

- Hole number must be included.

Desirable:

- Goals can be moved if the area around it becomes too worn. These moves can be difficult to do, so should be kept to a minimum.

- A cleared space 30 feet (9 m) in diameter is desired by some disc golfers. The more skilled prefer obstacles.

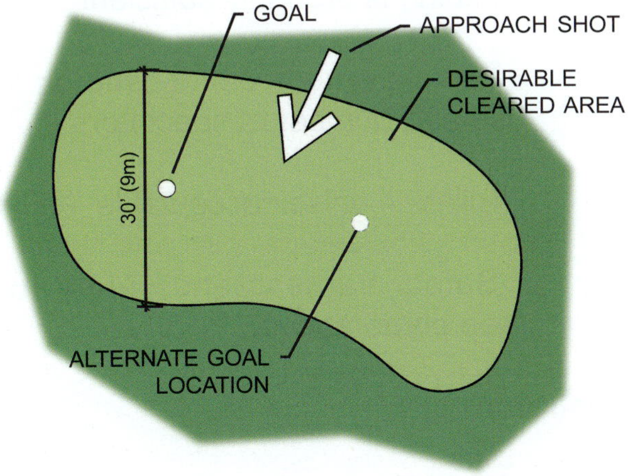

FIG. 9.9 – ALTERNATE GOAL LOCATION

Goal/hole (trees in front of goal are an effective obstacle) – French Creek State Park, Pennsylvania

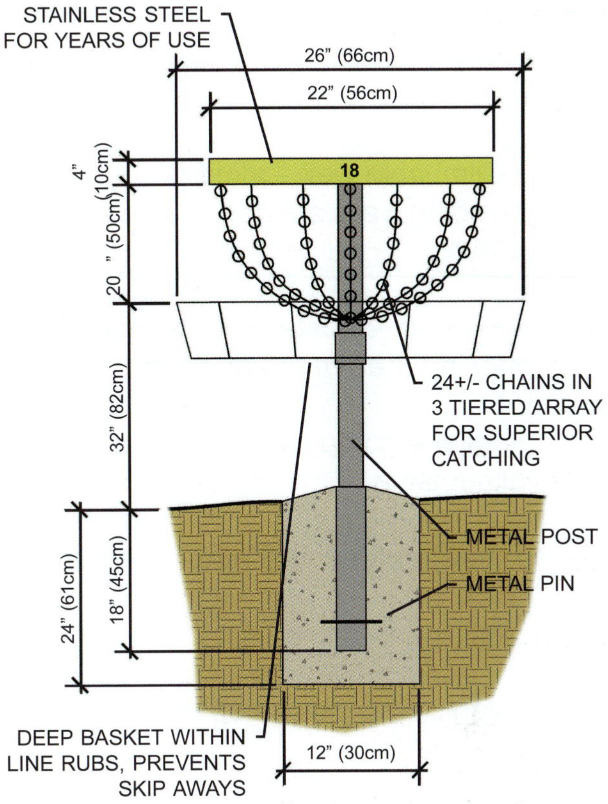

FIG. 9.10 – TYPICAL DISC GOLF GOAL [45]

Additional Desirable Features:

- Scoreboards should be provided on courses used in competitions.

- Scorecards.

MOUNTAIN CLIMBING

Mountain climbing, generally under controlled, artificially constructed conditions, is becoming popular. The activity required one of two conditions: (1) natural climbing wall or (2) cliff or manmade climbing wall. It should be clearly understood that this activity is dangerous! Utmost care must be taken to protect the participants as much as possible without diminishing the enjoyment of the climbing challenge.

NATURAL

Required:

- Climbable wall – most good, natural climbing walls are not located in typical parks.
- Parking – locate small additional parking area at top of climb.
- Toilet – composting and unisex are acceptable.
- Viewing area with attendant parking.

Desirable:

- Vehicle access at top of climb.

MANMADE

Portable manmade climbing tower located at a fairground

Requirements:

- Climbing wall with varying levels of difficulty. The higher and more difficult, the more challenging and the greater the enjoyment for most climbers.
- Six-foot high safety fencing with controlled access.
- 100 feet (30 m) x 100 feet (30 m) for climbing is probably sufficient.
- Parking – numbers depend on likely use and number of spectators.
- Toilets – unisex acceptable – flush.
- Safety harness and safety ropes (see photo above).

Desirable:

- Night lighting.
- Spectator viewing area(s).
- Control structure/fee collection booth.

SNORKELING AND SCUBA DIVING

Snorkeling and scuba diving are activities enjoyed by a wide age range. They can take place anywhere there is underwater scenery, either natural or manmade. The only requirement is that there is something of interest to see, usually plants and/or animals, especially fish. There are two types of facilities required.

1. UNDERWATER FEATURE(S)

This can be natural, e.g., stones, ledges, coastal trees, coral reefs, etc., or manmade, e.g., old shipwrecks, dumped rubble, sunken metal objects, etc. These formations and manmade objects provide for a concentration of favorable habitat for fish and other marine organisms. The larger the feature is, the greater the opportunity for natural, interesting systems to become established and the greater the attraction for snorkeling and scuba diving.

2. ON-SHORE SUPPORT FACILITIES

There must be a way to get to the water features. These can be either marina or beach related.

Marina:

Many viewing areas are accessible only by boat. This requires dock space at marinas for dive and snorkeling party boats and diving equipment. The number of boats will depend on the popularity of the underwater feature. The facilities can be located in one area or divided into several places.

Scuba gear at a commercial boating facility – Roatan, Honduras

• One parking space for each two people.

• Toilet facilities on shore and, preferably, aboard the dive boats.

• Interpretive facilities describing the feature to be seen and trip procedures.

• Sales area.

• Properly equipped dive boat with water ingress and egress facilities.

• Site anchoring capability – best with pre-positioned anchoring areas and or anchors.

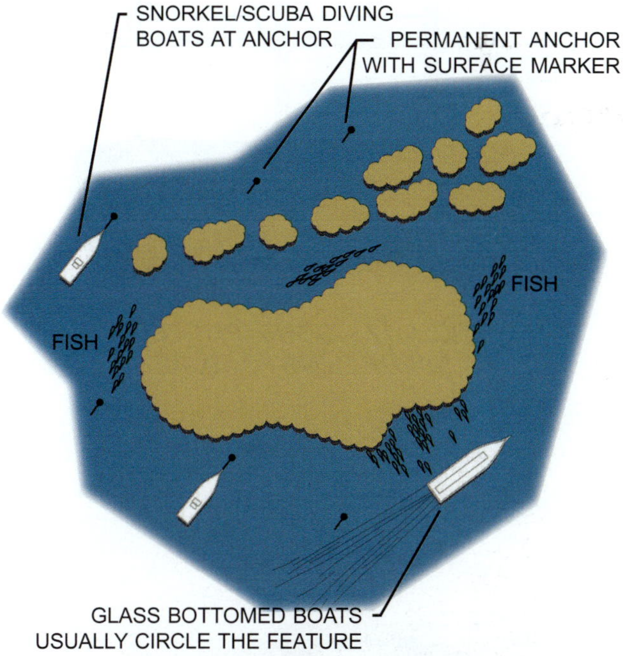

FIG. 9.11 – UNDERWATER VIEWING AREA WITH ANCHORAGE SYSTEM

Beach Access:

Underwater viewing, usually snorkeling, can also be done from the shore. Underwater enhancement of existing features is frequently needed. Figure 9.12 is an example of how a structure on pilings can be effectively used for water habitat enhancement.

Snorkeling from shore
Photo courtesy of Rowland family

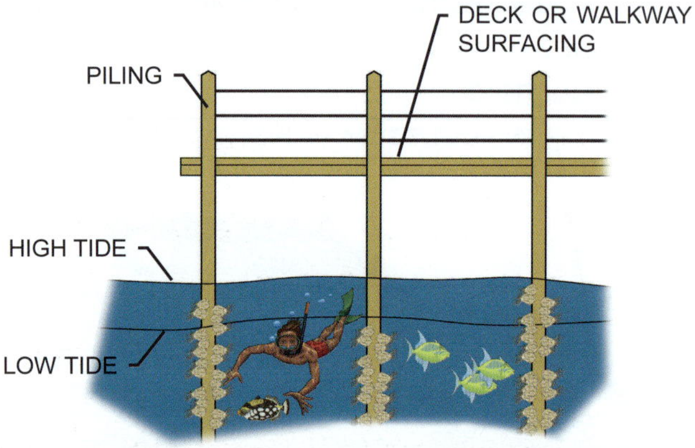

FIG. 9.12 – CONSTRUCTED SNORKELING FEATURE

Snorkeling from shore
– John Pennekamp State Park, Florida

MODEL AIRPLANES, BOATS, CARS, ETC.

CONTROLLED AIRPLANES

Tri-plane display area at model airplane field
– Collier County, Florida

Normally located in urban areas in large multipurpose parks or in places where noise will not be a problem. Could also utilize facilities built for remote controlled planes.

Required:

- Parking – within 200 feet (60 m) or closer to the use areas.

- Set-up and waiting space.

- Cleared, smooth space for takeoffs and landings (turf or asphalt); 150 feet radius (45 m), 75 feet radius (225 m) minimum.

- Safety barriers, preferably fencing a minimum of four feet (1.2 m) high, between flying area and surrounding uses, including spectators.

• Sanitary facilities within a maximum of 400 feet (120 m) of use area, but much closer is desirable. Unisex vault or composting-type toilets are acceptable.

Desirable:

• Spectator area (only if there are normally spectators).

• Small clubhouse and only if there is sufficient use.

These facilities will also serve for small model rockets, and, if paved, for remote controlled model cars, etc.

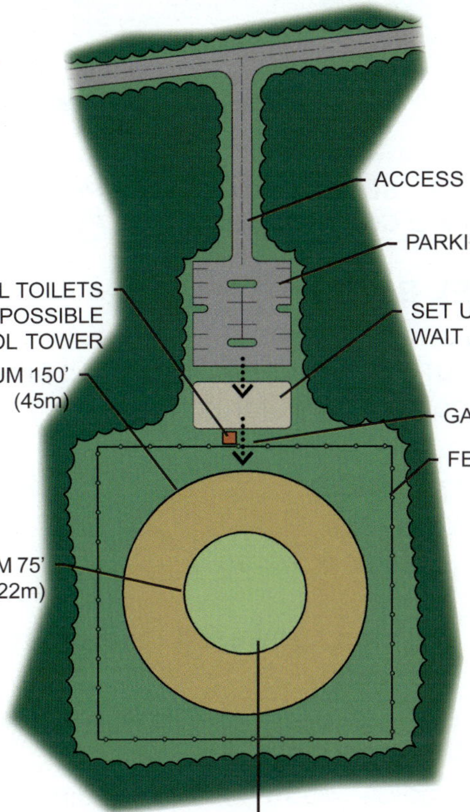

FIG. 9.13 – CONTROLLED MODEL PLANE FIELD

REMOTE CONTROLLED AIRPLANES

Remote controlled model plane flying field – Collier County, Florida

Required:

• Parking – gravel acceptable.

• Paved set-up, waiting-to-fly and plane display space.

• Paved access (taxiway to runway).

• Paved runway of a minimum of 100 feet (30 m) x 100 feet (30 m); 150 feet (45 m) x 150 feet (45 m) is desirable. The runway should be separated by fencing from all other areas at the model plane facility.

• Spectator viewing area.

• Control tower.

• Electricity.

• Sanitary facilities, possibly unisex. Preferably flush, but composting acceptable.

• Safety barriers to separate spectators and participants.

• Cleared area of approximately 1000 feet x 1000 feet (300 m x 300 m) with no major obstacles that would damage airplanes when they are forced to crash land.

Desirable:

• Clubhouse if sufficient numbers of users will support its inclusion.

• Water supply and sewage disposal.

• Spectator overlook platform to better see the takeoffs and landings.

• These facilities will also ideally serve for launching model rockets of all sizes and for other remote controlled model vehicle users.

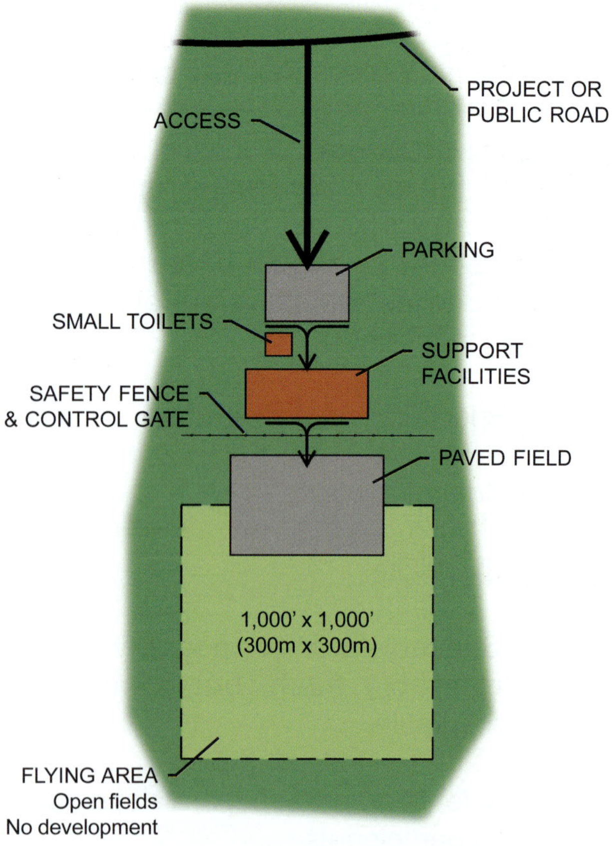

FIG. 9.14 – CONCEPTUAL REMOTE CONTROLLED MODEL PLANE AREA

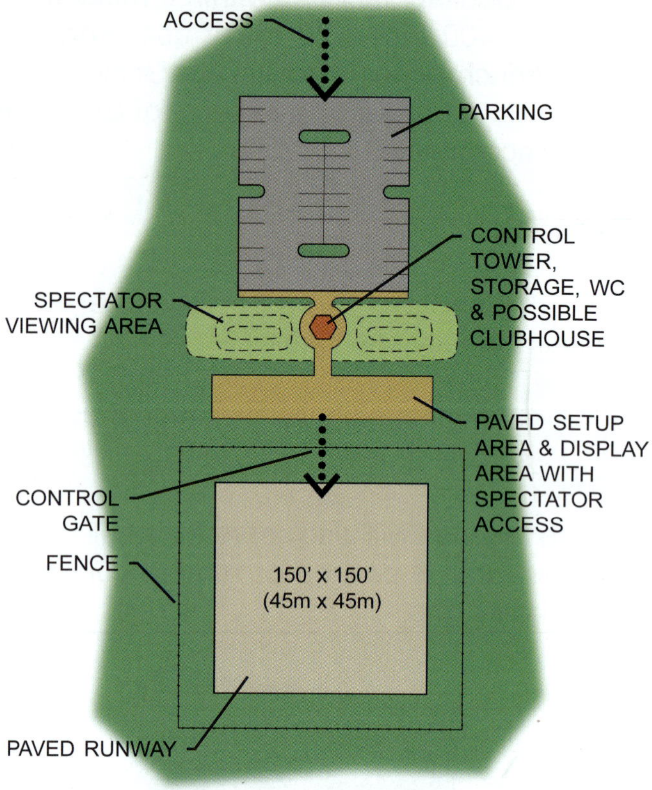

FIG. 9.15 – SUGGESTED MASTER PLAN LAYOUT REMOTE CONTROLLED MODEL PLANE FIELD

MODEL BOATS

Use of community borrow pits and development lakes for boating.

Types of boats:

• Motor powered.

• Wind powered (sailboats and iceboats).

Facilities needed:

• Launching area(s).

• Participants' model control location.

- Model set-up area.
- Spectator viewing area(s).
- Parking (the number of spaces needed is dependent on the amount of use and can vary from less than ten spaces to many times that.)
- Toilets – unisex probably the best if the number of anticipated users is small.
- Access around lake to pick up boats.
- Accessibility provisions for participants and spectators.

Possible other desirable facilities:

- Clubhouse/meeting room – could be shared with other groups.
- Picnic tables.
- Night lighting (if used for boating after sunset) – especially useful in the south where there is no freezing and winter days are short.
- Shade or an area to set up personal portable pavilions.
- Model display area.
- Sound system (only on larger sites).

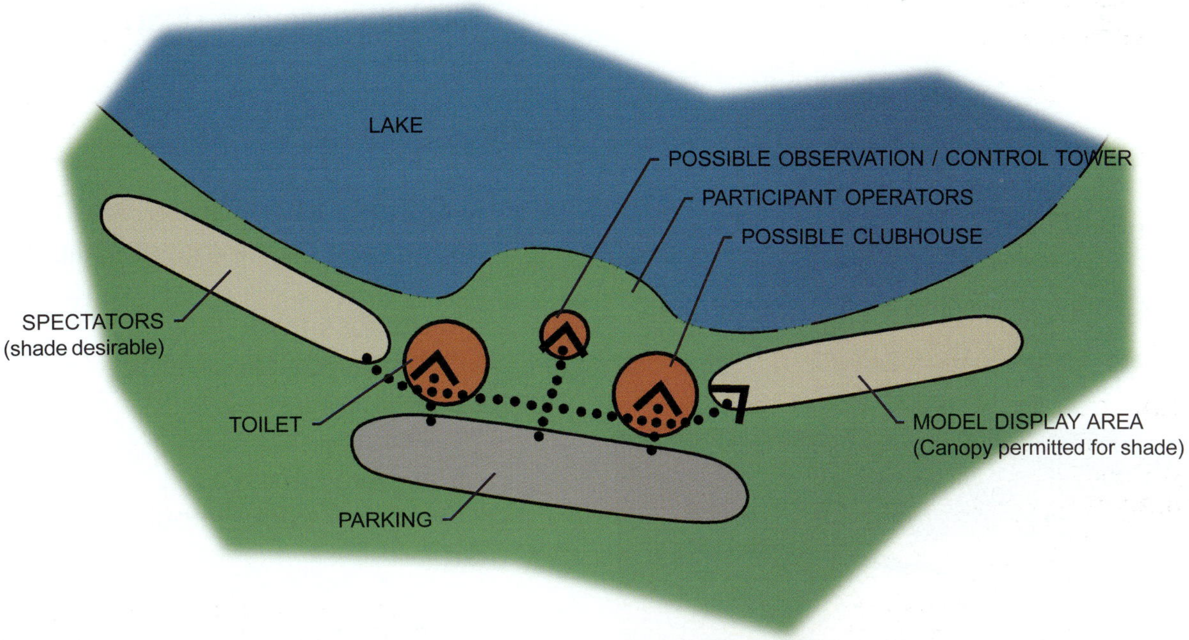

FIG 9.16 – MODEL BOAT LAKE WITH PARTICIPANT/SPECTATOR AREAS

CONTROLLED MODEL VEHICLE USE AREAS

Use of landfill sites is a good option. Need only a small space of one to two acres plus parking and other support facility needs. Size depends on the number of participants and spectators. Sound/noise of model motors can be a problem. Location of activities in a way to minimize or better eliminate the noise is a major factor in site location. New technology of electric motors may make noise less of a problem. An alternative to reduce model noise is to locate the activity on a slightly smaller facility indoors.

Types of model vehicles:

- Cars
- 4 x 4s
- Motorcycles
- SUVs and other OHVs
- Tanks and other military equipment
- Trucks

Young modeler controlling his OHV model – Golden Gate Community Park – Collier County, Florida

Remote controlled model park – Golden Gate Community Park – Collier County, Florida

- Farm equipment
- Construction equipment
- Just about anything that moves on the ground.

Facilities needed:

- Space to operate vehicles – appropriate for the model equipment to be used.
  - Motocross track
  - Construction site
  - Drag strip
  - Hill climb
  - Flat paved area
  - Oval race track – could be paved or dirt
- Model display area – must be accessible to both participants and spectators.
- Participants' model control area – frequently a raised platform or wide, elevated walkway.
- Participant set-up/repair area.

• Noise barrier if non-noise compatible facilities are located in the sound basin.

• Toilets – unisex might be the more desirable option.

• Participant parking.

• Accessible provisions for participants and spectators (only if spectator provisions are provided at the site).

Possible other desirable facilities:

• Clubhouse.

• Spectator seating.

• Spectator parking (If site is popular, spectator parking may become a necessity.).

• Shade.

• Night lighting (if significant night use is anticipated).

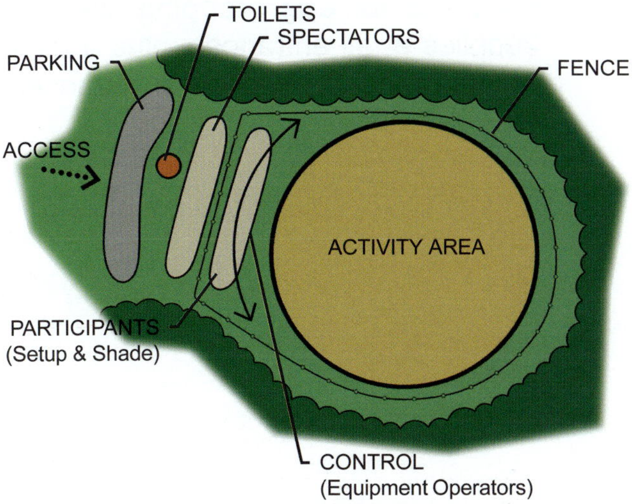

FIG. 9.17 – MODEL VEHICLE AREA

• Shaded model display area.

• Sound system (only on larger, heavily used sites).

Model set-up/repair area at track – Golden Gate Community Park – Collier County, Florida

DOG PARKS

CONCEPT

An enclosed space where dogs can be let off of their restraints to run freely and interact with other dogs. The park will have at least water for the dogs and sitting areas for owners.

Dogs can be free of restraints in fenced dog parks –Vienna, Austria

Space Needed:

Minimum: 3 acres (1.2 hectares).
Desirable: 5 acres (2 hectares).
Maximum: As large as desired.

Needed Facilities:

- Fence - 48 inches (1.2 m) high desirable; 6 feet (1.8 m) high maximum. Not recommended due to cost and poor aesthetics.

- Dog drinking fountain.

Dog drinking fountain – Vienna, Austria

- Entrances – foot and possibly service vehicle if facility is several acres (hectares) in size. Double-gated entrance is a desirable feature to keep dogs from getting outside of the dog enclosure.

Entrance and signs at fenced dog park – Vienna, Austria

Support Facilities:

- Benches.

- Toilets within site or desirable within a 300-foot (90 m) distance of the site or a maximum of 400 feet (120 m).

- Picnic area with picnic tables, people drinking fountain, and trash receptacles.

- Signs with dog park rules.

- A place for dog dropping cleaning supplies at all entrances, plus a trash receptacle for disposal at all entrances.

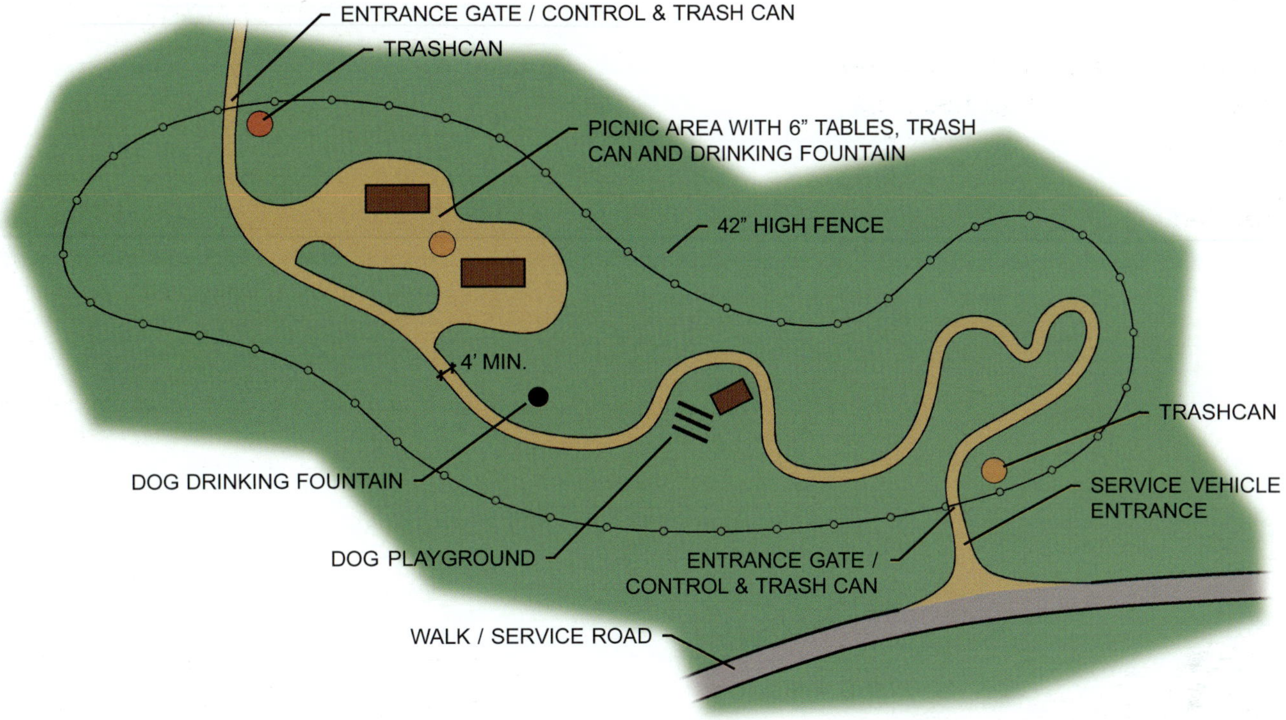

FIG. 9.18 – CONCEPTUAL DOG PARK

Chapter 10

OFF-HIGHWAY VEHICLES

MOTORIZED VEHICLE FACILITIES [25]

GENERAL

Many people like to recreate utilizing motorized vehicles, either as participants or as spectators. Powerboating (see Chapter 18, Boating), snowmobiles, off-road vehicles (ORVs), all-terrain vehicles (ATVs), motorcycles (track, cross-country, and sightseeing), sport utility vehicles (SUVs), dune buggies, swamp buggies, 4 x 4s, cars (sightseeing, drag racing, track racing, and rallying), and motorized models of all types (direct controlled and remote controlled) are but some of the activities that utilize mechanical equipment for the primary focus of the recreation activity. Many require site development and support facilities to be able to operate in an enjoyable and safe way without destroying the resources and endangering the users or spectators. Motorized models are covered in Chapter 9 at the end of Special Use Facilities.

Most motorized equipment is noisy and most can be destructive of the natural resources. Because of these two negative features, the majority of natural resource users and site managers object to their presence in natural resource parks and recreation areas.

Motorcycles, snowmobiles, powerboats, 4-wheel drive vehicles, and other motorized recreation vehicles continue to be sold in large numbers. Because of the continuous increase in sales, provision for facilities for the type of recreation activities this equipment generates must be considered in any complete outdoor recreation system. The facilities can be either public or private or any combination of the two.

In the U.S., continued population growth accompanied by urban sprawl and environmental concerns have produced a nationwide shortage of legal and appropriate use areas to ride and drive off-highway vehicles and powered models. Urban opportunities are particularly limited. Those facilities that are available usually only offer limited facilities and frequently do not adequately address environmental and social concerns. [28]

USER INTERESTS

All motorized vehicle users are interested in one or more of the following: (1) testing driving skills, (2) testing their equipment, (3) relaxing, or (4) enjoying the scenery.

FACTORS INFLUENCING SITE SELECTION AND DESIGN

• To reiterate, the most important factor in locating a motorized vehicle facility is noise! The location of any motorized vehicle area is first and foremost influenced by noise problems, real and/or perceived.

- OHV facilities, if they are located in a resource-oriented park, should be separated, both visually and acoustically, from the rest of the site's natural resources to minimize the disturbances to other users.

- Separated from desirable wildlife habitat or have little to no adverse impact on that habitat.

- Separated from other non-project surrounding land uses that require a more quiet atmosphere, i.e., residential areas, library, offices, etc.

- The size/amount of land needed is dependent on the type and number of OHV activities desired and the amount of use expected.

• Like most recreation activities, the closer to the potential users the facilities are located, the greater the likelihood for success in getting the projected numbers of users to the facilities.

• Accessibility must be provided to all buildings. Not all activities (e.g., hill climbing, motocross, etc.), however, need to be built to accessibility standards.

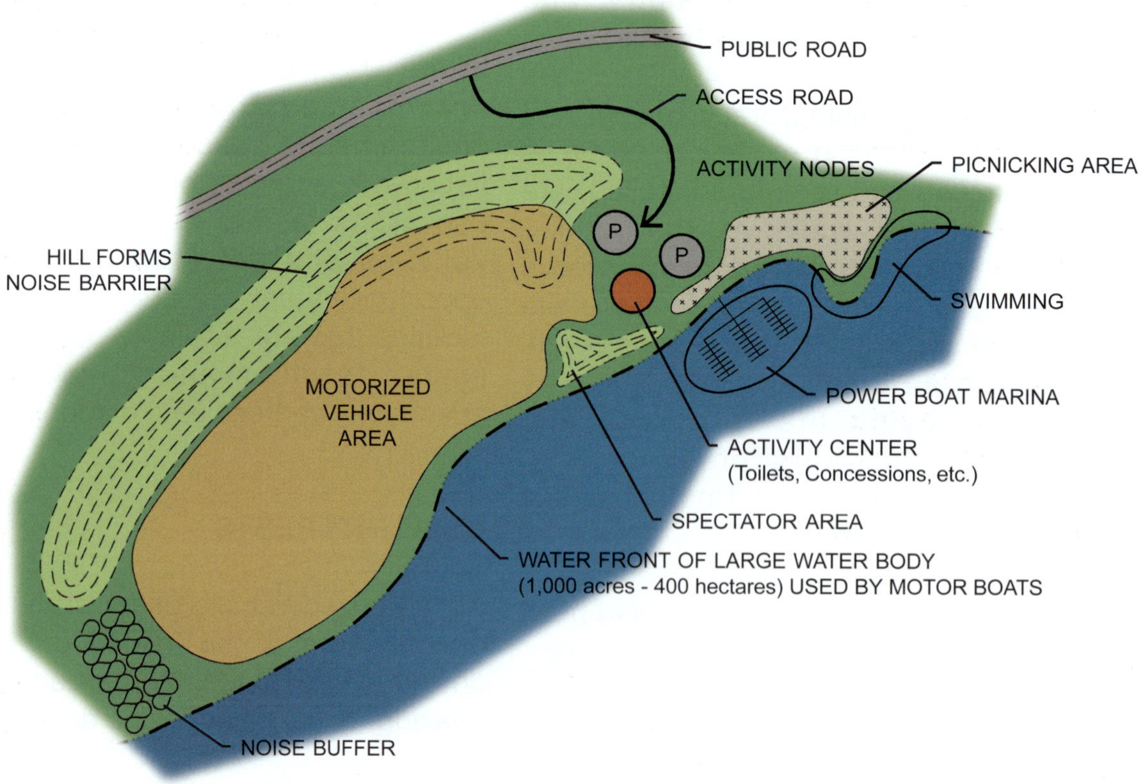

FIG. 10.1 – AN IDEAL MOTORIZED/OHV VEHICLE AREA LOCATION USING LAND FORM AND DESIGN AS A BUFFER

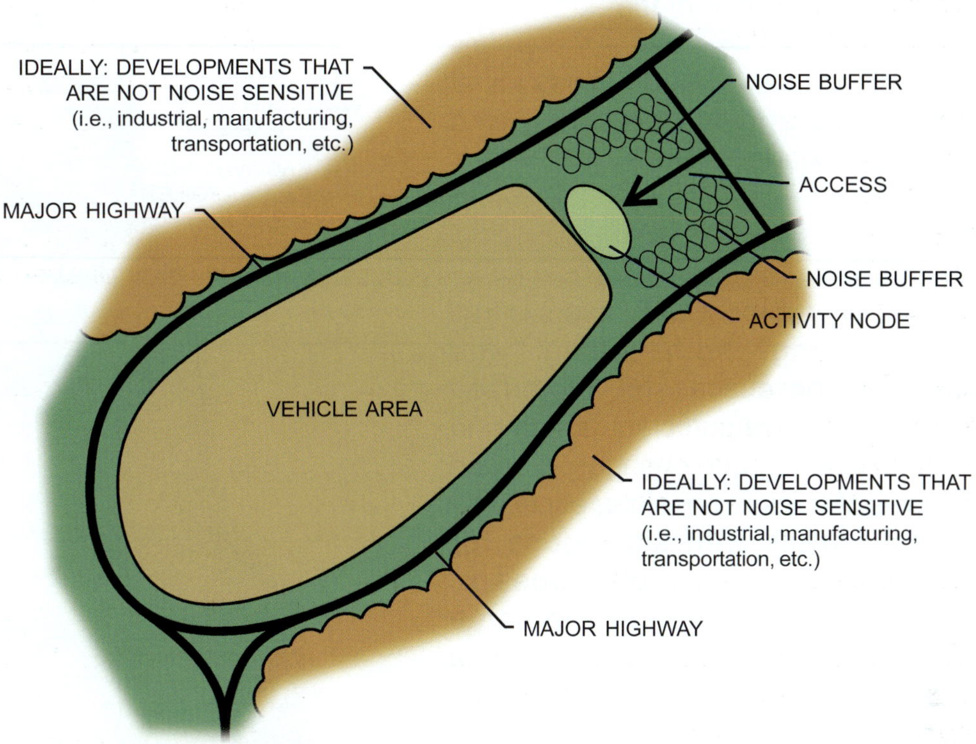

FIG. 10.2 – AN ALTERNATE MOTORIZED OHV LOCATION USING LAND USE AS A BUFFER

• Variation in topography is very desirable – some flat, some hilly.

• Access to the site is a necessity as it is in any resource site development.

• Adequate parking, both for participants and spectators, must be provided.

• Trailhead orientation signs are needed with details of use regulations, environmental concerns, and interpretive information.

FIG. 10.3 – TYPICAL TRAIL DIFFICULTY SIGN SYMBOLS

• Sanitary facilities are required as per any resource project development.

• Spectator viewing areas are desirable at any activity node, i.e., hill climbing, motocross, etc.

• Soil stability is a necessity for any non-trail activity site.

• Utilities: water, electricity, sewage, and telephone must be provided.

• Winter use by snowmobiles can utilize most typical OHV facilities.

• Other items to consider:

- Children's play area(s) – usually only in relationship to large activity nodes.

- Swimming (pool or natural beach), especially on any major use site.

- Shade – natural or manmade.

- Picnic facilities – need access for at least ATVs and motorcycles, and preferably shade.

TRAILS

The primary activity of most OHV users is trail riding and driving, both casual and competitive. To be successful, motorized vehicle trails must have sufficient length and frequent direction and grade changes. Shared or multiple use of trails is possible, especially on main trunk trails with side loops for specialty needs of the various types of vehicles. They basically follow the same criteria as hiking or equestrian trails on a conceptual basis. Major differences are as follows:

1. Trails are likely to have intensive use.

2. Much more damage occurs to the ground than on pedestrian trails; therefore, special care must be taken to avoid fragile and wet areas. Special features are not special when destroyed by overuse.

3. Special features should be by-passed by the main trail with side trails leading to them. This will make them much more special when you get there.

4. Trails will require regular and, frequently, intensive maintenance.

5. Switchbacks can only be used with extreme care due to size of vehicle turning radiuses.

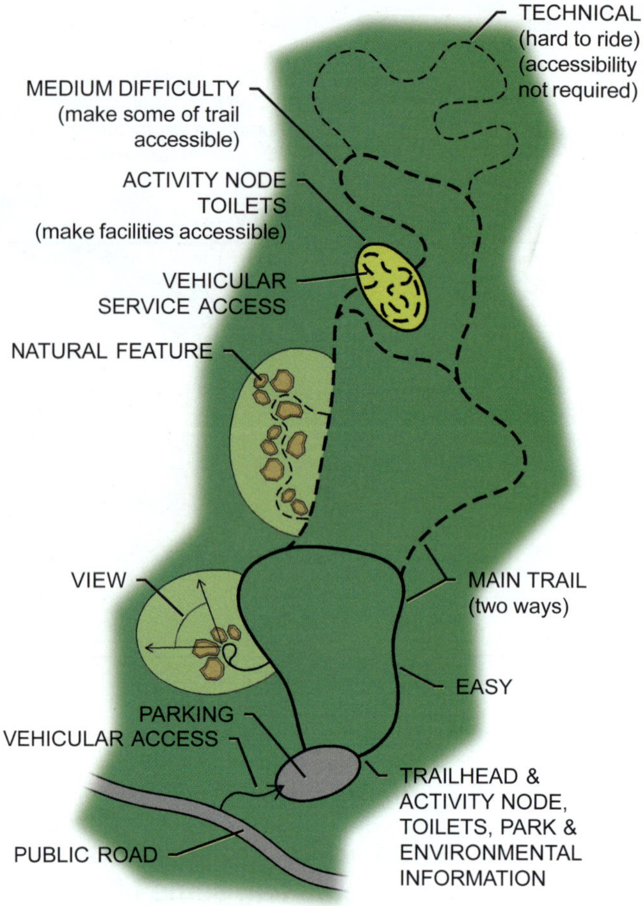

FIG. 10.4 – CONCEPTUAL TRAIL LAYOUT

6. One-way versus two-way trail systems: There is a major disagreement over the desirability of having a one-way or two-way trail system. Logic says that a one-way system is safer. User data says no – especially on longer trails. The reason is that on longer trails users may be able to enter from multiple entry points and may choose the “wrong” one-way even though it is signed correctly. A two-way trail system also doubles the experience opportunities depending on the direction of travel. It is strongly recommended by the National Off-Highway Vehicle Conservation Council, however, that a one-way system be used only on competitive venues and events. [28]

7. Trails must be designed to meet the intended uses, i.e., single-purpose (motorcycle, ATV, 4WD, snowmobiles), shared use (multiple OHV use and/or with non-OHV [site] visitors).

8. Trails need to use a standard signage system. See Fig. 10.3).

9. Like all resource-oriented facilities, mechanical vehicle/OHV parks need a comprehensive sign system. (See Chapter 13.)

10. Steep hill runs almost always suffer from severe erosion. Special care must be taken to accommodate this erosion, i.e., sediment ponds, changes in vertical alignment to allow for water removal.

Hill climb area at an OHV state park in Southern California

11. Utility rights-of-way are frequently utilized by trail riders. These are often not and, frequently, cannot be legally open to use. Utility companies must be contacted prior to any serious consideration of their use in the trail system.

12. There are many areas of an OHV park that need to be vehicle free. Barriers are usually required to accomplish this effort. They should be made as natural looking as possible and utilize materials occurring on the site or trail.

13. Activity nodes – large tracts of land up to several hundred acres (hectares) in size – can be a major asset to a motorized trail system, with areas for free riding and organized activities, as well as designated trail riding. Many riders enjoy competition, and the nodes, properly designed, can accommodate this activity.

ATV

All-terrain vehicles can basically go almost anywhere, even across small bodies of water, if necessary. On short trails, a one-way loop system is best. Some groups prefer two-way systems, and the prospective users should be consulted prior to design.

TRAIL REQUIREMENTS

Length – Approximately 20± miles (30 km±) or a 3- to 6-hour ride.

Surfacing – Can be varied and may include wet areas or rough areas, but the trail should be as dust-free as possible. All wet areas must be very carefully designed to keep areas from various forms of environmental damage. A boardwalk might be required.

Alignment – Should be varied and challenging; grades of over 75 percent should be avoided. Curves with 10 to 12 feet (3 to 4 m) radius are minimum with gentler curves better.

Width – Six feet (2 m) one-way; 10 feet (3 m) two-way. A 10-foot (3 m) trail can also serve (if it is not too steep) as a service/patrol road.

Clearing – Vertical – 8 feet (2.5 m); horizontal – trail width plus 1 foot either side of trail opening, and maintaining views is also desirable; higher, if the trail is used for winter activities.

FOUR-WHEEL DRIVE

There are two types of 4-wheel drive vehicles – the SUV (sport utility vehicle) and the more rugged 4WD.

Four-wheel drive (4WD) set up for eight passengers – Southern Caribbean

KINDS OF TRAILS

1. Trunk or main trail is for all ability levels. These can be two-way and are ideal for SUVs.

2. Primitive trails are for the more rugged 4WD and also for the expert user. They are for low volume use and can be made extremely difficult.

For both types of trails in a controlled site, a one-way system is best and, in fact, almost a necessity for safety, construction costs, and minimizing impacts on the environment. It should be noted, however, that many in the OHV recreation groups believe that two-way trails are preferred. This is an area that must be worked out with the users.

TRAIL REQUIREMENTS

Length – Depends on terrain; 50 to 100 miles (80 to 160 km) is minimum desirable. Utilize as many miles of existing dirt roads, old logging roads, and utility corridors as possible to keep costs down. A loop road system is not necessary if the designed-for-four-wheel-drive vehicles are normally licensed to travel on the public highway system. A multi-jurisdictional trail may have to be a two-way system.

Signing – Needed for both safety and information on trunk trail. Minimal signs needed on primitive trails except to warn the novices to stay off and to mark any safety concerns, and to provide interpretive information. Use standard trail signs. (See Fig. 10. 3.)

Surfacing – Rough.

Alignment – Do not duplicate public road conditions; make it difficult. Trunk trails – 40 percent maximum grade desirable; 60 percent and greater grade for short distances on primitive trails is permissible.

Width – Trunk – 8 feet (2.4 m) minimum on one-way systems; primitive one-way trails can be 6 feet (1.8 m) minimum. Eighteen feet (5.5 m) wide if two-way trails are developed – the space required is virtually the same as a standard rural roadway.

Clearing – Eight to 10 feet (2.4 to 3 m) – vertical; horizontal – trail width plus 2 feet (0.6 m) on both sides.

TRAIL BIKE AND OFF-HIGHWAY MOTORCYCLES

USER INTERESTS

Motorcyclists love the backwoods. It is fun to be there, and it is an escape. Further, most riders want challenging and/or interesting trails. All types of bikes can be and are used.

Motorcycles on the trail

Trail riding on motorcycles is usually physically demanding, especially on rough terrain. Basically, these trails are similar to "Four-Wheel Drive," and they can, in fact, readily use all four-wheel drive and most ATV trails. The trail should look unimproved, but must protect the rider's safety and the site from environmental damages.

TRAIL REQUIREMENTS

Length – Fifty to 100 miles (80 to 160 km), depending on terrain and ability of the likely riders; up to a 6-hour ride.

Surfacing – Trail must be resistant to soil erosion. Mud holes are acceptable, but must meet all environmental protections and constraints. Watch out for stream sedimentation. This frequently means constructed stream crossings. Ruts, bumps, boulders, and small logs are desirable on some segments.

Alignment – Grades up to 100 percent are possible, but have alternate routes for the extremely steep runs. Intersperse routes with easier segments. Many twists and turns are desirable.

Width – Three feet (1 m). Shoulders may not be necessary, depending on soil conditions and trail surface.

Clearing – Horizontal – 3+ feet (1+ m); keep it minimal; vertical – 8 feet (2.5 m); keep it minimal, but keep it open.

MECHANIZED VEHICLE AND/OR OHV PARK

A very desirable alternative to utilizing resource-oriented facilities for vehicular use would be to develop recreation areas specifically for mechanized vehicles. (See Fig. 10.1.) These could be located almost anywhere noise is not a problem, where the noise can be controlled by good design, or on strip-mined and other seriously disturbed lands, and could help in restoring the land. These lands would, of course, require careful evaluation and, where necessary, treatment to ensure that there is no pollution generated on the site that would harm surrounding lands.

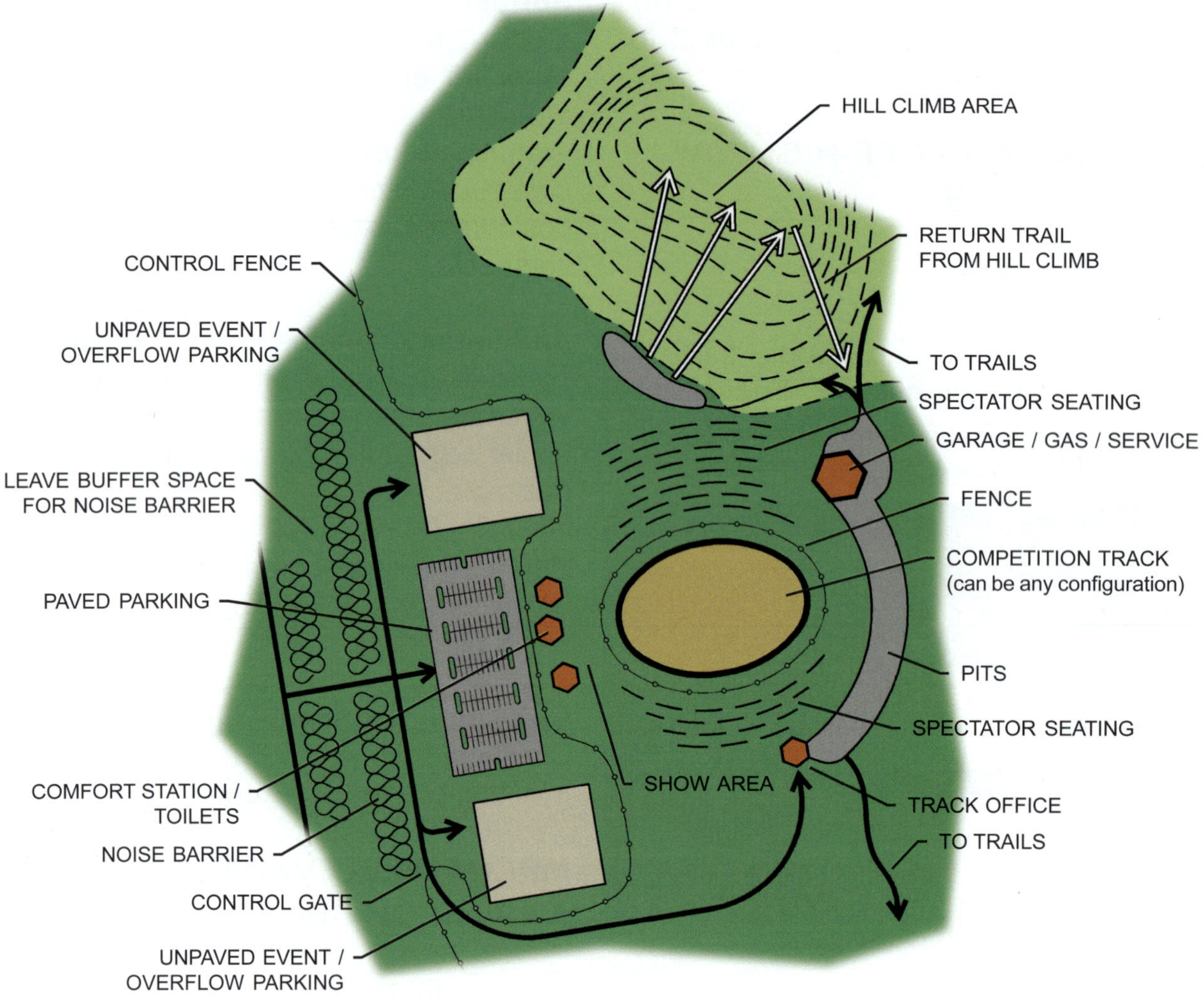

FIG. 10.5 – LAYOUT – MECHANICAL VEHICLE PARK

It should be understood that those who use mechanical vehicles for recreation have the same needs as the typical park user. A "mechanized vehicle/OHV park" should, in addition, consider providing space for several types of special OHV use, such as OHV training areas, ATVs, snowmobiles (in snow country), car racing, four-wheel racing, motocross tracks, mini-bikes, model airplanes, model cars, and model rockets, as well as motorcycles. The park, of course, would need special facilities over the above those previously mentioned for motorized trails and those found in typical resource facilities. They might include gas stations, garages, large temporary parking areas for events, visitor viewing areas, fire and ambulance facilities, etc.

A mechanical vehicle park must be located in a sound basin where the noise generated from its many activities will not disturb surrounding land uses. Areas between major highways or in industrial areas or in enclosed sound basins are examples of sites that might be suitable for mechanical vehicle/OHV parks. (See Figs. 10.1 and 10.2.)

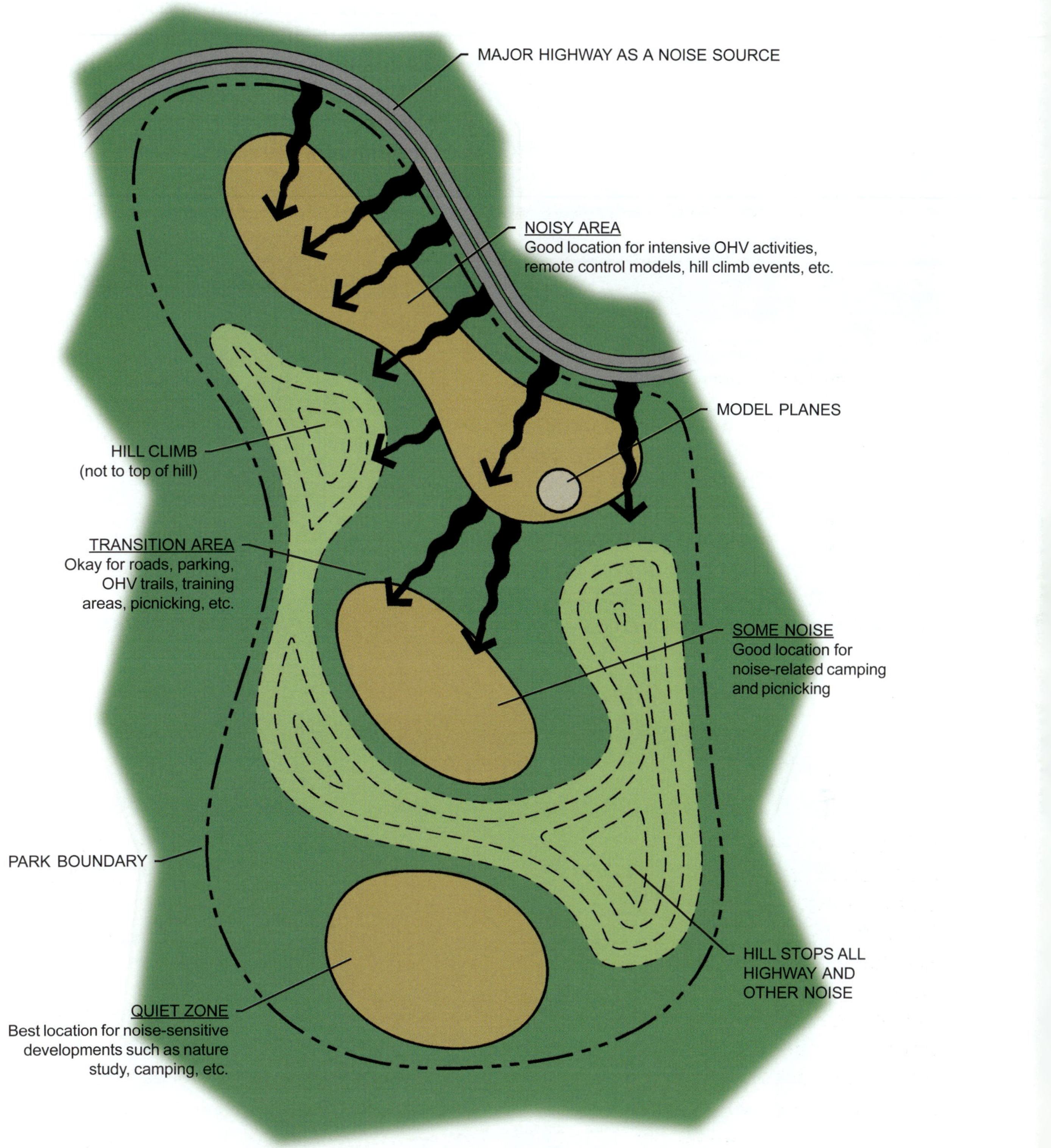

FIG. 10.6 – LOCATION OF ACTIVITIES IN RELATIONSHIP TO NOISE SOURCES

PARKING FOR OHV FACILITIES

Snowmobile parking – Spitzbergen, Norway

The ideal layout of a participant parking area is also significantly different than standard parking design (Chapter 11, Fig. 11.17 – Right angle parking.) Participant parking layout (Fig. 10.8) shows a desirable OHV parking area. Please note that this type of parking requires 1000± sq. ft. (90 sq. m) of area per parking space (including minimal vehicular access, pedestrian circulation, and landscaping). This amounts to 40+ car/truck and trailer parking spaces per acre, or approximately 1.7 times that needed for standard car/truck and boat trailer parking. It is 2.5 times the space needed for spectator parking.

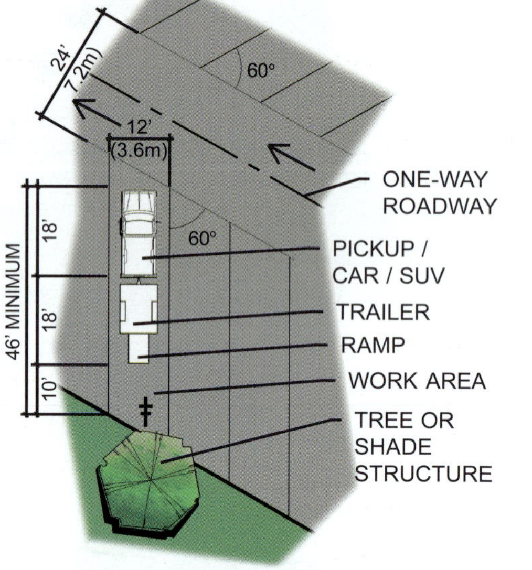

FIG. 10.8 – PARTICIPANT PARKING LAYOUT

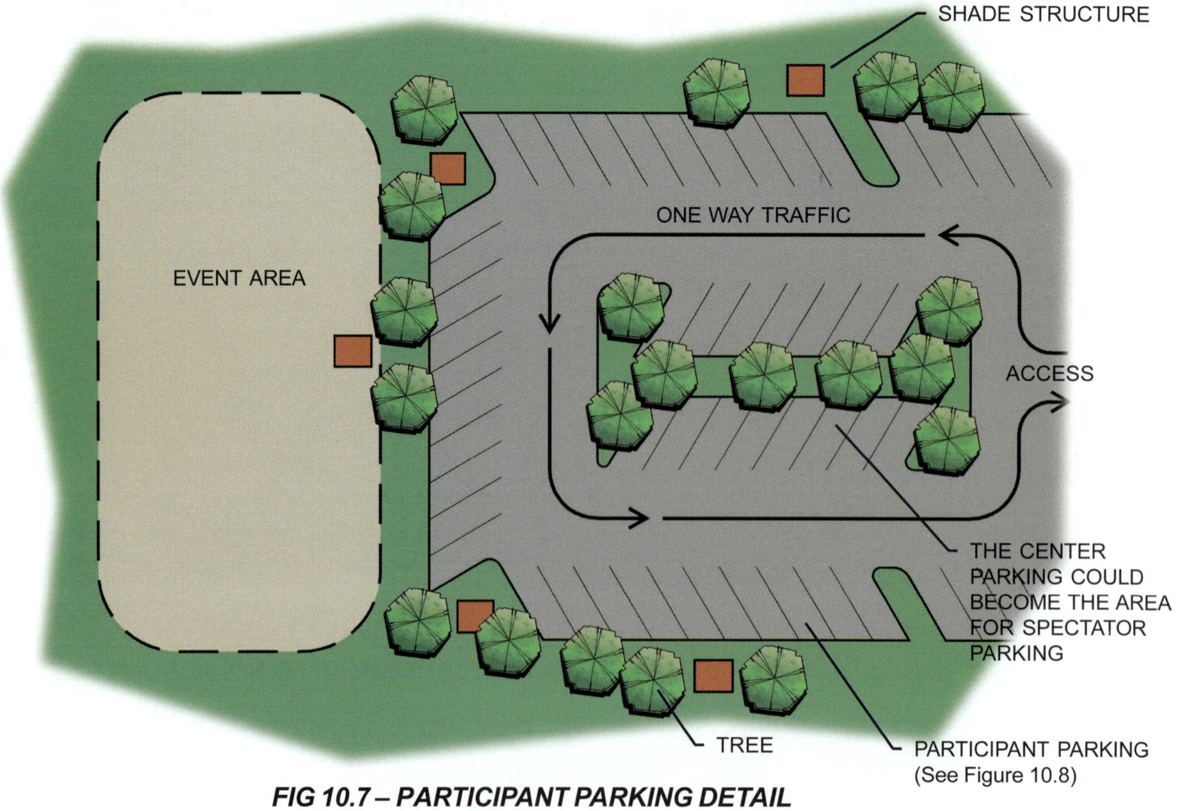

FIG 10.7 – PARTICIPANT PARKING DETAIL

MISCELLANEOUS OHV EQUIPMENT

There are many types of specialty OHVs, such as dune, sand buggies, and rails, swamp buggies and airboats. Each of these, and other special vehicles, require individual design considerations.

DUNE, SAND BUGGIES, AND RAILS

These specially built vehicles, like ATVs, can go almost anywhere, especially in loose, sandy soils.

Dune and desert environments are extremely fragile, easily damaged, and have a very long recovery period. It is, therefore, imperative in these environments to establish well-marked, clearly recognizable trails. Equally important is that "free-riding" areas be well defined naturally, and appropriately signed. Designated, free-riding areas should be located in spaces with little vegetation, and that vegetation which occurs should be protected with unobtrusive barriers. Trails, on the other hand, will likely traverse varied terrains and may have significant amounts of vegetation, which must be vigorously protected. A combination of appropriate natural and manmade barriers, interpretive/informational signing, and intensive regulations will be required.

SWAMP BUGGIES

Swamp buggies are self-powered, four-wheeled, very high clearance vehicles. These vehicles are primarily home built and designed for wet, flooded, muddy terrain. Privately owned swamp buggies are used to gain access to back-county areas for the tourist trade and hunting, fishing, camping, and wildlife viewing. Specially crafted versions are built specifically for competition at specially-designed mud tracks. Tour operators utilize multi-passenger swamp buggies to transport visitors into swampy areas not accessible by conventional vehicles.

Homemade swamp buggy

Where there is demand for, and sufficient suitable area available, an OHV facility may wish to consider opportunities for swamp buggies. It is extremely critical and difficult to sustain long-term environmental quality in these areas. To accomplish this, the activity must be restricted to designed and managed trails.

AIRBOATS

Airboats are flat-bottomed, shallow-hulled vessels with rear mounted aircraft propellers powered by noisy aircraft or automotive engines. They vary in size from one- or two-passenger personal boats to the much larger twenty or more passenger tourist vessels. They are popular for back-country access and tourism rides in shallow swamp and coastal wetland areas. They are extraordinarily noisy and disturb wildlife, especially wading birds.

Typical small tour airboat – Collier County, Florida

To sustain long-term airboat opportunity with desired resource protection requires a carefully designed and well-managed water trail system or area. The airboat's capability for high speed and the elevated levels of sound produced by the propellers and engine necessitates large areas designed to meet visitor needs while protecting wildlife and adjacent developed areas from undesirable noise. A very difficult task.

LEARNING AND PRACTICE AREA FOR RIDING OHVs

Learning to operate OHVs is no different than learning to drive highway-legal vehicles. There is a need to know and understand:

- how to physically operate the vehicle;
- the rules of safe riding/driving;
- how to be an environmentally responsible rider/driver; and
- what the mechanics of the equipment are, and how to make at least minimal repairs.

Youth OHV Training

OHV training areas are needed and should be considered for inclusion in all major OHV facilities. The only question should be, to what extent?

Design of learning and practice riding areas holds special importance for safety, training in trail etiquette, and environmental awareness. Training areas should be designed to allow sufficient space for the appropriate rider level. A safe area of usually one to two acres (less than one hectare) restricted from other more qualified riders is needed.

DESIGN CRITERIA

Site Designation – Signing should clearly indicate the purpose of the area and encourage use by appropriate riders. "Trail" or "loop" layouts are preferable to a "track" layout.

General Design – A tight, twisty loop layout with rolling bumps, but NO jumps, will teach skill, and control speed.

Boundary Fence – Fencing is necessary to prevent inadvertent entry or exit and increase safety.

Entrance/Exit Points – A single point of entry and exit will reduce wrong-way traffic and allow for better supervision by trainers.

Directional Signs – LARGE, bold arrows should be used to provide clear direction.

Signing – Trail signing should replicate what the riders will encounter when they are able to venture out on to regular trail systems. Signing should promote land ethics in addition to providing direction and identifying trail conditions.

Length/Width – Up to ¼ mile can provide an adequate loop and allow observers to see the entire loop area. The width of the trail should be approximately 8 feet (2.4 m) – enough to allow use and passing by off-highway motorcycles (OHMs) and all-terrain vehicles (ATVs).

Surface – A firm surface is critical. Sand, powered soil, gravel, and rocks are tiring and difficult for inexperienced riders. Excessive dust is undesirable for riders, observers, other park visitors, and adjacent communities.

Chapter 11

ROADS AND PARKING

The primary means of access to most large-scale park, recreation, and leisure facilities is and will continue to be by automobiles, trucks, and buses. The movements of vehicles to and through a site and their storage in the facility will continue to be a major item in the development's design. Vehicle sizes and horsepower are varied and likely to continue this way for the next several years. Access by chartered buses, especially by older people, is likely to continue to increase, particularly in tourism-related facilities.

Many forms of transportation within a resource area are possible, such as tramways, monorails, conveyor systems, buses, trackless trains, helicopters, hydrofoils, and hovercrafts. In most instances, roads are probably the most cost-effective means of moving people through a facility; however, a thorough and thoughtful determination should be made of the most meaningful way in which people can experience the resource before a road system is built. It should be noted that almost all non-conventional (non-car/bus) transportation requires considerable capital investments and, more importantly, incurs ongoing operation and maintenance costs. Unless a user fee is charged specific to the special transportation needs, it is unlikely that any form of transportation, other than cars/buses or other vehicles that use standard roadways, can be considered in any park/leisure time project.

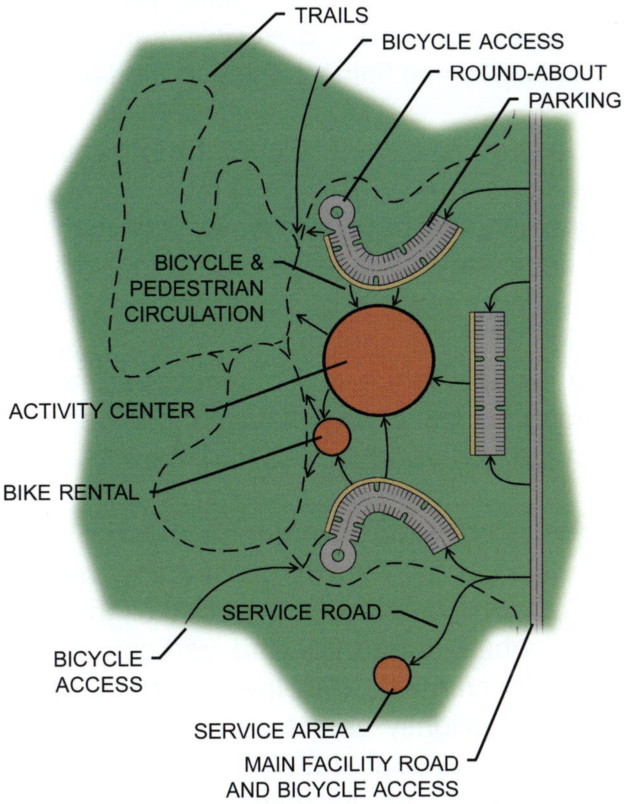

FIG. 11.1 – PARK CIRCULATION SYSTEM

All vehicular access and parking in a resource area should be handled in the most aesthetically pleasing manner possible. Major cuts and fills and log tangents must be minimized. In effect, the roads and parking should be molded to the terrain.

The various types of circulation systems (vehicular, pedestrian, bicycle, equestrian, etc.) should be kept separated, where possible, to avoid conflicts. This is particularly necessary for equestrian trails and OHV and pedestrian trails.

ROAD ALIGNMENT

Like all roads, park and resource roads must provide safe, efficient and economical transportation for the park visitors. In addition, however, leisure facility roads must also provide for the driver's pleasure and enjoyment while fitting closely to the land.

A roadway is a linear element that provides the opportunity for continuous rapidly changing visual experiences. As such, not only is it necessary to make the road safe, efficient, and economical, it is imperative that it be designed as a continuous series of good visual experiences. This necessitates a thorough visual analysis of what can be seen from the road, both near and distant.

For pleasing visual quality, there must be good coordination between horizontal and vertical curves. The best appearing road alignments occur when horizontal and vertical curves generally coincide, with the horizontal curve beginning slightly before and ending slightly after the vertical curve. From a visual standpoint, the roadway should be perceived as a constantly changing three-dimensional curve. Generally, long tangents should be avoided, especially in rolling topography, as well as "short dip" vertical curves on long tangents or horizontal curves.

In resource-oriented facilities, roads are also strong visual elements in the landscape, and their impact must be considered visually from the surrounding land uses.

A valley road that fits the site from an overlook.
– Norway

Roads alignments should result in a roadway that minimizes its adverse impact on the land. The alignment should:

1. generally run parallel to bold, linear landscape features, such as shorelines, rivers, estuaries, valleys, and hills, to complement natural spaces and forms and take advantage of these visual elements;

2. never cross hills and ridges head-on, but at oblique angles and crossing the top at naturally occurring saddles;

3. make rock cuts in irregular form and conforming to the geologic characteristics of the rock strata (occasionally some cuts may be cut clean for educational interpretive purposes);

4. avoid constant slopes in cuts and fills; and

5. provide transitional grading between cuts and fills and at the top and bottom of slopes.

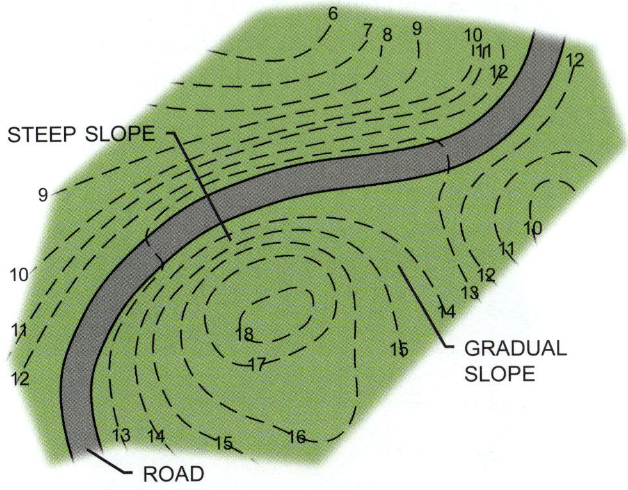

FIG. 11.2 – TRANSITIONAL SLOPES

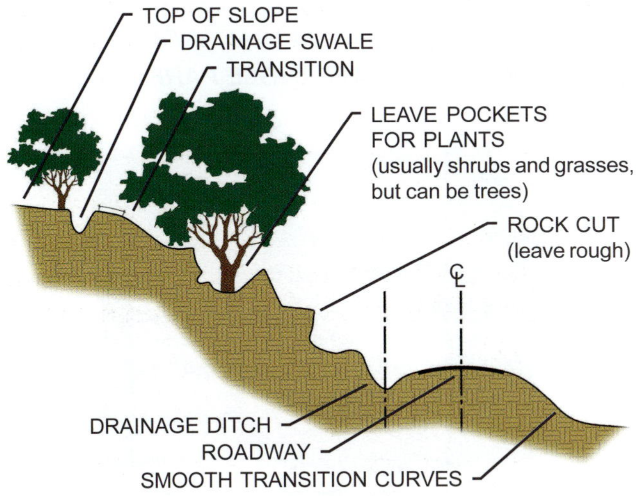

FIG. 11.3 – SECTION OF A CUT SLOPE THROUGH STONE

DRAINAGE

The primary reason for road failure is poor drainage. It is of paramount importance that adequate drainage of water off and away from the road section be done. All water intercepted by the road must be carried away from the road, and usually under the road in adequate-sized drainage structures; 18 inches (45 cm) is the minimum size necessary to enable the culvert to be easily cleaned, usually with a long-handled shovel.

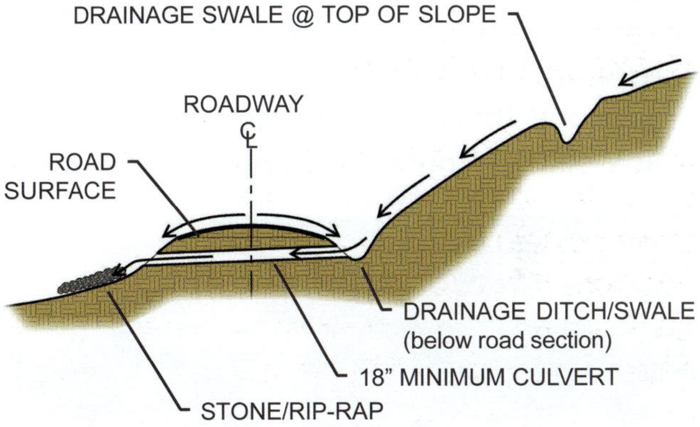

FIG. 11.4 – ROAD DRAINAGE

PARKING

Parking spaces should be located so that they are within 400 feet (120 m) of the activity they are intended to serve. Parking at distances greater than 400 feet will normally only be used on unusual occasions, such as beach access where no other alternative is possible, or a steep slope. If adequate parking cannot be provided within a reasonable distance of the activity, provision of alternative transportation to the site feature should be seriously considered, especially for handicapped, i.e., trams, buses, etc.

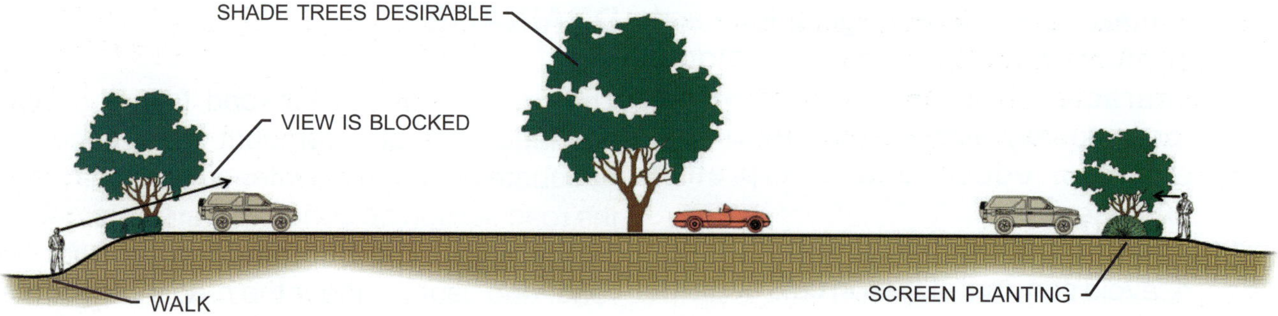

FIG. 11.6 – PARKING LOT SCREENED WITH PLANTS

Please note that changing vehicle sizes and shapes over time is a constant and must be considered in all vehicle facility designs. Where possible, parking areas should be screened from roads and activity areas. Please note that right angle parking is the most space-efficient parking system. It takes 10 percent less space than 60° parking and 20+ percent less than 45° parking. The size of parking lots should be a minimum of 60 feet (18 m) with a minimum of 9 feet (2.7 m)-wide parking bays. Spreading shade trees should be installed in the parking lot approximately as shown in Fig. 11.6.

Congested car and bus parking at a scenic tourist area in Norway

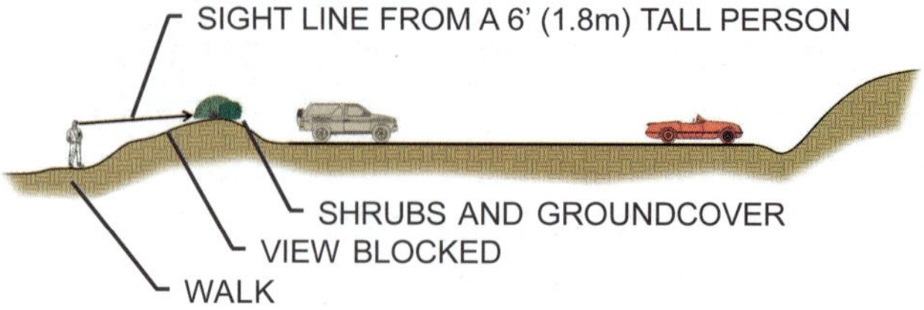

FIG. 11.5 – PARKING LOT SCREENED WITH GRADING

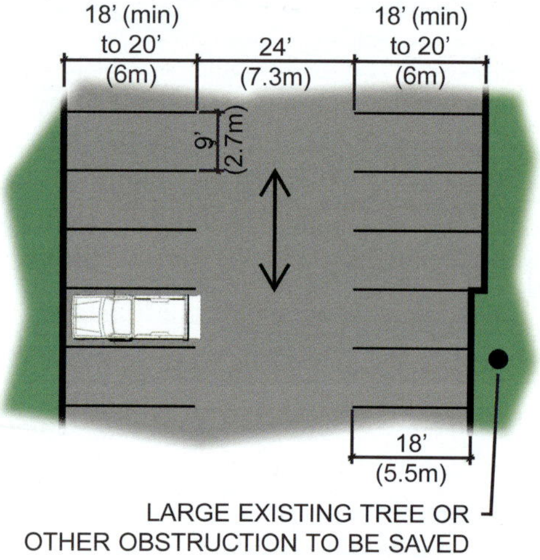

FIG. 11.7 – RIGHT ANGLE PARKING

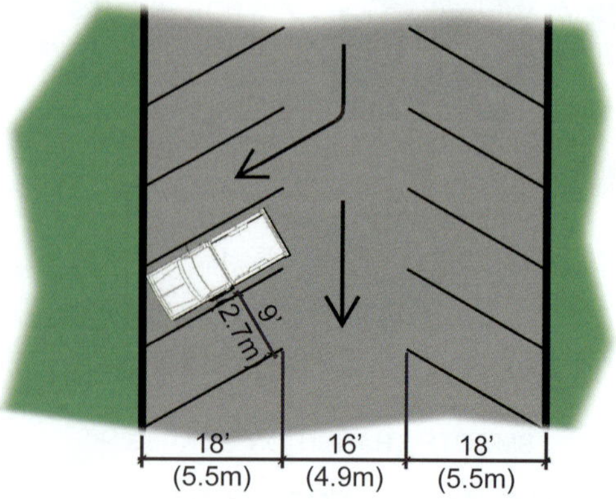

FIG. 11.8 – 60° ANGLE PARKING

Barrier free, signed, accessible parking spaces of 8 feet (2.4 m) in width, plus 5-foot (1.5 m)-wide pedestrian aisles must be provided throughout the facility in locations adjacent to accessible areas.

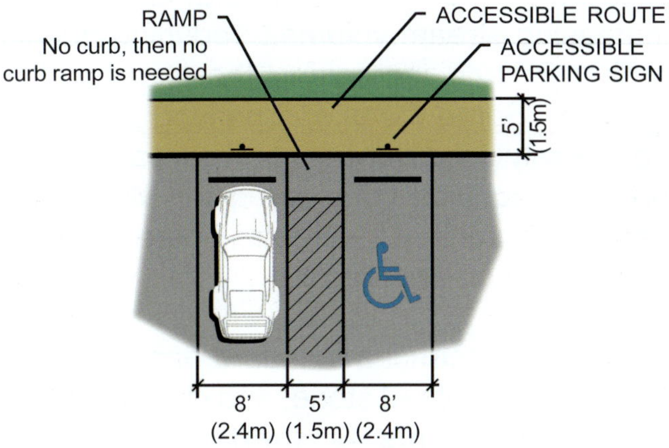

FIG. 11.9 – ACCESSIBLE PARKING

Accessible parking at Clam Pass County Park – Collier County, Florida

1. Car: gross area per 90° car space – 300 square feet (28 sq. m); approximately 140 cars per acre (250 cars per ha).

Multiple types of vehicles in a parking lot designed to accommodate them
Shark Valley at Everglades National Park, Florida

2. Car and boat trailer: gross area per space – 600 square feet (56 sq. m); 70 per acre (175 per ha).

There are two basic trailer parking types: (1) pull-through; easiest to use but very expensive in amount of needed land and construction costs, and (2) pull in - back out at a 60° angle; somewhat more difficult to use but requires less space and less construction costs. [2, 6]

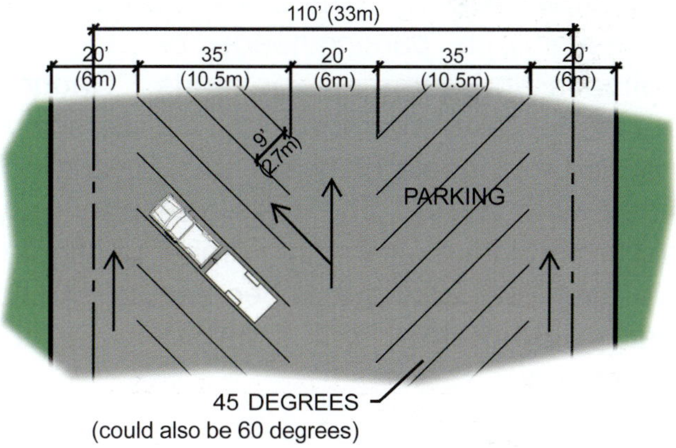

FIG. 11.10 – CAR AND TRAILER PULL-THROUGH PARKING

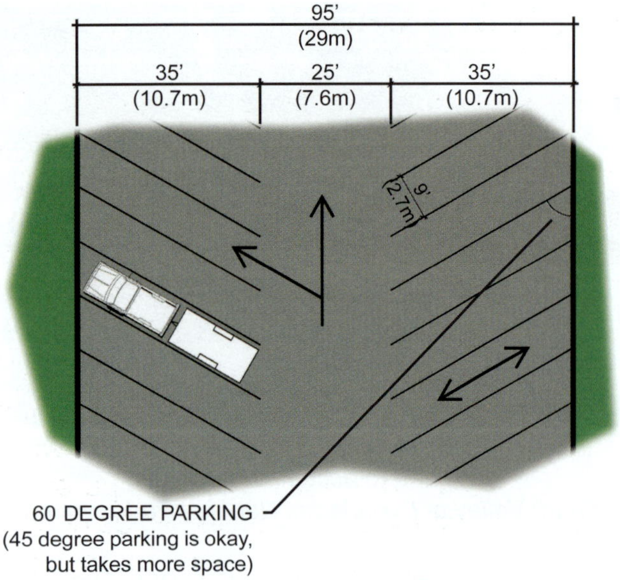

FIG. 11.11 – CAR AND TRAILER PULL IN – BACK OUT PARKING

3. Maximum desirable grade is five percent, with parking lots of ten percent grades possible under careful design.[(2)] Accessible parking must be essentially flat; maximum – two percent grade.

Where practical, it is advisable to provide overflow parking (on stabilized turf, if necessary), i.e., parking needed only for peak holidays and summer weekends. Caution should be taken that the extra activity space needed for people on major use days is not filled with cars. The resource can only accommodate a maximum number of people. No overflow parking and people use should be provided that will prohibit a quality experience.

ENVIRONMENTALLY-SENSITIVE SURFACING

Traditionally, paved roads and parking areas seal off the land from the environment. This creates 100 percent runoff of all rainfall, increasing stream volumes, reducing aquifer recharge, and increasing the likelihood of erosion. Some roads and parking areas are not heavily used throughout the year. Those areas should be considered for alternative permeable surface treatment. There are three currently used approaches.

1. Construct a standard base, surface with crushed stone, and choke with top soil. This is then seeded and maintained as an open field except during heavy use periods. See the preceding section on parking. A variation frequently used is to pave the roadway and leave the parking grassed. See Fig. 11.12.

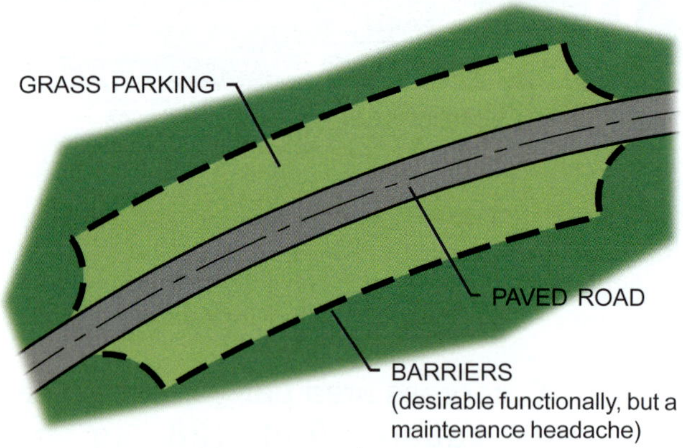

FIG. 11.12 – GRASS PARKING WITH PAVED ROAD

Sugden Park – Collier County, FL

2. Install porous paving surfacing.

3. Use of open grid-type pavers/topsoil and planting as per Fig. 11.13.

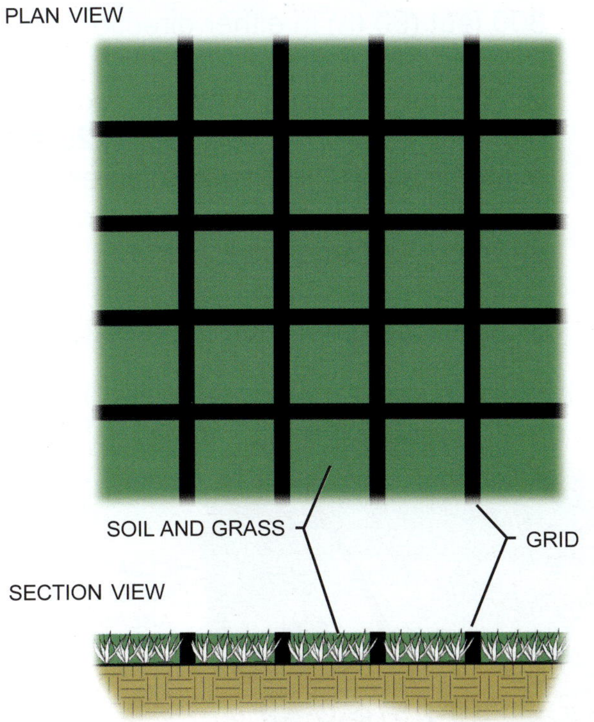

FIG. 11.13 – OPEN GRID CONCRETE PAVERS OR OTHER NON-CORRODIBLE MATERIAL

PROJECT ROADS

Road systems within the use area(s) (interior circulatory roads) should be so designed as to protect the safety of patrons using the use area(s) while preserving the site's aesthetic qualities. Interior roads are not meant for high-speed travel, generally not more than 25 mph (40 kph). A primary consideration in designing and constructing recreation roads is the principle that roads are made to fit the site's natural features and without untoward interference with other recreation pursuits. Balancing cut and fill on site should be done if possible. The types, number, and purpose of the potential users must be considered, as well as the capabilities of the road maintenance staff.

Road designs should keep the need for reduced maintenance constantly in mind, i.e., limit mowed areas and ornamental plantings requiring care, reduce the resurfacing frequency, etc.

Control gates should be provided for all facility access roads. This will enable the manager(s) to control effectively the numbers of participants. Facility roads should be classified. It is suggested that major, minor, and special-purpose (including one-way roads) be used. Please note that adequate drainage must be included in all road designs to prevent damage from erosion as well as wet road conditions.

DESIGN STANDARDS

Component:	Width 1-Lane*	Width Minor 2-Lane	Width Major 2-Lane	Parking Spur
Roadbed - including shoulders - w/o shoulders face to face of barriers or curbs	16'(4.9m) 12'(3.7m)	24'-26'(7.3m-7.9m) 20'(6.1m)	28'-30'(8.5m-9.1m) 24'(7.3m)	10'(3m) 9'(2.7m)
Surfacing	12'(3.7m)	20'(6.1m)	22'(6.7m)	9'(2.7m)
Shoulders	2'(0.6m)	2'-3'(0.6m-0.9m)	3'-5'(0.9m-1.5m)	2'(0.6m)

*Width of road surface at curves should be increased as needed, especially where campers and vehicular-pulled trailers are expected.

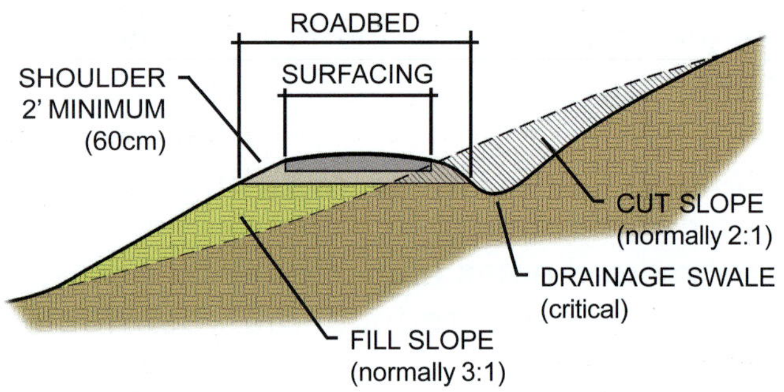

FIG. 11.14 – TYPICAL ROAD SECTION

SIGHT DISTANCES

1. At facility road intersections – 300 feet (90 m) in either direction.

2. At intersections with an exterior highway system – 400 feet (120 m) minimum, with the distance increasing with the amount of park use and speed on the road being intersected.

3. At places other than intersections – 175 lineal feet (55 lm).

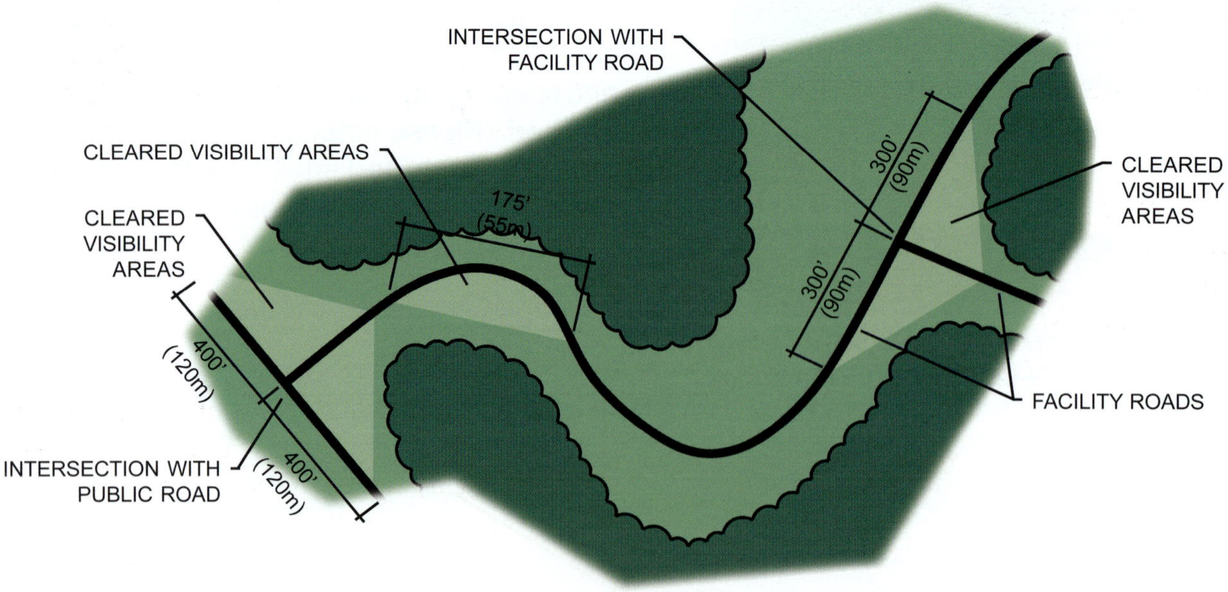

FIG. 11.15 – SIGHT DISTANCE (PLAN VIEW)

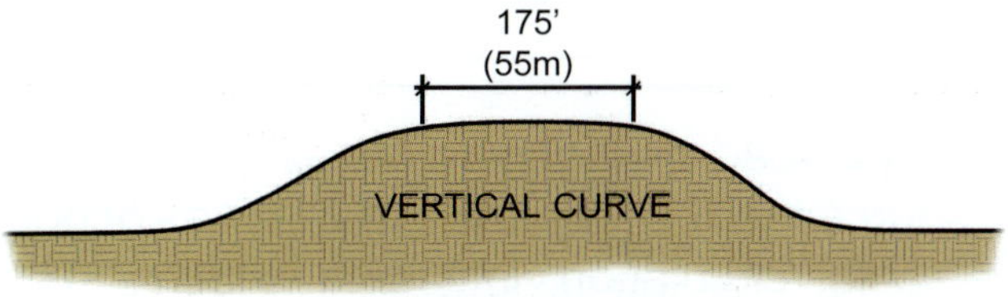

FIG. 11.16 – SIGHT DISTANCE (SECTION)

ALIGNMENT

Minimum radius	50 feet (15 m)
Minimum desirable radius	80 feet (25 m)
Road intersections	50 feet (15 m) radius desirable
	35 feet (10 m) radius minimum
Dead-end circle	40 feet (12 m) radius minimum
Turnaround	50 feet (15 m) radius desirable

GRADIENT

Maximum desirable – 9 percent. Short stretches of road may exceed the maximum desirable grade but careful consideration should be given to types of traffic, i.e., passenger cars, pickup trucks, passenger cars and pickups pulling trailers, and service vehicles, such as garbage trucks, etc.

SCENIC VIEWS

Locations that are outstanding for visual and for photographic purposes, particularly when separated from designated parking areas, frequently justify the development of pull-over parking. See Fig. 11.17 Scenic overlook.

Scenic overlook – Karingai, Australia

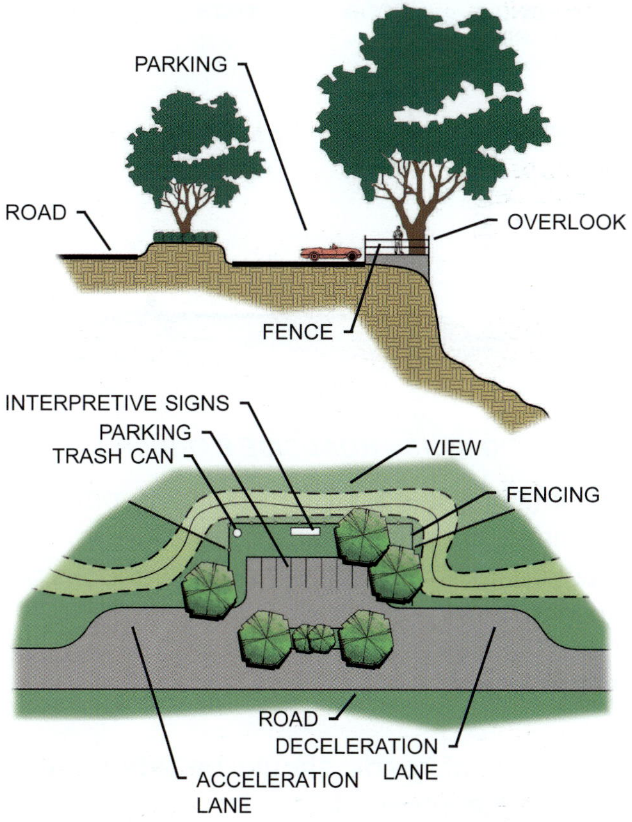

FIG. 11.17 – SCENIC OVERLOOK

TURNOUTS

Overall length – 100 feet (30 m) minimum; 50 feet (15 m) of two-lane width plus 25 feet (7.5 m) of tapered end sections.

BARRIERS

Barriers should be installed where needed to prevent unauthorized vehicular travel within the recreation area. Control of automobile traffic is important from the point of view of safety and also to prevent the deterioration of the terrain and vegetation of the recreation area. The barriers should be as unobtrusive as possible and still provide the necessary control. If wood barriers are used, they should be pressure treated with a wood preservative.

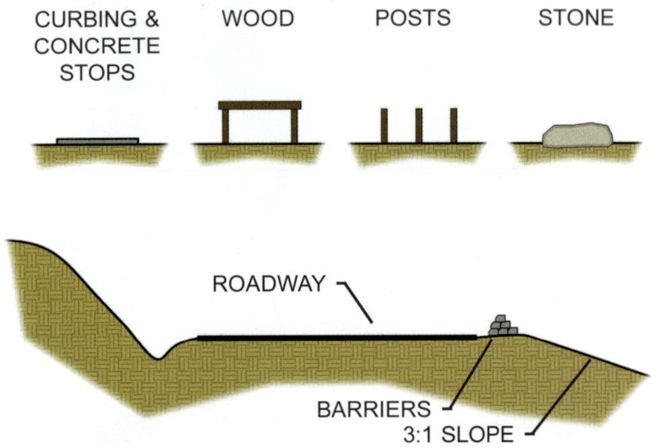

FIG. 11.18 – ROADSIDE BARRIERS

Barriers may keep out cars, but they come with the need to be maintained. In addition, care must be taken to ensure that all overlooks are accessible.

SURFACING

Surfacing of roads should be adequate to support the intended use.

The road systems within an activity area should have, as a minimum requirement, a stabilized surface to control dust. Low use roads can be gravel (requires annual maintenance). Higher use roads can be oil and chip or blacktop. Concrete is a very good low-maintenance surface, but it is not normally recommended due to high installation costs in most areas.

UNDERPASS

A major road or highway passing through a resource facility is a barrier to all types of non-vehicular circulation, including wildlife. This can be partially alleviated by the installation of culverts, sometimes over-sized, which include a wildlife and/or pedestrian underpass in addition to transporting water.

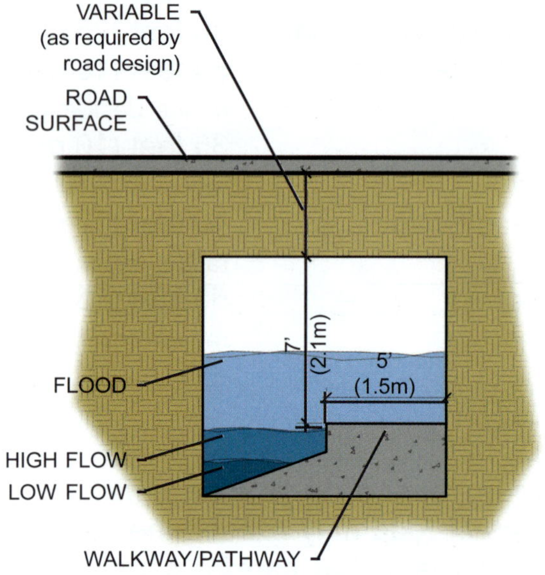

FIG. 11.19 – COMBINATION CULVERT AND PEDESTRIAN UNDERPASS

The multipurpose culvert should have the following standards:

1. The shape of the channel should maintain sufficient depth for fish during low flows.

2. The walkway/pathway will have a minimum 7-foot (2.1 m) clearance and be 5 feet (1.5 m) wide for acceptable pedestrian use at other than flood stage. A slightly larger space will be needed if used for part of an equestrian trail – 6 feet (1.8 m) wide x 10 foot (3 m) clearance.

3. The depth cover over the culvert from the road surface can vary except for the minimum required by the road design.

4. The drainage structure must be wide enough to contain an existing stream bottom in addition to the walkway/ pathway.

5. Construction of the walkway must be integral with the culvert so that washouts will not occur.

6. The walkway surface must be textured to minimize slipping.

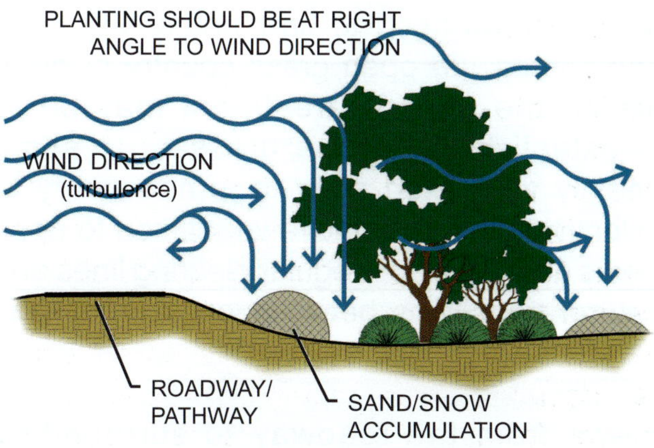

FIG. 11.20 – PLANTS CAN BE AN EFFECTIVE BARRIER FOR BLOWING SAND, DUST, AND SNOW

Plant material can readily stabilize sand movement. Al-Hassa, Saudi Arabia

ROADSIDE TREATMENT

"The roadside is an integral part of the total " road. "Roadside development is the treatment given to the roadside to conserve, enhance and display natural and cultural beauty." "... and features of interest ... through which the [road] passes."

The conditions on the immediate highway right-of-way are almost always manmade and may differ radically from the surrounding natural systems. Within these conditions, however, the addition of plant material should be used:

1. to stabilize the soil and reduce or prevent erosion;

2. to guide traffic and reduce roadside distractions;

3. to screen objectionable views;

4. for snow control (and sand control in deserts);

5. to transition from the rigid geometry of the road to the natural surroundings; and

6. for visual enhancement by enframing vistas, creating selective views, or break monotonous stretches of roadway.

Plant material can consist of trees, shrubs, wildflowers, and grasses, and should, wherever possible, be closely associated with the existing surrounding vegetation.

Not all areas need to be planted with trees and shrubs. In open grass country or other areas, the primary treatment may be to re-establish the native grasses. In some heavily vegetated sites, it is necessary to selectively thin or remove vegetation to open views and develop irregular clearing lines and natural transitions between open areas and the dense woods.

Views from the roadway to surrounding features must be maintained over the years or much of the road value will be quickly lost to blocking plant material.

Brazilian Pepper blocks views on a portion of US 41 – Southwest Florida

View on the opposite side of US 41 – Southwest Florida

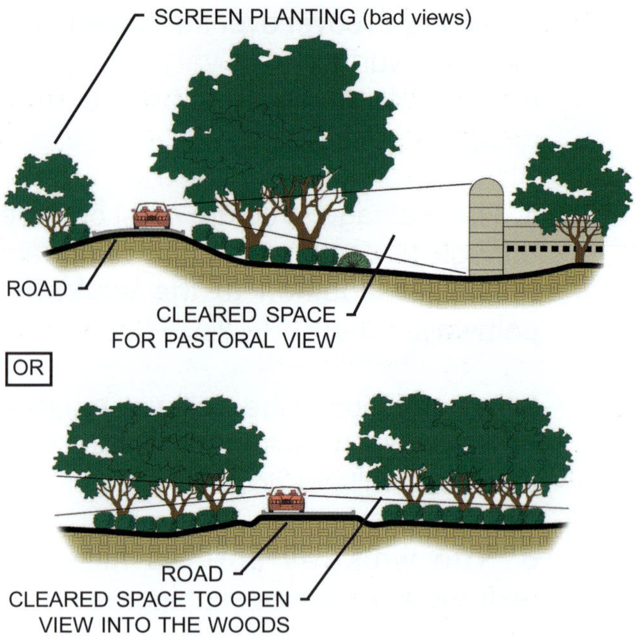

FIG. 11.21 – VIEWS ARE IMPORTANT AND MAY REQUIRE CLEARING SOME ROADWAY VEGETATION

ENTRANCE STATION

The prime functions of an entrance station are for:

Control

- Collect entrance fees
- Issue use permits and/or assign campsites
- Regulation of visitor numbers
- Protection of visitors and the environment
- First aid, as needed

Information

- Directions
- Communications

DESIGN FACTORS

• Adequate vehicle backup space must be provided commensurate with the expected use.

• The design of an entrance station must be predicated on the need to move people through this likely bottleneck quickly and efficiently.

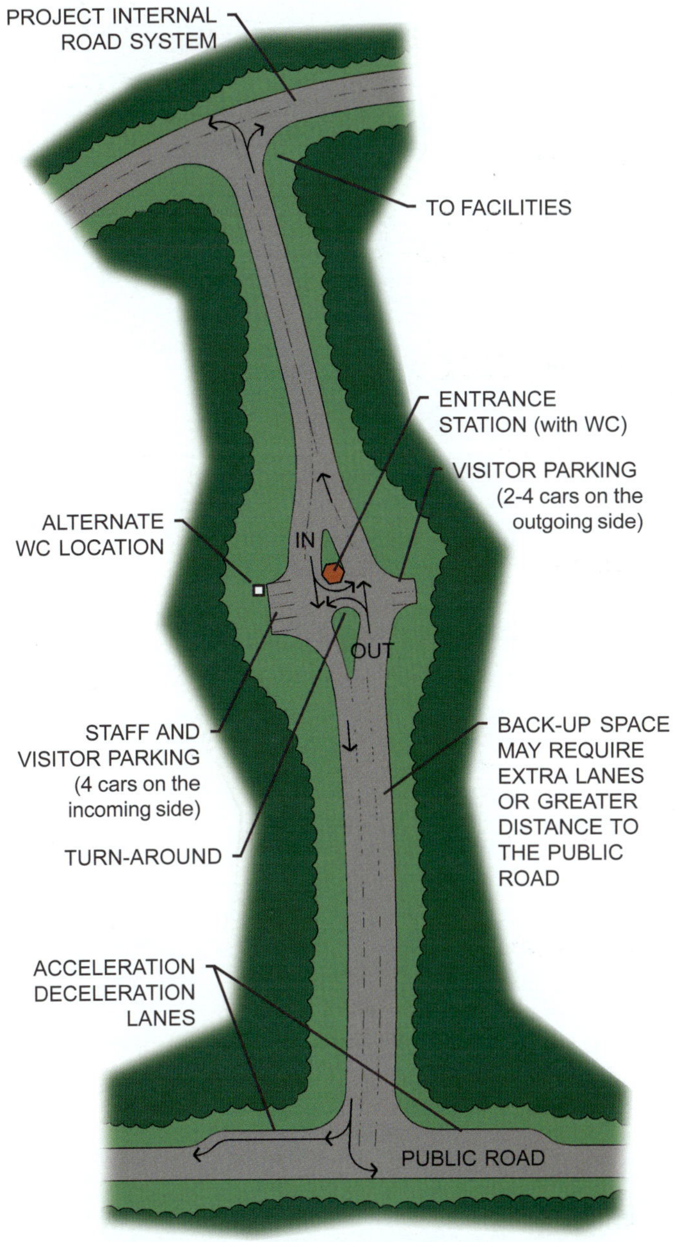

FIG. 11.22 – CONTROLLED PARK ENTRANCE

• Electricity, phone (cell phone is alright if there is good reception), and sanitary facilities for the staff must be available. In addition, a public pay phone should be provided.

• Water and sewer connections are desirable.

• Parking for staff is required.

• Parking for visitors with a minimum of three vehicles is desirable, and more if use indicates a need.

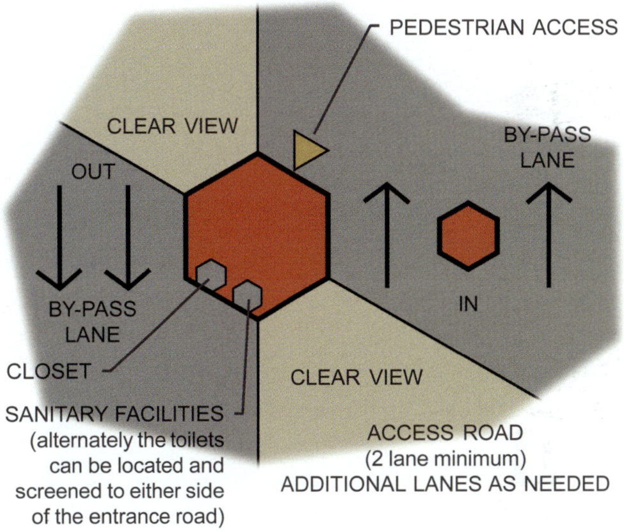

FIG. 11.23 – PARK ENTRANCE STATION

Chapter 12

UTILITIES

Facilities in the Grand Canyon

GENERAL

The significance of providing utilities as an integral and indispensable part of every leisure facility cannot be over-emphasized, especially in light of ecological and environmental consequences and environmental regulations. The utility systems' concept development as an integral part of a project at an early stage of planning will save considerable time and money. Inadequate preliminary work as to the location, aesthetics, capacity, arrangement, and site considerations will be detrimental to all succeeding project design phases, and failure to adequately address utilities may endanger the successful completion of a project.

Investigations and surveys for early planning stages of a project are broad in nature, with emphasis on covering all factors relating to utilities as an integral part of the project. Some planning considerations are as follows:

1. The extent of the area and population to be served and the pattern of present and future facility growth.

2. The estimated present and future utility needs.

3. Off-site utility services should be actively considered if existing or proposed plant capacity is available and the lifecycle cost of the project to be connected to them, especially in regards to long-term operation and maintenance costs, are equal or less than are off-site facilities.

4. General arrangement of the utility system to best serve the user needs.

5. Excavation for utility lines is expensive and should be considered at the earliest planning stages with adequate subsurface investigations.

6. The re-use of treated waste water for non-consumptive purposes must be evaluated and, where possible, used.

WATER SUPPLY

An evaluation of available water sources should be made. Generally, it is most cost effective to utilize an existing municipal service. The second most desirable source for a water system is wells, because they generally produce a consistent quality of water at reduced treatment costs. This does not preclude, however, the use of lake or creek water. In fact, in certain situations, these might be the only feasible sources of water and **must** be considered. In the event that alternative water sources are available, they should be considered, and the best system chosen on the basis of environmental and lifecycle costs, including operation and maintenance costs and not merely on initial costs. All possible water conservation techniques, such as self-closing faucets, low volume flushing accessories, reduced pressure showerheads, etc., should be considered during the detail design phase of a project.

The use of any surface water source will require adequate treatment and disinfection, and will require a state permit and be subject to public health regulations.

The quantity of potable water storage is dependent upon the amount and reliability of the water source and variations in use patterns. As a general guide, storage should be provided for a maximum of a three-day weekend period. With good quantity and quality of water, storage might be held to the **maximum** day use. The minimum operating level of water storage and distribution line size should be such that a minimum pressure of 20 p.s.i. exists throughout the water system. It is generally preferable to use an elevated storage/gravity system over a mechanically maintained pneumatic pressure system. That way water pressure can at least be temporarily maintained during a power outage.

Using a high point on the property minimizes tank construction costs.

Elevated storage structures, such as water tanks and standpipes, are usually out of character with the project's landscape, especially in natural-type facilities. Location of these storage tanks is of extreme importance in a leisure facility's environment.

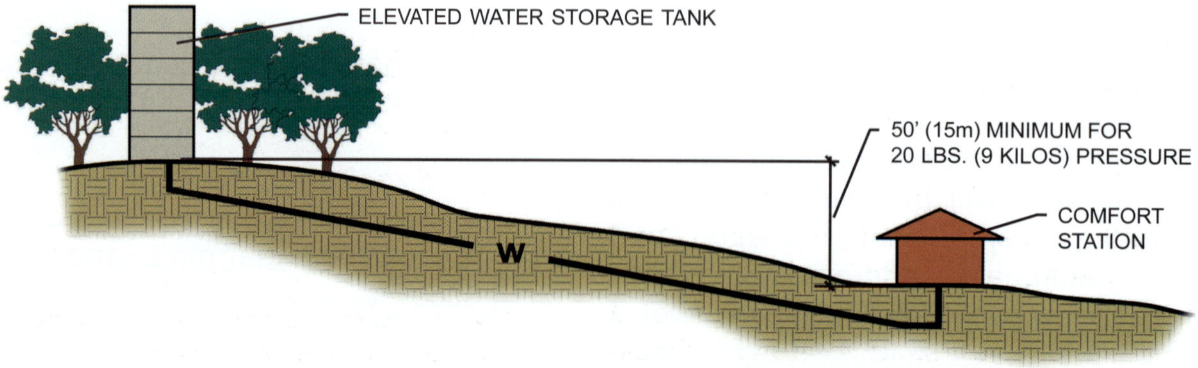

FIG. 12.1 – A GRAVITY WATER SYSTEM IS THE MOST DESIRABLE

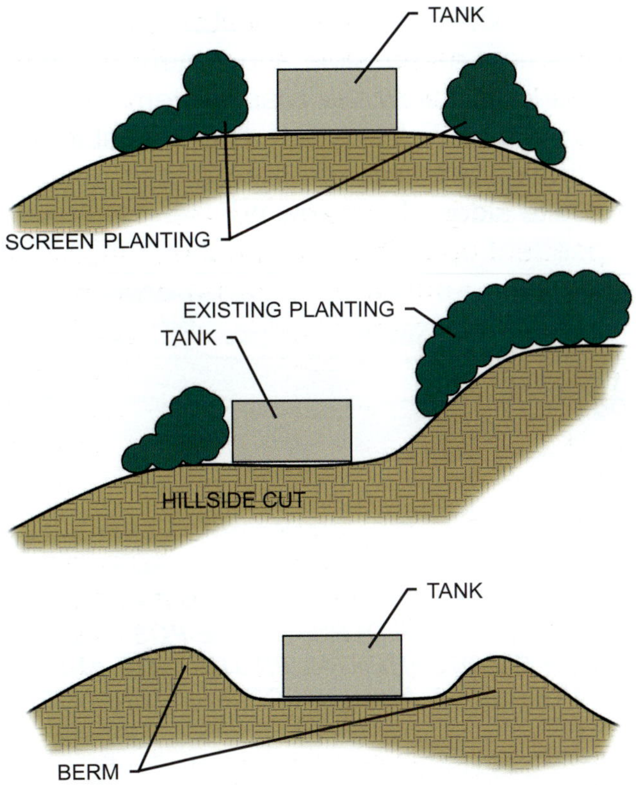

FIG. 12.2 – SCREENING STORAGE TANKS

Careful site selection is necessary. Making maximum use of existing trees and topographic features, balancing structural dimensions and site excavation with landscaping, cutting out the bank and keeping a low storage tank profile, and selection of a color to blend with the surrounding landscape are ways to enhance tank aesthetics while the water utility's functional needs can be satisfactorily met.

If gravity storage is not possible, a hydropneumatic pressurized system can be used to force water directly into the water distribution system with no other outlet than the water actually consumed.

Whenever possible, adequate visual screening and a security gate at the entrance to the site of water storage tanks should be provided. The water storage facilities should be on a fenced and secure site to deter tampering. The site should be sufficiently far back from the road as to be out of view, and a minor service road provided. This road should be so laid out with the use of curves that a view of the facilities will not be possible at the intersection with the site's road.

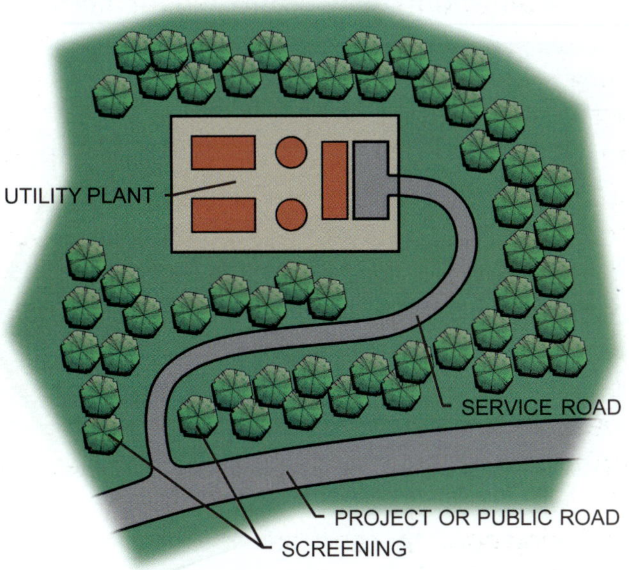

FIG. 12.3 – UTILITY PLANTS SHOULD BE SCREENED

In areas of high fire danger or of historic or other valuable structures, provision should be made for adequate water supply, pipe sizes, and outlets for fire suppression. The need for additional water supplies for fire flow should be evaluated and coordinated with local authorities.

Fire hose storage and fire water connection – Hopewell Furnace National Historic Site, Pennsylvania

Wherever cold climate, winter use of leisure facilities is planned, suitable means in the water storage tanks and distribution piping to guard against freezing of water must be provided. Frequently, on the distribution system, this may mean insulating the pipes and/or putting them in below the frost line.

Insulating pipes under construction – Spitzbergen, Norway

SANITARY

A leisure facility is like a small community, only it has a transient population and is complicated by severe seasonal sewage flow fluctuations.

Sanitary water treatment and disposal of treated waste water are crucial aspects of a leisure facility's development. Adequate treatment of all waste is a necessity, and a leisure facility's development and expansion cannot proceed without these capacities. The type and extent of the system should be discussed with the responsible health and environmental agencies in the area in which the development of the facility is to occur. A state permit will be required.

NOTE: All available data strongly points to a public desire/demand for flush toilets.

All sewer lines should be located for as much gravity flow as possible and, where feasible, they should follow the road system. Sewer lines must be well separated from potable water lines and are usually located on the opposite sides of a roadway.

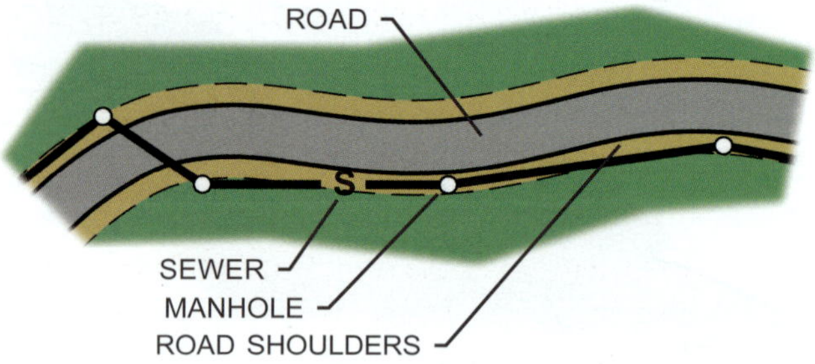

FIG. 12.4 – UTILITY LINES SHOULD BE PLACED IN ROAD SHOULDERS, WHERE POSSIBLE, FOR ENVIRONMENTAL PROTECTION AND FOR EASE OF ACCESS FOR MAINTENANCE

Where it is not possible to follow roads, trails can frequently be developed over utility lines.

Manholes should be set to make sure rainwater does not enter the system – use sealing manhole covers.

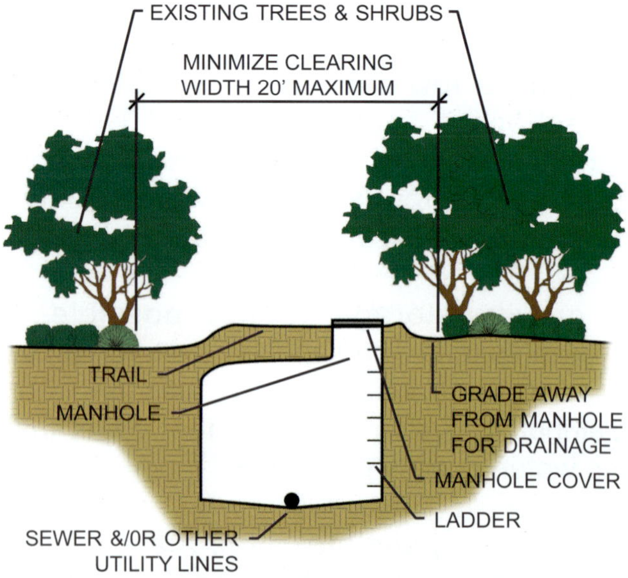

FIG. 12.5 – A TRAIL ON TOP OF A UTILITY LINE

MECHANICAL TREATMENT SYSTEMS

All wastewater treatment systems permitted by state agencies must be designed by a licensed professional engineer. There are several options for treatment and disposal.

- Tying into an area-wide waste system should be considered as the first choice, even if the initial costs are somewhat higher than other disposal systems, provided it proves economical on a "capitalized costs" basis. For this purpose, a 20-year design life for the collection and conveyance facility is typically anticipated.

- Major facility developments may be fairly economically served by constructing a sewage treatment plant. The plant, if it is chosen, should be located downstream of use areas to take the best advantage of gravity collection. It can be prefabricated and placed in a container and the "package" set in the ground. It is desirable to plan for one properly located treatment plant, even if the initial cost is somewhat higher than having two or more treatment plants in the same site because of the economics of scale and the excessive operational and maintenance demands placed on the facility's resources, personnel, and finances by the latter system.

A wastewater treatment plant or management technique can be designed to provide advanced treatment and high-level disinfection such that the treated effluent is suitable to reuse.

Small sewage treatment plant – French Creek State Park, Pennsylvania

NATURAL TREATMENT SYSTEMS

In certain resource facility situations, aquaculture, or the production of aquatic organisms (flora and fauna) under controlled conditions, can be utilized for treatment. Aquatic plants remove nutrients and the pollutants from the wastewater. The plant material is periodically harvested and can be used as fertilizer, soil conditioner after composing, animal feed, and a source of methane when anaerobically digested. The system is frequently suitable for recreational facilities due to the warm season nature of these recreational facilities. Water hyacinth (Eichhornia crassipes) is one good plant; however, **extreme** care must be taken to ensure that the plant cannot get into the natural waterways due to its prolific growth habits. It grows in about 50° F. (10° C.) water temperature and flourishes when the water temperature is approximately 70° F. (21° C.). Alternative native plants are much more desirable from an environmental standpoint. Basin depth should be adequate to maximize the plant's rooting and water absorption. A detention time of 4 to15 days average and a space of 2 to15 acres (1 to 6 ha)/mgd are required.

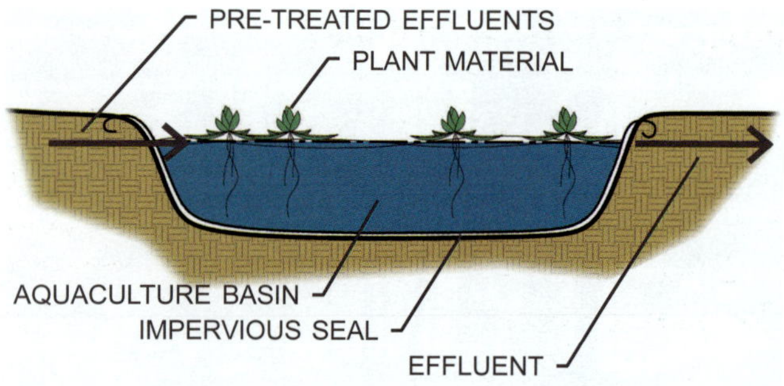

FIG. 12.6 – AQUACULTURE

Please note that although aquaculture is a desirable treatment method, permitting will not be easy. Any discharge of effluent, even effluent of very high quality, to a natural water body may impose permitting difficulties.

LAND APPLICATIONS

Where suitable land is available, treatment by land application is an attractive alternative. It is not known, however, whether any of these following applications will be acceptable to the states where the need exists, but cost-wise it is worth exploring. The technology has been widely and successfully utilized for more than 115 years. Sewage is applied to land to nourish vegetation and purify the partially treated liquid wastes. There are three commonly utilized methods – irrigation, overland flow, and rapid infiltration.

1. **Irrigation** (especially good technically in arid areas where irrigation is needed for good vegetative growth) — Liquid is applied to ornamental planting, crops, golf courses or to forests (silviculture) by sprinkling, flooding or ridge and furrow methods. The liquid is sometimes disinfected before land application. This process is limited by soil type and depth, topography, underlying geology, climate, plant material, and land availability. **Slopes should be less than 15 percent to minimize unintended runoff and erosion.** Typical equipment needed are pipe, pump, valves, gates, and spray nozzles. Required field area is 56 to 560 acres (20 to 200+ ha) per million gallons per day. Application rates, if the process is acceptable to the state and/or approving authority, are governed by state requirements – generally, 0.5 to 4 inches (1.2 to 10 cm) per week, i.e., 2 to 20 feet (.6 to 6 m) per year is allowed. A soil depth of 2 to 5 feet (.6 to 1.5 m) and soil permeability of 0.06 to 2 inches (.15 to 5 cm) per hour are desirable. Most states have requirements of pre-application treatment varying from a minimum of primary treatment to secondary degree of treatment.

2. **Over-land flow** – Liquid flows through vegetation on a graded slope. The runoff is collected at the bottom and reused or discharged to a river or stream. Other considerations and design criteria are the same as for the irrigation system.

3. **Rapid infiltration** – Partly treated sewage is applied in controlled doses to sandy soil, i.e., deep and permeable soils. Three to 56 acres (1.2 to 20+ ha) per million gallons per day are needed. Application rates of 20 to 400 feet (6 to 120 m) per year or 4 to 92 inches (10 to 230 cm) per week are normally allowed. Soil depth of 10 to 15 feet (2 to 4.5 m) or more and soil permeability of 0.6 inches (1.5 cm) per hour or more are desirable.

LAGOONS

Lagoons are large holding reservoirs, frequently several acres (hectares) in size with detention periods of several weeks. They are used to biologically treat wastes. Treatment capacity can be increased by oxygenating the ponds. The amount of space needed depends on the amount and characteristics of the wastes, the location (temperature affects biological activity), adequate site conditions, and effluent discharge requirements. Generally, the effluent is disposed of by spray irrigation of crops, golf courses, or other landscaped areas. Lagoons that adequately consider aesthetics can be a very attractive facility feature.

ALTERNATIVE SEWAGE TREATMENT SYSTEMS

There are many other types of sewage treatment systems that might be suitable for serving a specific facility or unit within a facility. Most alternative systems are small and use less energy, water, and materials than the larger central treatment systems. Such systems are almost always more cost-effective than a conventional central sewage treatment system and should be seriously considered where they are technically and environmentally feasible. The following is a discussion of some of the alternative systems that can be used in developments.

SEPTIC TANK SYSTEMS

There are several variations of the basic system depending upon the site soil conditions. In all these variations, a septic tank is followed by a distribution box and some type of effluent disposal (dispersal).

1. **Septic Tank and Soil Absorption Field (Trench):** Most common on-site systems are of this nature. It is suitable only for certain soil types. It generally requires level ground to moderate (less than 10 percent) slopes. All states and many municipalities have design requirements for such systems. In the trench system, liquid from the septic tank flows to the distribution box then through perforated pipes in trenches and through the surrounding crushed rocks or gravel and soil to the groundwater.

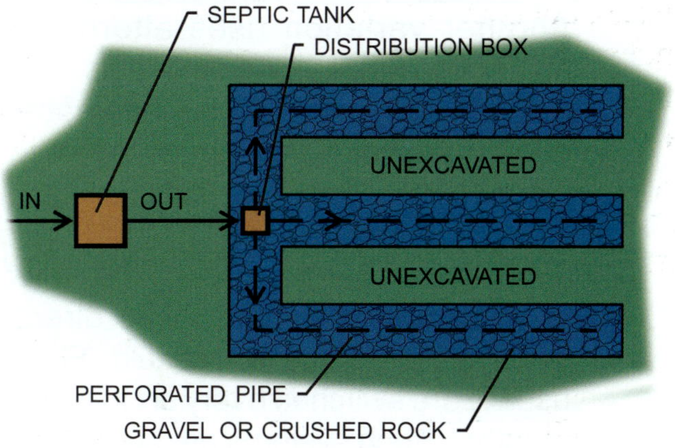

FIG. 12.7 – SEPTIC TANK AND SOIL ABSORPTION FIELD (TRENCH)

2. **Septic Tank and Soil Absorption Field (Bed):** This system is similar to the trench type. It uses a smaller field. In this system, the total field is excavated. This is useful where the space is limited. It requires nearly level ground (2 to 5 percent slopes).

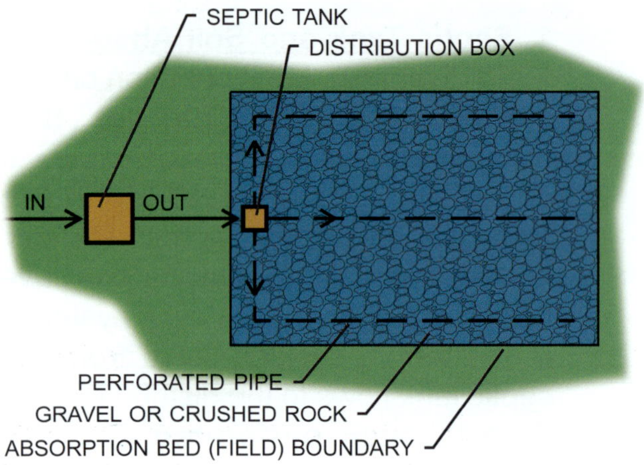

FIG. 12.8 – SEPTIC TANK AND SOIL ABSORPTION FIELD (BED)

3. **Alternating Absorption Field:** Another variation uses alternative absorption fields. One field rests while the other is in use. This alternating pattern allows a field to renew itself, extends life of the field, and provides a standby if one unit (field) fails. Two distribution boxes following the valve box are needed. The valve directs sewage liquid to the proper field. Fields usually are switched every six to twelve months. Such systems are suitable for heavy use areas and could be used together for major use days, i.e., holidays.

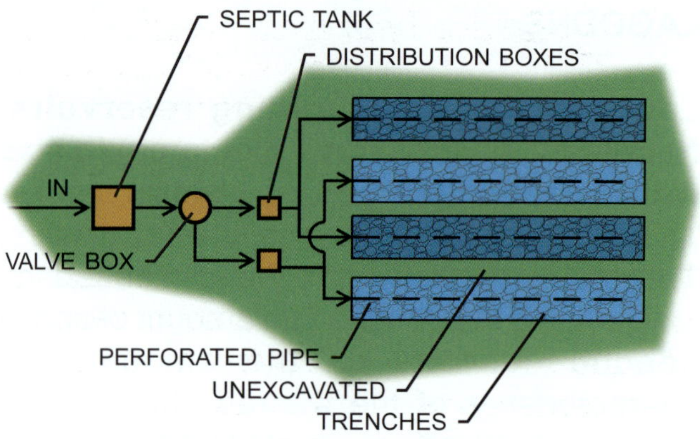

FIG. 12.9 – SEPTIC TANK WITH ALTERNATING ABSORPTION FIELD

4. **Dosing System:** This variation of the septic tank system refinement uses a pump or siphon to force liquid through perforated pipes in controlled doses. All pipes, therefore, discharge liquid almost at the same time (dosing), and the system better utilizes the entire field. This procedure allows a spreading of the liquid evenly over the field and gives the field a chance to dry out between dosings. The absorption field could be an open or closed loop type.

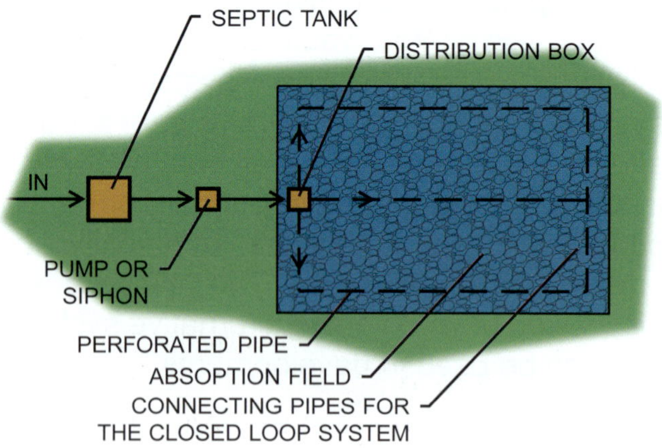

FIG. 12.10 – DOSING SYSTEM

5. **Septic Tank with Sloping Field**: This type uses the serial distribution technique where the absorption field is sloping (10 to 15 percent). A pump forces liquid through perforated pipes in the contoured absorption field. Drop boxes regulate liquid flow. The highest trench fills up first and lower trenches fill up last. Plastic fittings are sometimes used instead of drop boxes to regulate flow.

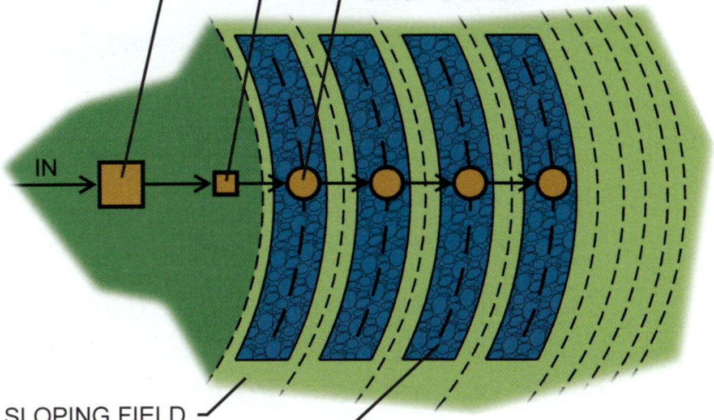

FIG. 12.11 – SEPTIC TANK WITH SLOPING FIELD

6. **Septic Tank with Seepage Pit**: For limited space but good soil conditions, a seepage pit instead of leach field could be used. Liquid from the septic tank flows to a pit that has open-jointed brick or stone walls surrounded by rocks. The system allows liquid to seep through walls or holes of pre-cast tanks and through rocks to the surrounding soil. Such pit sites need a periodic cleaning to avoid clogging.

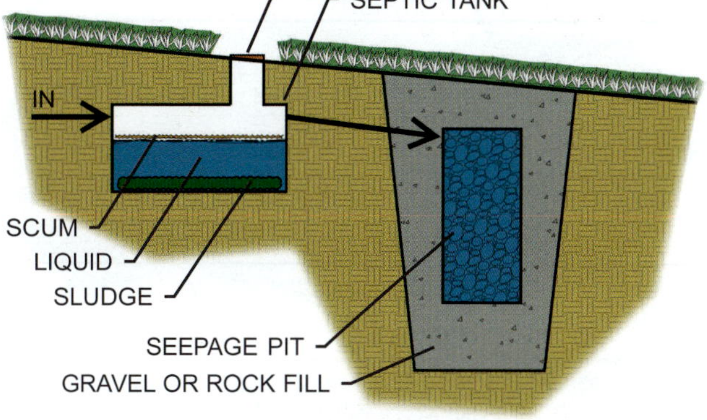

FIG. 12.12 – SEEPAGE PIT FOLLOWING SEPTIC TANK

AEROBIC SYSTEM AND SOIL ABSORPTION FIELD (basically replaces a septic tank system)

In some soil conditions, where septic tank/ leach field systems are not suitable, an aeration tank instead of septic tank is provided. In this tank, air is blown through the wastewater. Such a system, although requiring more attention and periodic maintenance, provides a better degree of treatment than standard septic systems. Water is thus provided a higher degree of treatment before going to absorption fields. Such systems use more energy and require utility connections.

SEPTIC TANKS / SAND FILTER / DISINFECTION AND DISCHARGE

In certain soil conditions, treated effluent discharge to surface water is utilized. A septic tank discharges liquid onto sand filters. The filter could be at ground level but usually is in a buried sand pit due to use and aesthetic considerations. The liquid enters by perforated pipe at the top of the sand and filters through the sand and gravel to the bottom pipe. The under-drain pipe conveys the liquid to the disinfection unit.

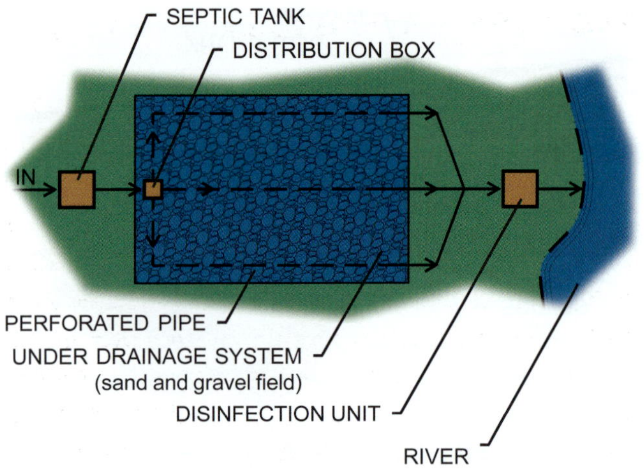

FIG. 12.13 – SEPTIC TANK / FILTER FIELD / DISINFECTION / DISCHARGE

Subsurface sand filters should not be installed in areas where bedrock is encountered or the seasonal high groundwater table is within three feet (1 m) of the surface. The size of sand filter should be determined on the basis of loading rate and the estimated volume of maximum flow per day. The loading rate of 1.15 gallons per day per square foot (900 sq. cm) of filter area is generally utilized. At least two inches (5 cm) of ¾ inch to 1½ inch (2 cm to 4 cm) size gravel should surround under-drains and distribution pipes. A six-inch (15 cm) layer of gravel should be placed on top of the two inches (5 cm) of bedding gravel over which 24 inches (60 cm) of clean sand of approximately 0.12 inches x 0.24 inches (0.3 to 0.6 mm) effective size should be used.

MODIFIED SAND MOUND SYSTEM

Where existing soil conditions (rocky or tight soil of high water table) are not suitable for disposal systems and effluent discharge to surface water (stream or ditch) is not possible, a sand mound or evapotranspiration bed system can sometimes be used. Such systems could be used with septic or aerobic tank units.

1. In the sand mound system, liquid is transported from the storage tank through perforated plastic pipe in the sand mound that covers **plowed** (scarified) **ground**. Liquid flows through rocks or gravel and then sand to natural soil. Mound vegetation helps evaporate liquids.

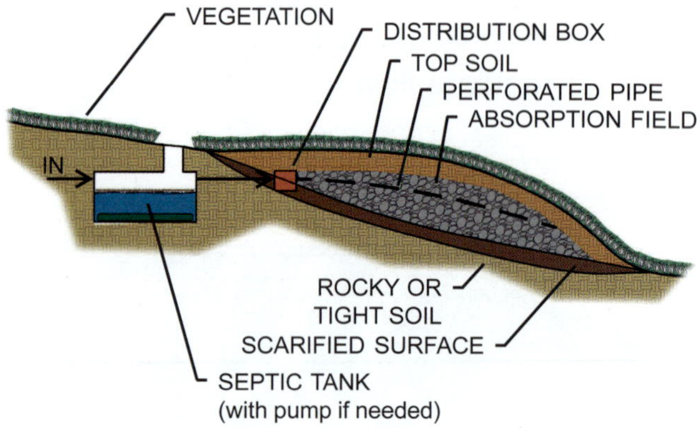

FIG. 12.14 – SAND MOUND

2. In the evapotranspiration bed variation, the sand bed is lined with plastic or other waterproof material. The bed can be mounded or level. Liquid evaporates because it is prevented by the liner from filtering through the natural soil. Plants help in the evapotranspiration process. Mounds for such systems can be creatively located where desired and can be used to screen use areas.

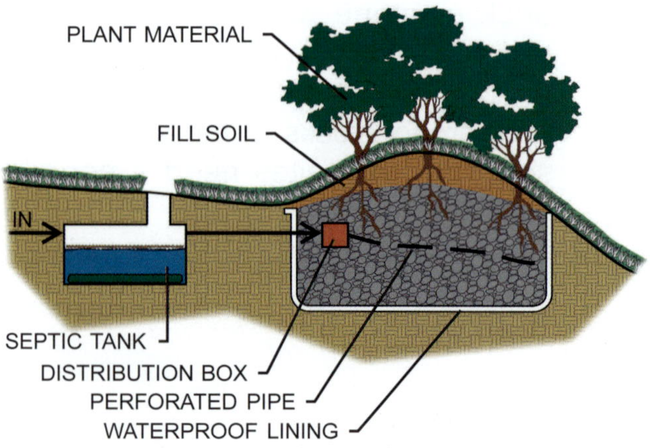

FIG. 12.15 – EVAPOTRANSPIRATION BED

CLUSTER BED

Where more than one use area of a facility lies in proximity of each other, a cluster system approach could be used. Several such facilities could be served by a common treatment and disposal system.

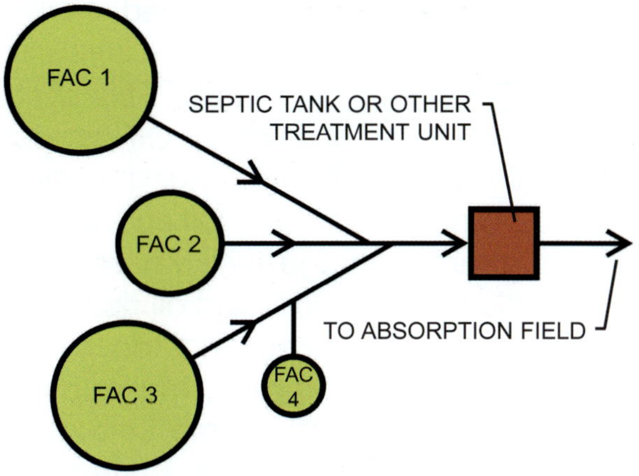

FIG. 12.16 – CLUSTER SYSTEM

Several combinations are possible. Each building could be connected to its on-site septic or aerobic tank, and treated liquid connected to a common absorption field by a small diameter gravity system. Such clusters could also use other alternative systems, such as mounds, pressure sewers and sewage treatment lagoons.

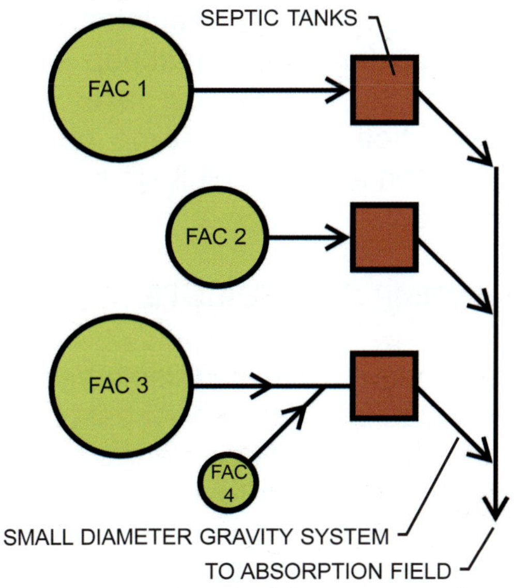

FIG. 12.17 – ALTERNATE CLUSTER SYSTEM

PRESSURE SEWERS (Grinder Pumps)

Pumps that grind solids in the sewage are installed at the storage tanks at each building to enable wastewater to be pumped through small-diameter pipes to a central or alternate treatment and disposal system. The grinder pump could be installed in the storage tank that collects wastes from multiple buildings. Yet, in another modification, multiple buildings, each served by septic tanks, could discharge to a storage tank by gravity from where it is pumped, with the aid of grinder pumps to additional treatment and/or disposal.

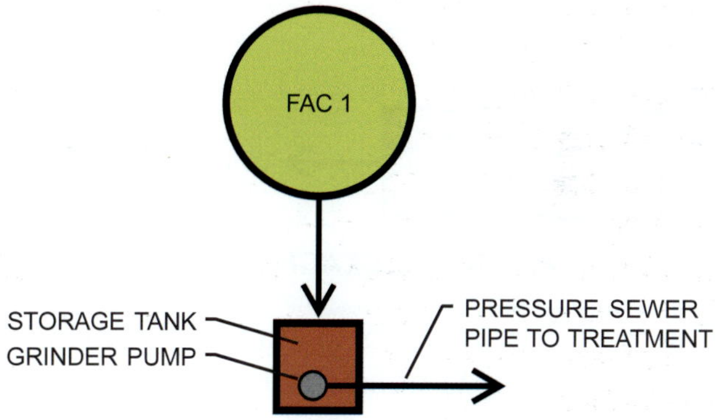

FIG. 12.18 – NO SEPTIC TANK

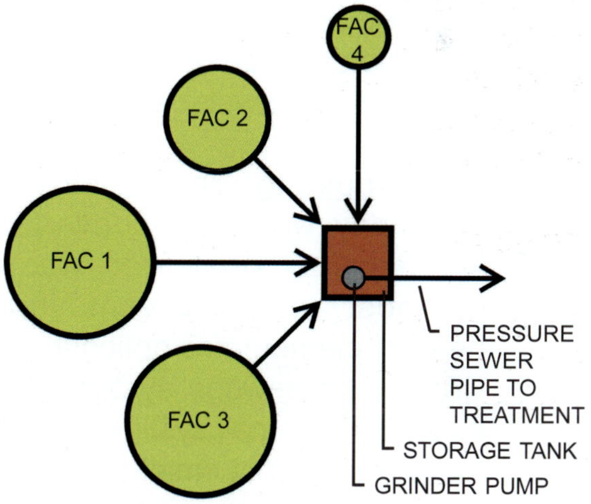

FIG. 12.19 – CLUSTER SYSTEM NO SEPTIC TANK

DUAL SYSTEMS

Dual systems are the systems that segregate "black water" and "gray water" and handle them separately. The term "black water" is used to describe wastes from toilet fixtures and is usually handled by waterless or low-water toilet systems.

The term "gray water" is used to describe other wastewater from the kitchen, laundry, etc. Such water needs less treatment and can be treated or disposed of by septic or other approved treatment and disposal systems.

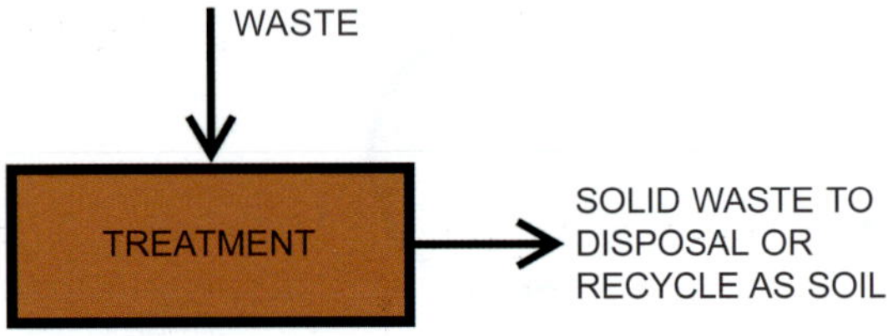

FIG. 12.20 – BLACK WATER

The main advantage of using the dual system is the necessity to handle only a small fraction of wastewater compared to conventional waterborne systems. Because of its inherent water conservation, it also reduces the need to provide large amounts of water and is particularly useful in remote areas and sites where there is limited water availability.

1. **Composting:** This system does not need any water. It converts toilet wastes and most food wastes to compost. Electric vent, fan, and heating element are optional on large waterborne sewage systems, but are essential on small systems that will be the case in most small and/or remote resource facilities. The use of solar (photovoltaic) panels is strongly recommended as a means of providing the limited electricity necessary. Proper care of such a system is essential.

2. **Incineration:** This system also does not involve any water. Electricity, gas, or oil burns solids and evaporates liquid. Ash will need to be removed on a periodic basis depending upon the load on the incinerator. A roof vent and proper maintenance are needed. This system is not recommended.

3. **Recycling Oil Flush:** This system does not use any water. Oil instead of water is used for flushing. It is similar to airline flush toilets. Oil and waste go to a large storage tank where wastes settle to the bottom and oil rises to the top. Oil is filtered and recycled for flushing. Periodically, makeup oil is required and, after some time, the oil needs replacing. This system uses electricity and requires proper care and attention. In remote areas the use of solar panels is recommended.

4. **Recycling Chemical:** These systems use small amounts of water. A water-chemical flush mixture is used instead of water in the toilet bowl. Mixture and wastewater go to a storage tank and are filtered with the chemicals being re-circulated. A water hookup for adding makeup water is needed; chemicals are added periodically. The same care and attention as in the oil flush system are needed.

VAULT / PUMP-OUT TOILETS

Low-use primitive areas and use areas within floodplains can often be served best by vault or portable chemical toilets. Vehicular access is, however, necessary to service the units. These types of toilets are very frequently used to provide supplemental toilets for events.

Vault toilets at Iwo Jima Memorial – Arlington, Virginia

Comfort station – Paris Mountain State Park, South Carolina

COMFORT STATION REQUIREMENTS

Suggested fixture unit requirements for the various recreation activities are given in their respective sections. Most states have strict requirements in this field, and they should be determined very early in the design work. Although most sanitary requirements do not provide for it, the number of fixture units actually needed in the comfort stations is normally greater for women than for men.

A man takes approximately 1.1 minute to use a urinal and approximately 1.8 minutes to use a toilet.

Men in day use areas use a urinal 3 to 4 times more frequently than they use a toilet. (36)

A woman takes approximately 2 to 2.5 minutes to use a toilet.

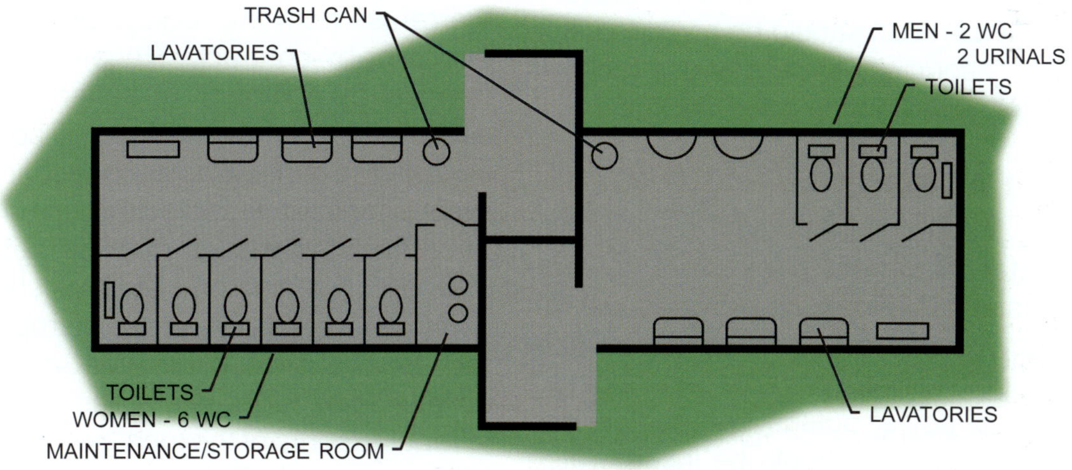

FIG. 12.21 – THE NUMBER OF FIXTURE UNITS NEEDED IS USUALLY GREATER FOR WOMEN THAN MEN

All sanitary facilities located on handicapped accessible routes shall have handicapped-accessible facilities provided, including doorways, lavatories and WCs. At least WC stall for each sex shall be approximately 60" (150 cm) wide by 60" (150 cm) deep, with grab bars and outward opening door. Refer to ADA requirements.

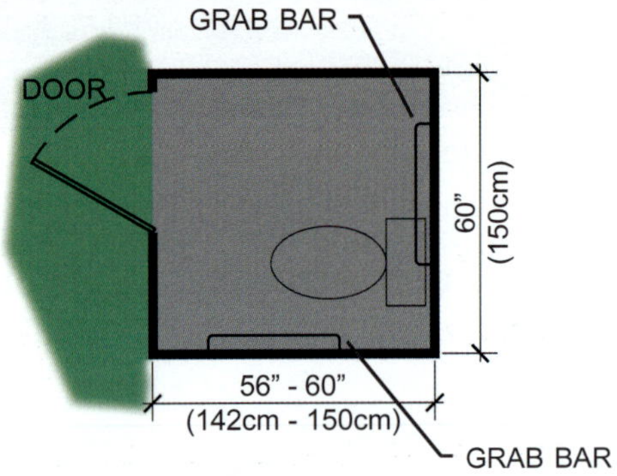

FIG. 12.22 – WC STALL WITH GRAB BARS

Hot or tempered running water has normally been provided at most comfort stations and at all comfort stations with showers. Because of fuel costs, consideration should be given to eliminating hot water in all day-use comfort stations, including showers at beaches. Where hot (tempered) water is necessary, strong consideration should be given to using solar heat, especially since day-use facilities are primarily used during good weather.

MISCELLANEOUS

Wastewater treatment plants and sewage pumping stations should be provided with an emergency generator unit or with a suitable outlet for hooking into a portable generator unit at the time of power outage. An audible and visible alarm system should be incorporated outside the lift stations to indicate high level alarm conditions. Telemetering the status of remote facilities to a central control station should be done if at all possible.

When budget permits, a central control system located at the treatment plant should be considered.

Security is important and can be enhanced by:

1. proper screening of the treatment facilities from public view.

2. provision of a gated, fenced barrier.

3. night lighting.

4. intrusion alarms combined with telemetering status to a central location.

SOLID WASTE DISPOSAL

Solid waste disposal is a continual and often overlooked problem of major proportions, and should be planned for when developing a leisure facility. The best solution is to remove the refuse from the facility, either with facility forces or by contract. Recent trends are for removal by contract. In either situation, it is necessary to know the kind of equipment to be used in solid waste collection before a system for trash receptacles can be designed. In some instances, it may be necessary to dispose of wastes on site. This should be by whatever method is least disruptive to the facility and should be located away from downwind of public-use areas. Conformance to requirements of the local health department will be required. This type of disposal should only be considered as a last resort option and only after all other solutions have been thoroughly investigated.

Adequate numbers of trash receptacles (in this case, recycled 55-gallon drums) of some type are necessary – East central coast of England

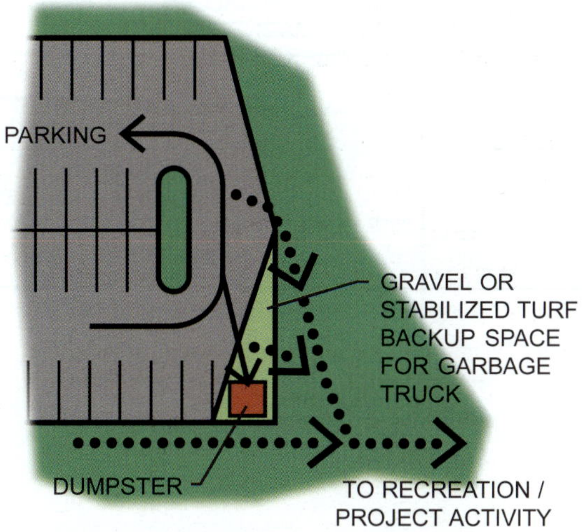

FIG. 12.23 – TYPICAL DUMPSTER SITE

Adequate solid waste collection facilities should be provided. These can best be located adjacent to walks, roads, and service drives to facilitate mechanical pickup. In recent years, more leisure facilities have been forced, due to economics, into utilizing a few strategically located dumpsters instead of the more familiar and widely dispersed trash cans. It should be noted that walks used by service vehicles must be designed to withstand the intended use. This will usually mean more base material and wider paved surfaces and larger-radius horizontal curves.

Trash pickup truck – Sweden

ELECTRICITY AND TELEPHONE

All major day-use installations and all overnight areas, except primitive areas, should be serviced by electricity. Primitive overnight and low-use areas can frequently be served by solar-generated electricity, thus eliminating the need for what can be extremely expensive electric line installation.

To reduce the maintenance costs, **all** power lines, phone and other communication should be placed underground unless special conditions make such installation costs truly prohibitive. Whenever possible, electric and telephone lines should be placed in a common trench and, where feasible, in conjunction with water and/or sanitary lines.

All underground utility lines should be marked with non-decomposing, electronically detectable markers. Plastic tape identifying the utility below is the best and least expensive technique.

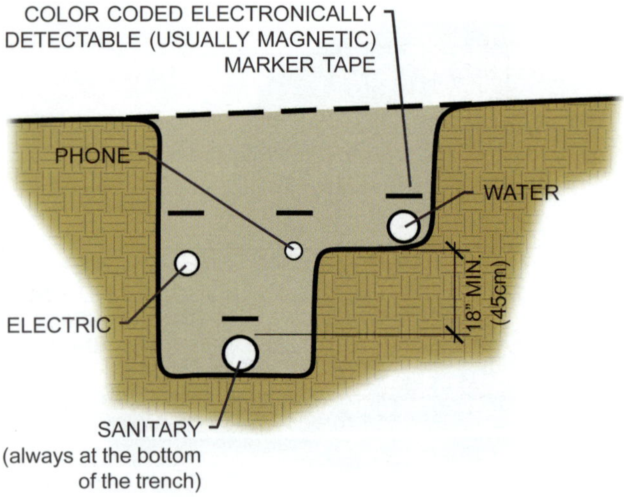

FIG. 12.24 – MULTIPLE-USE UTILITY TRENCH

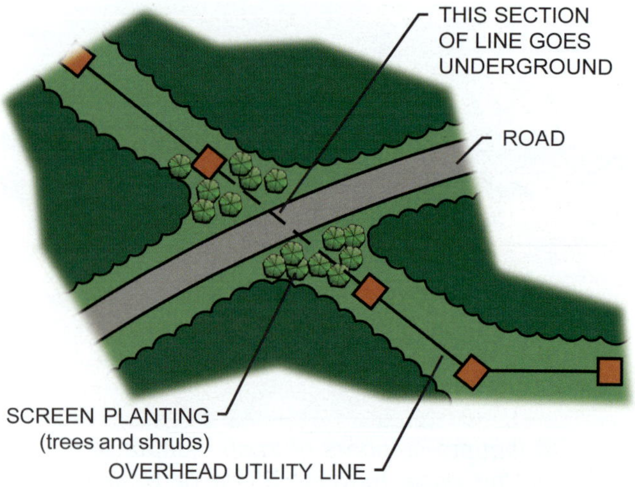

FIG. 12.26 – ALTERNATE ROAD/UTILITY LINE CROSSING

Public toilets in day-use areas that are closed at dusk do not normally require night lighting.

When overhead lines become imperative, special care must be taken to break up long views down the right-of-way. This basically means that road and trail crossings should be at right angles to the roads and pathways. These rights-of-way and clearings should be kept to a minimum and planted with view-blocking vegetation to minimize this undesirable visual intrusion.

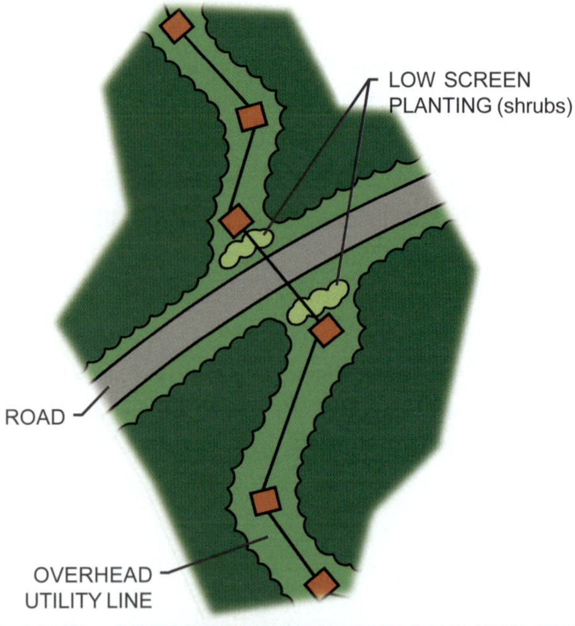

FIG. 12.25 – ACTIVITY ROAD/OVERHEAD UTILITY LINE CROSSING FOR PUBLIC PROJECT ROAD

Photovoltaic panels – usable for all sorts of low level electrical service – Vienna, Austria

Celluar phones have become so prevalent that they are surpassing land lines for emergency service.

Any facility that has events requiring television filming must have adequate electrical and communications systems.

Media coverage of a small tennis tournament – Naples, Florida

Chapter 13

SIGNS

OK – Where am I? The Mall, Washington, D.C.

GENERAL

Signs are a necessary part of the total circulation system of any facility and, as such, they should be effective aids to the public in understanding and enjoying their visit. **All signs in a facility should be unified in character** and relate to the total design theme of other resource facilities. Pay careful attention to the design and placement of signs; they can add significantly to the facility's aesthetic experience or they can detract from the visit. In addition to specific facility signing, it is necessary to have adequate "trailblazer" signs to direct the visitor to the overall resource. The design of these signs and their placement must be coordinated with the affected highway department(s).

The primary sign concept in use in many large-scale facilities today consists of word messages and usually accompanied by visual graphics. The sign blanks are usually stained or painted a particular color with the message in white or other sharply contrasting color. These signs are effective in conveying their messages, but they require costly reworking at regular intervals, frequently every five to seven years.

Informational sign – Clam Pass Park, Collier County, Florida

Informational sign – London, England

Many resource agencies have now decided to rely more on graphic symbols and color associations. This type of sign system consists of an arrow and symbol, frequently using standard highway symbol graphics on a color field. (See photo of sign cluster.) It should be basic, functional, and should, in most instances, **not** attempt to decorate the landscape.

Graphics in a sign cluster

These graphic signs are frequently made of metal with applied decal-type symbols and lettering as used by highway departments.

The graphic sign system used by the federal government and, in particular, the National Park Service and shown in detail in its publications, is a slight modification of the standard international sign system and is strongly endorsed. It is particularly useful in areas where more than one language is used.

DESIGN

Signs are almost always mounted centered on their supports. Figure 13.1 shows an alternative placement that could provide better directional guidance.

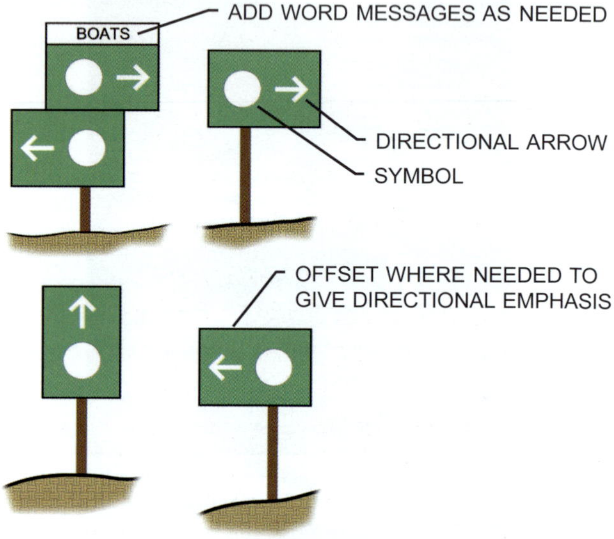

FIG. 13.1 – SIGN PLACEMENT ON SUPPORTS

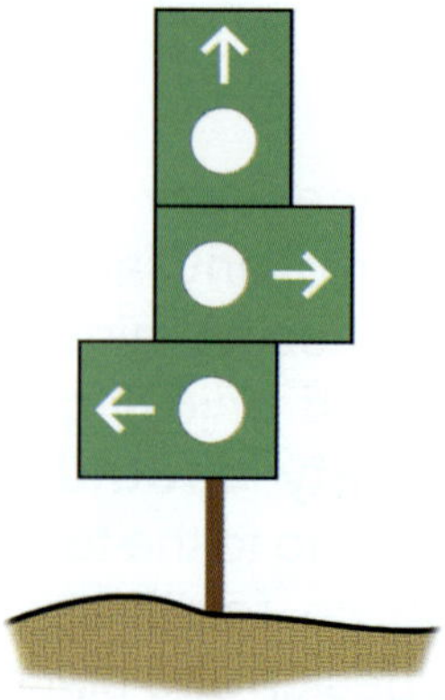

FIG. 13.2 – SIGN CLUSTER
(shows how multiple directional signs can be effectively mounted on a single support system)

All sign components used in the construction of signs should be readily available and long-lasting (seven to ten years minimum). Other than the main entrance sign, all signs should be easily fabricated (e.g., by the resource staff or local highway sign shop) and easily maintained by the local staff.

Main entrance sign
– Springettsbury Township Park, Pennsylvania

The design of individual use symbols is not recommended, especially for facilities that will serve foreign visitors. However, if the design of sign symbols is undertaken, especially for local-use parks, it should produce a locally, clearly understandable message that is rapidly communicated to the intended facility user.

FIG. 13.3 – SYMBOLS

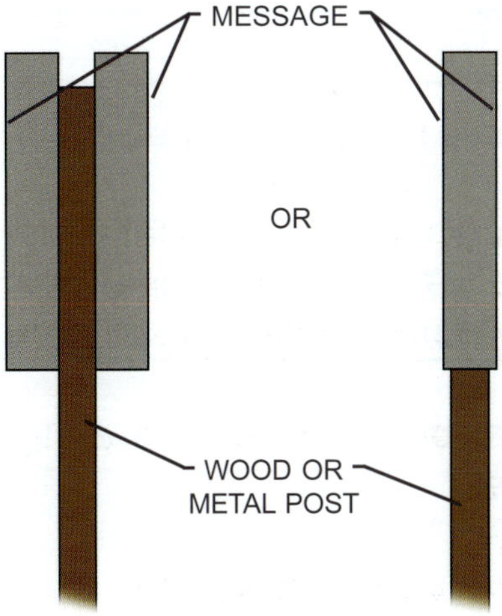

FIG. 13.4 – TWO-SIDED SIGN

Directional arrows must be clear. Do not try to invent your own. Use the international federal highway standard. It works!! Yours may not! Make sure the arrow color and background color are sharply contrasting.

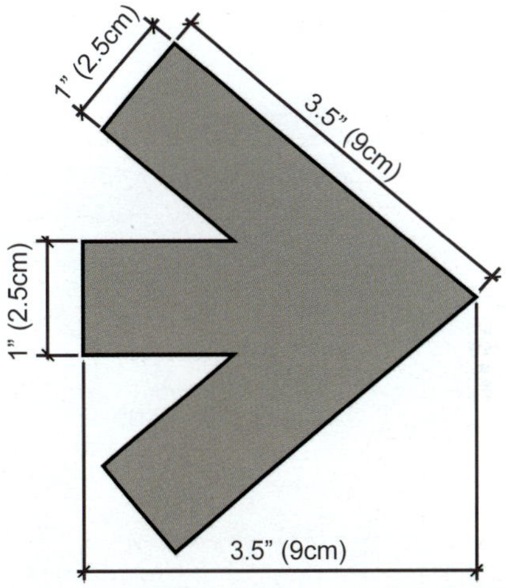

FIG. 13.5 – DIRECTIONAL ARROW

LAYOUT

Sign layouts must be planned.

In general, a minimum number of signs should be used. Good facility planning can help reduce the number and kinds of signs needed.

Factors to be considered in a sign system layout are:

- Visual distance and reaction time (number of feet needed between reader and sign, and sign size increases as speed increases).

- All speed limit, stop, or other motor vehicle regulation and control signs must be legally enforceable to be of real value. Therefore, the signs must meet the specifications and standards of or be acceptable to the local traffic-enforcing authority.

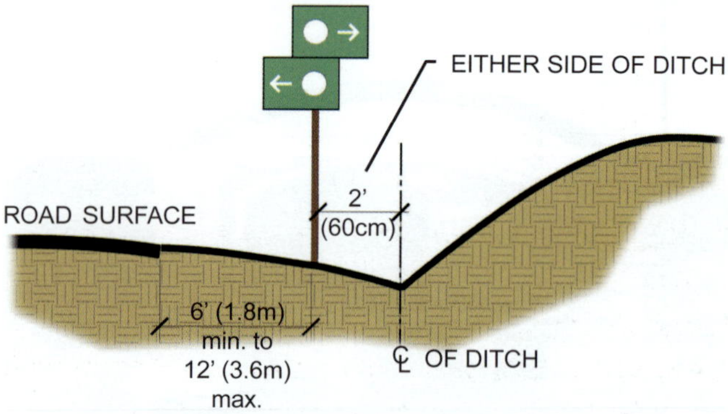

FIG. 13.7 – SIGN PLACEMENT LOCATION

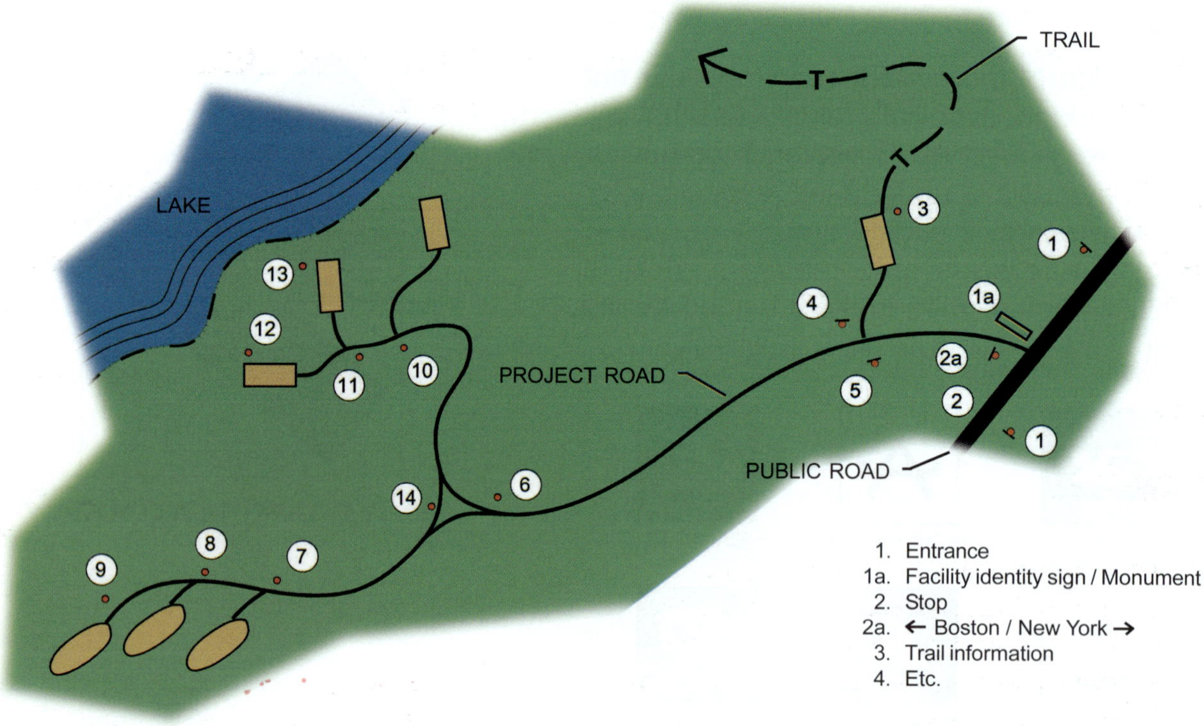

FIG. 13.6 – SIGN PLAN

Chapter 14

OVERNIGHT USE

Extended stay desires of the participants, relative inexpensiveness of camping and communing with nature, and people's mobility have led to a continued need for "camping." People have demonstrated an ongoing interest in the out-of-doors and "getting away from it all." To satisfy this need, public and private camping facilities have been developed and some continue to be built almost everywhere. Proper planning and design are particularly important to the preservation of the natural setting (one of the main reasons for most campgrounds being), and for effective, economical campground operation and maintenance. There is some indication that the number of "campers" may be stabilizing, while at the same time overall tourism is increasing.

GENERAL

Before looking for areas suitable for overnight use, a determination must be made as to the need for such facilities. A survey of the use of surrounding overnight facilities should be made that would include kinds of facilities, location, and number of overnight units. The number of capacity nights and the number of turn-aways may be more difficult to obtain, but its availability will immediately tell you if you need to build a campground. If the survey shows a need for overnight accommodations for the resource users, the type of facilities desired should, if possible, be determined. Most small campgrounds having less than 100 sites are questionable; due to their high operating costs, they frequently operate at a loss.

TYPES OF OVERNIGHT ACCOMMODATIONS

Many types of overnight stay can be provided. These experiences vary from primitive, walk-in camp sites to modern, full-service hotel/lodge facilities. A variety of types of overnight facilities is generally desirable in any major use facility and might include any or all of the following:

- Primitive walk-in sites; few or no amenities – one of the few types of overnight use where there has been sustained growth.

- Walk-in sites; water and sanitary facilities provided from vault toilets and wells – some sites may be able to provide flush toilets and running water economically.

• Trailside shelters; limited water and sanitary facilities. As the name implies these are located along trails.

• Typical family campground; limited water and sanitary facilities.

• Typical family campground with flush toilets, showers, and laundry tubs.

Campground set into a forest
– French Creek State Park, Pennsylvania

• Typical family campground with complete utility hookups at each camp site (basically, trailer courts) — almost exclusively in private ownership and management.

• Housekeeping cabins.

• Lodges/hotels with complete service. They may include pool, restaurant and or cafeteria, and other amenities.

In addition, there are special types of overnight uses, such as:

• Group tent camping – water and sanitary only; usually and infrequent resource use.

• Caravan camping areas – limited sanitary facilities to full-service group campground. (See Fig. 14.24.)

• Campventions – large organized groups, i.e., Boy Scouts, Girl Scouts, National Recreation Trailer Association.

• Organized group camps – complete lodging and dining facilities provided. Limited new organized camps are being developed due to construction costs and high ongoing O & M costs. Usually uses old CCC facilities, which are costly to maintain.

• Transient camping – usually along major tourist highways; most frequently privately owned.

• Youth hostels. Overnight facilities infrequently utilized in the U.S., and are usually done in conjunction with historic or old building renovation.

The use of private or non-governmental funds for the construction and operation of the more elaborate, financially viable types of overnight facilities, such as group camps, lodges, cabins, trailer courts, and youth hostels is normally considered and encouraged. The reasons for this are to avoid competition with private enterprise, while providing additional complimentary-use facilities to the typical leisure facility recreation activities.

GENERAL LOCATION FACTORS

Initial considerations in determining the location of overnight use areas include:

- Relationship of the facility to the resource as a whole.

- Location of the site with respect to other internal recreational facilities.

- Location of the site with regard to related facilities, such as access roads, potable water supply, and other utilities.

- Terrain that is level or gently rolling, well drained, wooded and/or partially shaded. Certain adverse conditions can often be overcome with imaginative design.

- Size of campground and potential for expansion should be determined. It is generally not desirable to design campgrounds with less than 150 sites due to more expensive per site construction costs and, especially, more expensive operational costs.

GENERAL SITE REQUIREMENTS

The design of a camping area is necessarily dictated by the particular characteristics or natural environment of the site.

Topography is the most compelling of the characteristics, followed by vegetative cover, soil conditions, drainage, and rock outcrops. Visual separation between camp sites is desirable. It is necessary to screen camping areas from other resource uses.

TOPOGRAPHY

Gently rolling with good drainage, one to five percent is desirable. Fifteen percent maximum slope permitted, one percent minimum – anything less will require extensive site modifications for drainage, and is expensive.

VEGETATION

Vegetation with canopy for shade and understory for screening is best. Mature timber stands are undesirable because of likely loss due to age or disease. Thinning of canopy and other forest management practices should be considered, when possible, prior to development to improve vegetative conditions.

SOILS

Soils should be such that water permeates quickly to avoid wet and/or muddy conditions. The area should be able to take repeated traffic without adverse compaction or erosion. Depth to high or seasonably high water table should be enough so as to not adversely affect construction or ongoing use, and so that standing water is not present during inclement weather in the use season.

CHARACTERISTICS

Young adult campers without children are the most likely to seek remote camping (backpacking, etc.). As families begin to rear children, they are likely to modify their camping style to the traditional family camping with some backpacking. During the period when their children are between 5 and 14 years old, families are most likely to do only roadside camping. However, as their children mature and leave home, some parents will again seek out remote-only camping experiences. Most will leave the camping market altogether or will utilize some type of recreational vehicle.

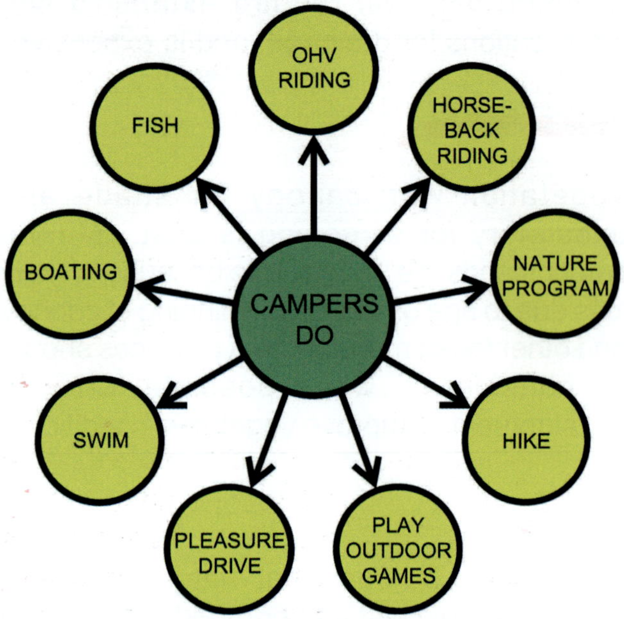

FIG. 14.1 – CAMPERS DO OTHER ACTIVITIES BESIDES CAMPING

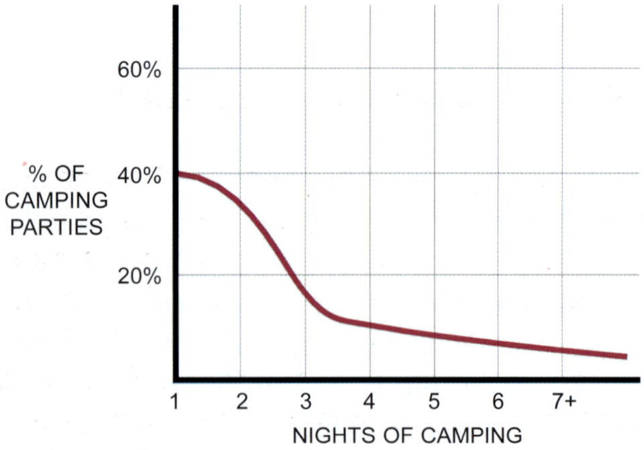

FIG. 14.2 – LENGTH OF STAY

Length of stay is extremely variable. Most campers go out only for the weekend – arrive on a Friday, camp Friday and Saturday nights, and leave during the day on Sunday.

ATTITUDES

• Camping is...

for 10%, a social experience, not a physical one.

for 27%, a physical experience, not social.

for 28%, neither physical nor social.

for 34%, both a social and a physical experience.

• Screening between campsites is considered by many to be more important than spacing.

• There is a diversity of desires for campground experiences.

• **Water** – both the availability of water oriented activities and of campsites in sight of water are, overall, the most dominant factors in campground and campsite attraction.

TRENDS IN CAMPING

• Many people (possibly 40 percent) during the camping season camp with friends. Consideration should be given to providing accommodations (10 percent of sites) for more than one family site complex, possibly two to three units together. (See Fig. 14.11.)

• Off-season camping use may be declining; it generally averages between 10 percent and 20 percent of total camping attendance.

• Trailer and camper to tent ratio varies according to type of campground and section of the country. Generally, in the east, it runs about two to one; the figure is stable at this time. Four to 13 percent of sites had two or more cars.

• Activity peaks at camps: 1:00 p.m., 5:00 p.m., and 9:30 p.m., with 50 percent of the campers never leaving the campground.

• Friday and Saturday are, by far, the most heavily used camper nights; weekdays about one-half capacity. The three major camping weekends for most are Memorial Day, the Fourth of July, and Labor Day. Some facilities run at 100 percent capacity for several days at a time; however, recent trends have been for campground occupancy to vary anywhere from 10 percent to 20 percent in small, rustic areas to approximately 50 percent, except on holiday weekends. Approximately 85 percent to 90 percent of the campers in Pennsylvania stay three nights or less. Off season they stay only one-and-one-half days.

• Fireplaces are seldom used for cooking (hot dogs, coffee, and marshmallows are exceptions), and their prime function is for heat and evening atmosphere.

Typical camp stove. It can be used for small campfire, as well as cooking, and can also be tipped up for cleaning.

• Private campgrounds continue to upgrade their campsite facilities with a greater number of full hookup sites to meet their clientele's demand for full amenities. This includes expanding the amperage from 15 to 30 amps due to more electric appliances in the campers.

• The distance traveled for camping trips is reducing.

TYPES OF CAMPING EQUIPMENT

There are significant regional trends in the use of recreational vehicles, with the west and the plains country having a very high percentage of camper trucks; the remainder of the country using a combination of travel and camping trailers. This regional difference is important when preparing the campground layout and, particularly, the individual camp spurs and their living spaces. The size of a vehicle and its functional characteristics dictate how the arrangement of the living area should be developed.

RECREATIONAL VEHICLE OWNER PROFILE

In general, recreational vehicle owners fall into three categories: skilled, professional, and retired. Nearly one-half of the owners have no children at home. Of the families with children, one-third have one child, one-third have two children, and the remainder three or more. The average camper with children had two children, ages 0 – 17, with 82 percent of the parties having two children, ages 7 – 12. Recreational vehicle owners are generally affluent. Median age of household head is 50, with 70 percent between 36 and 65, and 11 percent over 65.

Distance traveled is being reduced due to high gas prices and available time. This information was based on 2,500+ replies – divided 80 percent travel trailers, 10 percent truck campers, 5 percent camp trailers, and 5 percent miscellaneous.

Rental continues to be an alternative to ownership of this expensive equipment, and should be recognized as a factor that will influence the kinds of campers and their camping needs.

WATER AND SANITARY FACILITIES

The minimum type of sanitary facilities provided in the family campground should be sealed-vault latrines. This would include toilets for the women and urinals and toilets for the men. Hand-washing facilities need to be provided as per public health requirements. A minimum of a hand pump for potable water supply is necessary; potable water supply from faucets is desirable.

Campground comfort station with informational bulletin board – French Creek State Park, Pennsylvania

The more modern camping facilities would be washhouses or a combination of washhouses and comfort stations. The washhouses include water showers (usually tempered water), flush toilets, tempered and cold running water in the lavatories, electric receptacles, and night lighting. The building may be heated for winter use if the campground is to be used in the northern climates for off-season use. In the deep southern portion of the United States, Mexico, and the Caribbean heating is not an issue.

Night lighting and electrical receptacles in comfort stations are almost a necessity. In remote areas, photovoltaic collector panels with storage cells may be a feasible way of providing for necessary minimal electrical requirements.

If extended-stay camping is expected, coin-operated washers and dryers can be provided in the washhouses or a centrally located camp center facility. The comfort stations should have flush toilets, tempered and cold running water in the lavatories, and electrical receptacles. A comfort station may be heated depending on need.

A potable water supply should be provided with freeze-proof faucets in cold climate areas (where camping is permitted during the winter) within 50 feet (45 m) of each campsite.

WATER SUPPLY

- With showers and flush toilets: 25 to 30 gallons (95 to 115 l) per camper day is needed. [4] With flush toilets only: 15 to 20 gallons (60 to 75 l) per camper per day is needed. [4] Without showers and flush toilets: 5 gallons (19 l) per camper per day is needed. [4]

- Emergency water storage is usually required by governing agencies: estimated at double the anticipated average maximum day use for the capacity of the water storage reservoir.

- Distance from drinking water to most distant camp site: 300 feet (90 m) maximum; 150 feet (45 m) optimum.

SANITARY FACILITIES

- Distance from comfort station to farthest unit: 500 feet (150 m) maximum; 300 feet (90 m) desirable maximum.

- Distance from washhouse to farthest unit: 600 feet (180 m) maximum; 400 feet (120 m) desirable maximum.

- In cold climates, at least one washhouse should be heated in campgrounds that are to be used during the winter season. The remainder of the toilets should be able to be winterized.

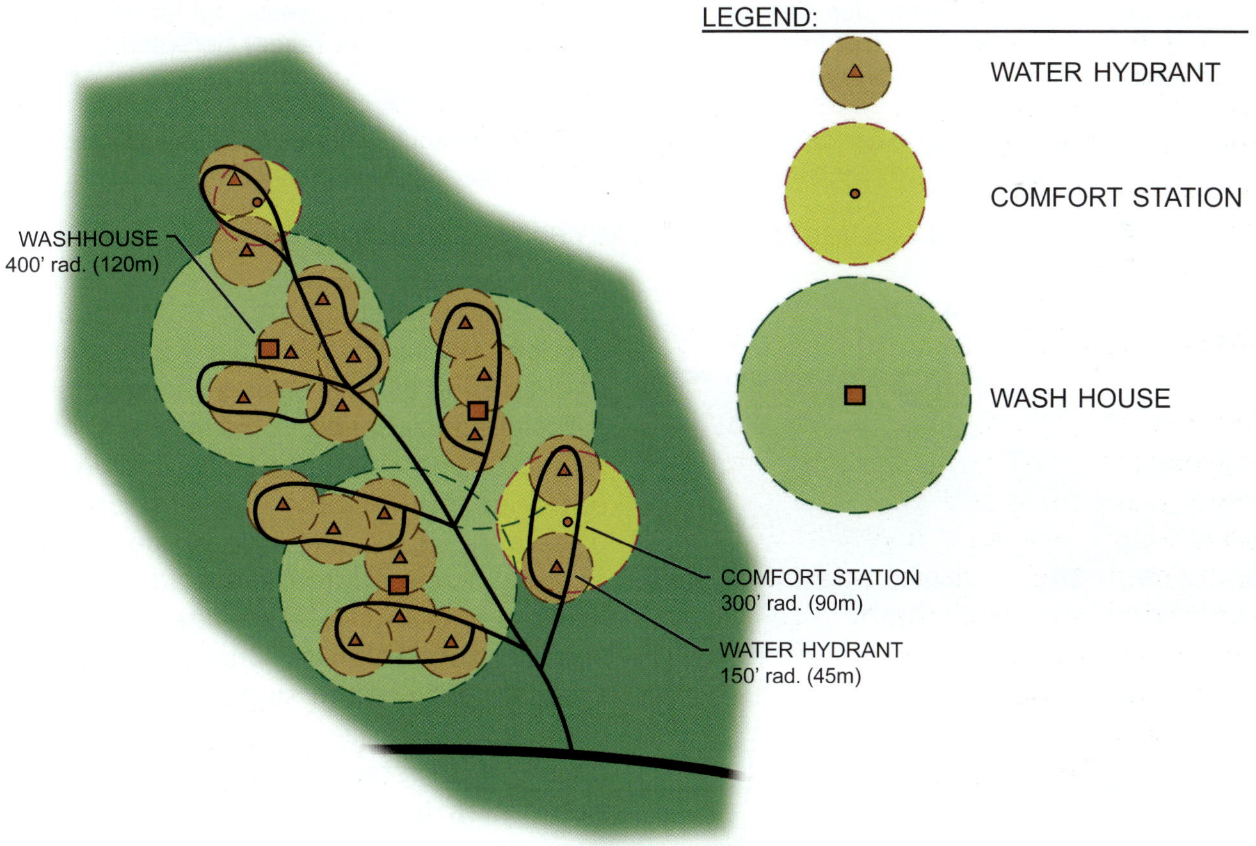

FIG. 14.3 – LOCATION OF CAMPGROUND WATER AND SANITARY FACILITIES

No. of Tent or Trailer Spaces*	No. of Toilet Seats Male/Female**		No. of Lavatories Male/Female		No. of Urinals Male	No. of Showers+ Male/Female		No. of Sanitary Stations
1-15	1	1	1	1	1	1	1	1
16-30	1	2	2	2	1	1	1	1
31-45	2	2	3	3	1	1	1	1
45-60	2	3	3	3	2	2	2	1
61-80	3	4	4	4	2	2	2	1
81-100	3	5	4	4	2	3	3	1

Suggested Sanitary Requirements – Assumed a 50 percent male/50 percent female user breakdown. Most states have standards that must be followed.

*For recreational areas having more than 100 tent or trailer spaces, there should be provided one additional toilet seat and lavatory for each sex per each additional 30 tent or trailer spaces; one additional men's urinal per each additional 60 sites; and one additional sanitary station per each additional 100 tent or trailer spaces or fractional part thereof.

**Urinals specifically designed for females may also be provided in lieu of toilet seats, but for not more than one-third of the required number of toilet seats. American women have not readily accepted this type of fixture, which is frequently provided and used in Europe.

+ A centrally located washhouse can be substituted for individual bathhouse shower facilities – this facility can be concession-operated and may be part of a camp center complex.

FIG. 14.4 – SUGGESTED SANITARY FIXTURE REQUIREMENTS

TRAILER WASTE STATION

Campground trailer waste station
– French Creek State Park, Pennsylvania

The trailer waste station is a necessary service to campers, providing for the dumping and cleaning of their sewage holding tanks in a designated location. This station should be located, wherever possible, between the entrance station and the first campsite, preferably on the exit side of the road, and properly screened from the road. One trailer waste station should be provided for each 100 sites or fraction thereof. Check with state and/or local public health standards to verify any standards for trailer waste stations. Also check with state and local approving authorities to determine if there are any unwritten standards for these facilities. Proper sewerage inlets to accommodate drain hoses and water facilities for cleaning the trailer tank should be provided. Instructions as to use and health hazards should be displayed. Locate, when possible, so that connection to the campground sanitary system can be made. (See Fig. 14.8 for suggested location.)

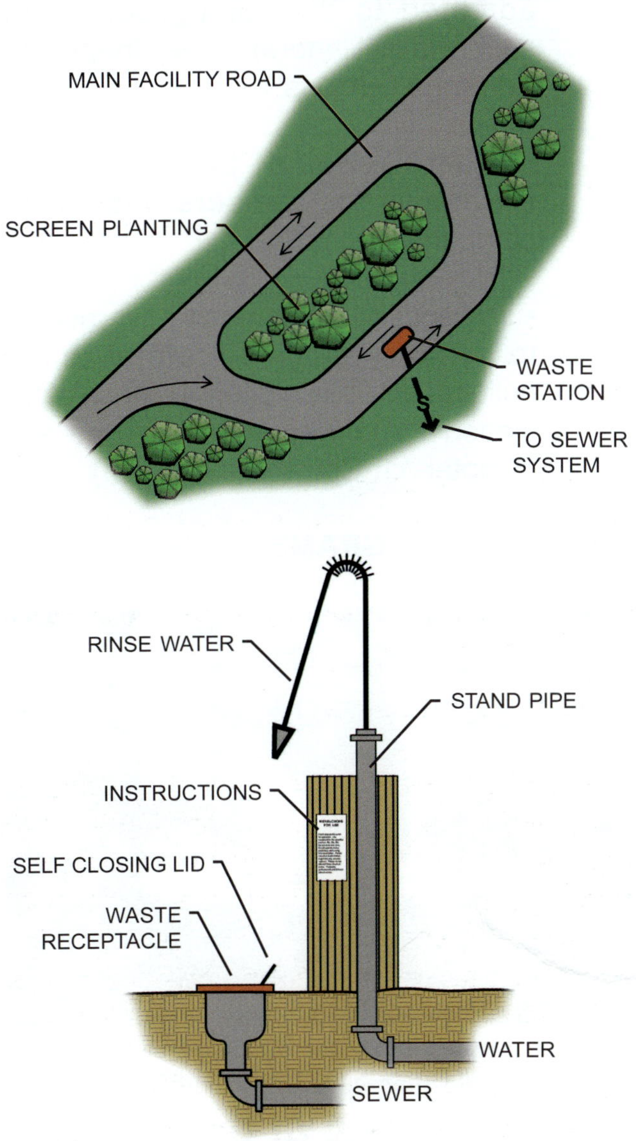

FIG. 14.5 – TRAILER WASTE STATION

ELECTRICITY

- Required for all public-use buildings in modern campgrounds. In areas where public electrical service is difficult and/or expensive to secure, consider photovoltaic supply.

- All-night lighting is desirable at all comfort stations.

- Electrical service to individual campsites is a frequently requested camper amenity. It should be made available in some highly developed campgrounds and, especially, in private camp areas.

CAMPING ROADS

The main camping area entrance road should be two-laned and located to permit easy, safe ingress and egress relative to site distance and grade from the public road.

Roads within the developed area should be designed to fit into the landscape with as little disturbance as possible. All roads should receive an appropriate surface treatment to minimize maintenance and dust problems.

Roads should not exceed a 12 percent grade where camp vehicles are permitted. Grades to 18 percent may be possible in tent-only areas under unusual conditions. Road width will depend on unit design, traffic flow, topography, and the vehicular circulation pattern. It is necessary to lay these roads out by eye at the site or, at a minimum, field check after a survey to make any desired adjustments that will save trees and other natural features of the area, as well as to obtain maximum usage of the site.

One-way loop roads throughout the campsite area, where possible, will provide a minimum intrusion on the landscape, reduce through traffic, and improve circulation. (See Chapter 11 Roads and Parking for road details.)

ENTRANCE STATION

The purpose of the entrance station is to control the numbers of campers and to organize the operations of the campground. These operations include the collection of fees and the issuing of camping permits, dissemination of campground information, security for the campers, and provisions for emergency communications for those without cell phones. Experience indicates that contact stations should be so designed as to allow issuance of permits to the camper sitting in his car and also allow space for parking for some car-camper units for campers to stop and walk back to the contact station to obtain additional information. The details associated with the contact station are as follows:

Campground entrance station
– French Creek State Park, Pennsylvania

• The backup space length should be determined by anticipated use and operational characteristics of each campground. One guide is to provide for ten feet of backup space for every campsite.

• There should be a bypass lane around the contact station for campers already admitted to the campground, and separate exit lane(s). (See Chapter 11, Entrance Stations.)

• There should be turnaround provisions for campers finding the campground full.

• Entrance stations must have access to sanitary facilities, either in the building or within a short distance of the station - 100 feet± (30 m). (See also Chapter 11, Entrance Stations.)

CAMPFIRE PROGRAMS

Interpretive/campfire facilities
– French Creek State Park, Pennsylvania

Provision of facilities for evening campfire programs should be considered for all campgrounds, especially those over 100 or more units. This facility can also serve as an environmental and OHV lecture area and should:

- be within walking distance of the overnight accommodations.

- have adequate visual and sound separation from campsites.

- be within 400 feet of a parking lot. The number of parking spaces needed is determined by the distance the amphitheater is from the campground. The greater the distance to the amphitheater, the greater the percent of parking spaces for overnight units that is needed.

- be accessible for people with disabilities.

- have lighting at campfire and along main access walkway.

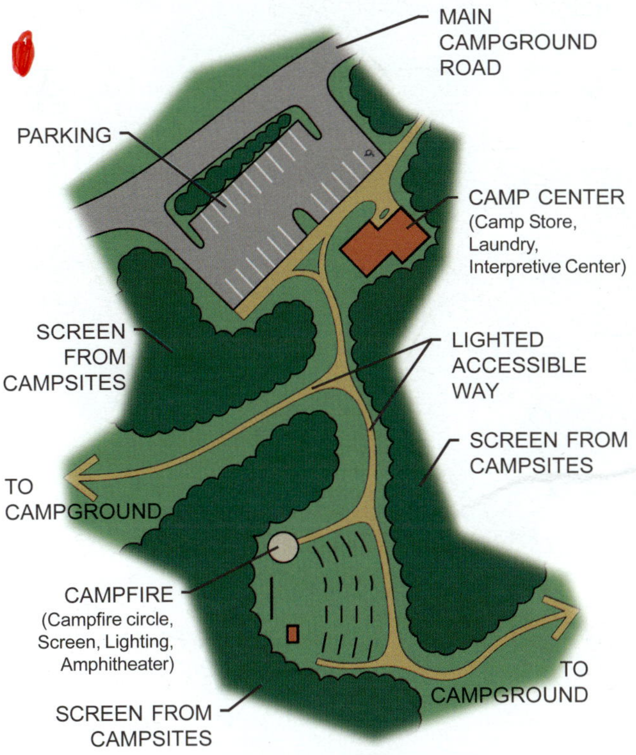

FIG. 14.6 – LOCATION OF CAMPING SUPPORT FACILITIES

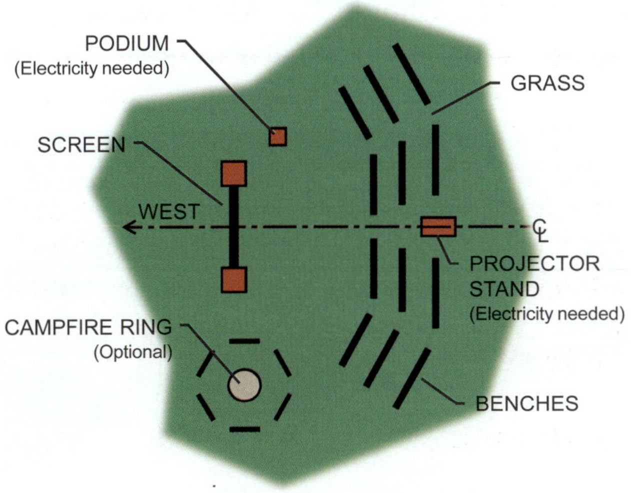

FIG. 14.7 – ORIENTATION OF CAMPFIRE PROGRAM FACILITIES

In a larger campground (200± sites), an alternative would be a rear projection system.

Campfire ring at interpretive facilities – French Creek State Park, Pennsylvania

GENERAL AMENITIES

Laundry Facilities (coin-operated): Desired by most campers staying longer than two days. They can be located in the bathhouse(s) or centrally located in a camp center complex.

Camp Store: Should be centrally located on the main campground road. All major campgrounds (200+ sites) should have such a facility unless there is a local store where camper supplies and parts can be purchased.

Firewood: Should be made available to campers, possibly on a fee basis by the concessionaire.

Firewood – Paris Mountain State Park, South Carolina

Telephone: All overnight facilities should have access to pay telephone(s), even though cell phone coverage may be excellent. The phones can be located as needed but, as a minimum, one should be provided at each contact station and camp center complex.

Accessible Facilities: Some campsites (a minimum of 10 percent suggested) must be accessibly designed and marked for use by the disabled.

FIG. 14.8 – A TYPICAL FAMILY CAMPGROUND LAYOUT

Pedestrian Access Routes: In overnight use areas, trails are as much an integral part of the facility as roads. Pedestrian access routes should connect all washhouses or toilet buildings. They should also connect to the play area(s) and open play fields, the central camping complex, and amphitheater/campfire area.

Play Areas and Play Fields: Play areas are of importance in campgrounds that cater to families. (See Chapter 15, Play Areas and Play Fields.)

Boat Launching: Facilities for launching boats, where possible, in the campgrounds located on navigable water bodies and waterways. Generally, these facilities should be less elaborate than standard boat facilities and should be for campers only.

Rubbish: One trash receptacle is needed per two-to-three campsites, depending on the frequency of rubbish pickup. If dumpsters must be used in lieu of trashcans, position them on a prepared surface at the campground's centrally located sanitary facilities.

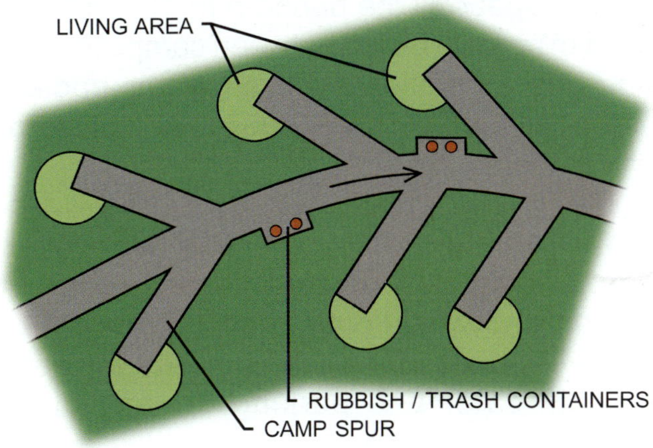

FIG. 14.9 – CAMPGROUND LIVING AREA

LIVING AREA

Location: In the East and Midwest, it is desirable to locate 90 percent of the living spaces to the left of the spur (facing the spur from the road) since the most used recreational vehicles' doors are located on the right side of the camper or camper tents. However, in the West and Southwest, a significant percentage of the campsites should be located in the rear of the spur to accommodate the prevalence of pickup campers. In hilly areas it will be necessary to locate the living areas where the land permits. These sites should be reserved primarily for tent campers.

Living area – campground at Paris Mountain State Park, South Carolina

Tables: Generally, a 6-foot long table is adequate for a typical family-type campground. Eight-foot long tables would be useful in OHV campgrounds and campgrounds serving large four or more person camping groups. Tables should be secured in permanent locations or they will be relocated by the campers causing overall site compaction and subsequent loss of vegetation.

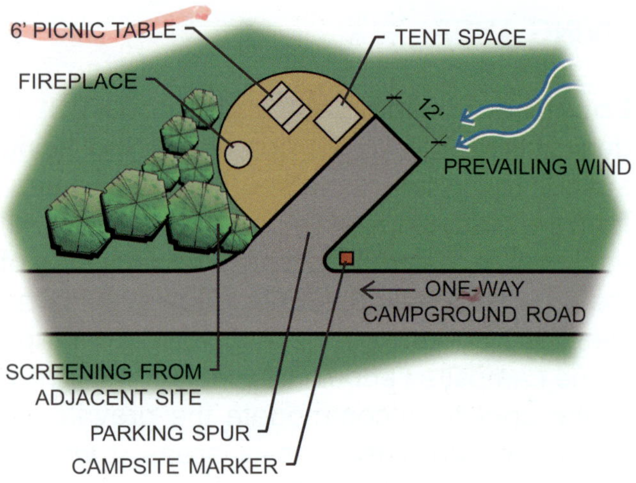

FIG. 14.10 – LIVING AREA

Living Space: Six hundred ± square feet (55 SM) of space is desirable; 400 ± square feet (40 SM) is the minimum space needed for a picnic table, cooking unit, and pitching a tent; 300 square feet (30± SM) should be leveled to 1 percent ± for tenting.

Multiple Family Sites: Ten percent or more of sites should be designed to accommodate two or more families.

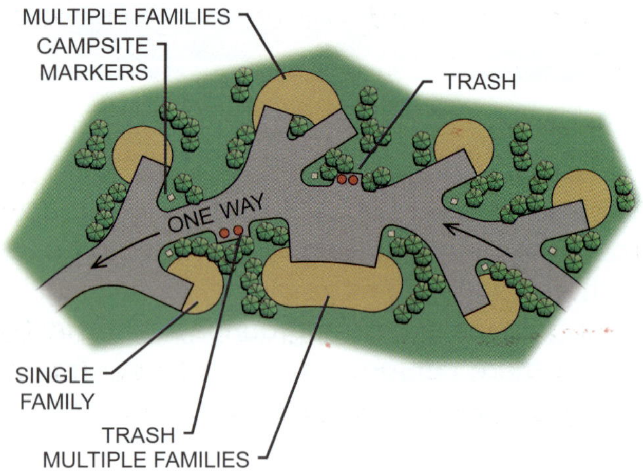

FIG. 14.11 – MULTIPLE FAMILY SITES

Campsite Surfacing: Campsites should be well drained, free of large rocks, and have a surface that does not become muddy but will accept tent stakes.

Parking Spur: Campers prefer their parking spur to be well drained and surfaced sufficiently to prevent erosion and muddy conditions.

Site Spacing: Sixty feet ± (18± m) on center – more space is generally desired by campers, but construction costs become too high the further apart the sites are placed.

One-way camp road and camp spurs – Paris Mountain State Park, South Carolina

Buffer Space: One hundred to 150± LF (30 to 45 m) should be left between campsites and any site amenities such as water bodies, viewpoints, etc. This is public use space for all campers.

Extra Parking: Parking space for two or three cars should be provided at each comfort station and washhouse, and 10 percent or more of spaces for each campsite for each amphitheater and parking for any other special use facilities.

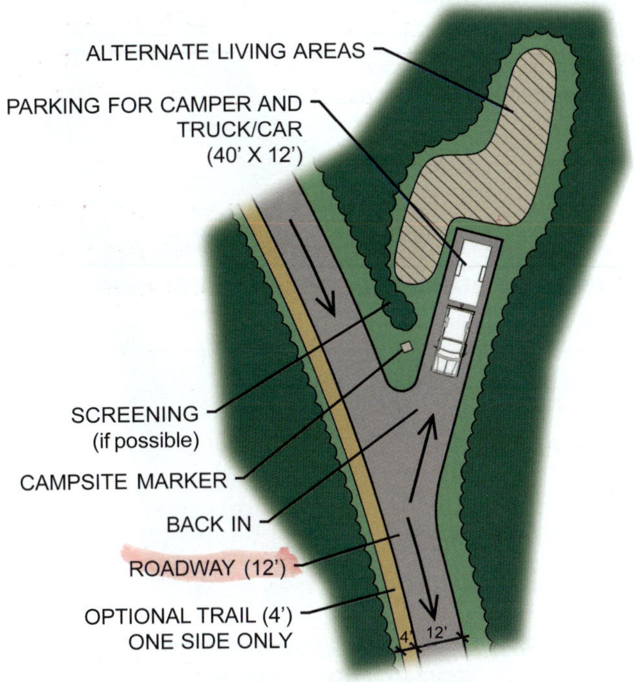

FIG. 14.12 – TYPICAL CAMPSITE/PARKING SPUR

Typical campsite showing 24'-wide parking (2 vehicles), camp stove, tent pad, picnic table, water and electrical outlets.

PARKING SPUR

- Sites should be 60± (18 m) feet on center with a level "living" area adjacent to the parking spur; two percent maximum grade desirable over the last 25 feet (7.5 m). Total length of spur should be 40 feet (minimum space for two vehicles); width, 12 feet (3.6 m).

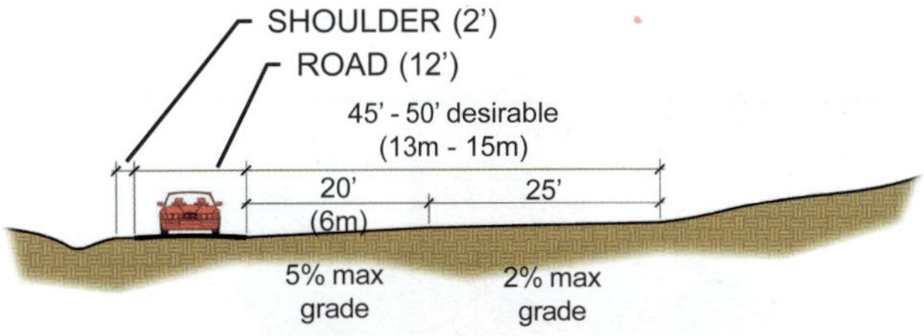

FIG. 14.13 – SECTION CAMPSITE PARKING SPUR

- Seventy percent of the spaces should be developed to accommodate one car truck and camp trailer.

THE SITE

Privacy: Generally, campers prefer a sense of privacy.

Units Per Acre: Six to ten units spaced about 60 feet ± (18 m) on site centers are optimum. The number of units per acre varies according to results desired, the topography, existing vegetation, and general land character. Ten to fourteen units spaced 50 feet (15 m) on site centers are maximum development, and still keep any sense of camping.

Living Space: The actual camping area (living space) should be 400 SF to 600 SF (37 SM to 56 SM) to accommodate a 6-foot (1.8 m) picnic table, stove, and tent space.

Site Identification: Campsites should be numbered so the numbers can be seen from cars and patrolling security personnel.

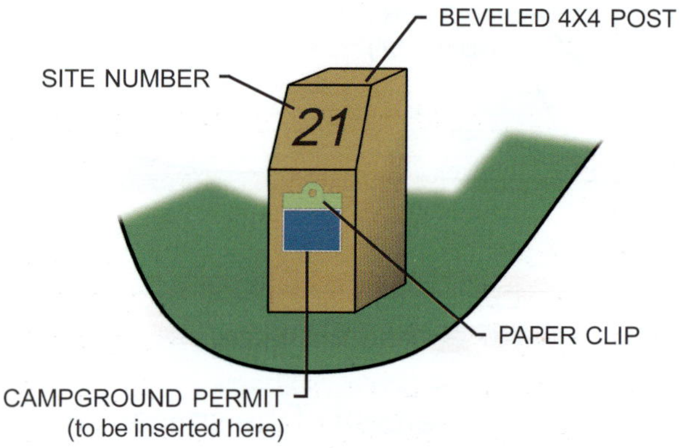

FIG. 14.14 – CAMPSITE IDENTIFICATION

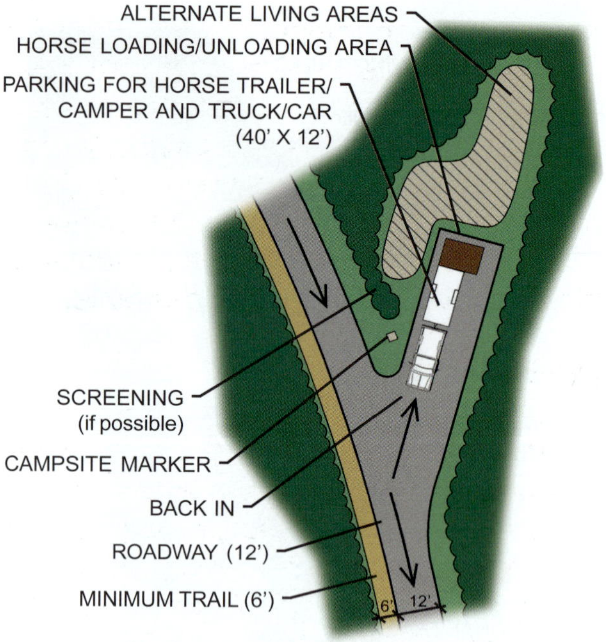

FIG. 14.16 – CAMPSITE MODIFIED FOR EQUESTRIAN USE

EQUESTRIAN CAMPING

The basic type of equestrian camping unit, as in all other camping, consists of a cleared and leveled area for a table, fireplace, tent, camping trailer, and horse trailer.

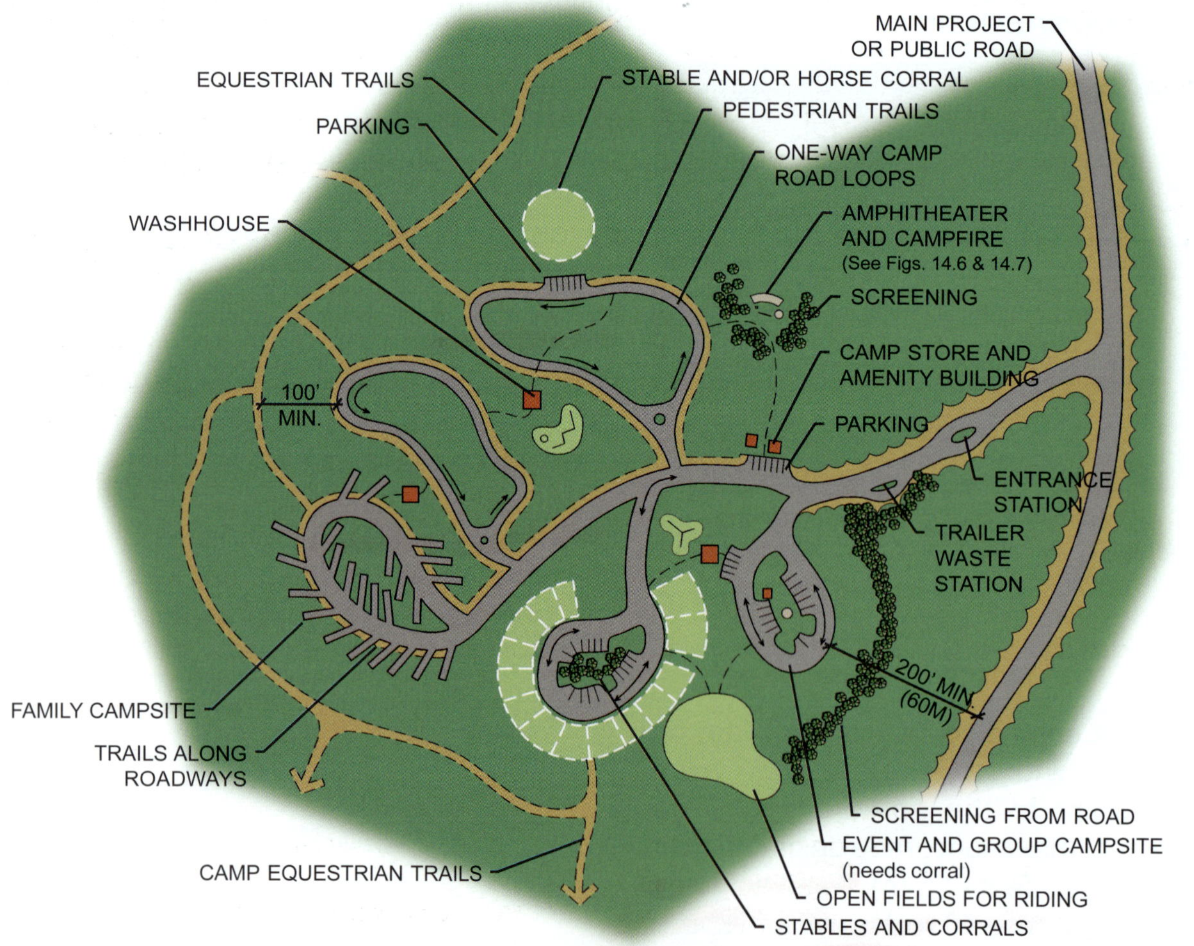

FIG. 14.15 – A TYPICAL FAMILY CAMPGROUND LAYOUT MODIFIED FOR EQUESTRIAN USE

A typical family campground modified for equestrian use has a number of distinctive differences. There is a need for, as a minimum, larger parking spurs, corrals, fenced areas for holding horses overnight, feed storage, water for the horses, manure removal, and equestrian trails access. In addition, stables and event facilities are desirable.

PARKING SPUR

- Sites should be 60 feet (18 m) minimum on center with a level "living" area adjacent to the parking spur; if possible, use two percent maximum grade over the last 25 feet (7.5 m). Total length of spur should be 60 feet (18 m) (space for two vehicles), end to end; width, 16 feet (4.8 m) for space to hold horses at the site and for loading and unloading horses. Access to the camp's roadside equestrian trail(s) is necessary.

- Seventy percent of the spaces should be developed to accommodate one car/ truck and one equestrian trailer.

THE SITE

Privacy: Generally, campers prefer a sense of privacy.

Units Per Acre: Six to 10 units spaced about the same as family camping or slightly further apart (10 feet ± (3m) or greater). As in family camping, the number of units (i.e., degree of privacy) varies according to results desired, topography, vegetation, and general land character. Ten to 14 units spaced 50 (15 m) feet on site centers are the maximum development, and still keep any sense of camping. The maximum density is not recommended.

Living Space: The actual camping area (living space) should be the same as standard family camping - 400 SF to 600 SF (37 SM to 55 SM) to accommodate a 6-foot picnic table, stove, and tent space. It is desirable, but not necessary, to have a space to tie up your horse(s) at the campsite during the day.

Site Identification: Campsites should be numbered as per family camping sites.

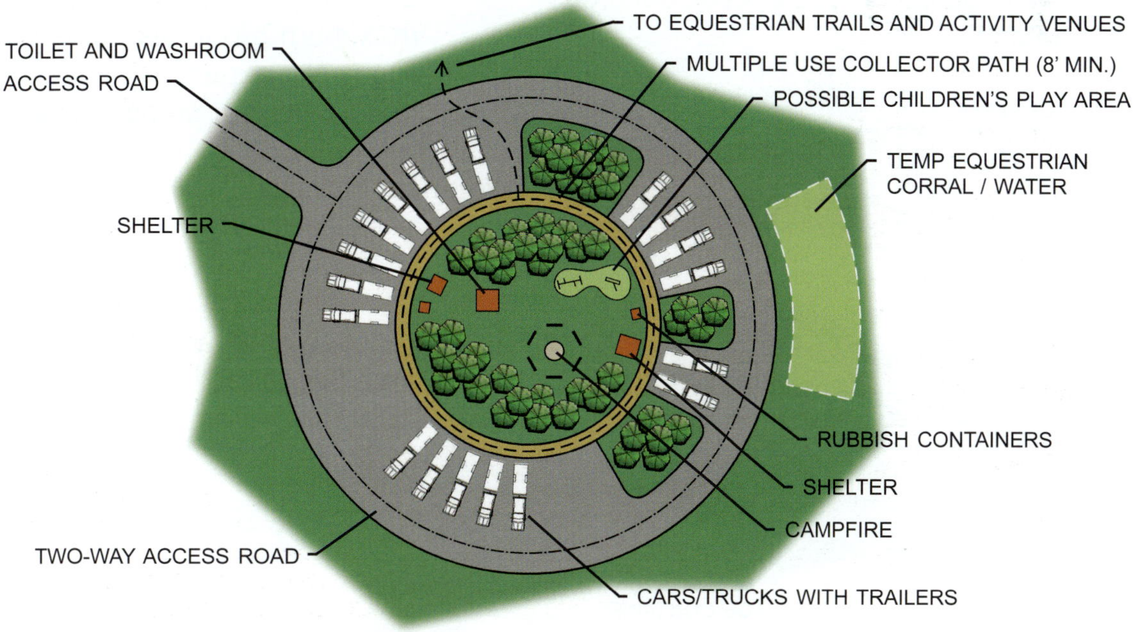

FIG. 14.17 – EQUESTRIAN EVENT AND GROUP CAMPING

EQUESTRIAN OVERNIGHT AREA

Horses need a place to stay when not being ridden. It is desirable for most that it be separate from the campsite. This place must have accessible drinking water, a place to individually store feed, ease of mucking, a space for saddling, and, of course, trail access.

Water: It is absolutely critical that 24-hour-per-day water be readily available for all equestrian assembly and stabling areas. The water at the stalls, corrals, and picket lines is preferable, but not absolutely necessary.

Feed: Access is needed to all overnight spaces for bringing feed to the horses.

Cleaning/Mucking/Bedding:

- Access is very desirable for getting bedding material to the overnight corral/stables area.

- A place to put horse droppings and used bedding is necessary to prevent unacceptable buildup of used odiferous material.

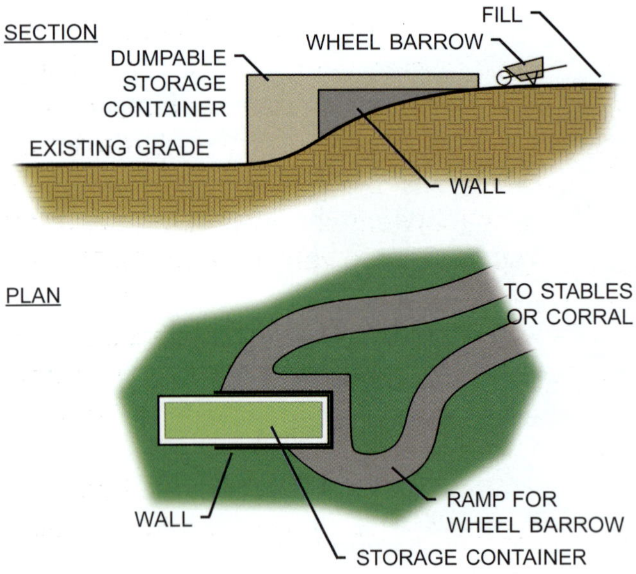

FIG. 14.18 – MANURE DISPOSAL

Saddling:

- Individual and group saddling space is desirable; however, individuals can easily use the group space.

- A lockable space for tack storage at the corral/stables is desirable.

RIDES STARTING AREA

Saddling:

- An area relatively flat and near the corral/stables area is desirable for the saddling area.

- Drinking water for horses is necessary.

- Immediate trail access is necessary.

- A rain shelter for people is desirable.

Assembly:

- Space for "X" number of horses x 20 percent. Depends on expected maximum group size plus some extra room for expansion and for special once-a-year or so special events.

Water for Horses:

- Water.

- Please note: an after-ride wash down area is desirable.

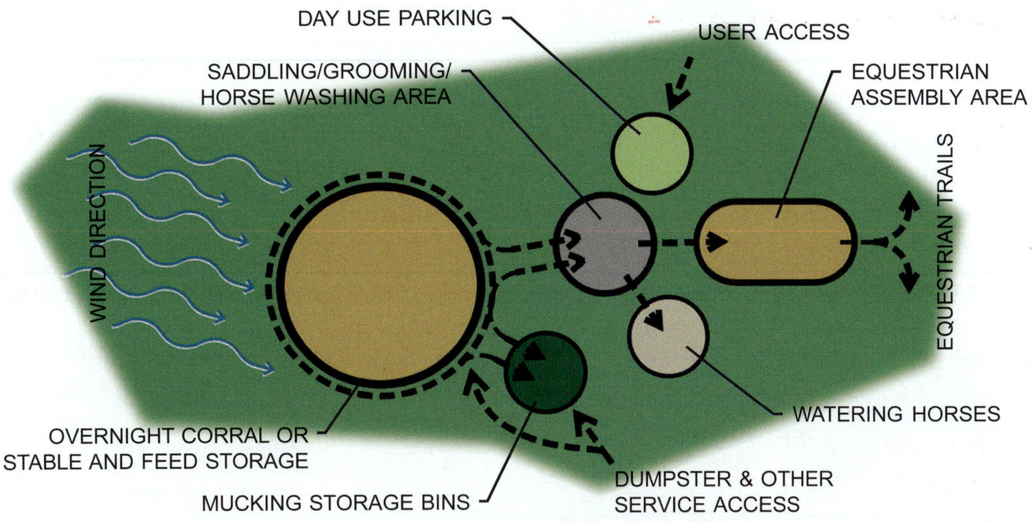

FIG. 14.19 – EQUESTRIAN ASSEMBLY/RIDE STARTING AREA

EVENTS AREA

A space near the equestrian assembly area is desirable for:

- giving instructions.
- awarding prizes.
- saddling horses.

GROUP/OVERNIGHT PICKETS

Temporary or permanent fencing is needed for all horse holding areas. This can be:

- a picket line.
- corrals (either permanent or temporary).
- stables.

OHV CAMPING SITE

See Chapter 10, Off-Highway Vehicle Facilities, for additional OHV details.

The basic type of OHV camping unit consists of a cleared and leveled area for a table, fireplace, tent, camping trailer, OHV trailer, and OHV equipment parking and an OHV work area.

PARKING SPUR

- Sites should be 60 feet (18 m) minimum on center with a level "living" area adjacent to the parking spur; if possible, use two percent maximum grade over the last 25 feet (7.5 m). Total length of spur should be 50 feet (15 m) (space for two vehicles); width, 16 feet.

- Seventy percent of the spaces should be developed to accommodate a single car/truck and trailer (camp or OHV).

- Thirty percent of spaces should be developed as typical family camping sites.

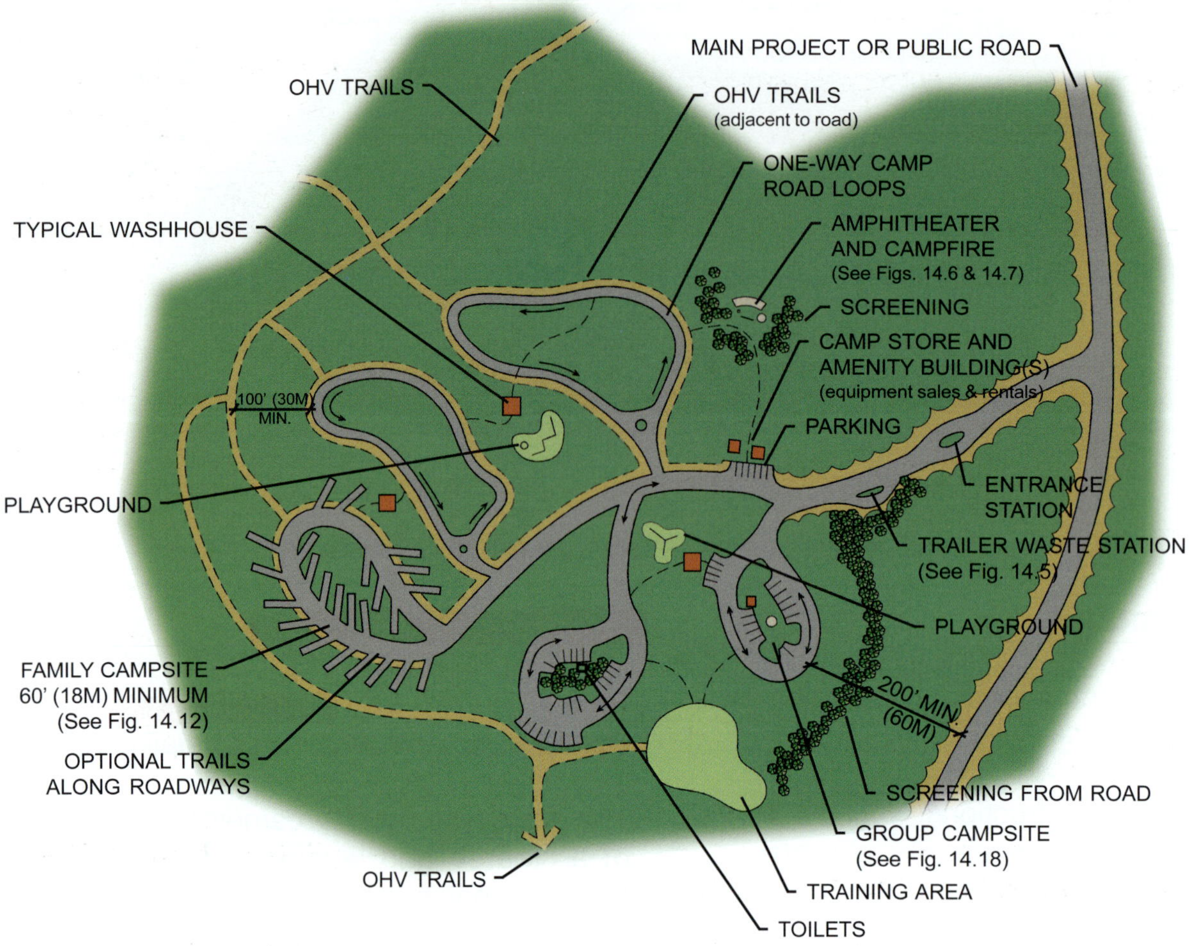

FIG. 14.20 – A TYPICAL FAMILY CAMPGROUND LAYOUT MODIFIED FOR AN OHV PARK

THE SITE

Privacy: Generally, OHV campers, like almost all campground users, prefer a sense of privacy.

Units Per Acre: Six to 10 units spaced about 60 to 70 feet (18 m to 21 m) on site centers are optimum. The number of units varies according to results desired, privacy or togetherness, topography, vegetation, and general land character. Ten to 14 units spaced 50 feet (15 m) on site centers are the maximum density development can be, and still keep any sense of "camping." The maximum density is not recommended.

Living Space: The actual camping area (living space) is the same as in all types of camping.

Site Identification: Campsites should be numbered so the numbers can be seen from the cars and camp patrol vehicles as per family campgrounds. (See Fig. 14.14.)

GROUP CAMPING

An area for groups, usually with self-contained camper units.

Requirements:

- Large grassed or surfaced level site a minimum of approximately 180 feet (55 m) in diameter and roughly circular in shape, with a minimum of one washhouse per 100 camper units.

- Shade – trees and/or shelters.

- Central campfire circle.

- Separated from family campers.

- Rubbish receptacles at a minimum of 200 feet (60 m) on center; alternatively, but not as desirable, dumpsters at the toilet building(s).

- Recreation facilities – horseshoe pits, open play area for children, sand volleyball and, possibly, softball, etc.

- Direct connection to trails and activity venues.

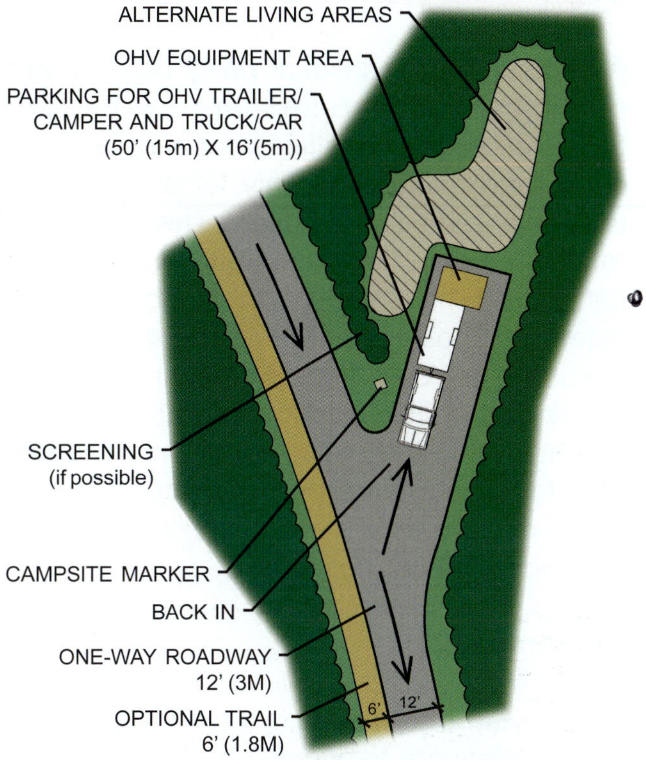

FIG. 14.21 – CAMPSITE MODIFIED FOR OHV USE

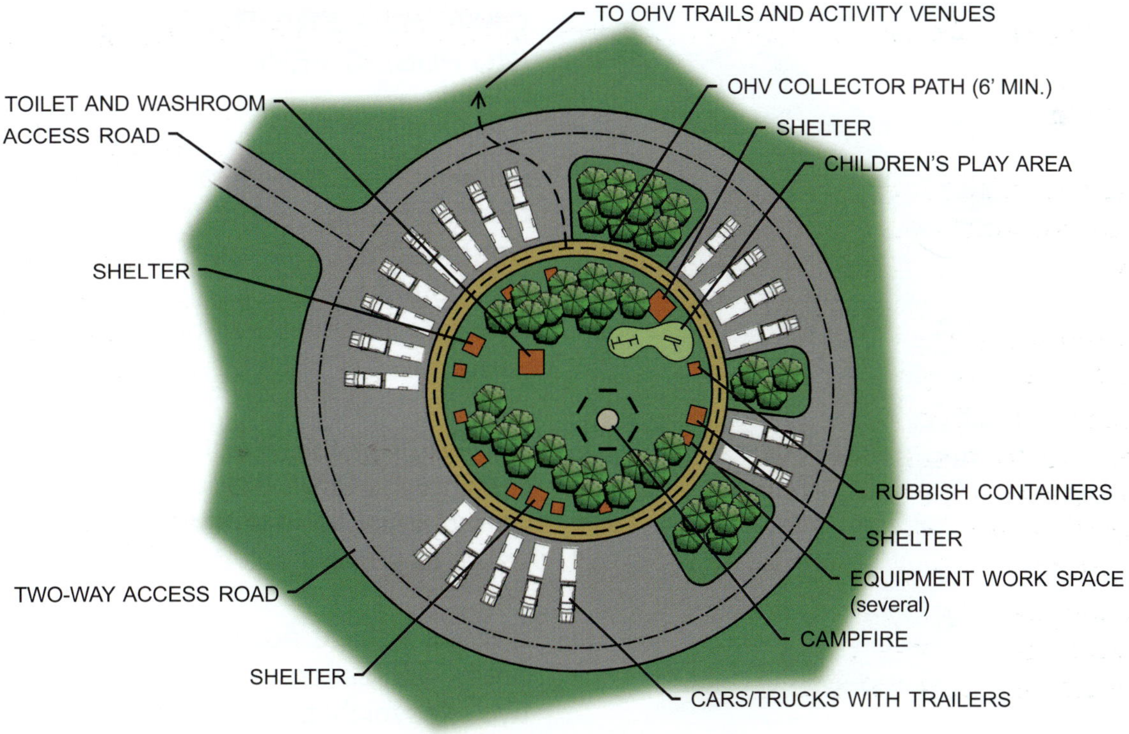

FIG. 14.22 – OHV GROUP CAMPING

CAMPING – BOAT-IN UNIT (ACCESS FROM WATER ONLY)

A campsite for individual party use on land adjoining rivers, reservoirs, lakes, and protected ocean coastlines not accessible by car. Cleared shoreline only for boat access, tent site, table and stove. The areas are relatively small, accommodate but very few camp units, have water-tight pits or chemical toilets, and no developed water (except where a source is readily available and may be developed at little cost); some areas should be retained in a primitive condition. A service road for maintenance purposes, such as toilet pump-out, firewood supply, etc., to the area is desirable, but not necessary.

Requirements:

- **Minimum area** is a level space adequate to accommodate a tent and, possibly, a table and camp fireplace. Ample buffer space between units should be provided.

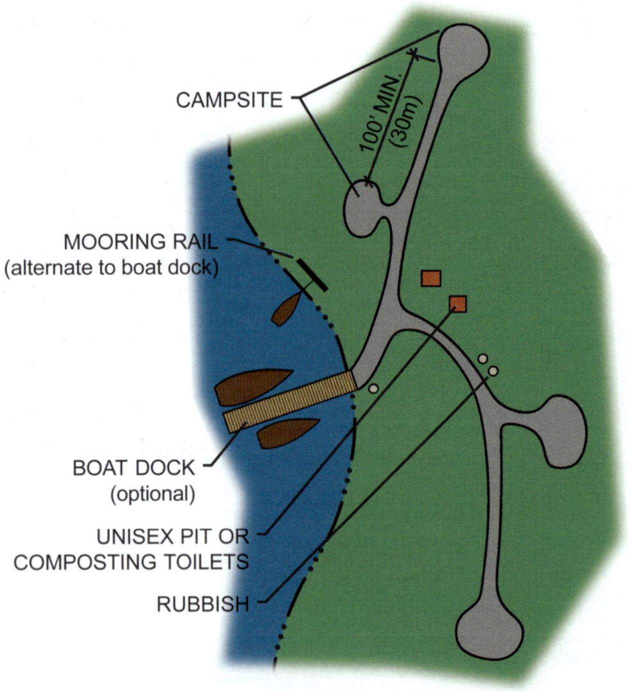

FIG. 14.23 – BOAT-IN CAMPING

- **Number of people** – 8 – maximum; 3.0 – average.
- **Units per acre** (ha) – variable to fit site with two to four per acre (four to eight per ha) being average.
- **Distance between units** – 100 feet (30 m) – optimum; this is generally greater than the 60 feet (18 m) in a typical campground.
- **Toilet facilities** – one pit composting chemical unisex toilet to four camp units.
- **Rubbish receptacles** should be placed at each boat area; one per four campsites minimum unless a carryout policy is enforced.
- **Boat tie-up** – adequate space should be provided – either a boat dock or mooring rail.

CAMPING – PRIMITIVE (NO PUBLIC VEHICULAR ACCESS)

A campsite similar to a boat unit, the difference being that one walks to the area from a central parking space rather than boating to it. At some locations, these campsites may be adjacent to riding and hiking trails and could be utilized by the trail users.

Frequently, no facilities of any kind are provided under these conditions. Tight control must be maintained on the number of users to prevent site deterioration.

Service vehicle access is desirable to camp areas with several sites. An area with one or two sites might be serviced by horseback, trail bike or ATV.

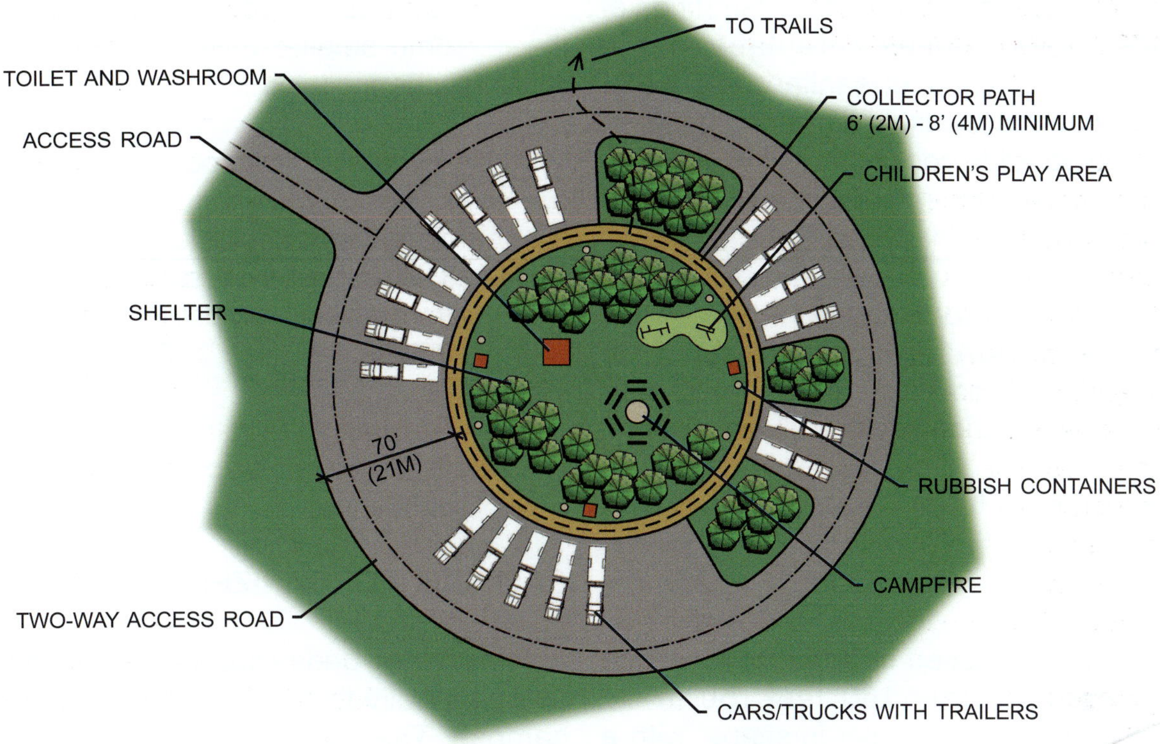

FIG. 14.24 – CARAVAN CAMPING

ORGANIZED ADULT GROUP CAMPING

An area for groups of self-contained camper units may be desirable in larger destination facilities. This is not a commonly provided facility. See Equestrian and OHV Camping for a more commonly needed group camping facility. Make sure there is a demonstrated demand before including space for this activity in the development plans.

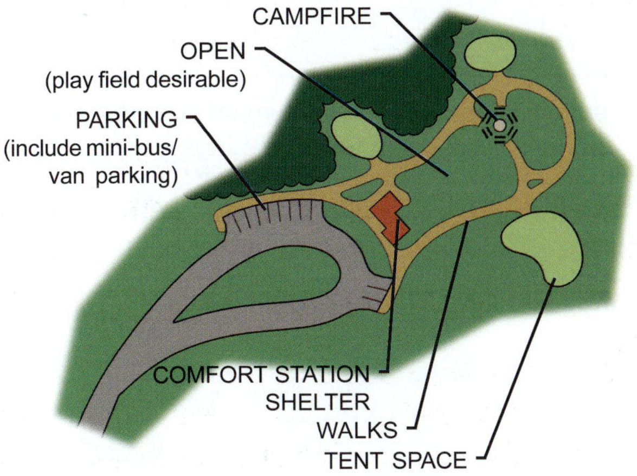

FIG. 14.25 – GROUP TENT CAMPING

GROUP CAMPING

Groups, including equestrian and OHV use, vary in size from four or five units to one hundred or more, with most groups being less than fifteen units. They are frequently noisy and like and need privacy. Because of this, group camps should be separated from other public-use facilities and be able to accommodate various numbers of people. It may be desirable to develop several smaller units within an area, which could accommodate several small organized groups separately or, by combining units, a large group could utilize the entire area. The group campsites should be for ten to eighty persons and include space for tent sites, camp rigs of various types, tables, fireplace rings, campfire circle, parking, sanitary and water facilities, internal roads, trail system, barriers, signs, and possible cooking/meeting shelters. These units require a minimum of five acres (two hectares).

Suggested Sanitary Requirements* - Most states have standards, which must be followed. The following are patterned after those of the Commonwealth of Pennsylvania.

Requirements:

- Parking – one area for 15 to 20 cars.
- Large grassed or surfaced level site approximately 160 feet (50 m) in diameter and circular in shape, with a minimum of one washhouse per 200 camper units.
- Central showers and sanitary facilities.
- Central campfire circle and possibly some smaller units for more intimate gatherings.
- Separated from other campers.
- Rubbish receptacle(s) at a minimum of 200 feet (60 m) on center or, alternatively, dumpsters at the comfort stations.
- Recreation facilities – i.e., horseshoe pits, area for badminton, volleyball, softball, etc.

CAMPING – ORGANIZED GROUP

A primitive or undeveloped-looking area set up specifically to handle formal organization camps. They are frequently concession-operated and sometimes even user or concession built. Operation by the primary user organization is common. They usually consist of sleeping space (cabins, tent platforms or even tent areas), washhouses, lodge/activity space(s), dining hall, staff residences, first aid, office, and parking.

No. of Persons	No. of Toilet Seats Male/Female		No. of Lavatories Male/Female		No. of Urinals** Male	No. of Showers Male/Female	
1-20	1	2	1	1	1	1	1
Each Additional 20 persons	+1	+1	+1	+1	+1	+1	+1

*Organized camps that do not provide overnight lodging and serve a maximum of one meal per day are not usually subject to this minimum number of sanitary facilities, but should provide toilet and lavatory facilities.

**Urinals for males may be provided in lieu of toilet seats, but for not more than one-third of the required number of toilet seats.

FIG. 14.26 – SANITARY FIXTURE REQUIREMENTS FOR GROUP CAMPING

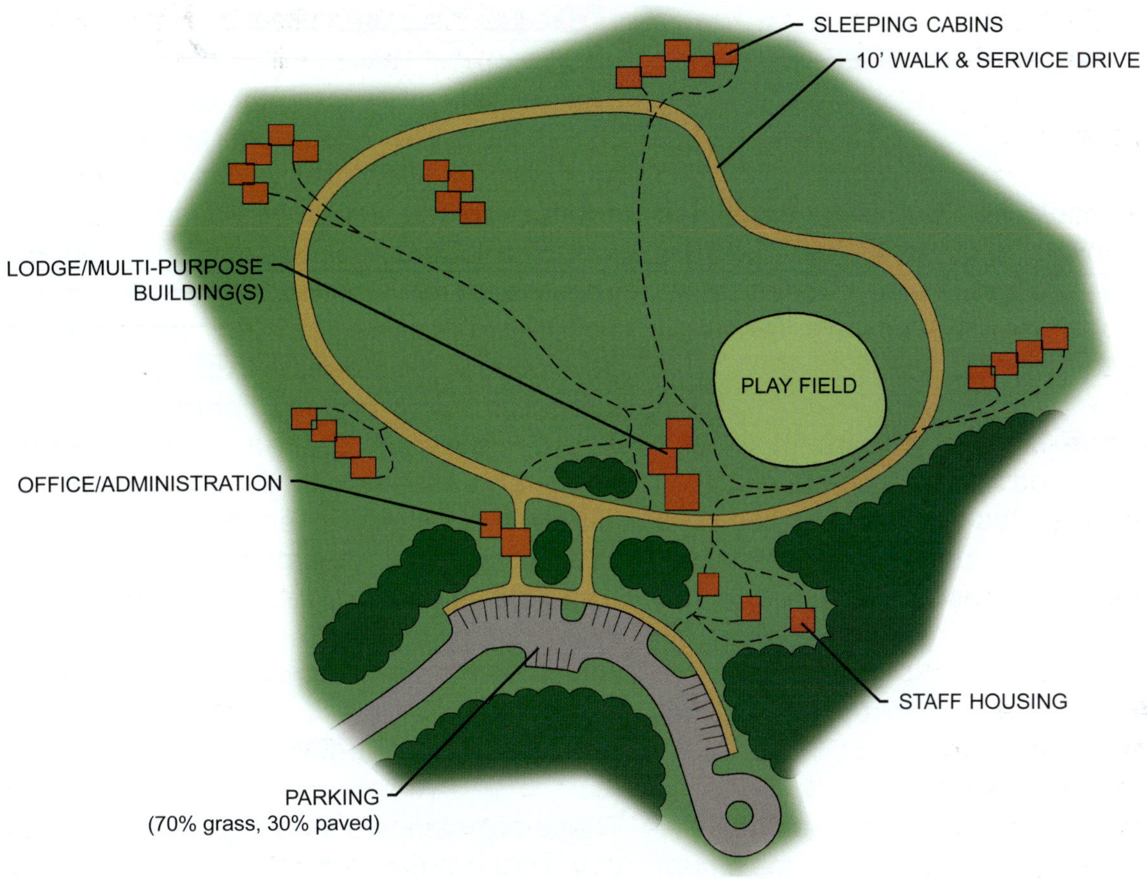

FIG. 14.27 – ORGANIZED GROUP CAMP

Requirements:

• Maximum distance from sleeping and use areas to sanitary facilities – 300 feet (90 m); desirable – 200 feet (60 m) or less.

• Maximum distance to showers – 1000 feet (300 m); desirable – 600 feet (180 m) or less.

• Maximum distance to dining hall – 1000 feet (300 m).

• Dining hall or separate weather screened area(s) is needed for inclement weather activity space(s) for all of the users. They can, and probably should, be divided into more than one space.

• Minimum site size – 5 acres (2 ha); usually much larger.

• Paved parking space for 10 percent of the number of beds, and grass overflow parking for an additional 20 percent.

TRAILER AREAS – SPECIAL TRAILER FACILITIES

Requirements:

- Ten units/acre (25 units/ha) calculated as follows: width – 40 feet (12 m) x length – 70 feet (21 m) + 25 feet (8 m) for road = 4000 square feet/unit (360 sq. m/unit).

- Design factors: 8 percent or less slopes, good access, adequate utilities – picnic tables and stoves (campfire space) not required, but desirable. Comfort stations not required to the extent needed in camping areas.

- Complete utility hookups required at each site.

- Central showers and washhouse – 600 feet (180 m) desirable maximum distance from trailer units.

- Private capital normally used for construction and operations.

- A combination recreation room, office, and store is usually provided.

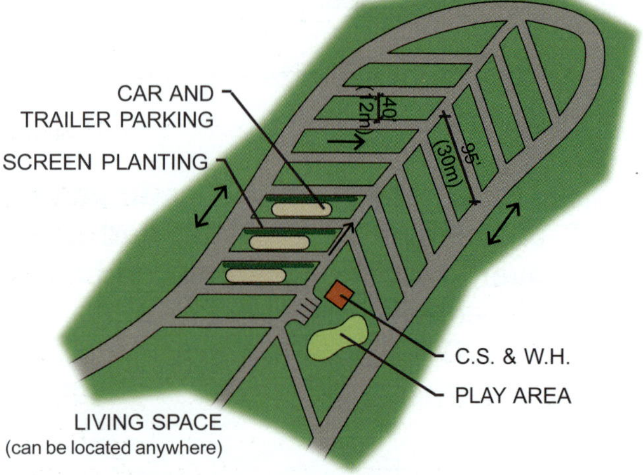

FIG. 14.28 – TRAILER AREAS (usually in commercial areas only)

LODGES, CABINS, TENT PLATFORMS

The larger, more heavily used resource-oriented facility developments need to consider all types of overnight accommodations in addition to the usual "park"-type facilities, including lodges, cabins, and tent platforms. These basically manmade types of overnight accommodations should normally be developed and operated with private funds with adequate using agency controls to ensure quality service at reasonable prices. Long-term leases (30 years or more) are usually necessary to encourage adequate capital for this type of development. A complete analysis of potential user desires must be done before undertaking these capital and labor intensive facilities.

TRANSIENT CAMPING

These are campers who only stay overnight, one night in a campground, while in route to a destination area. Standards for this type of overnight user are typical of family camping with the following exceptions.

1. The site density may be very high, with camp units located as close as 40 feet (12 m) on center and camp roads 150 feet (45 m) on center.

2. They should be located only when in proximity to a major transportation route or destination site and have easy access to other available uses and to the main highway.

3. Recreation facilities should be limited to children's play areas (use native material where possible).

4. Interpretive facilities and programs would be minimized.

Chapter 15

PLAY AREAS AND PLAY FIELDS

Most large-scale parks, recreation, and leisure facilities are intended for use by a variety of age groups. These groups have different needs and interests in addition to the major recreational activities of picnicking, swimming, etc. This is especially true for younger people, although older people's needs must also be considered. Levels of ability and capability within the various age groups, as well as the law, make it imperative that at least some of any facilities provided must be accessible.

PLAY AREAS

Play areas should be developed for various age levels and designed to meet the ability and the interest of the intended users. They should be as safe as possible for the ages of the users, while still being environmentally friendly. Recommended age groups are pre-school (ages 3 to 5), elementary (ages 6 to 10), and older children and young adults. Where possible, play areas for the different age groups should be separated since the interests and abilities of the three age groups are NOT compatible.

PRE-SCHOOL AGE

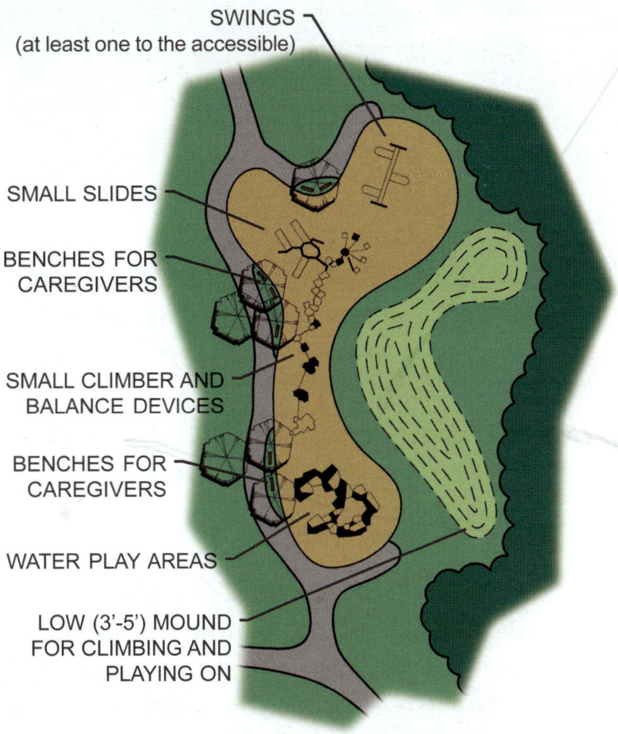

FIG. 15.1 – PRE-SCHOOL CHILDREN'S PLAY AREA

1. Locate out of general traffic patterns but still close to areas of adult activity and, if possible, adjacent to grass fields.

2. Separation from all vehicular circulation areas, either by distance – 200 feet (60 m) or more – of usually by a 42-inch (1 m) high chain link fence.

3. Accessible for the very young.

4. Design to accommodate little people with minimum supervision.

5. Few moving parts.

6. Locate in partial sun in northern climates, while shade is necessary in southern areas.

Playground with swings, water play area, and caregiver benches for 3- to 5-year-old children – Vienna, Austria

7. Provide benches for supervising caregiver.

8. Should have sand for playing and digging, climbing, slides and, possibly, small swing(s), and water play area. The area should blend into the surroundings and utilize materials and designs not commonly found in the neighborhood parks.

9. Keep separate, if possible, from older children's play areas.

ELEMENTARY SCHOOL AGE

1. Locate within sight of adult activity areas, but somewhat away from picnic sites due to noise. Possibly locate in conjunction with a playfield.

Playground adjacent to open playfield – French Creek State Park, Pennsylvania

2. Design to accommodate active, inquisitive children who, although seeking a challenge, also need to succeed. Make it clearly more challenging and interesting to older children so they will not be tempted to use the pre-school area. Please note that the more capable and adventurous 3- to 5-year-olds will utilize the older children's play areas.

3. Moving parts are acceptable and of major interest to this age group.

4. Design for safety of user.

5. Limited adjacent seating needed for caregivers.

6. Accessible facilities are required by law.

7. Some shade desirable, especially in southern states.

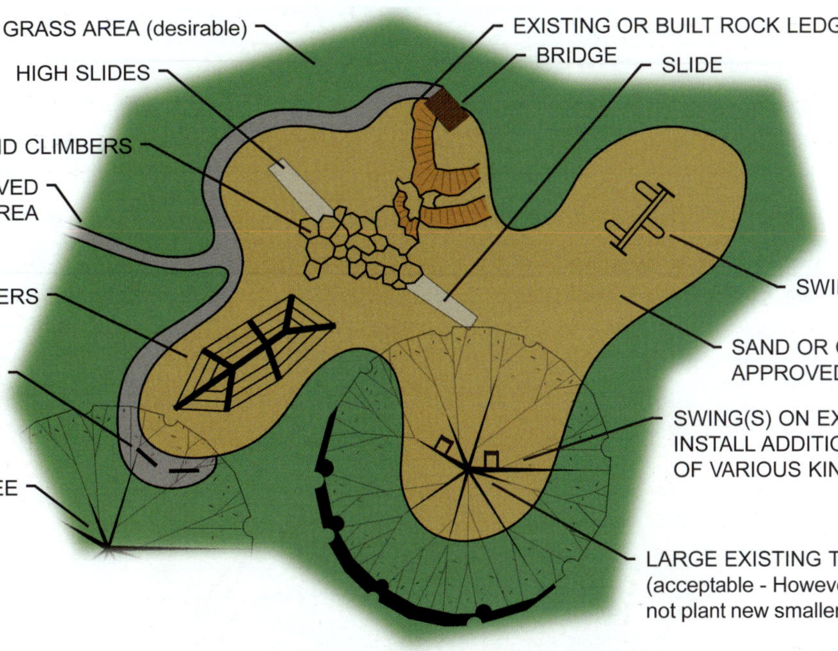

FIG. 15.2 – ELEMENTARY SCHOOL-AGE PLAYGROUND

OLDER CHILDREN AND YOUNG ADULTS

1. Locate only in parks where there is a desire to have this age group present. Especially desirable in areas of urban concentration in conjunction with beaches and swimming facilities.

2. Separate but visible from family activity areas.

3. Facilities to consider might include weightlifting, parallel bars, high bar, rings, adult-size swings, volleyball, and skateboard ramps.

4. Viewing – spectator area(s). This can be a significant feature because young people like to be seen and to see others.

5. Facilities must be accessible.

PLAYFIELDS

A large, open, free-form space 200 feet x 200 feet (60 m x 60 m) – minimum; 300± feet width x 600± feet length (90 m x 180 m) – desirable; gently sloping for drainage – two percent slopes – desirable; five percent – maximum. Locate, where possible, in existing open fields or in poor timber stands where trees can easily be removed without environmental damage. However, if necessary, good trees must be removed. Care should be taken in locating these open space facilities to minimize environmental damage from vegetative removal and/or grade modifications.

FIG. 15.3 – PLAYFIELD/PICNICKING

Playfields would normally be located in conjunction with picnic areas, beach areas and all group-use areas. The space should be designed to allow for softball/baseball, football (pickup-type), Frisbee throwing, and volleyball (probably sand surface). In addition, special use spaces for regionally important activities, such as soccer, should be considered. Volleyball areas are frequently located on beaches. When they are part of a beach project, see Chapter 17, Swimming Areas.

OLDER PEOPLES' SPACES

Provide space for visiting, sitting and viewing park activities, board games, and probably tennis and golf if they are offered for younger ages. These facilities should be in close relationship to other activity areas or made integral to the younger peoples' facilities so that the users will be part of the whole recreating scene. Some separation might be useful so that they can enjoy their activities at their own pace.

Older people frequently are benefited by accessibility standards. Particular care should be utilized throughout any older people areas to make them accessible.

One or more accessible picnic pavilions with tables should be considered for special equipping for older users, such as with board games, etc.

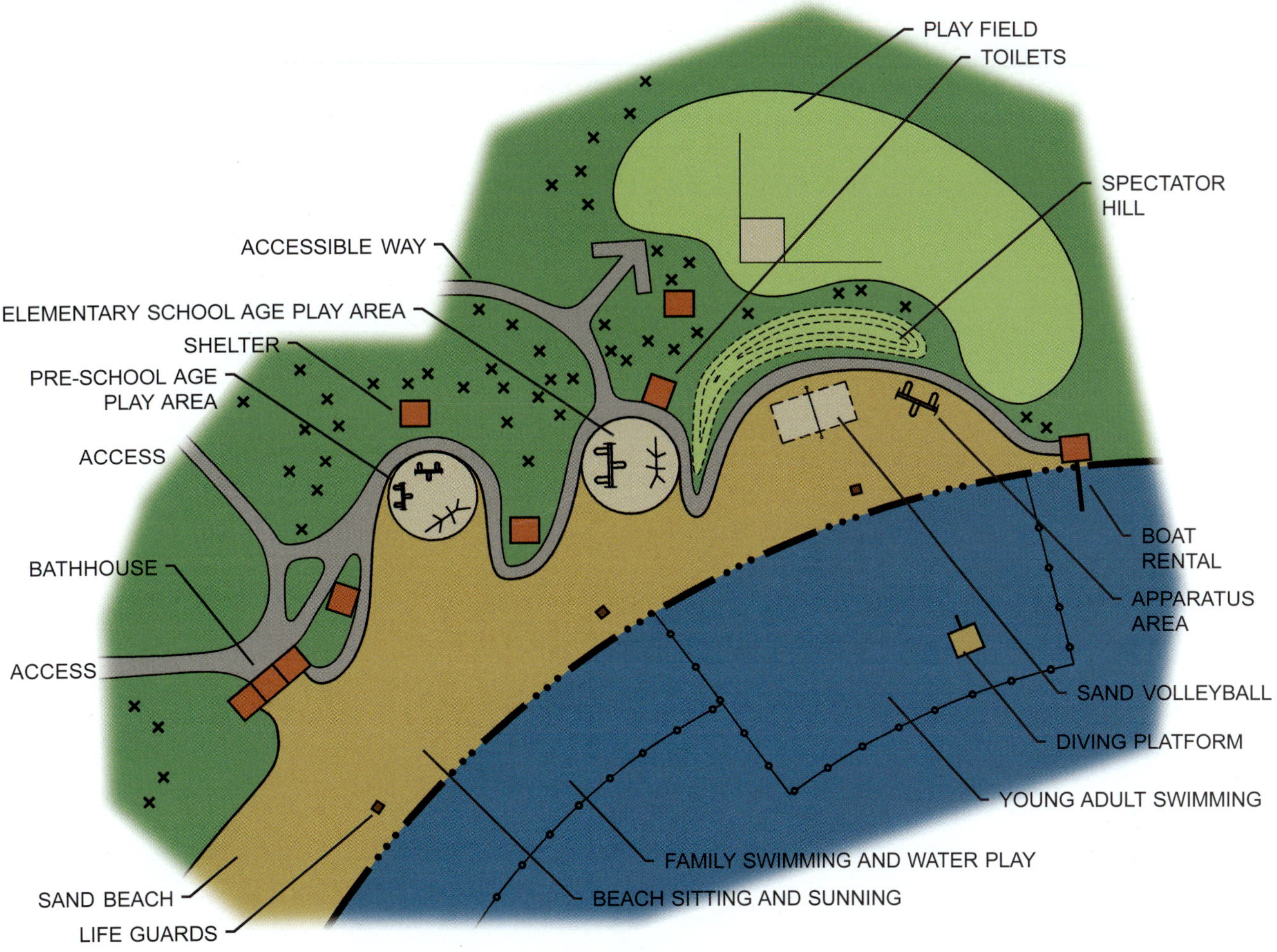

FIG. 15.4 – PLAY AREAS IN CONJUNCTION WITH SWIMMING

Chapter 16

PICNICKING

This type of use appeals to all ages, particularly to urbanites, and normally originates within one to one and one-half hour's drive of the site. The day-use party participates in an average of 2 to 2.5 activities. About 10 to 20 percent of visitors, **excluding** sightseers/transients, participate in only **one** activity. Sixty-five to 70 percent of picnic use occurs on weekends during the primary use season – normally summer, except in the mild winter areas of the southern states. For more locally oriented urban facilities, the use is likely to be slightly more evenly distributed over the week.

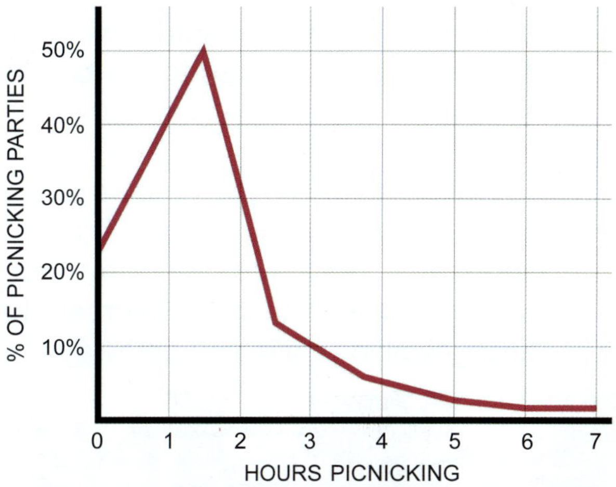

FIG. 16.2 – PERCENTAGE OF PARTIES WHO PICNIC FOR VARIOUS TIME PERIODS

ACTIVITIES

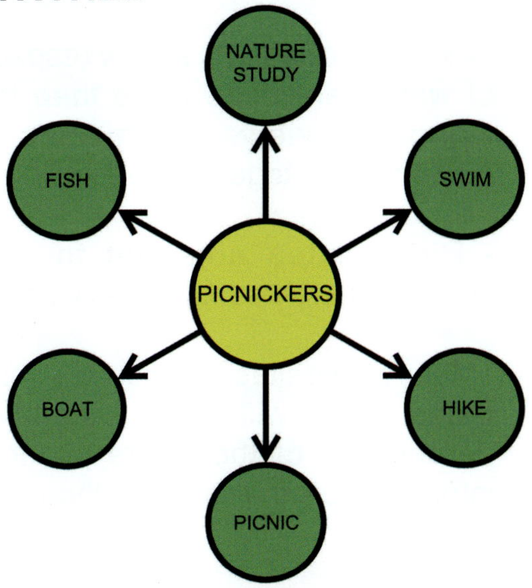

FIG. 16.1 – PICNICKERS DO VARIOUS ACTIVITIES

ATTITUDES

Picnickers -

- prefer tables located where there is some shade and, to some extent, a sense of privacy. Picnic shelters are most desirable, followed by open areas with scattered trees.

- have a definite preference for tables near their car or access point. Use drops off greatly over 60 feet (18 m) beyond an access point (about the length of many backyards) and, given the opportunity, many picnickers will drive right up to the picnic table.

• will spread their lunches on the grass rather than walk 400 feet (120 m) to a table.

• will choose to be as close to a water body as they are allowed or to which they can physically get.

GENERAL

• The typical visitor to a leisure facility gets as close to his final destination as possible by vehicle and then goes to his major objective (beach, picnic table, stables, etc.), and then to the comfort station.

• Most park visitors prefer to be able to have an opportunity to swim. One in two wants playfields and play areas nearby. One in three is interested in hiking/walking trails and pathways.

Picnic site adjacent to play areas and parking – Paris Mountain State Park, South Carolina

• Most picnickers have a variety of equipment that may include an ice chest, supplies, cooking stove or grill, chairs, blankets, radios, etc., depending on what they expect to have provided at the site. This means that the closer to the picnic table, the better.

Picnickers frequently bring a lot of gear (Note accessible picnic table and accessible way)

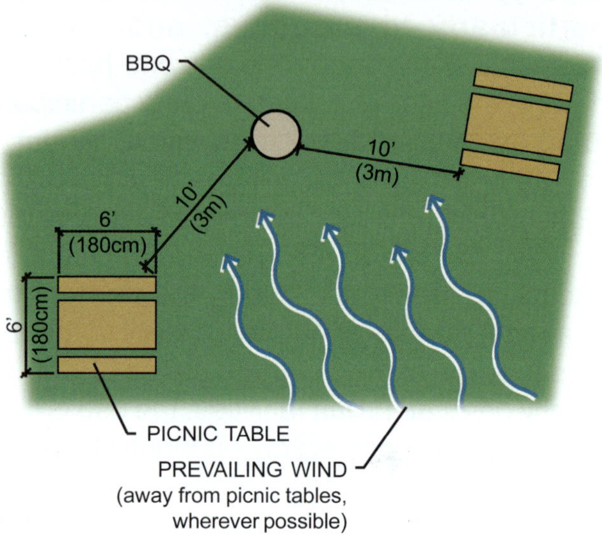

FIG. 16.3 – TYPICAL 6-PERSON PICNIC SITE

• Picnic facilities with a view (especially of water) are used more than those without a view. Picnicking and swimming go together.

• Picnic sites adjacent to beach swimming are usually heavily used.

• Many picnic sites with partially shaded grass areas will have a significant percentage of the users picnicking informally on the grass without using the tables.

• Accessibility to ten percent or more of the sites is necessary from the accessible way. Twenty percent of sites with accessibility would be better.

Urban lawn picnicking – Pittsburgh, Pennsylvania

• Desirable slope – 2 to 15 percent, with slopes over 5 percent requiring terracing. Maximum slope – 20 percent - requires terracing. Picnic table needs to be approximately level.

PICNIC SHELTERS

Groups prefer shelters. When provided, these popular facilities should be built to minimize operating and maintenance costs. They should be considered for all heavy-use areas. Size and number of shelters depend on the normal weather conditions and local interest. In all cases, the shelters must be designed to be compatible with the existing or proposed facility architecture and the surrounding environment. Most leisure facility agencies reserve pavilion space for a fee.

Vehicular access to shelters is required to drop off supplies and equipment, and for service. As a minimum, work counters, picnic tables, trash cans, and barbecue units are needed.

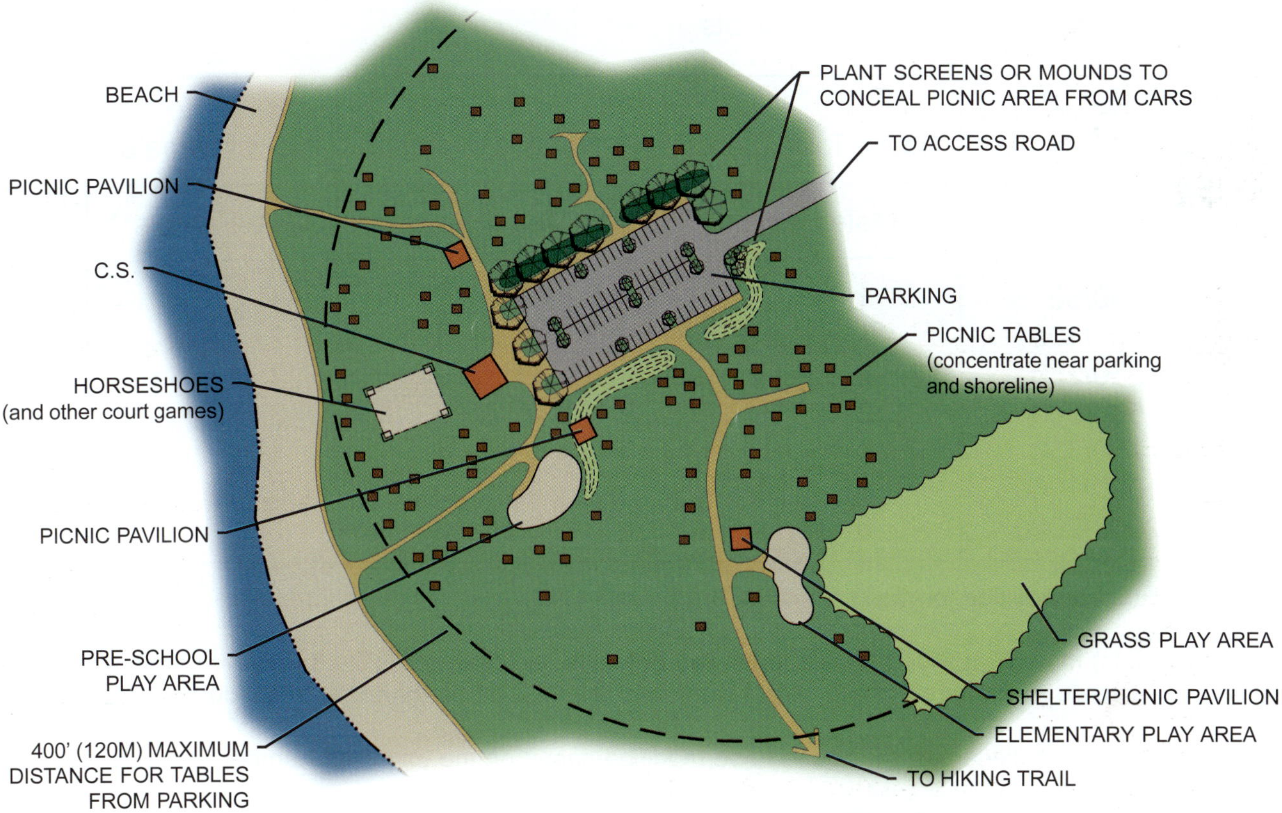

FIG. 16.4 – CONCEPTUAL LAYOUT – PICNIC AREA

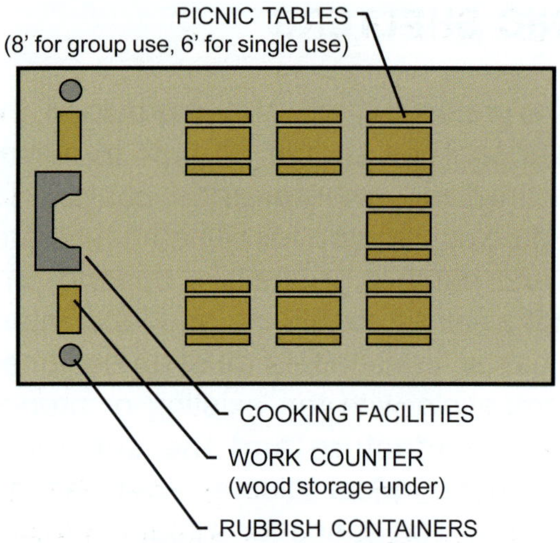

FIG. 16.5 – PICNIC/GROUP PICNIC SHELTER

SANITARY FACILITIES

- Distance from restroom to picnic tables – 300 feet (90 m) – optimum; 400 feet (120 m) – maximum.

- Sanitary facilities for picnic areas should generally be located in relation to the use area, not the parking lots.

RUBBISH DISPOSAL

Desirable: One rubbish can per four units located within 150 feet (45 m) of the picnic tables. They should be easily accessible to motorized equipment to facilitate trash pickup. Due to operation costs, this type of rubbish disposal has frequently been replaced by dumpsters located at parking lots. Rubbish cans are still needed, however, in areas of high use and along major walkways.

Acceptable: Dumpsters located at parking lots. They must be located on a stabilized surface and accessible to large rubbish disposal trucks. They should be painted in a color compatible with the leisure facility colors. Location must be visible to all using the picnic area while not becoming a major visual focal point. An easily accessible enclosure is desirable from an aesthetic standpoint, but may reduce its ease for trash disposal if it is difficult to use.

No. of Males/Females	No. of Toilet Seats***		No. of Lavatories		No. of Urinals*
	Male/Female**		Male/Female		Male/Female**
50/50	1	2	1	1	1
100/100	1	3	1	1	2
250/250	2	4	2	2	2
500/500	3	6	2	3	3
750/750	4	8	3	4	4
1000/1000	5	10	4	5	6
2000/2000	6	14	5	6	7

*Urinals should be provided for men.

**Urinals (bidets) may be provided for women in lieu of toilets, but may not exceed one-third the number of required toilet seats (see men's urinals). Most women in the U.S. do not normally use bidets.

***The mix of toilets male/female may need to be modified based on the expected number of males and females.

FIG. 16.6 - SANITARY FIXTURE REQUIREMENTS

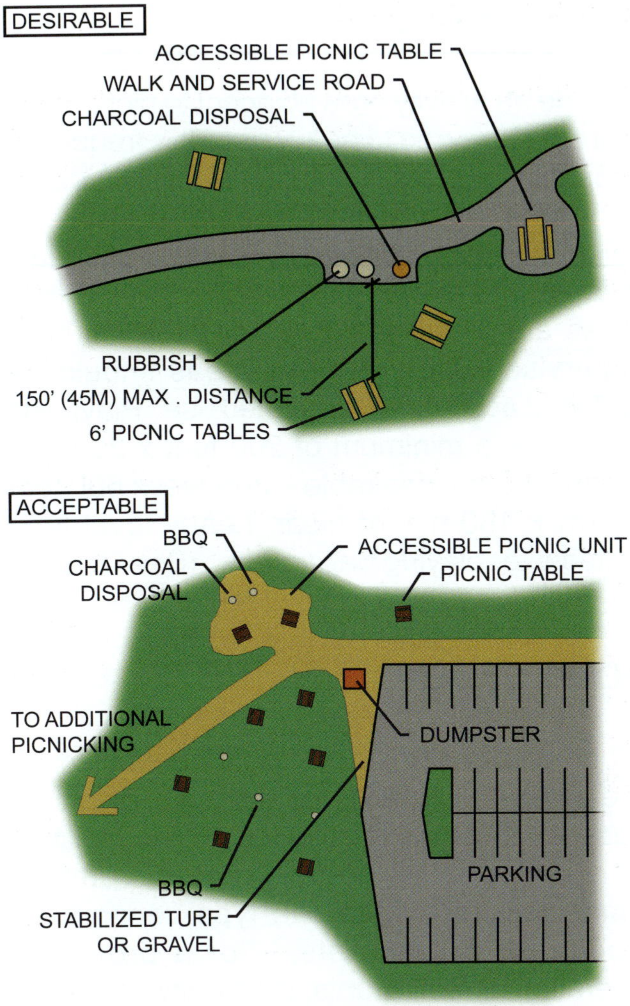

FIG. 16.7 – LOCATION OF RUBBISH DISPOSAL RECEPTACLES

CHARCOAL DISPOSAL

Used charcoal disposal facilities located within 100 feet (30 m) of every charcoal cooking area table. The charcoal disposal unit nearest to accessible picnic facilities must also be accessible. This can be a major safety problem if not properly handled because small children can mistake the coals as sand and be severely burned by the sometimes still hot coals.

WATER SUPPLY

- Distance from drinking water to farthest unit: 300 feet (90 m) - maximum; 150 feet (45 m) - optimum.

Amount of water needed:

- Five gallons (19 l) per person per day (with flush toilets).
- Two and one-half gallons (9.5 l) per person per day (without flush toilets).

SOILS

It is extremely important that heavily used recreation facilities be sited on soils that can sustain the intended use and still retain desired vegetation.

PARKING

- Located or screened to minimize visual intrusion on the picnic area.

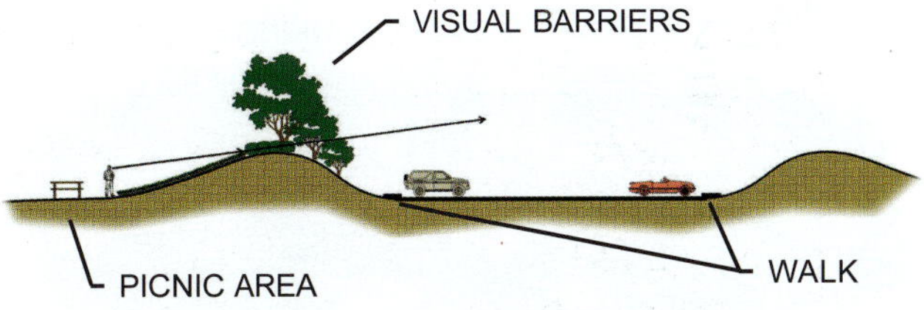

FIG. 16.8 – PARKING IN USE AREA

- Maximum distance from parking to picnic table – 400 feet (120 m); 250 to 300 feet (75 to 90 m) – desirable.

OVERFLOW PARKING

- Usually gravel or turf, frequently called "stabilized turf." It should be considered part of the total design capacity, and should be provided in all heavily used picnic areas. This type of parking can be inexpensive to build, but may be expensive to maintain. It will, however, minimize the visual impact on the facility when it is not at maximum use. The amount of overflow parking can be arrived at by determining the average heavy-use day and then providing the additional holiday and heaviest day parking as overflow. Under no circumstances should a resource-oriented facility be permitted to exceed its total design capacity.

- **Overflow parking must not use open fields normally used for recreational activities. These are most needed for their intended use during heavy attendance.**

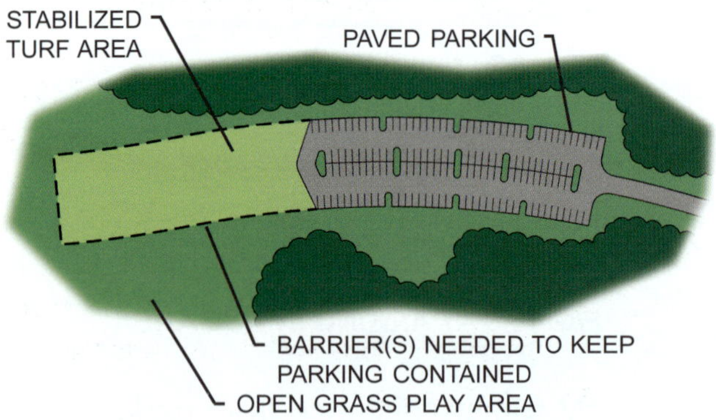

FIG. 16.9 – OVERFLOW PARKING

ACTIVITY AREA

Provide an activity area adjacent to picnic sites that are subjected to heavy use. It is frequently desirable to provide additional facilities and/or space for various activities such as children's play, soccer, volleyball, baseball, softball, and possibly horseshoes, etc. (these areas are to be designed for informal, non-supervised use). All use areas should be surfaced according to intended use. Playfields should be a minimum of 200 feet x 200 feet (60 m x 60 m); desirable – 300 feet x 600 feet (90 m x 180 m), of clear, nearly level land suitable for playing ball games. (See Chapter 15, Play Areas and Playfields.)

FOOD SALES

All areas of heavy use should be studied for the need to provide for the sale of picnic supplies and/or prepared food. The facilities can range from coin-operated vending machines, to mobile cart-type vendors, to traditional restaurants. For a profitable operation or restaurants, the facility should be located so as to maximize visitor access, while not adversely affecting the resource of facility function.

Mobile food service vendor – Eastern Europe

Requirements for Restaurants:

- Market analysis to determine if there is adequate clientele to support the proposed operation.

- Adequate parking.

- Service access, including delivery trucks.

- Water, sewer, electric, and telephone services.

- If a year-round operation, the facility must be winterized and heated in cooler areas, and air conditioned in warmer areas.

- The size and type of eating facility is dependent upon the number and type of clientele.

- Provide an enclosed and, preferably, screened rubbish area.

FAMILY UNIT

Designed for typical family groups of 3.5 to 8 people.

Requirements:

- Minimum area: 225 square feet (20 sq. m).

- Minimum 8-foot (2.4 m) table spacing: 20 feet (6 m) on center; 40 feet (12 m) – desirable. Tables should be 6 feet (1.8 m) - 8 feet (2.4 m) in group areas only – and fixed (non-movable) in heavily used areas; they may be fixed or movable in normal developments. At least 10 percent of tables in every picnic area should have accessible design and be located on an accessible way.

Picnic unit – French Creek State Park, Pennsylvania (still needs accessible way to the excellent, accessible picnic and barbecue)

- Units per acre (hectare): 40 (100) - maximum, only if extremely heavily used facilities and then only when site conditions will permit; 10 to 15 (25 to 35) - desirable maximum.

- Water: one hose bib-fountain combination within 150 feet (45 m) of all picnic sites.

- Parking: two cars per picnic unit in urban areas; 1.5 cars per unit in non-urban areas. This will provide for some lawn picnicking.

- Adequate shade from 11:00 a.m. to 5:00 p.m. is normally needed. In cool areas, such as the coastal area of central and northern California, Oregon, Washington, and British Columbia, the opposite would be necessary - adequate sun plus wind protection from 11:00 a.m. to 5:00 p.m.

FAMILY LAWN UNIT

Lawn picnicking takes place on portions of lawn or turf areas and consists of turf, shade and/or sun, and parking area. People density may be greater than family units. All other facilities provided for table picnicking will be needed.

Lawn picnicking in a tourist area – England

GROUP UNIT

A picnic area for groups with a minimum of 25 persons constitutes a group picnicking unit. The maximum number of people that can be accommodated in a group area must be determined by availability of space and demand for group facilities by large organizations. Facilities described here will accommodate fifty persons. For groups of different sizes, these facilities can be adjusted proportionally. A fee is almost always charged for the reservation of group sites.

Shaded group picnic facility – Naples, Florida

Requirements:

- Minimum area: two+ acres (1 ha), usable land exclusive of recreation support facilities.
- Should be located adjacent to a playfield.
- Barbecue stove and serving table; must have vehicular access.
- Water: Hose bibs adjacent to tables and stove area.
- Sanitary facilities.
- Play area(s).
- Picnic tables: adequate to seat 75 percent of a group at one time – 8-foot (2.4 m) tables are acceptable.

- Fire rings for evening programs are desirable.

- Adequate shade and rain shelter.

- Accessibility is required for each picnic group.

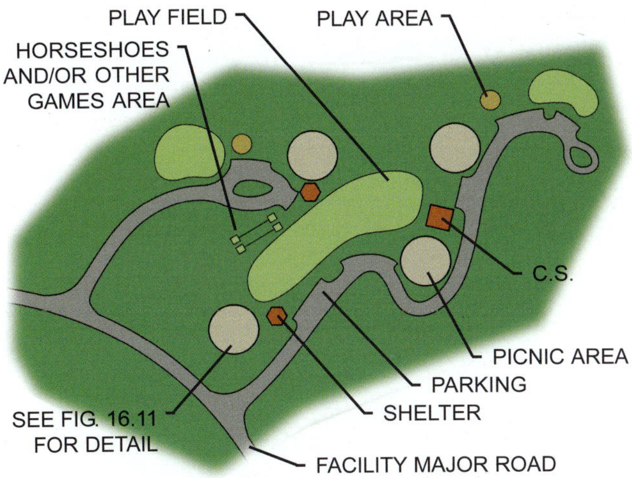

FIG. 16.10 – GROUP PICNIC UNIT

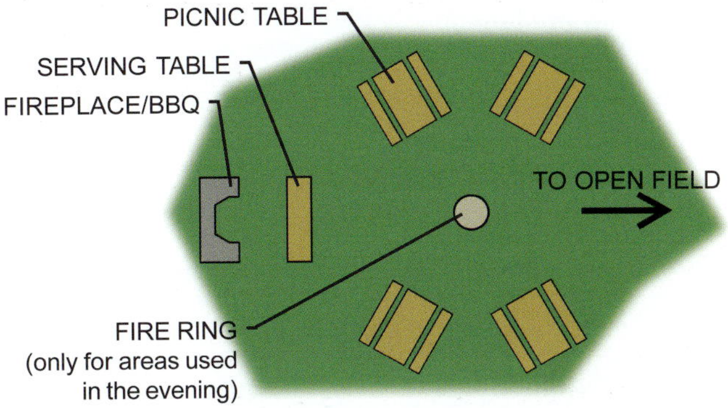

FIG. 16.11 – BLOWUP OF USE AREA

Small group picnic shelter
– Paris Mountain State Park, South Carolina

BOAT UNIT (ACCESS BY WATER ONLY)

A picnic site for use on land adjoining large bodies of water not accessible by car, with cleared shoreline for boat access, table(s), and fire ring. The areas are small, accommodate but few picnic units, have watertight pit or chemical toilets, no developed water (except where a source is readily available and may be developed at little cost), and retain a primitive nature. Service road access should be provided, where possible, to facilitate maintenance; if not possible, area must then be able to be serviced from the water via boat. Accessibility must be provided for at least one picnic unit, including its provided support facilities, such as toilets or barbecues.

Chapter 17

SWIMMING AREAS

CHARACTERISTICS

Three of every four Americans ages 18 to 24 can swim. This proportion drops as one gets older to only one-third of those over 65 years old able to swim; however, this percentage is increasing. There are three basic types of swimming-related activity areas: (1) freshwater natural swim areas (lakes and rivers), (2) salt water beaches, and (3) swimming pools. Each type has its own kind of users and its own special design needs. The majority of users of swimming areas does not swim per se or do not swim only. They usually sit in the sun, visit with friends, play in the water, beachcomb, etc.

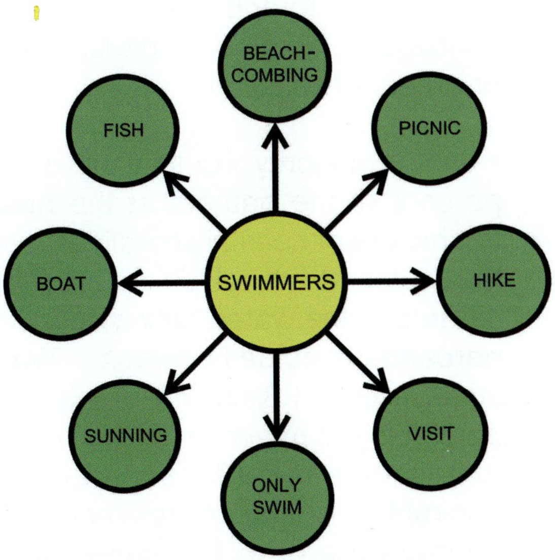

FIG. 17.1 – SWIMMERS DO OTHER ACTIVITIES

Clam Pass County Park – Collier County, Florida

It should be clearly understood that very few people actually swim. Most swimming in leisure facilities is actually water play, and/or just standing around in the water, visiting for adults and playing games for children.

ATTITUDES

- There is no evidence that the availability of beach facilities per se attracts certain types of individuals or repels others. Over time, certain areas become known for one group or another. This emphasis for group-type segregation can be enhanced or negated by management practices and specialized facility development.

• Natural beauty characteristics of a beach appear to be of more importance to visitors with high socio-economic attributes (e.g., high pay, high education, professionals) than with low socio-economic attributes.

• The availability of food facilities on or immediately adjacent to the beach seems especially conducive to attracting teenagers and older youth; so do beaches with distinct entrances and boundaries, and beaches that can be "surveyed" by youths cruising on foot or in cars.

• Teenagers and young adults seem to express a strong positive reaction to crowding on beaches. They also want/ need a place to play games such as volleyball, paddleball, Frisbee, etc.

GENERAL

• In natural-type facilities there is a strong relationship between picnicking and swimming. Where possible, picnic and swimming areas should be located adjacent to each other, with no vehicular separation. For those going to saltwater beaches, picnicking generally occurs on the beach and is much more limited in extent.

• Sixty-five to seventy percent of the bathers in inland waters are likely to be on the beach at any given time. The remainder of the bathers is either in the picnic areas or going to and from other areas of activity or their parked vehicles. Forty-five square feet (4 sq. m) of the beach (above water) per person is the minimum. Ninety square feet (8 sq. m) of beach per person for most beachgoers is more desirable.

• Activity patterns of coastal beaches vary significantly from freshwater swimming facilities. People will walk considerable distances to get to beaches from their parking – up to one-half mile or more. Shelling, sand sculpture, and walking along shorelines are very popular activities. Picnicking per se is almost impossible; however, some food is frequently consumed by most beach party groups. Cell phones are common.

Sand sculpture (alligator)
– Clam Pass County Park, Collier County, Florida

• Almost ninety percent or more of the coastal bathers are likely to be on the beach and/or in the water. The remainder of the beachgoers can be found going to and from their cars, at concession facilities, on piers, shelling, or on boardwalks, etc.

• Only a minority, up to thirty or forty percent of the bathers at the beach, freshwater or coastal shorelines, are in the water at any given time. Of the bathers in the water, only a very small percentage actually swims. Twenty square feet (1.8 sq. m) of water per person is the minimum space needed; forty square feet (3.6 sq. m) is more desirable. Minimum desirable water temperature is in the upper 60's F. (above 20° C.).

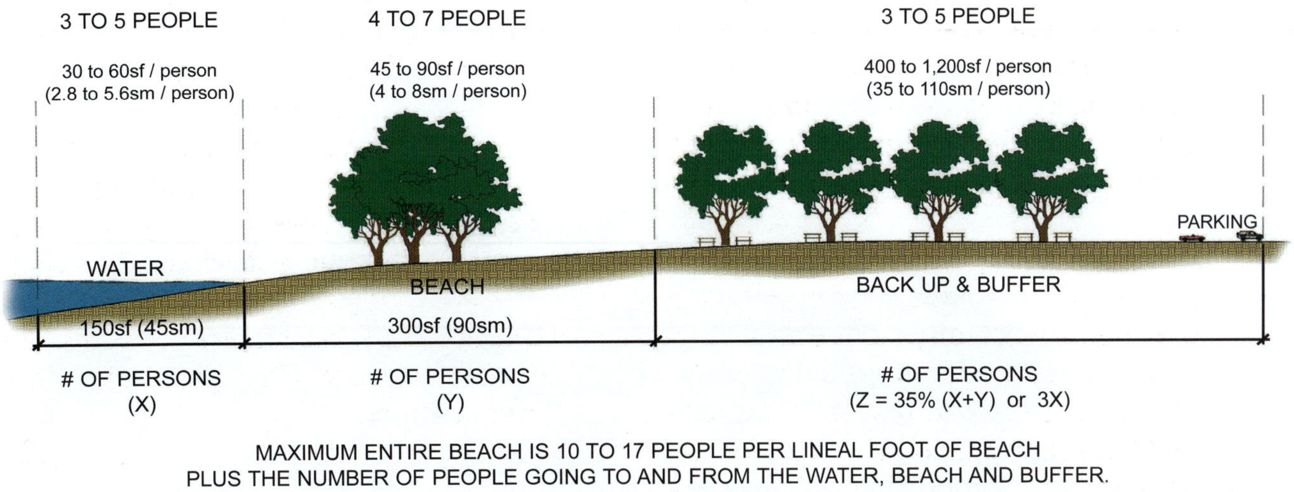

FIG. 17.2 – THE NUMBER OF PEOPLE A LINEAL FOOT OF BEACH CAN ACCOMMODATE AT ANY GIVEN TIME

• Where practical in fresh water areas, diving/jumping areas should be provided. These should be separated from the main swimming/wading areas and require a minimum of thirty square feet (2.8 sq. m) of water per person with a desirable 50 square feet (4.6 sq. m) of water.

Further, the number of people supported by one lineal foot (meter) of beachfront could be derived from the schematic cross section of the areas as shown below.

Total number of persons/lineal foot (meter) of beach = (x + y + 2) or approximately 4 times x.

FRESHWATER BEACHES AND POOL COMPLEXES

Type of Area	Square Feet (Sq. m) Needed Per Person							
	Water		Beach		Backup and Buffer		Total	
	ft.	(m)	ft.	(m)	ft.	(m)	ft.	(m)
High Density	30	(2.8)	45	(4.0)	400	(35)	475	(45±)
	minimum							
	20	(1.8)						
Median Density	40	(3.6)	60	(5.6)	800	(75)	900	(85±)
Low Density	60	(5.6)	90	(8.0)	1200	(110)	1350	(125±)

FIG. 17.3 – SQUARE FEET (METERS) OF AREA NEEDED PER PERSON

FIG. 17.5 – BEACH COMPLEX – STABLE WATER LEVEL

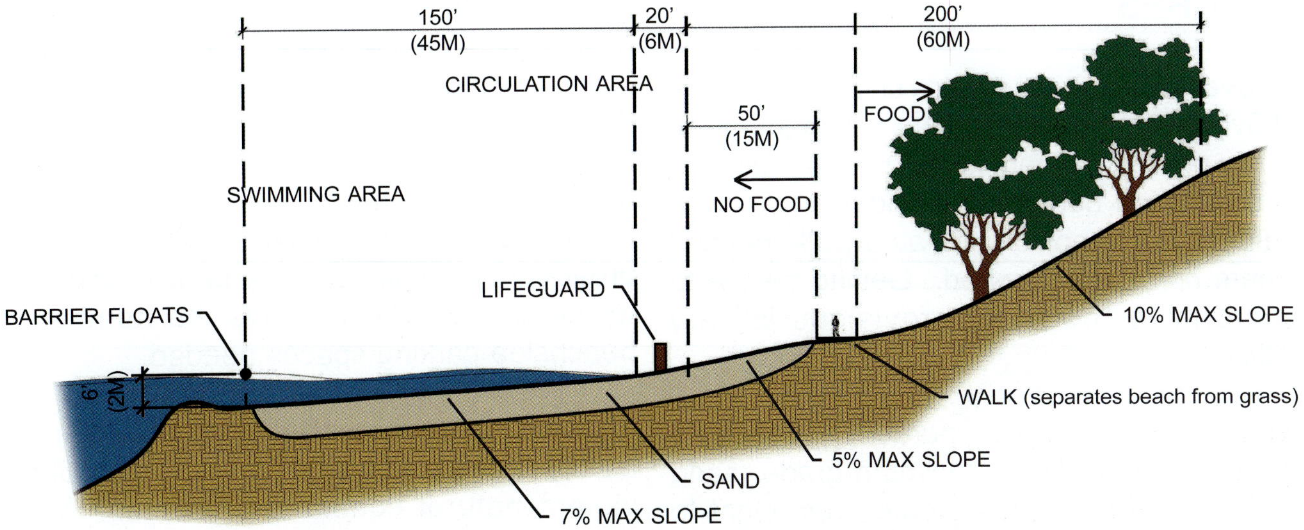

FIG. 17.6 – SECTION THROUGH A FRESHWATER BEACH

The preceding guidelines are on the conservative side and each particular situation will have to be viewed on its own merit, depending upon its individual topographic and other site characteristics.

- Government/public facilities generally use low and median density figures.

- The first 10 to 40 feet (3 to 12 m) of beach is an active-use area and is not suited for sunning. This is the main walkway and the location where the people walk to see and to be seen. It is also, on saltwater beaches, the shelling and beachcombing area. The majority of beach use will be found within 200 feet (60 m) of the swimmable area(s).

- Water area activities have a turnover of people three to nine times per day.

- Beaches have a turnover of people, which varies and may be zero in one area and one-half to two times per day in another.

- The maximum desirable number of people a swimming complex should serve is 4000, due to distances from various activities and support facilities. If more people are expected, provide additional swimming complexes.

- Site development – grass area slopes adjacent to beaches should be ten percent or less.

- Safety – the two most important factors in swimming safety are the very young and sex (male or female). Forty percent of all drownings are of children under age four. The next largest group is men – three to four times as many more drown as women. Swimming areas that attract these groups need special safety precautions, i.e., life guard facilities, first aid, and easy emergency vehicle access to the beach.

- Walkways should be a very light color for protection of bare feet.

BEACHES

Above Water: Sand surface should be a slope of five percent or less, with a minimum grade of two percent. Where local rules prohibit food and drink on beaches, consider providing a definite visible point, such as a walk, beyond where no food is allowed. Getting people to conform to "no food" provisions is very difficult.

Below Water: Seven percent – desirable grade; ten percent – maximum grade (sand will not stay on slopes greater than eight to ten percent); five percent – minimum grade (slopes less than five percent are too shallow and become too wide for easy guarding). Beaches below water level should have an adequate base similar to that of a walkway or road to prevent the area from becoming muddy. Maximum water depth - 6± feet (180± cm), except in diving areas. Most importantly, make sure that there are no sudden changes in grade and no unexpected holes or obstructions on which people could injure themselves or, much worse, drown.

COASTAL BEACHES

Most coastal developments are linear by the very nature of the resource. They vary from the most urban of waterfronts to those almost untouched by man. All are important resources that must be carefully protected, while still providing public access to this most desired of resources.

Because of their linear qualities, they differ in their design approach from the cluster-style developments at most pools and lakes. Effective site utilization requires numerous, relatively small access points located at intervals along the beach. This, in turn, disperses the users and their needed support facilities. Also, unlike most developments discussed in this book, a substantial percentage of the users of resort and urban- oriented beaches are people who walk to the beach. This affects the number of beachside parking spaces needed.

In all beach developments it is necessary to clearly understand and relate to the sometimes violent natural coastal processes. Wind, waves, sand, erosion, littoral drift, flooding, corrosion, saltwater intrusion into freshwater aquifers, and coastal vegetation are all vital parts of the dynamics of the coastal ecosystem.

Man has made many mistakes in trying to tame this system that will not be tamed. We, as users of the coastal resource, must be willing to live with it, not fight it. In other words, beach facilities must be movable and/or easily replaceable. See Chapter 4, Environmentally-Sensitive Design for some techniques for working with the environment.

The users generally fall into two categories: (1) young people who frequently congregate in one or more areas, and (2) family groups utilizing other beach segments. Both groups of users generally bring food, drinks (of all kinds), beach chairs and/or blankets and, frequently, some type of flotation device, radio, and cell phone. They, like most facility users, "stake out" their piece of territory immediately on arrival.

Group of young people waiting for permission to swim – Paris Mountain State Park, South Carolina

Shelling – Clam Pass County Park, Collier County, Florida

Most older adult users will walk along the beach or sit and watch other users; from time to time they will take a brief dip to cool off. Family groups (frequently three generations) will stay together, and some of the members will be playing in the water (usually the children) during most of their stay. Younger adults and teenagers will spend their time in a number of ways, from listening to music (sometimes quite loud), sunning and walking along the beach to see and be seen, swimming, playing volleyball, Frisbee, paddleball, and other games. Although both groups will probably spend some time in the water at water play, they will, however, spend **very** little time, if any, actually swimming.

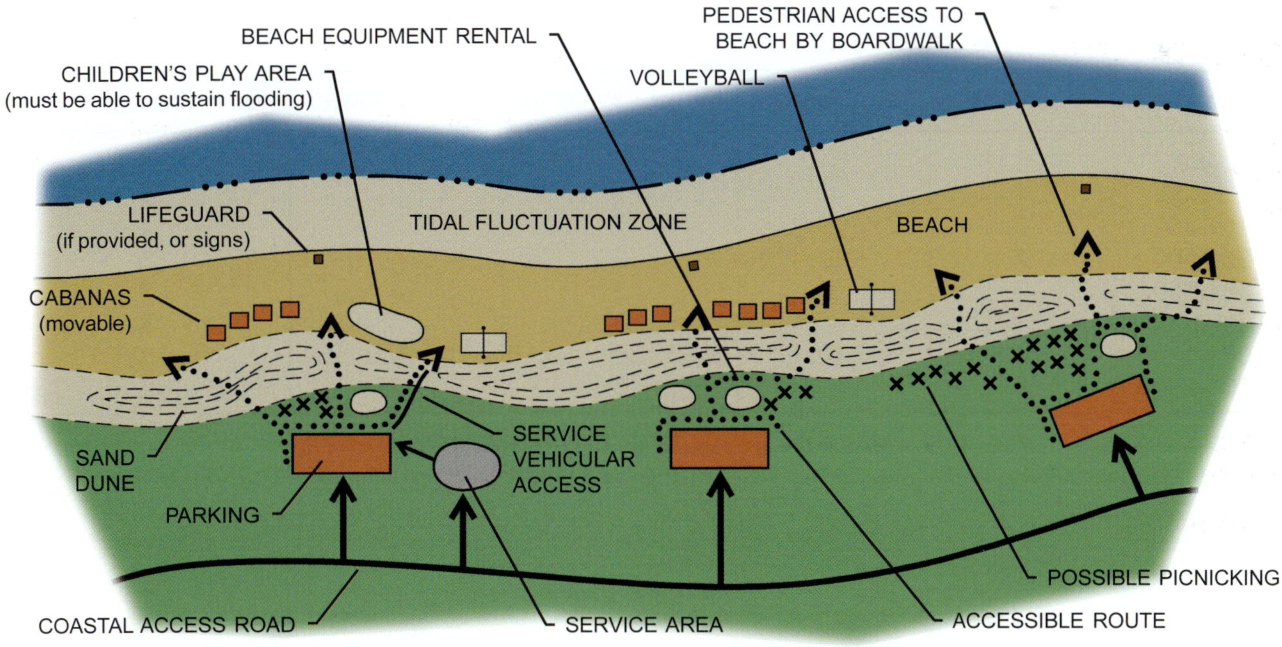

FIG. 17.7 – SCHEMATIC LAYOUT OF COASTAL BEACH FACILITIES

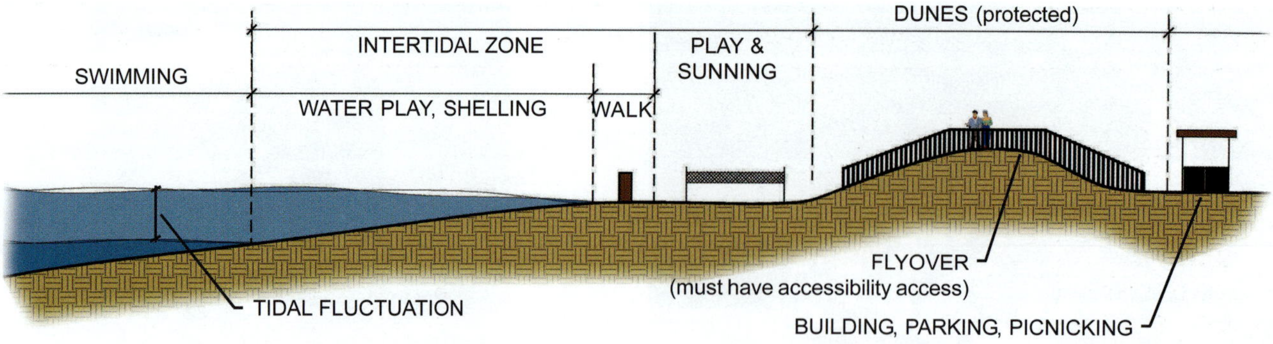

FIG. 17.8 – SECTION THROUGH A COASTAL BEACH

SURFBOARDING, SURF SAILING & PARAGLIDING

Information on these topics is located in Chapter 18, Boating.

BEACH MAINTENANCE

Most heavily used beaches require cleaning and grooming on a regular basis. This is usually done with a vehicle-drawn rake and/or some kind of debris pickup device. This type of maintenance will have an effect on the features (i.e., lifeguard, cabanas, boat rental, etc.) that might be placed on the beach and/or their design. It also requires vehicular access to the beach.

SANITARY FACILITIES

The number of sanitary fixtures required in a bathhouse complex in a swimming area (beaches or swimming pools) is governed by the prevailing regulations in the area in which it is to be constructed.

The following requirements are recommended:

No. of Males	No. of Toilets	No. of Urinals	No. of Lavatories	No. of Showers	No. of Change Rooms
1-50	1	1	1	1	1
51-100	1	1	1	2	2
101-250	2	2	2	3	4
251-500	2	3	2	4	6
501-750	3	3	3	4	7
751-1000	3	4	3	5	8
1001-1500	4	5	4	6	10
1501-2000	5	6	5	7	12

FIG. 17.9 – MALE BATHHOUSE FIXTURE REQUIREMENTS (5) *

No. of Females	No. of Toilets	No. of Lavatories	No. of Showers	No. of Change Rooms
1-50	1	1	1	1
51-100	2	1	2	2
101-250	3	2	3	4
251-500	5	2	4	6
501-750	6	3	4	8
751-1000	7	3	5	9
1001-1500	9	5	6	11
1501-2000	11	5	7	13

***FIG. 17.10 – FEMALE BATHHOUSE FIXTURE REQUIREMENTS* [5] ***

*Foot washing facilities are necessary at sand beaches. They should be located immediately behind the beach on the walk system leading to the parking lot and, preferably, before the comfort station/bathhouse. Fresh or saltwater may be used. Self-closing valves are a necessity.

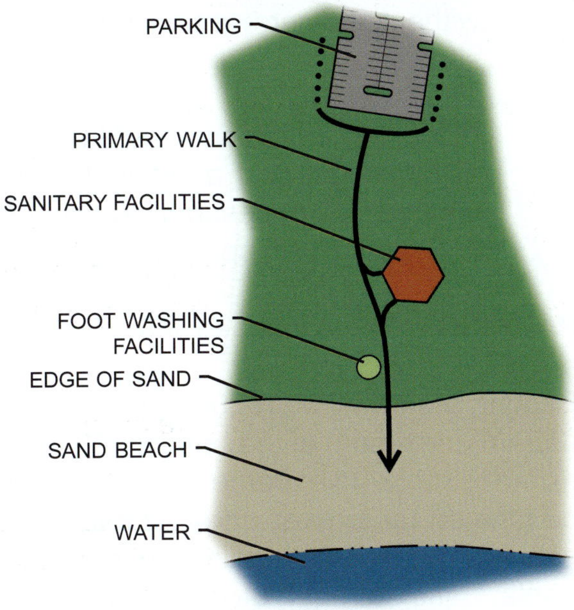

FIG. 17.11 – LOCATION OF FOOT WASHING FACILITIES

In picnicking/swimming combination areas, adequate sanitary facilities should be provided on either the beach or in the picnic area. There should be no overlapping of facilities. The number of sanitary fixtures required in comfort stations to serve picnickers' needs can be obtained from the following tables. [5]

The figures in the preceding tables could be extrapolated on a straight-line basis to obtain fixture units for more than 2,000 persons.

The distance from the water's edge to the restrooms should be at least 200 feet (60 m) so as not to interfere with the various beach-related activities; 500 feet (150 m) – maximum. Maximum distance apart – 1,000 feet (300 m).

No. of Males	No. of Toilets	No. of Urinals	No. of Lavatories
1-50	1	1	1
51-100	1	2	1
101-250	2	2	2
251-500	3	3	2
501-750	4	4	3
751-1000	4	5	3
1001-1500	5	6	4
1501-2000	6	7	5

FIG. 17.12 – MALE COMFORT STATION

No. of Females	No. of Toilets	No. of Lavatories
1-50	2	1
51-100	3	1
101-250	4	2
251-500	6	3
501-750	8	4
751-1000	10	4
1001-1500	12	5
1501-2000	14	6

FIG. 17.13 – FEMALE COMFORT STATION

Dressing Rooms:

• Should be located in close proximity to the beach, where possible.

• Where picnic and beach combinations are planned, dressing rooms should be located between the picnic area and the beach.

• Wherever possible, dressing rooms should be combined with sanitary facilities and showers.

• Showers can be located outside of the building and, possibly, at the same location as the foot washing. These showers cannot use salt water.

• Limited coin-operated lockers or other checking facilities should be considered for inclusion in the dressing areas. Most people seem to prefer to keep their clothes with them on the beach or at the pool. If lockers are deemed necessary, it is suggested that five percent of beach capacity be considered for calculating the number of lockers.

WATER REQUIREMENTS

• Five gallons (20 l) per person per day without showers; ten gallons (40 l) with showers.

• Drinking fountains should be located at buildings, and additional fountains located, as necessary, to provide for 250 feet (75 m) spacing.

PARKING (often combined with picnicking)

Parking areas will be required within 800 feet (250 m) maximum of the beach; 500 feet (150 m) – desirable. In extreme cases, parking can be located up to over one-half mile from the beach. This does not hold true for swimming pools. The number of cars needed in the parking area should not be greater than the capacity of the beach plus thirty percent. For picnic/beach combinations for coastal beaches, it should not exceed the carrying capacity of the beach. (See Chapter 11, Roads and Parking, for details and Chapter 1, Methods for Determining Visitor Demand, for number of people per car.)

FOOD SERVICE

These facilities should be provided at all major beach areas. The extent of the facilities can vary from a small vending machine area to a large snack bar, and even to a restaurant complex. They should be located between 250 and 500 feet (75 and 150 m) from the water and can often be integrated into the dressing room/comfort station complex. It is desirable, if combined with a beach picnic area, that the food service facility be so located that it will serve the picnic area. An eating area should be provided, preferably adjacent to the food service area and with a view of the beach. This will minimize the carrying of food onto the beach area.

SAFETY FACILITIES

Adequate safety facilities must be considered for all swimming areas. There are no standards and, because of interpretation of liability laws, the safety services provided vary from posting a notice stating there is no protection and swim at your own risk to extensive lifeguard and emergency care facilities.

Lifeguard Chairs: No existing standards; 400 feet (120 m) on center – suggested.

Lifeguard stand – Southern California

Beach Patrol: Many coastal beaches do not provide lifeguard services. They, instead, may utilize rangers who patrol on all-terrain or other vehicles. This type of patrol will have an effect on the features that might be placed on the beach and/or their design. It also will require vehicular access to the beach.

Safety Floats: To demark the swimming area and keep swimmers inside and boaters and fishermen outside 150 feet (45 m) from shoreline.

Swimming Floats or Platforms: Locate, if possible, at the outer edge of the swimming area. Normally used only on stable water bodies, such as inland lakes.

Lifeguard Room: Many large beach areas and most pool complexes provide a lifeguard room or building. It should have visual control of the beach/pool area. Vehicular access to the lifeguard building/room for emergency vehicles is necessary.

Telephone Service: Cell phones are normally now used for phone service; however, land line service must be provided for safety reasons. This line should also be available for other facility communications.

Turbidity: Constructed beaches and beach nourishment projects should be built with sand containing as few "fines" as possible to limit turbidity and thereby enhance safety by making it easier to find people in the water who are in trouble.

PUBLIC TELEPHONE

It is desirable to have public pay telephones provided in a prominent location in all beach areas.

ACCESSIBLE FACILITIES

Accessibility standards must be provided to the water's edge even on fluctuating bodies of water. Ingress and egress to and from the water for disabled persons must also be available in all pools and constructed water features.

ACTIVITY AREAS

It is desirable at all "swimming" areas to designate and set aside land for various recreation activities, such as children's play, volleyball, and turf fields. These facilities should be located in close proximity to the swimming area, where possible. In coastal areas, they are usually located on the beach, but must be so designed that they can take the adverse coastal conditions or that they can be moved during storms. Where picnic and beach combinations are provided, the activity area should be located between the picnic area and the beach.

Sand volleyball behind the beach – Naples, Florida

Rental facilities, such as bicycle, boats, paddle-boats, cabanas, umbrellas, etc., are desirable additions to larger beach areas. They should be located at the periphery of the use areas and along major pedestrian walkways. Vehicular service (walks) access must be provided.

Boat rental
– Clam Pass County Park, Collier County, Florida

FIRE RINGS

Most heavily used beaches do not permit fires. In places where they are permitted, fire rings should be placed in groups away from the swimming area toward the rear or extreme ends of the beach area. The individual rings should be about 100 feet (30 m) apart. These should be considered only where beaches are open in the evening hours. **Note**: This type of development is likely to attract more teenagers and young adults.

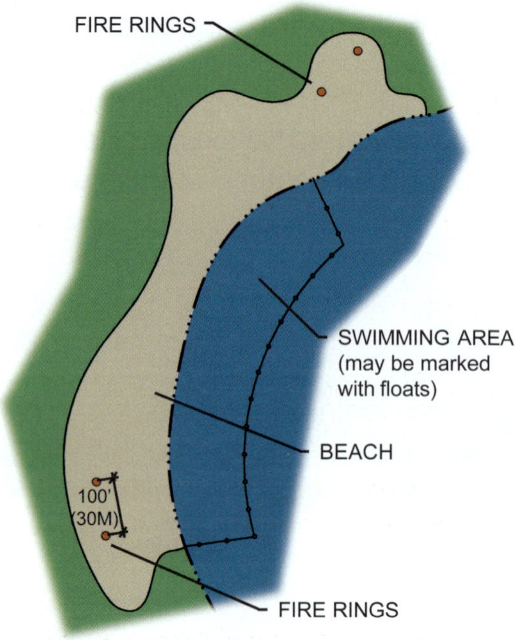

FIG. 17.14 – LOCATION OF FIRE RINGS

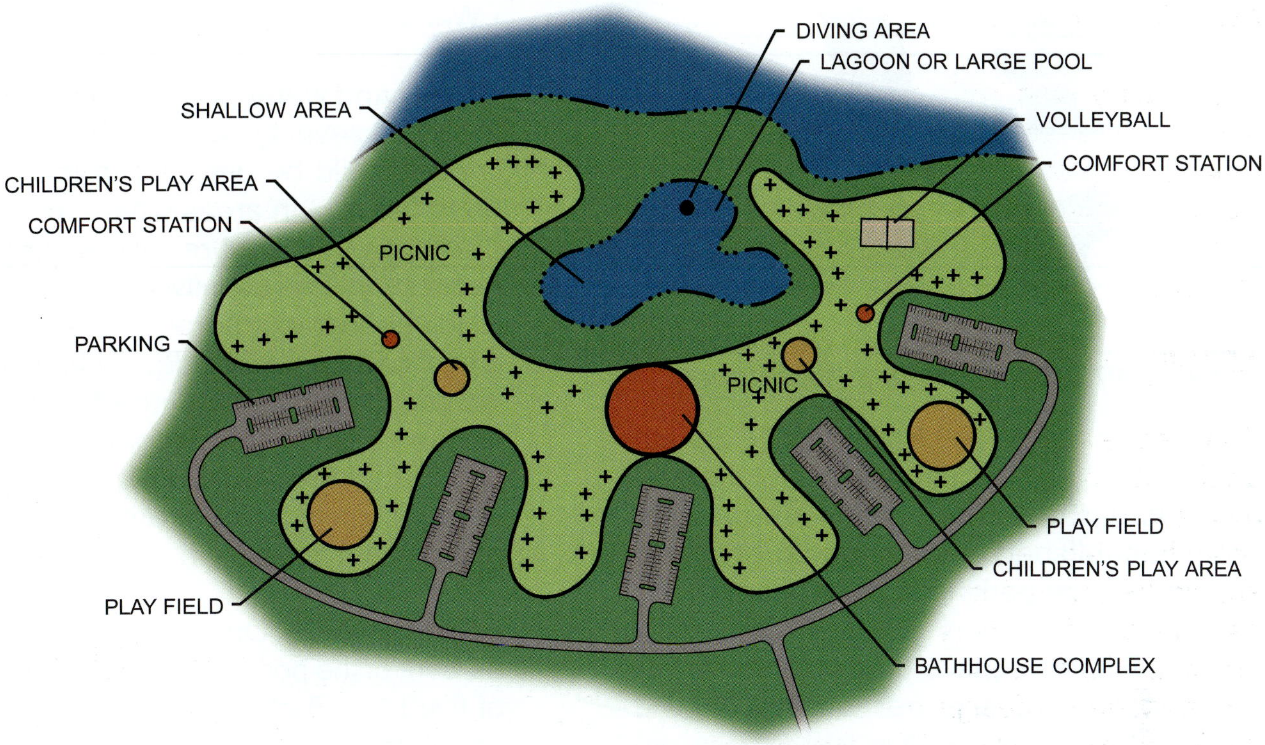

FIG. 17.15 – LAGOON AND LARGE POOL COMPLEX CONCEPT

SWIMMING LAGOONS AND LARGE POOL COMPLEXES

Swimming lagoons or large pool complexes should be considered where water quality, water level fluctuations, or lack of large water bodies are a problem. Details are the same as for freshwater beach areas plus the following:

1. Water quality controls, including circulation and/or recirculation of the water, will probably fall under the same controls as swimming pools and could make lagoons impractical from a cost standpoint.

2. Water treatment (chlorination) may be necessary as per public health regulations.

3. Lifeguards will probably be required by public health rules.

SWIMMING POOLS

Swimming pools, when used, should fit the character of the remainder of the facility development. Pools do not have to be rectangular, but they do have to have lifeguards. Straight lines are easier to build. Corners are more difficult to guard from a safety standpoint. The size of the pool can be tailored to fit the projected numbers of people. The concept of wading pools has pretty much been passed by the spray pool phenomenon. Wading pools have high water treatment criteria – frequently four times the rate as swimming pools. This makes it necessary to have separate equipment and water, and do not recirculate. They also do not need lifeguards – another advantage.

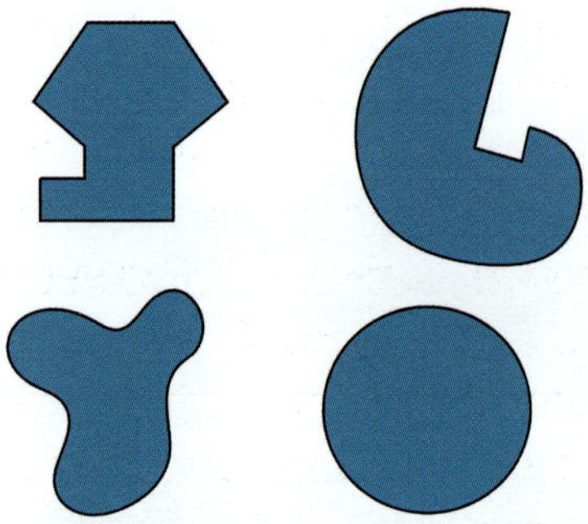

FIG. 17.16 – SWIMMING POOL CONFIGURATIONS ARE LIMITED ONLY BY YOUR IMAGINATION

• Because of the limited space around pools, a maximum capacity for the pool and its related uses should be established. Maximum suggested: 1200 car parking or 2500 people.

• Fifteen square feet (1.4 sq. m) of water surface per person is the minimum; twenty-five feet (2.3 sq. m) is desirable.

• Deck surface needs to be a minimum of twice the water surface

• Grass sunning area should be equal to the entire pool and deck area.

• A diving or jumping area should be provided, when possible, especially in areas subject to heavy use by young people. Diving areas require safety precautions, which usually include a lifeguard.

• Twenty-five square feet (2.3 sq. m) is the minimum space needed per person; forty square feet (3.7 sq. m) is desirable for water surface in the diving areas.

• Provisions for the disabled to enter and to exit the pool, surrounding areas, and supporting facilities must be included in all projects

• Water uses:

- Water and water play should amount to sixty to seventy percent of pool. The depth should be one foot to four feet (.3 to 1.2 m). In areas where freezing of the ground occurs, winterizing is necessary. This usually, at a minimum, requires draining the pool. Placing on a pool covering is also desirable. Pools with depths less than three feet (1 m) may experience severe damage due to freezing and thawing. Special construction techniques are required to overcome this problem.

- Swimming – Only twenty to thirty percent of the pool should be at a depth of five to six feet (1.5 to 2 m) to easily accommodate the few people who swim. Lap swimming is fairly common and needs a minimum depth of three+ feet (1+ m) throughout.

- Diving – Ten to fifteen percent of the surface area of the pool will likely be needed if diving is provided, and depth is as required by height of diving boards and platforms.

Swimming pool (note almost all use is in the shallow end of the pool). Photo by Michael Fogg

• Spray pools/spray grounds – If a separate area is desired for pre-school and young children, it is recommended that spray pools or spray grounds be used in lieu of wading pools. Spray pools and/or spray grounds require no recirculation of the water. Wading pools need a high level of treatment – usually a two-hour turnover. Provide benches with shade for parents.

Spray/wading pool
Collier County, Florida
(Most spray areas do not now have standing water)

• Water recirculation and filtration should be as simple as possible to minimize operations and maintenance costs. Recommended - pipeless, i.e., an integrated water recirculation and scum gutter system with a sand filter system. Local pool health requirements must be adhered to, and the pool must meet local and state regulations.

• Fencing is required and should be at least 42 inches to 48 inches (1.2 m – 1.4 m) high, with adequate lockable gated openings to and from use areas. This will provide adequate warning to people of a possible danger while still keeping the effect of an open site. Locate the fence to be as unobtrusive as possible, and screen with planting where it is visually objectionable. Almost all governments have requirements for safety fencing.

• Where fees are charged, or may be charged in the future, a six-foot (1.8 m) fence with a single controlled entrance will be required. Emergency exits will also be needed for safety purposes.

AQUATIC COMPLEXES

There are a number of multipurpose aquatic swimming complexes located throughout the U.S. and other countries. They consist of a variety of water-related experiences from super slides and wave-activated pools to spray pools and spray grounds, tubing areas, and waterfalls. They should only be considered for locations where the potential users have undergone a thorough market analysis to ensure adequately that the facilities will be used and that they will be economically viable. The pools' support equipment and operational requirements are very costly, making it imperative to charge sometimes substantial entrance fees for their use.

Chapter 18

BOATING

Boating is a major, generally expensive recreation activity. Most areas have inadequate "boatable" water to meet present demands. All available sources of boating water should be considered for development commensurate with reasonable use densities and good design. Horsepower limitations should be considered when planning for lakes in natural-type leisure facilities, or bodies of water less than 800 surface acres (300 ha), due to noise, pollution, and safety problems. The water area required per boat increases as the horsepower increases. Therefore, many small bodies of water may need to prohibit entirely power boating or, at the very least, restrict the motor horsepower. Environmental factors are of particular importance in the consideration of building boating facilities in estuarine environments, and sometimes may preclude an otherwise desirable area from being used for boating and its necessary onshore support facilities.

VISITOR CHARACTERISTICS (8)

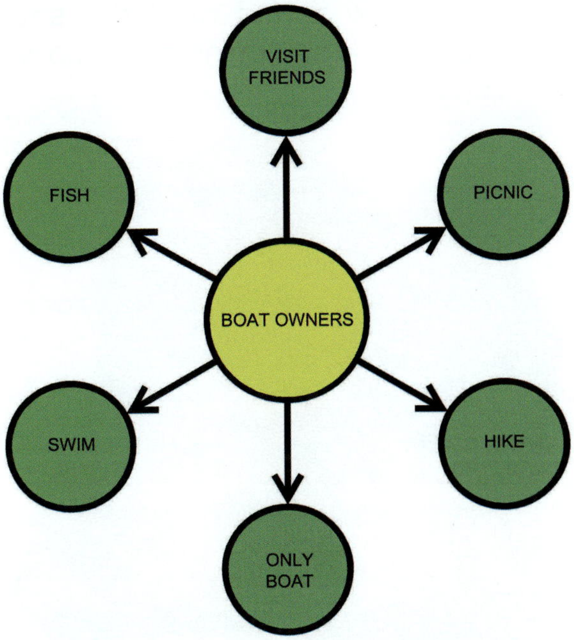

FIG. 18.1 – NON-RENTAL BOATERS FREQUENTLY PARTICIPATE IN OTHER ACTIVITIES

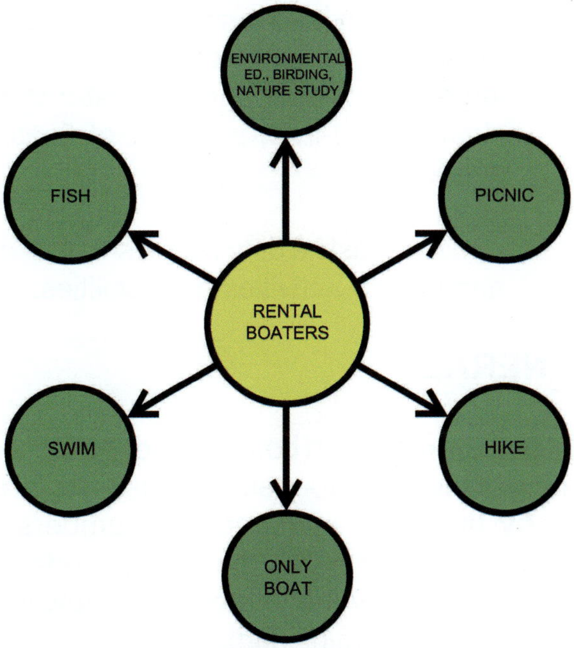

FIG. 18.2 – RENTAL BOATERS FREQUENTLY PARTICIPATE IN OTHER ACTIVITIES

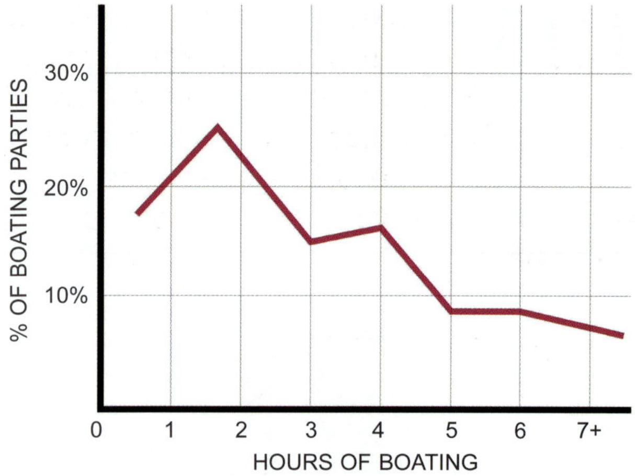

FIG. 18.3 – BOATERS BOAT FOR VARIOUS LENGTHS OF TIME

Note: These charts and graphs are conceptual only. No recent data has been found to establish the percentage of users who participate in one or more of these activities.

- Rental boating is most popular with the younger facility visitors; non-rental boating with the older visitors. (8)

- Boaters, like other leisure activity users, prefer to have their boating close to home. In lake reservoir access, the users prefer their boating area to be as large as possible and the water to be clean, weed-free, and free of floating debris.

- Boaters dislike dirty water, small lakes, and lack of activities and facilities.

GENERAL

Where extremely high boat use is experienced, zoning of the water for particular uses, by area and by time, will increase the numbers of boaters who can safely be accommodated. The enjoyment by the boaters may, however, be significantly diminished.

Factors to be considered when designing boating facilities include:

- Prevailing wind conditions – especially important when sailing is being considered, and on large bodies of water. Storm wind direction is particularly important for location of breakwaters and/or the location of the docking and launching facilities.

- Open reach of water.

- Sheltering headlands.

- Current – primarily on river marinas.

- Water maneuvering areas.

- Depth of water in maneuvering areas.

- Silting – can be a major maintenance problem.

- Special use zones such as for fishing only, slow zones near the shore, especially in swimming areas, no wake zones, etc.

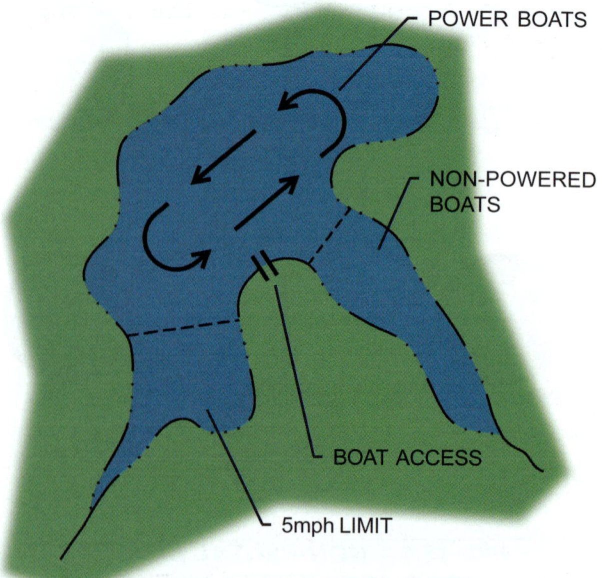

FIG. 18.4 – LAKE ZONING

• Economics – how the facility is to be financed, both construction and, especially, operation.

• Seasonal lake draw downs in reservoirs.

• Fluctuating water levels – can make launching and marina facilities very difficult to operate.

• Vehicular access to water for boat launching.

• Available usable land for onshore support facilities, especially parking.

• Accessibility to main water bodies, i.e., bridge clearance, tidal mud flats, etc. The closer to the main water surface area, and the more barrier-free, the better.

BOAT LAUNCHING

Boat launching should be considered at all protected coastal areas and on lakes and rivers wherever there is adequate space for boating over and above that required for boat rental facilities.

Boat launching ramp – Coastal Southern California

Vehicular access to boat launching facilities is required. It should be located to keep vehicles pulling boat trailers from entering into other use areas. The access to the boat launching area should be one of the first areas to be reached after entering a multipurpose leisure development.

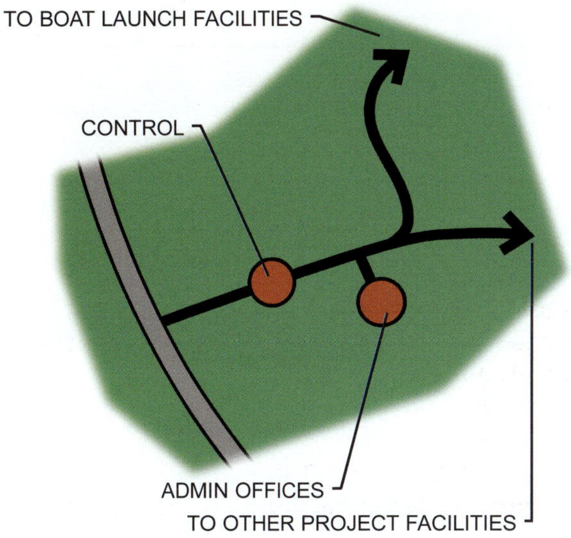

FIG. 18.5 – VEHICULAR ACCESS TO BOAT LAUNCHING

Adequate parking space must be provided adjacent to the launching facility. Note that many people come to meet friends and/or just to watch the boating activity.

Many boating parties have members who do not boat. Where possible, provide picnic facilities near boat ramp area at the rate of at least one table per ten parking spaces.

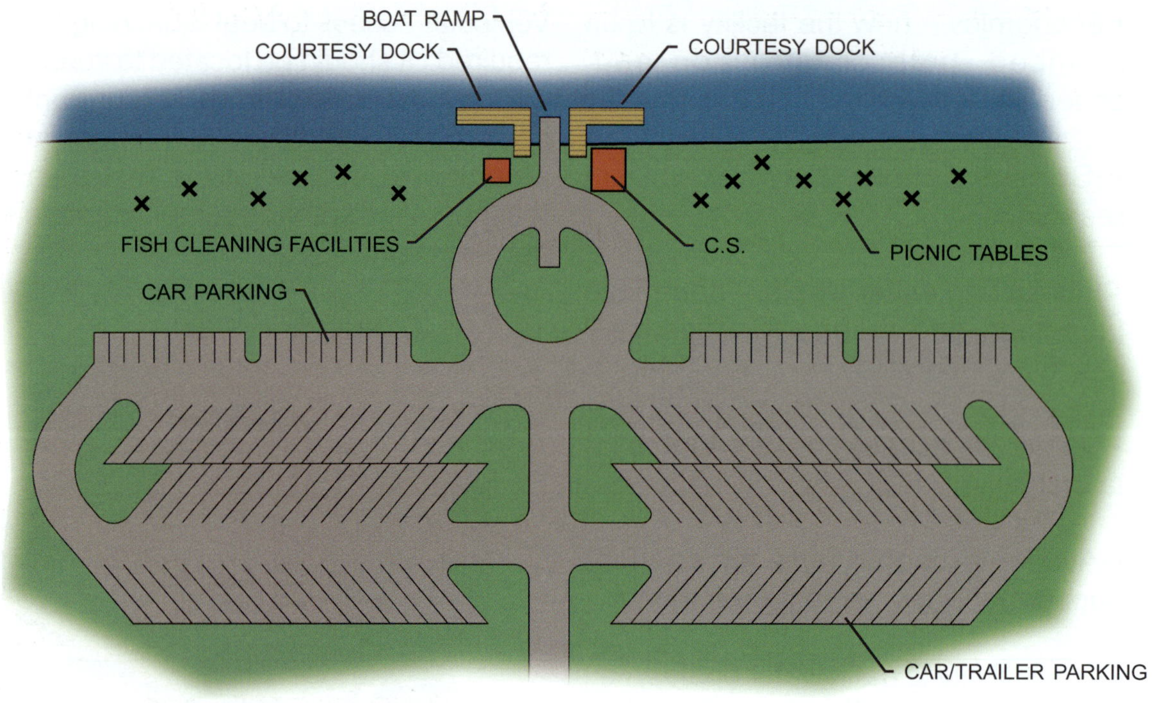

FIG. 18.6 – BOAT LAUNCHING AREA

LAUNCHING RAMPS

This is the most commonly used method of launching boats. It takes three to six minutes to launch or retrieve a power boat, plus the time to park or retrieve the vehicle and trailer. Please note that it generally takes twice as long (ten to fifteen minutes) to launch a sailboat.

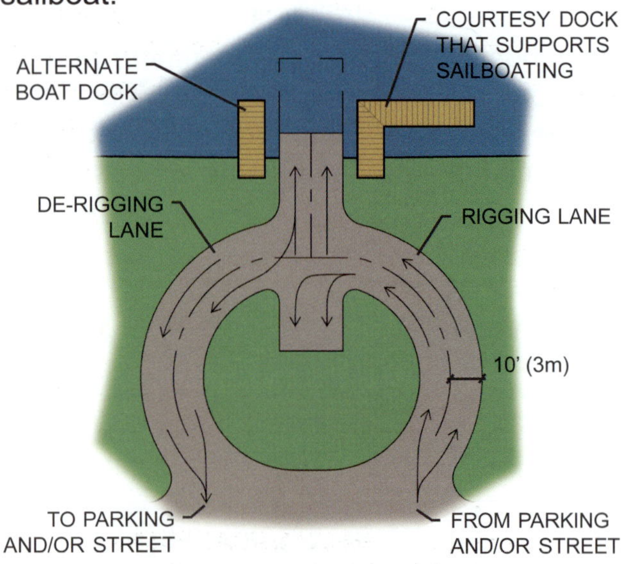

FIG. 18.7 – LAUNCHING RAMP

A rigging and de-rigging lane is needed to prevent the boaters from tying up the launching ramps for a long time period. This is especially necessary where sailboating occurs.

- **Percent slope for boat ramps**:

Minimum	7 percent
Desirable	13 to 14 percent
Maximum	15 percent

Less than 7 percent ramp slopes frequently causes the rear of towing vehicles to become submerged. More than 15 percent can cause vehicles to have problems getting the boat and trailer out of the water and, sometimes, ends up with the towing vehicle slipping down the ramp and coming to rest underwater at the end of the ramp slope.

- **Width of launching lane**: 12 to 15 feet (3.5 to 4.5 m). Multiple-land launching ramps can be constructed: four-lane – desirable maximum; ten-lane – maximum.

- **Parking**: 40 to 60 car and trailer parking is required for each lane of launching depending on the kind of boats and the distance to the parking lot. (See Chapter 11, Roads and Parking, for details.) An additional 10± percent parking is needed for second boat party cars and sightseers in inland waters, and, possibly, more extra second car parking is needed at coastal waters. Existing local boat ramp/parking use patterns should be checked to determine the amount of extra parking needed.

COURTESY DOCKS

These docks need to be provided at each launching area at the minimum rate of one 40-foot (10 m) dock per two lanes of launching, and, preferably, one 20-foot (5 m) dock per lane. They should be located in a manner that will permit continued use of the launch ramp while the boat is being held. An "L"-shaped dock is desirable if there is significant sailboat activity.

SANITARY FACILITIES

Toilets should be provided as needed and of sufficient size so as to avoid undue wait and/or walk of more than 300 feet (90 m) from the launching ramp. Approximately one fixture per sex per 150 cars should be provided. All launch areas must be provided toilets, with a minimum of one fixture per sex or with unisex fixtures.

BOAT SERVICE FACILITIES

Docking, gasoline, supplies, and food services should be considered at launching areas serving more than 300 boats or where there are fewer boats and no alternative areas for service. They should be located so that they are easy to operate from a central control point, preferably located in conjunction with other concession facilities, i.e., a marina or boat rental.

Boat service facilities
– Naples City Dock, Naples, Florida

ALTERNATIVE TYPES OF LAUNCHING

Mechanical means of launching (such as hoists, tractors, etc.) can be considered in special areas. These are usually only in private marinas or concession-operated public marinas where boats are stored in high density conditions, and where income generation is at least adequate to cover costs.

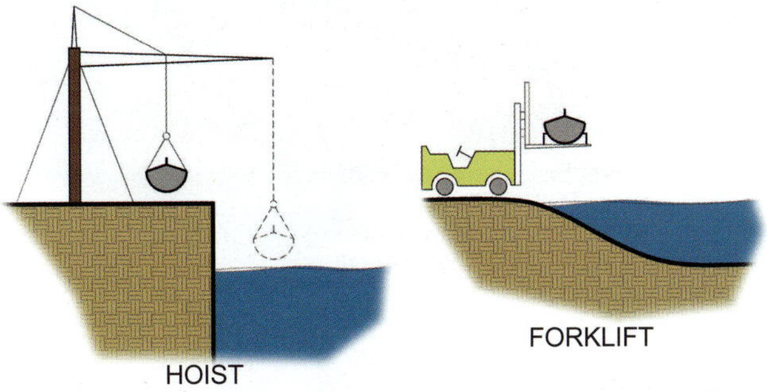

FIG. 18.8 – MECHANICAL MEANS OF BOAT LAUNCHING

NON-BOAT RAMP LAUNCHING

Car top and other non-ramp required launching may be desirable and, in fact, may be the only type of launching needed. This type of launching is almost always for small, non-powered boats, such as canoes and kayaks, and it is usually required in small bodies of water or streams and rivers. It requires an unloading space adjacent to the shore with gentle slope (frequently grass) into the water. On streams, locate both the launching and take-out points at a stream pool or eddy.

SAILBOATING

Sailboaters are frequently clannish and will often form clubs and indulge in racing. Other factors to be considered are as follows:

- Sailboat facilities need special attention to wind conditions.
- Different types of sailboats may have significantly different space and operating requirements.
- Wherever possible, separate sailboating from power boating, both on shore and in the water.
- Many sailboaters prefer to store their boats on shore, especially those who race, to prevent the buildup of speed-reducing algae growth. (7)
- Design of courtesy docks should consider wind direction and might be hexagonal or some other angled form to allow for different wind directions. (7)
- It is desirable to have a large grass or sand beach with some type of mooring anchor or rail to pull up and secure boats during the day and for launching car top boats. (7)

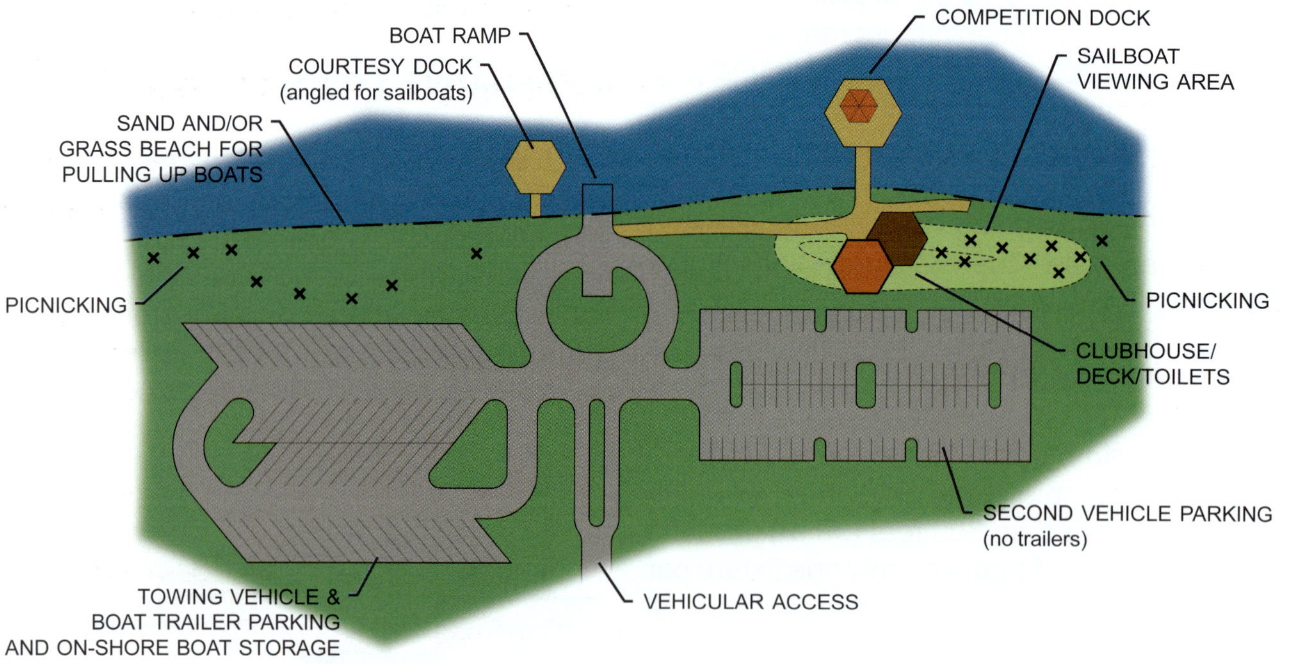

FIG. 18.9 – SAILBOAT FACILITIES

• Provide extra rigging and de-rigging space for boat ramps that serve significant numbers of sailboat enthusiasts. It takes three times as long to rig a sailboat as a power boat.

• If a yacht club or some other type of club is established or is already in existence, a clubhouse may be a desirable feature. These buildings are best located at a higher area than the water to better view the boat racing activities.

• In coastal areas, light-weight sailboats are frequently stored at the upper edge of the beach (above high tide) and then pulled or pushed into the water. This is particularly the case for surf sailing and small catamarans. This type of mooring is well served by a mooring rail.

Temporary shore storing of boats – Naples, Florida

SURF SAILING

This is an extremely popular activity among teenagers and young adults. It requires little special facility development, except a reasonable distance to the parking lot (200 to 400 feet (60 to 120 m), and needs to be located at one end of the beach for safety reasons. Surf sailing can take place in areas having extremely cold water by the use of wetsuits and has even become popular among the more hearty as far north as Anchorage, Alaska.

JET SKIS

These frequently are available for rent at marinas and beach boat areas. Jet skis are very fast and maneuverable and must be kept separate from swimming and other water play areas. They are compatible with other power boating and water ski activities. Very noisy and should be separated from any nature study, interpretive and quiet areas.

PARAGLIDING – BOAT TOW

Same requirements as water skiing. (See Chapter 9, Special Use Facilities, for more information on Paragliding.)

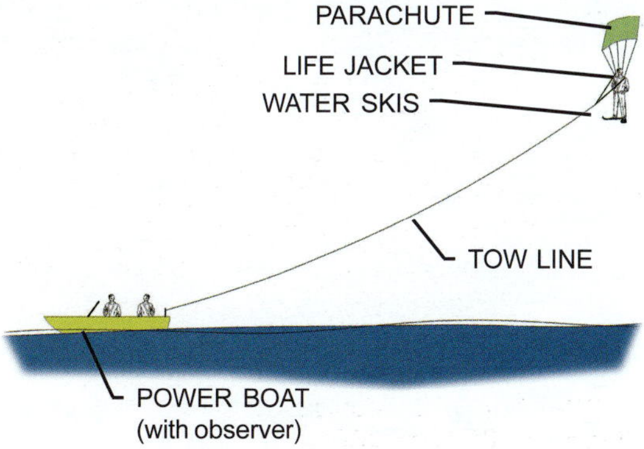

FIG. 18.10 – PARAGLIDING

WATER SKIING

No special onshore facilities are required. A sandy or grass beach can be used for a starting area, but is not needed. It is necessary, however, to have a large, low-use area for the actual water skiing – 100 acres (40 ha) or more space is needed, with 500+ acres (200+ ha) being much more desirable.

Water skiing in Northern Wisconsin
Photo Courtesy of the Fethke Family

SURFBOARDING

Yet another popular activity among the teenagers and young adults. Except for competitive events, no special facilities are required for surfboarding other than those normally provided for beach activities. This activity is not compatible with other water-oriented beach uses because of the safety problems with surfboards. An ideal setup would be to reserve the beach segments with the best waves for surfing only. Surfing is dictated by the availability of waves and may even take place during periods of inclement weather, and the normal off-season for swimming. Surfers winterize themselves with insulated wetsuits and can be found out in almost any weather in any water temperature, although most commonly during times of warm weather in warm water.

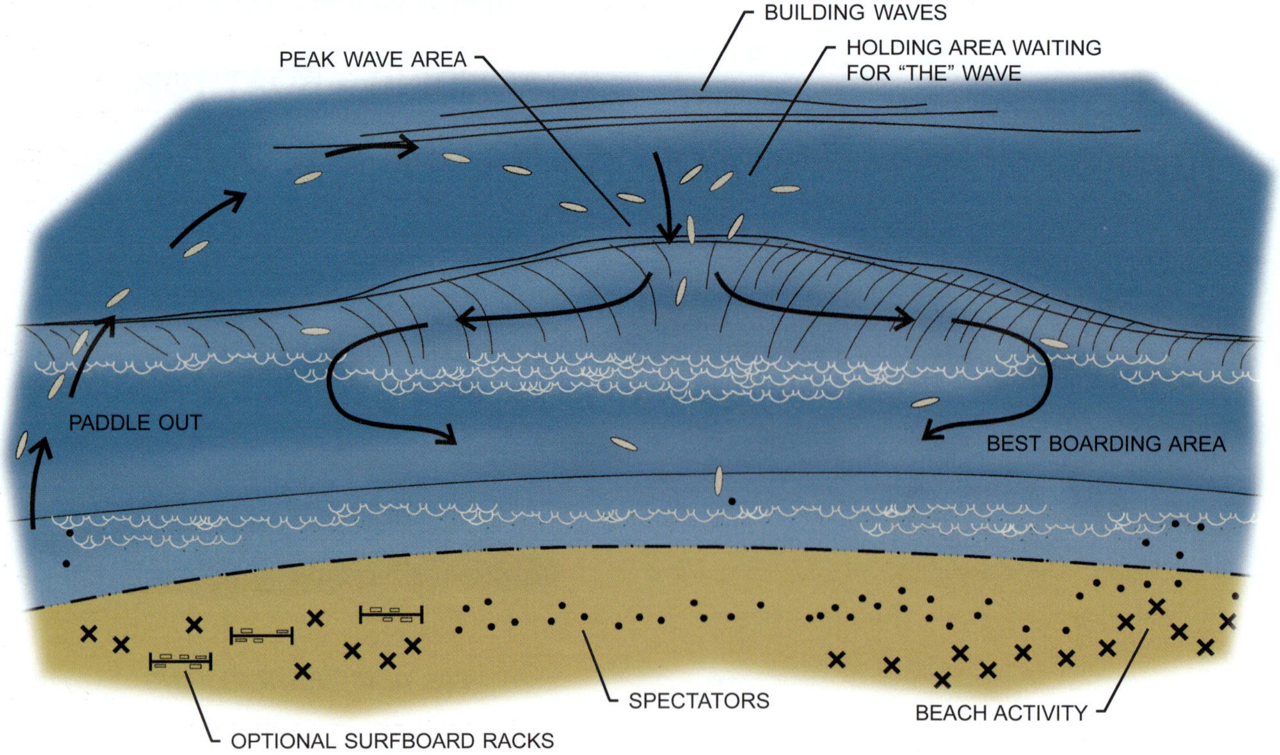

FIG. 18.11 – SURFBOARDING AREA REQUIRES MINIMUM FACILITIES

Required:

• An area along a beach with good waves. If there are no good waves, there is no surfboarding. There is no minimum wave height; however, two- to three-foot waves are necessary to provide any kind of ride and preferably larger – six to eight feet. For the very experienced, ten-foot or more waves are desired.

• Separation from other water activities.

• Close to parking
- 300 feet (90 m) or less desirable
- 500 feet (150 m) maximum.

• Sanitary facilities – see Swimming Areas.

Desirable:

• Surfboard rack(s) as needed.

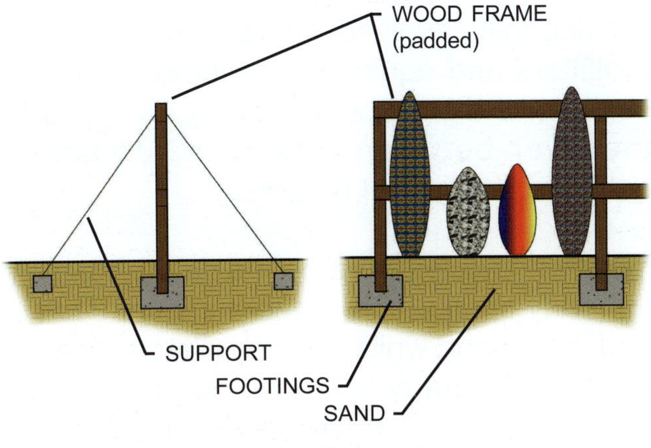

FIG. 18.12 – SURFBOARD RACKS

• Spectator viewing area – ideally from a vantage point above the beach. Normally along the shoreline in front of the surfing area.

• Boogieboard area – a place with shallow, smooth water for using the small surfboard called a boogieboard. Required 300 feet± (100± m) of shallow, very gentle sloped area of six to twelve feet (1.8 to 3.6 m) of water. Not desirable at the swimming section of the beach.

• Surfboarding is inherently challenging and dangerous. The danger can be compounded by strong rip currents during good surfing conditions. It can also become hazardous when sharks are in the area. A warning system is needed to make the surfers aware when these adverse conditions are present.

RIVER AND STREAM ACCESS

Most rivers and many streams offer tremendous boating potential for small boats. Level of boating difficulty is classified by A, B, C and 1, 2, 3, 4 and 5, with letters being relatively flat water and the numbers designated in ascending order of difficulty. The more difficult water with a Level 5 designation is very dangerous and for experts only. Use frequently starts at one area and ends many miles downstream. To be considered are:

• **Vehicle access** and parking must be available at the beginning and ending points of the trip.

• **Launching site** must be of sufficient size and be accessible to a person(s) carrying the boat. Boat ramps normally are not needed for water courses where power boating is not possible or is not permitted. (See Car Top Launching, this chapter.)

• **Water and sanitary facilities** are necessary but are frequently primitive (e.g., pump-out vault type), and may be unisex.

• **Information signs** with data on the stream, level of boating difficulty (A, B, C, etc.), including locating and giving the approximate time to take-out points, and especially information on dangerous water areas, rules and regulations, safety tips, etc.

• **Portage areas** should be identified at the put-in point with information on rough or impossible-to-boat section(s) of stream, including identifying take-out point(s), connector trail, and put-in points.

• **Stopover points** on longer stream runs for picnicking and camping.

- These areas should be located at appropriate distances, which can only be determined by running the water course.

- These areas should have, where possible, vehicular access for servicing, especially the toilets.

A stopping point on a raft trip down the Colorado River – Grand Canyon National Park, Arizona

- Where possible, primitive water and sanitary facilities should be provided.

WHITEWATER BOATING

This is an established recreation activity with many regular and frequent participants. The participants are usually young (teenagers to the 40s), tend to be in the upper income category, and often are going to college or college-educated. They are interested in the challenge, skill, comraderie, excitement and, to a lesser extent, their surroundings. Whitewater tubing has become popular, especially in urban areas. Whitewater boating is inherently dangerous and should be carefully controlled to minimize the number of injuries and deaths.

There are three basic types of whitewater boating – inflatable rafting, hardboats (kayaks and special whitewater canoes), and, recently, inflatable kayaks, referred to as rubber duckies. Because of the skills needed and the expensive equipment, whitewater boating is frequently involved with private enterprise (outfitters and equipment renters). There is sometimes a great deal of rivalry for space on the river between private hardboaters, outfitters, and rental boaters.

Most whitewater streams are at their best in the early spring (snow melt and spring rains) and, for a short while, after any heavy rainfall. Frequently many streams have good fall water due to fall draw downs of upstream reservoirs in preparation for necessary flood storage needs in the spring. Also scheduled dam releases for electrical generation and navigational purposes, etc., can make some rivers very boatable during normally dry periods, e.g., the Youghigany River in Maryland and Pennsylvania. Almost all streams have a maximum boat capacity, which,

Rubber ducky kayak on the mighty Colorado River within the Grand Canyon National Park, Arizona

if exceeded, will almost certainly cause a major reduction in user enjoyment and make it very likely that severe injury and, possibly death, will occur.

The best way to determine the river capacity is to verify, by observation, the number of boats that can go through a given point (the most likely bottleneck) during any specific time period, i.e., 50 boats per hour. In addition, certain prime whitewater locations are favored by hardboaters, and these areas can become congested, requiring on-site management. The number of boats per hour is then multiplied by the number of hours available to run the river. Four-hour run – start at 7:00 a.m., off at 11:00 a.m.; start 3:00 p.m., off at 7:00 p.m. (at dark) latest, or eight hours. Fifty boats times eight hours = four hundred boats per day.

boats/hour x # of hours
(total hours available = number of boats/day)

If the number of boats anticipated is greater than the resource capacity, scheduling and reservations will be needed. The boaters must be evenly distributed over the available time, e.g., start times similar to golf course start times complete with a starter shack.

Whitewater enthusiasts will travel great distances to participate in their activity on quality whitewater. Therefore, overnight accommodations are needed for good whitewater rivers. Boaters frequently come in groups, are noisy, and should, if possible, be separated from other overnight visitors, especially family campers.

All whitewater boating areas must be kept free of submerged logs, sharp metal from bridges, and, especially, debris from the frequently river-paralleling railroad embankments in the eastern half of the U.S.

Another area where whitewater boating takes place is in big surf areas. See Surfboarding in this chapter for guidelines.

Requirements:

- **Length**
  - A typical one-day run would be 9 to 12 miles (15 to 20 km) and longer for hardboats. Approximately on-river time of 5 to 6 hours. Most whitewater boaters are not in good enough physical condition to take longer runs.

- **Equipment and supplies**
  - Rafts and inflatable kayaks (at least two separate inflatable chambers are required) or hardboats/flotation devices.

  - Wetsuits, and more recently dry suits (a waterproof suit) in cold weather to prevent hypothermia.

  - Life jackets (an absolute necessity).

  - Safety equipment – including ropes and first aid kit (another absolute necessity)

  - Food – where possible.

• **Information** sign or display at river – includes information on the class of water, danger points, etc.

• **Desirable facilities**

- Control point at the beginning of run – reservation desk/starter's shack.

- Phone service, especially at take-out point.

- Shuttle service to/from put-in and, especially, the take-out point.

- River gauge – to determine the water level and subsequent river safety and floatability.

• **Boat put-in location**

- Private boaters
    * Equipment drop-off point.
    * Set-up space free of obstructions; 20 rafts and 20 hardboats use 2000+ square feet (200 sq. m).
    * Put-in access to water, preferably an eddy or slack water area.
    * Parking – one car/raft (4 people) if overnight facilities are nearby, otherwise one car per two people.
    * Sanitary facilities, including change house.
    * Orientation area.

- Commercial boaters
    * Preferably separate from private boaters.
    * Equipment set-up space.
    * Electricity for pumps to inflate rafts.
    * Shaded space for inflated raft storage – 5 ft. x 15 ft. (1.8 m x 4.5 m) x number of boats. If space is limited, they can be stacked four or five high.
    * Talk-up area – to instruct boaters on what to expect and how to use equipment.
    * Truck parking – one truck (stake body) per 20 or so 4-man rafts.
    * Bus drop-off, pick-up points.
    * Sanitary facilities – includes change house.
    * Telephone service.
    * Reservation desk.
    * Parking – one car/two people maximum.
    * Put-in access to an eddy or slack water area with the greater the number of rafts and the larger their size requiring greater amounts of space.

• **Spectator viewing areas** are a desirable extra if terrain and parking space permit. These can be at put-in points and at any interesting rapids.

• **Concession facilities** – food (snack) service, photo service of river trips, equipment rental and sales, souvenirs, shuttle service for private boaters. (See Private below).

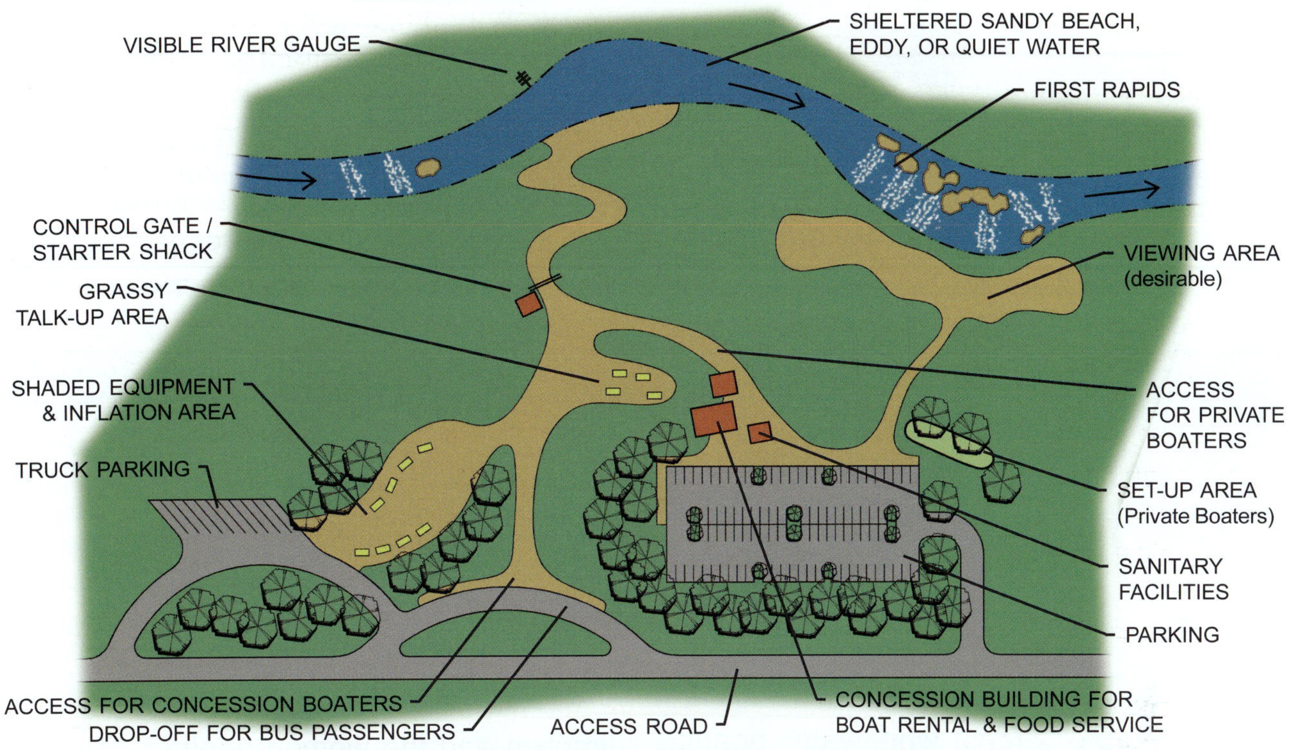

FIG. 18.13 – WHITEWATER BOATER PUT-IN AREA

- **Take-out location**

- General

  * Vehicular access to within 300± feet (100 m) of the river desirable and closer, if possible, with no steep gradients from river.
  * At the first accessible slack water at end of best whitewater – limit stretches of flat (slow moving) water between end of the whitewater and take-out point. One mile (1.6 km) – maximum desirable; less is better.
  * Sanitary facilities (vault and unisex toilets acceptable).
  * Trash receptacles (dumpsters).
  * Changing facilities and warming hut and/or hot showers are desirable, especially when cold water and cold weather conditions are encountered during the use season.

- Private

  * Parking for shuttle cars – one (4 people) in rafts and one (2 people in hardboats).
  * Equipment pick-up within 300 feet (100 m) of river and closer, if possible. No steep gradients, if possible, from river to pick-up point(s). Boaters are usually tired and the equipment is heavy.
  * Bus pick-up (shuttle service back to starting point) is desirable and requires space (trailer or special bus design) for rafts and hardboats.

- Commercial

  * Truck parking – one truck per 25 to 30 4-man rafts.
  * Bus pick-up (shuttle service back to starting point).

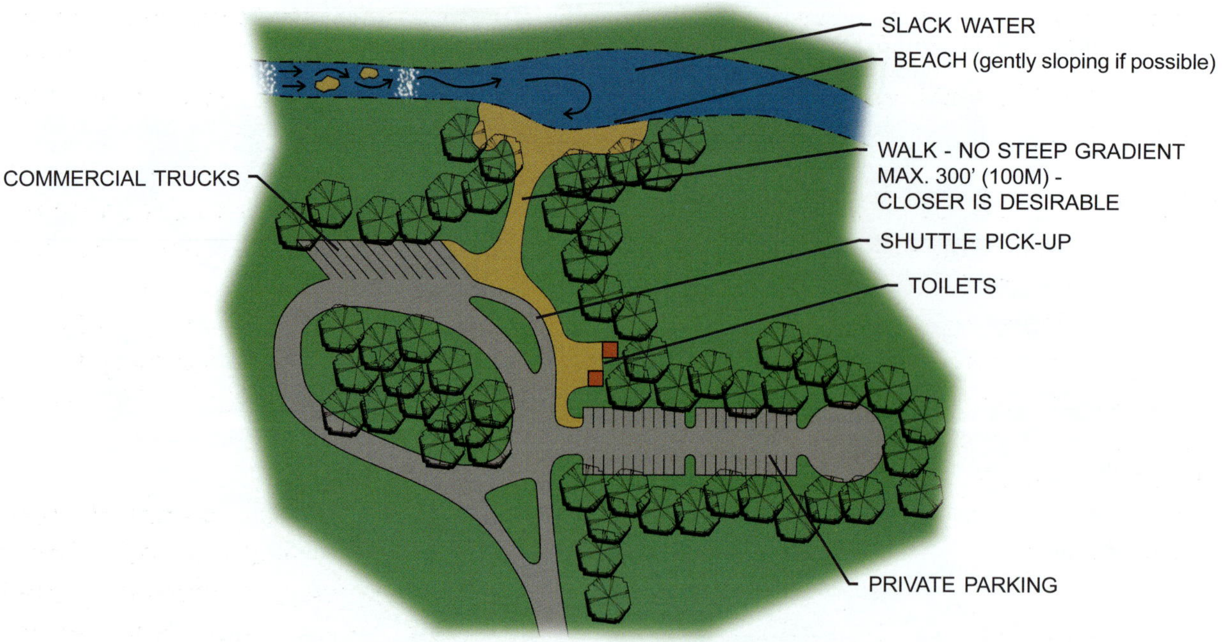

FIG. 18.14 – WHITEWATER BOATER TAKE-OUT

• **Stops** - most whitewater boating includes stops along the way. Areas suitable for the following activities should be identified, especially for group users:

- Eating – locate within the normal high water area and preferably on ledges or rocky ground to minimize boater impact.

- Swimming – in pools or chutes. In heavy-use streams it cannot be in constricted spaces where the swimming would interfere with boating.

- Sightseeing – side trips to special views, falls, vegetation, geologic features, historic, archaeological sites, etc.

If service access is easily available, vault toilets should be provided at popular stopping spots. If not possible, portable toilets can be carried in by the rafters. Normally, the boaters just go behind the nearest tree or bush and, if it is a large group, men go one direction and the women another. This can and does cause pollution problems on heavily used streams and rivers.

Access to whitewater rivers is frequently difficult and expensive. Innovative approaches must be considered for both ingress and egress. Parking may be especially difficult near the river, and shuttle buses to the river may be necessary from satellite parking areas.

WATER OR BLUE TRAILS

Non-powered boating – especially canoeing and, recently, tubing, rafts and kayaks – is continuing its rapid increase in popularity. As the numbers of users increase, more pressure is put on known boating areas. Water trails can be easily and economically provided for diversification of activity.

Water trails must be identified, accessible (ingress and egress available to the public) and boatable. They can be established on streams, rivers, lakes, and lagoons, and may be seasonal in nature. (See Chapter 7, Interpretive Facilities, for additional information on how to interpret the trail and its surroundings.)

Many, if not most water trails will, at least, partially abut private lands. Although most waterways in the U.S. that can be boated are legally available for "navigational" use, this privilege does not normally extend to the shoreline. In other words, stay off the shore in private ownership areas unless owner approval is secured.

Requirements:

- **Adequate water depth** – one foot (.3 m) is necessary, preferably year-round to float a canoe/2 people and gear or, where appropriate, small powered boats.

- **Length per day**
  - Fast-moving water – 13 to 18 miles (20 to 30 km);
  - Medium-moving water – 11 to 12 miles (17 to 19 km);
  - Slow-moving water – 8 to 10 miles (13 to 16 km);
  - Flat water - 4± miles (6± km).

Guided trail through the mangrove swamps – Caribbean Islands

- **Limit conflicts** between boating and fishing, especially on heavy fishing days – e.g., opening day of trout season.

- **Safe passage** – This includes removal of snags, dangerous logs, and sharp metal from bridges and railroad embankments, etc.
  - Clearing height – 6 feet (2 m) above normal boating water height
  - Clearing width – 12 feet (4 m) desirable.

Use discretion on the amount of clearing – clear only the space needed. Too much vegetative removal can cause degradation of the natural environment and reduce the aesthetic experience.

FIG. 18.15 – CANOE TRAIL CLEARANCE

- **Portage** – This is necessary where water is too dangerous, shallow or obstructions prohibit safe passage. Space must be provided – preferably on public land – for taking the boat out of the water, using a trail around the obstacle and putting the boat safely back in the water.

• **Put-in area**
- Parking – 1 car/boat

- Access needs to be at a slow water area.

- Sanitary facilities – desirable; vault and unisex toilets are acceptable.

• **Stopping places** – rest areas, eating places, overnight camping (see boat-in camp sites), and swim areas, in addition to the previously mentioned interpretive stops, are all desirable features that should be considered for water trails, depending on the length of the trip and the shoreline conditions. If special stopping places are provided (or developed by the boaters on their own), vault and unisex toilets may be desirable, but only if access for service vehicles is easily possible. Rubbish should be brought out by boaters!

• **Take-out** – places should be easily recognized – e.g., a bridge, dam, etc.

- Have easy access from water.

- Parking – 1 car/2 boats is normally sufficient. Boaters usually work on a shuttle basis with one car left at take-out point before the trip and the remainder of the cars at the put-in point.

- Sanitary facilities – hot showers desirable, but not necessary. Try to locate out of flood plain or make them floodable.

- Rubbish containers.

- Shelter/fireplace – desirable in cool or cold areas for use by those waiting to be picked up by shuttle.

• **Trail information**
- Signs or information at put-in point describing the water trail are necessary. These signs should warn people of any potential danger areas.

- Warning markers of signs must be placed at dangerous points so that boaters may get to shore and scout and/or portage the danger.

- Identify take-out point(s).

WATER USE DENSITY

BOATING

• **High-speed boating** – water skiing; one boat per three acres (1.2 ha) – desirable; one boat per two acres (.8 ha) – maximum density; 100 acres (40 ha) or greater is minimum recommended size for water skiing.

• **Low-speed boating** – ten horse-power or less; one boat per acre (2.5 ha) – maximum density.

Punting at Cambridge University – England

Sculling competition in the calm estuary waters of Southern California

- **Non-powered boating** – four boats per acre (10/ha) – maximum density; two boats per acre (5/ha) – desirable.

- **Special uses** – amount of space is determined by the type of activity, e.g. punting on a river – several boats per acres; or sculling – several acres of calm water per boat, etc.

FISHING

One boat per acre (2.5/ha) – optimum density. One boat per two acres (1.2/ha) when trolling. From four to six boats per acre (10 to 15/ha) for anchored fishing.

SAILBOATING

Four boats per acre (10/ha) – maximum; one boat per acre (2.5/ha) – desirable.

Chapter 19

MARINAS

Most water bodies have need for boat storage. These facilities may vary in size and the types of service they provide, from several boats to a thousand or more. A marina may include any or all of the following: in-water boat storage, on-land boat storage, under-cover boat storage (both in-water and/ or on-land), boat ramps, fuel sales, boat rental, boat sales, boat equipment sales, comfort station, shower facilities, clubhouse, restaurant, snack bar, boat repair, marina office, harbormaster, transient boat docks, fish cleaning area(s), ice and bait sales, picnicking, overnight housing, marina maintenance building, and Coast Guard, etc.

The location and design of a marina is dependent on the size and type of water body to be served, water depth, wind direction, access (land and water), user need, and amount of usable land on shore for the necessary support facilities. Boating facilities are expensive to build and operate, and almost always charge user fees. Marinas frequently are built with private capital, and those built with public funds are often operated by private enterprise. Because of the high costs involved, a thorough market analysis should be conducted prior to beginning any development.

Marina on the coast of Maine – by Stanley Fogg

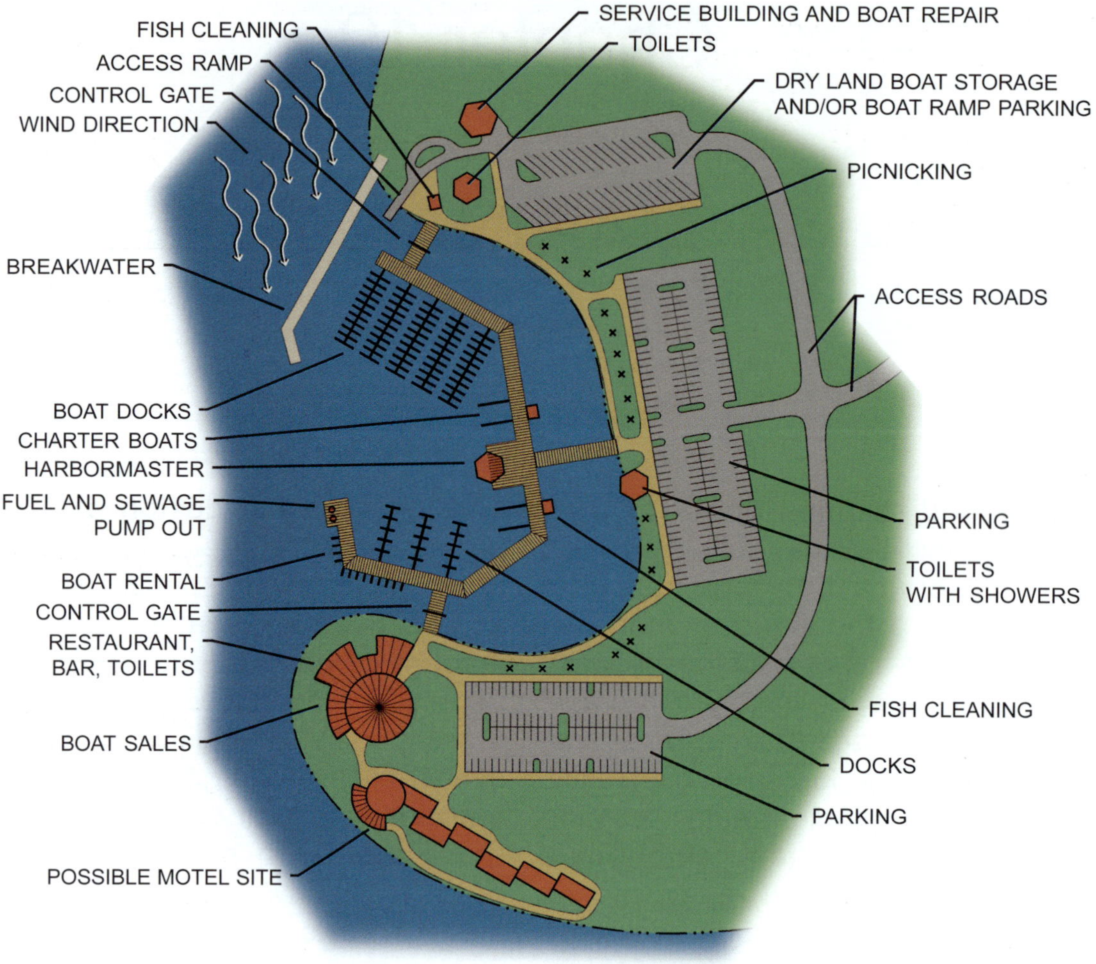

FIG. 19.1 – MARINA COMPLEX

Marina – Southern California coastal estuary

GENERAL

SIZE

Two hundred and fifty slips are usually sufficient for a profitable operation where powerboats are involved; one hundred± slips for small boat docking is a marginally profitable operation.

FOOD SERVICE

This activity should be considered in larger marinas. A study of surrounding eating facilities is necessary before deciding what level of service, if any, is to be provided. Types of service that could be provided vary from vending machines, fast-food service, snack bar, to sit-down short order or full-service restaurant. In addition, cocktail lounges and bars are sometimes provided. An unknown amount of additional personal vehicle parking will be required to serve non-marina patrons and staff.

ON-SHORE BOAT STORAGE

This type of facility should be considered where water fluctuations or other adverse conditions prohibit the economical construction of floating docks. In addition, many sailboaters, especially if they participate in racing, prefer to store their boats on shore due to algae build-up on their boats. On-shore boat storage can be multistory buildings or can be designed the same as car and trailer parking. It must have easy access to boat launching ramp(s). Separate these areas, if possible, from day-use boat launch vehicle/trailer parking. Provision of security is a necessity for on-shore boat storage due to the expense of the boats. As a minimum, fencing and security lighting are needed.

LONG-TERM USERS

Owners of larger boats frequently desire to stay on board on weekends and may even make use of the boat as a second home during the recreation season. If this type of use is permitted, additional on-shore support facilities will be required. Showers in the comfort station, water and electrical hookups, and all-night ingress and egress to the marina are minimal considerations.

BOAT DOCKS

Boat docks are basically in-water boat parking lots. They are approximately equivalent in arrangement and circulation

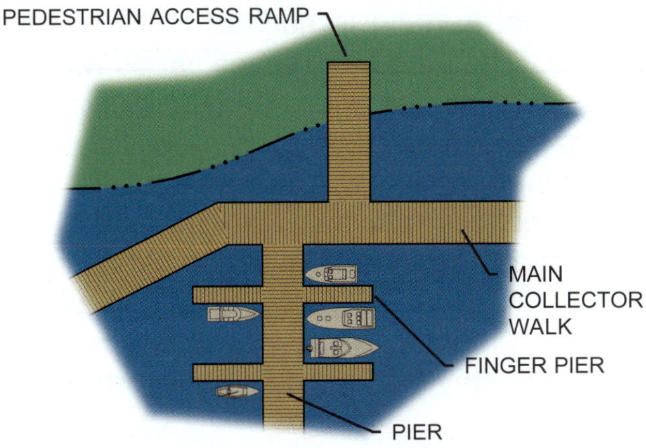

FIG. 19.2 – BOAT DOCK TERMINOLOGY

requirements to typical car parking lots. The only difference for all except the smallest boats is that more space is needed.

Sufficient anchorage to secure the dock in place is necessary to resist the various forces acting on the docks **and boats** when all berths are filled. Wind, current, wave, ice (vertical and horizontal) action, and water level fluctuations must be included in the calculations. It is necessary to determine carefully the type of boats to be berthed in the marina before any calculations are made, e.g., houseboats have a great deal more wind resistance than small motorboats.

PARKING

Most marinas have less than fifty percent and generally less than forty percent of the boats in use at any given time. Many boating parties arrive in more than one car. Therefore, marina parking capacity is determined by multiplying 1 ½ cars (the number of cars per boat in use) x 40 percent of the marina capacity (the maximum number of boats likely to be in use at any given time), or 0.6 cars per boat berth.

Additional parking is needed to store boat trailers. The amount of space varies with the type of marina operation. Boat trailers require the same amount of space as car parking. Additional parking will be required if a boat rental service is provided at the rate of at least one space per rental boat and, quite possibly, 1.2 or more spaces. Also, parking, in excess of that for marina users, will be necessary for patrons of any food service that is provided.

SANITATION

ON-SHORE COMFORT STATIONS

There are no standards available. Suggest one fixture unit per sex for 150± people. Additional fixture units will be needed if eating facilities are provided (refer to local health standards for food service facilities).

SHOWERS (if needed)

Determine the number of people normally staying overnight and then use the chart in Chapter 14, Overnight Use.

BOAT SANITARY DUMP STATION

Many states require these facilities. Check state and local standards to see if they are required. Suggest at least one per marina with provision for expansion if use warrants. A dockside sanitary dumping station should be provided wherever large-size boats with sanitary holding tanks are permitted. Locate at service dock or fuel dock.

Water will be needed to rinse out holding sewage tanks and portable toilets.

BOAT FUEL

Access for fuel for boats (both docked and those using the launching ramp) must be easy, and near a manned marina facility for joint use of marina staff. Fuel storage tank must be underground and accessible to delivery trucks. Installation of fuel tanks frequently requires special permits.

RENTALS AND SUPPLIES

Most marinas provide boat rentals and sale of fishing gear and/or supplies and miscellaneous minor boating equipment sale and rentals. These services should be located in the vicinity of the major pedestrian traffic pattern. Additional parking will be required for boat rental customers. (See Parking in this chapter.)

SERVICE AREA AND LAUNCHING

A boat repair and service facility is needed for each 300 or more boats. The repair staff could likely also handle fuel and other boater requirements.

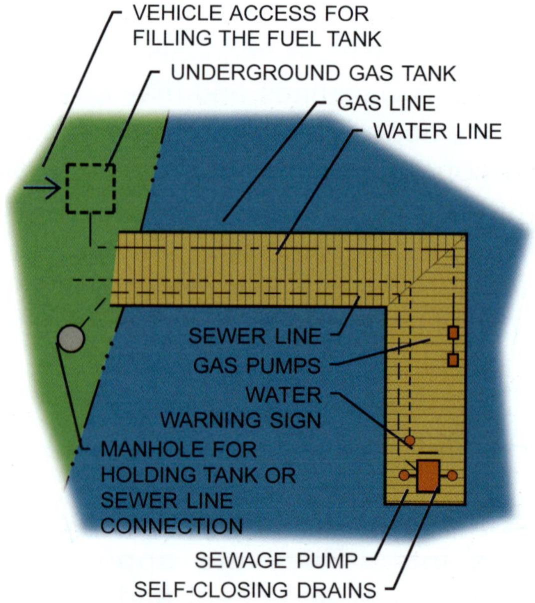

FIG. 19.3 – SERVICE DOCK

Large marina maintenance area – Southern California

Required:

- Service ramp for use only by marina patrons. (See Chapter 18, Boating, for ramp details.)
- Locate away from the main pedestrian circulation.
- Must have easy vehicular access.
- Visually screened from other boating activities.
- Utilities – water and electricity.
- Maintenance building.

ADDITIONAL FACILITIES TO BE CONSIDERED

BOAT CHARTERS

The rental of a boat with crew and usually all the necessary equipment to carry out the rental activity. The boats are usually larger than most private boats and are chartered most days of the use season, sometimes for more than one trip per day.

GENERAL

Required:

- Boat dock with easy access to shore and shoreside parking.
- Sales area – usually a small booth of 3 feet to 4 feet (90 cm to 120 cm) square.
- Water and electrical hookups plus optional access to sewage pump/left station.
- Access to sewage pump station for toilet pump-out.
- Phone service needed to sales area.

Desired:

- Phone connection to boat when tied up.
- Small, shaded sitting space for early arrivals for trip.
- Place to weigh fish.
- Fish cleaning facilities.

Charter boats – Naples, Florida

Charter boat displaying day's catch – Naples, Florida

TYPES OF CHARTER BOATING

Sailing

• Deep water needed – over 5 feet (1.5 m) usually needed at low water levels.

Evening sunset sailboat cruise – Key West, Florida

Sightseeing

• Shaded waiting space for next group.

Fishing

• Two types: (1) party boat – normally 10 or more people and frequently 20 or 30 or more – usually for bottom fishing and for 8 hours or less; (2) charter – small groups of 2 to 6 or slightly more – usually to go sport fishing. Desirable for the charter area to have a large scale for weighing large fish.

• Access to live bait and other supplies is needed.

• Fish cleaning is usually done on the boat by the crew on the way to the boat dock, therefore, fish cleaning facilities frequently are not needed.

Diving

• Same as fishing, only normally a fish scale is not needed.

Shelling

• Same as fishing, only a fish scale is not needed.

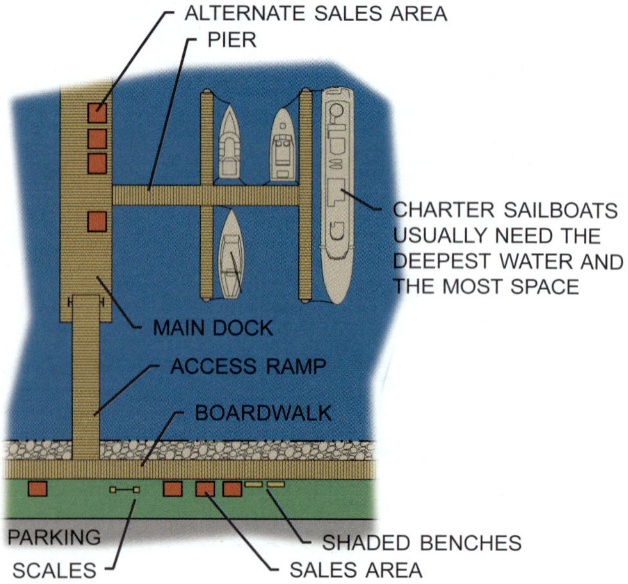

FIG. 19.4 – CHARTER/PARTY BOAT FACILITIES

MOTELS

Overnight accommodations may be feasible and desirable. Standard on-shore motel could be sufficient, but it should be designed and located so that maximum connection to the marina is maintained, or with boat docks (especially in coastal waters).

SALES

Boat and boating equipment sales are desirable, especially at larger marinas.

COVERED MOORING SPACE

Both on shore and in water are possible and could be economically feasible.

Covered mooring (boathouses) – Naples, Florida

UTILITIES

- Marina de-icing equipment in areas with winter ice problems is needed to prevent damage to permanent dock facilities and to any boats left in the water over the winter. An alternative is to have removable floating dock facilities, which are stored on shore during the winter. This moving of docks in and out of water can cause damage quickly.

- Water, electricity and, possibly, sewage connections should be considered on docks with large boats; especially where overnight use is permitted. Additional fees would be charged. These services must be considered in the early study stages, since the facilities can be extremely costly to provide.

- Underground and under dock electric and telephone services are desirable in all marinas.

- A beacon light is desirable at marinas located in larger bodies of water – 1000+ acres (400+ ha) to assist boaters in finding their dock facility at night.

FISHING CLEANING FACILITIES

Where productive fishing is anticipated, it is desirable to install fish cleaning facilities near the boat docking and/or launching areas. These facilities are essential to control odor, insects, and pollution, which would result from indiscriminate cleaning of fish and the disposal of waste material into reservoirs, streams, and along shorelines. Some jurisdictions do not allow fish cleaning at docks. The following elements should be considered in planning for fish cleaning facilities.

- Preferably, fish cleaning facilities should be located in a screened enclosure, although normally it is not done.

- Lighting should be provided whenever night use is anticipated.

Fish cleaning facility at the Naples Pier – Naples, FL

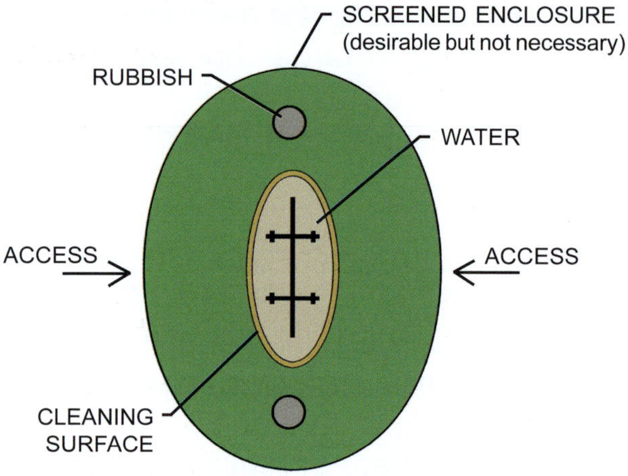

FIG. 19.5 – FISH CLEANING FACILITY

• Water under pressure should be provided to facilitate the cleaning of fish and for general cleanup.

• Disposal of waste: rubbish containers; garbage disposal in salt water areas could dispose directly into the water body if health rules permit, or have non-metallic containers.

BOAT WASHING

Where water quality causes the boats to become dirty, it is necessary to provide a place near the launching ramp or in the mooring service area to wash the boats. It must be located so that it does not impede launching or traffic flow.

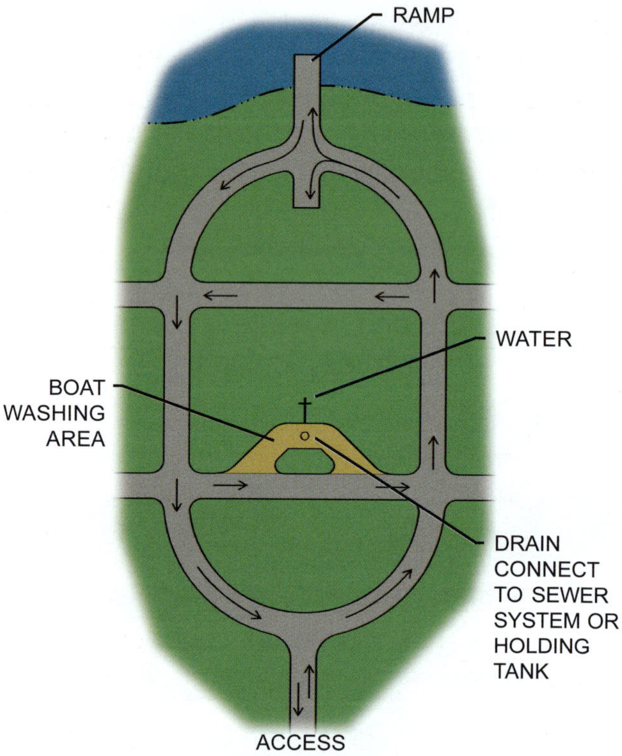

FIG. 19.6 – BOAT WASHING LOCATION

MOORING RAIL

A mooring rail should be provided for limited (up to 25) overnight storage of small boats where desirable. This is particularly needed at small lakes and urban coastal beach areas. Day mooring near picnicking/swimming areas should also be considered. Mooring rails in saltwater areas must be made from non-corrosive material. They may be made from metal on inland lakes and water bodies, but it is not recommended. All rails must be sufficiently sturdy to prevent theft of locked boats and the blowing away of boats in storms.

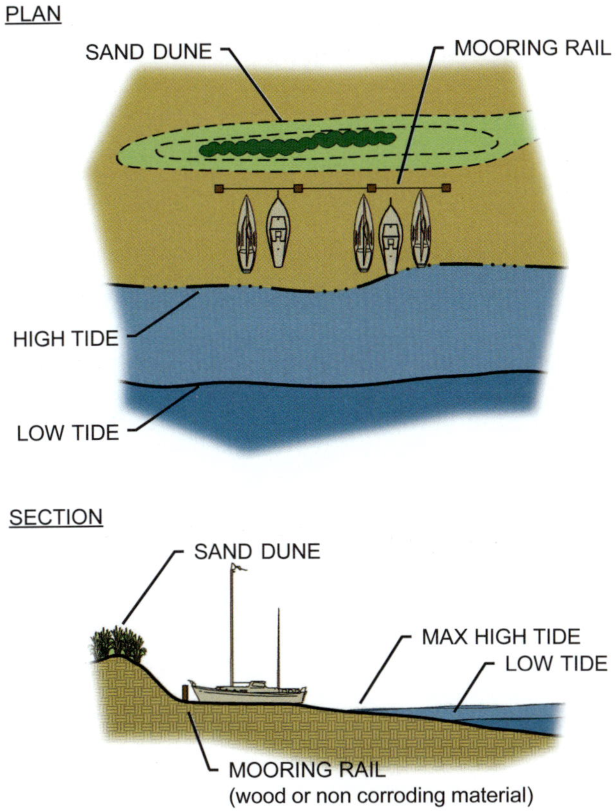

FIG. 19.7 – MOORING RAIL COASTAL BEACHES

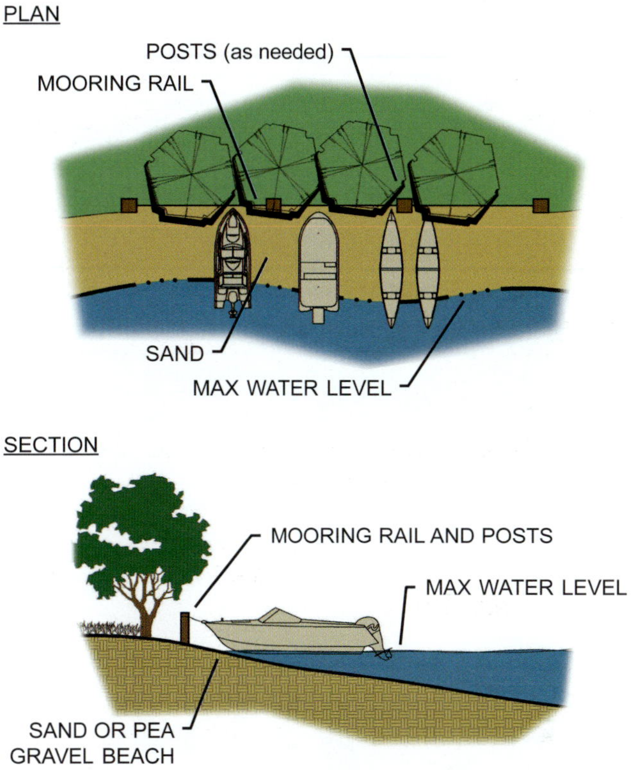

FIG. 19.8 – MOORING RAIL STABLE WATER AREAS

Boat mooring rail
– French Creek State Park, Pennsylvania

Chapter 20

GOLF COURSES

Many larger recreation, leisure facilities, and planned housing developments have or have planned adequate space suitable for golf courses. Golf courses and their support facilities take up a lot of space and are expensive to build and maintain. Before deciding to include a golf course in any project, however, a survey of the surrounding region should be undertaken to determine the need. The study should provide information on the number and type of courses and the amount of use each gets in the service area. Existing and proposed facilities should be included in the study. Information on the extent and success of the kinds of auxiliary features offered at each course to be included in the proposed course, i.e., tennis, driving range, swimming, practice putting greens, dining, bar(s), etc., should be obtained to the extent data is available or can be observed.

USER CHARACTERISTICS

Golf is a game of power, skill, and judgment – power to hit the ball as far as possible, skill to hit it where it is needed to go, and judgment to decide where to hit the ball and what club to use to accomplish it. Of equal importance for most golfers, it is a place to enjoy the golf experience and to meet and socialize.

It takes approximately four hours or more for four players to play eighteen holes of golf and about two plus hours to play nine holes. The time is not materially affected by the use of golf carts. The time needed per hole is approximately twelve minutes. A maximum of two foursomes can be on each hole at one time. During peak use periods, starting times for foursomes must be a minimum of six minutes apart. This means a maximum of ten foursomes per hour or forty people per hour can be accommodated. The total number of golf rounds that can be accommodated by an eighteen-hole golf course then is forty times the number of daylight hours minus four hours (the time to play a round). Therefore, during the winter in southern states (the prime season in the south), approximately 240 people maximum (10 hours sun light minus 4 hours of playing time or a maximum of 6 hours x 40 people per hour), while in northern states, during the summer (the prime season in the north), over 360 (13+ hours minus 4 hours x 40) could be accommodated. Normally, private clubs and resorts schedule only 200 rounds per day, while public courses will schedule up to 250 to 300 rounds.

According to the National Golf Foundation, 21.7 million people played golf in 1987. A total of 37.9 million people played golf in 2003 – up 16.2 million or 74 percent from 1987, (35) (20) or about 4.3 percent per year. The rounds of golf in 2003 were approximately 5 percent greater than in 2003. Core golfers (those who play at least eight rounds per year) are 13.2 million – up 5 percent from 12.6 million in 2002.

Gulf Harbor golf course – Lee County, Florida

The number of rounds of golf played per year has increased, principally by the addition of juniors and women. (35)

Approximately 90 percent of golfers play all eighteen holes. (20) It should be noted that people with disabilities play golf and many more say that they would like to play. (36)

Figuring only a 4 to 4.5 percent increase in rounds per year, it would require in the hundreds of new eighteen-hole courses per year to satisfy the continuing growth of golfing needs, with each course satisfying approximately 17,000 rounds (75 capacity days) per year. If the number of capacity days was increased to 100 or even 150 days per year, a minimum in the U.S. of over 100+ courses per year would be needed.

The demographics of golfers are as follows. (20)

By household income:

3.8% of golfers	less than $10,000
12.9%	$10,000 to $19,999
17.7%	$20,000 to $29,000
20.5%	$39,000 to $39,000
44.9%	$40,000+ per year.

By age:

	Age	
4.0%	5 to 14	11% of golfers and they play
7.2%	15 to 19	6.7% of rounds played
27.3%	20 to 29	73% of golfers and they play
22.2%	30 to 39	62% of rounds played
14.1%	40 to 49	
10.2%	50 to 59	15% of golfers and they play
5.4%	60 to 65	31% of rounds played
9.6%	over 65	

By sex:

77.4% men
22.6% women - however, 41% of the new golfers in 1987 were women, which could, if the trend continues, have a major long-term impact of increasing the percentage of women playing golf.

Another way of looking at who the users are is to determine the frequency of play.

20.2% of the golfers play only 1 to 2 rounds per year and account for 1.5% of the rounds played;

29.5% of the golfers play 3 to 7 rounds per year and account for 6.5% of the rounds played;

27.8% of the golfers play 8 to 24 rounds per year and account for 19% of the rounds played;

22.5% of the golfers play over 25 rounds per year and account for almost three-quarters (75%) of the rounds played.

From this information, it is apparent that a very few golfers play most of the golf. These golfers are likely to be mostly mature men and, lately women, who are well off financially. [20]

By law, golf courses must also be accessible to those with limitations. All courses must be designed with ADA accessibility guidelines in mind. In addition to golf, golfers like to eat, drink, and socialize while at the course. Golfing for exercise is not a primary goal of most golfers.

CHIP AND PUTT GOLF COURSE

There are usually eighteen holes at this type of course. The length of holes is from 25 to 120 yards (23 to 100 m) long; all holes are par three. Tees usually include rubber mats with rubber tees in place for the hitting area. The greens are usually 2000 to 3000 square feet (185 to 280 sq. m) in size. Sand traps are used very sparingly because of the shot difficulty involved with sand. These golf courses are usually lighted for night play. Only a limited number of natural and manmade hazards are included in this type of course because of the slow play that results. Irrigation systems, although expensive, should be included, especially for the greens, if they are sod instead of the much more common artificial grasses.

SPACE REQUIREMENTS

	Minimum Acres (Hectares)	Desirable Acres (Hectares)	No. of People Per Day **
Driving Range	10 (4)		
Chip and Putt Course	20 (8)	30 (12)	
Executive Course	50 (20)	70 (30)	250 to 300
9-Hole Regulation Course	50 (20)	85 (35)	200 to 250
18-Hole RegulationCourse	120* (50)	170* (70)	200 to 300

* The amount of land required for a golf course is being reduced wherever possible because of the high cost of land acquisition.
** Weather permitting.

FIG. 20.1

EXECUTIVE GOLF COURSE

The course is usually similar to the regulation golf course, except as many as eight to ten par three holes are included and one par five, making the par for the course about 60 to 62. This type of golf course provides late afternoon and evening rounds of golf of about 2 ½ to 3 hours duration. It requires the same demands and talents necessary to score well as on a regulation golf course, but the required acres of land needed are much less. All in all, the lesser time to play and the resultant lower scores because of the reduced par for eighteen holes interests the time-pressed portion of the golfing community. Most executive golf courses are eighteen holes and require the same thought and planning effort as a regulation eighteen-hole golf course. Depending on the demand for evening play, night lighting should be considered.

REGULATION GOLF COURSE

This course provides the ultimate challenge and variety for the golfer. A majority of the regulation golf courses built today are at least eighteen holes. Each nine should be from 3200 yards to a maximum of 3600 yards (2900 to 3300 m), depending on the intention planned for the golf course – championship or regular length. Usually total yardage for championship courses is about 7000 to 7200 yards (6400 to 6600 m); regular courses are from 6400 to 6900 yards (5800 to 6300 m).

High costs of maintenance and availability of water for irrigation are causing some courses to reconsider the amount of the course to be maintained in grass and plantings outside the fairway. Often the roughs are allowed to become "rough," and native non-maintenance plants either planted or allowed to grow naturally. Many courses are also considering reducing the fairway width, where possible, and making the course more like the early target-type European courses.

SITE SELECTION

In the selection of a golf course site, the land should ideally be gently rolling with a variety of tree stands and open areas. Land that is too hilly is tiring for the golfer, and it is difficult to maintain in turf. Maintenance vehicle and golf cart accessibility to and through the site should be easy. Major thoroughfares adjacent to the golf course provide the opportunity for good advertising. The soil condition of the site is important because good soil leads to good turf on the fairway, which will increase the popularity of the golf course. A soil analysis, therefore, is a necessity to first determine the need for modifying the soil for tee and green construction and even fairways and, secondly, how to modify the soil to support the required plants, especially grass growth. Electric power supply, water availability for irrigating, and sewage disposal are all necessary for a golf course and its accompanying amenities. Water availability for irrigation is especially critical, and lack of water can make it difficult to grow and maintain the grass and, quite possibly, make it undesirable to build a course at all. Any site selection must, therefore, take these factors into careful consideration.

A continuing trend of golf course development is combining of golf courses with various types of housing developments, such as single-family, condominiums, and resorts. These courses are normally operated as private courses with limited membership of 350± people. All golf courses need to be carefully studied in relationship to the environmental affects of the course construction. A great course might be possible on a given property, but the required environmental considerations may preclude its development or make its cost prohibitive.

CLUBHOUSE COMPLEX

The location of the entrance drive, clubhouse, and/or pro shop/locker room, practice area, practice putting green, first tee, and auxiliary features are important items to consider. The clubhouse is generally located away from the highway but convenient to it, with adequate site features to permit the development of a functional complex. It is desirable to locate the first tee, ninth green, tenth tee, and eighteenth green near the clubhouse/pro shop and parking lot area. Lighting is necessary for parking lots, access roads and walkways, and desirable for "highlighting" special features. For those courses within a planned community, the clubhouse becomes the social center for the development.

TENNIS

Two lighted courts are basically the minimum number, with four courts being more desirable. Courts with some limited shaded viewing space located near a parking lot are desirable. In addition, drinking water, benches, umpire's chair, and other standard amenities normally associated with tennis courts are needed. Lighting is needed, but not required and may be by coin-activated metering. This facility is normally used by non golfers and is frequently a money loser. In private clubs, however, it is a necessary extra for the convenience of non golfing family and guests, and for prestige purposes.

SWIMMING POOLS

Pools are frequently provided for the interests of the golfer's family. Size is dependent on the intended use. They are best located so the pool can be used by non golfers without interfering with golfing activities. Night lighting is very desirable, especially in southern tourist areas. Separate shower and change rooms from golfing may be desirable.

BAR/SNACK BAR

Minimum food service must be provided. View of the golf course is a necessity. This should be a convenient place to sit and visit, and is a major revenue generator.

DINING

These facilities are desirable and generally needed in major complexes. They can be rented out and can generate considerable income. Access to parking and a view of the course is a necessity. Golf clubhouses are sometimes utilized for receptions, parties, and meetings. A decision must be made prior to design on whether to provide for these activities.

PARKING

Space for a minimum of 100 cars is needed for private golf clubs, and 120 cars for public facilities; desirable - 120+ for private and 140+ for public. Valet parking is a very good idea for upscale courses.

GOLF CARTS

Golf cart on the golf cart pathway at a tee on Quail Run Golf Course – Naples, Florida

Most golf courses provide golf cart rental. This is a **major** revenue generator. Storage facilities, including battery recharging capacity, are needed. The clubhouse must have a golf cart staging area. For courses with their mandatory use, space is needed for approximately 80 to 90 carts. In addition, separate roofed and screened space must be provided for their upkeep – generally in the golf course service yard. Paved walks and drives must be provided at the tees and greens. For courses with heavy use of golf carts, walks and drives should be considered for the entire length of the course.

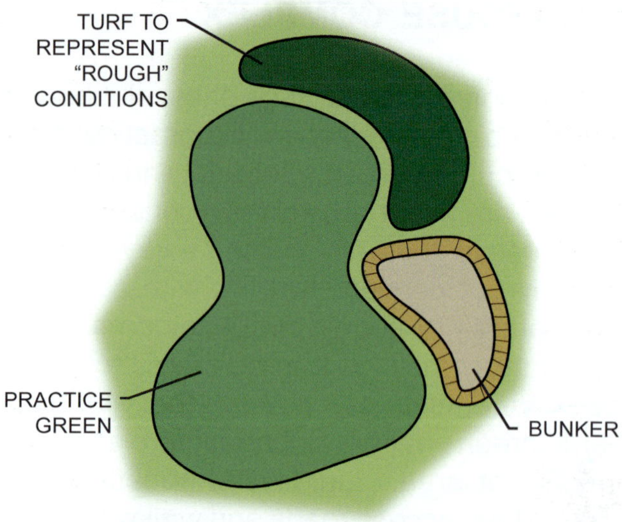

FIG. 20.2 – PRACTICE GREEN

PRACTICE GREENS

These greens are a basic requirement for any good course. They are used for putting practice, especially while waiting to start your round. Several holes (cups) are provided. The greens should be a minimum 10,000 square feet (930 sq. m); 12,000 to 15,000 square feet (1100 to 1400 sq. m) is desirable.

2-Hole practice green on a lighted, private course – Naples, Florida. Photo by Wayne Hook

TYPICAL CHIP AND PITCH PRACTICE GREEN

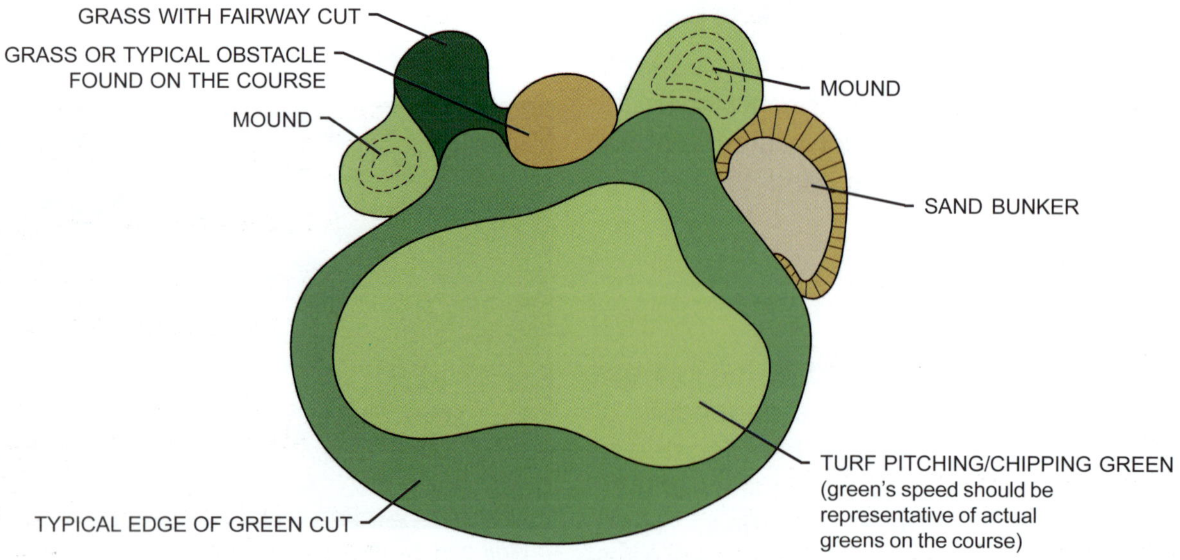

FIG. 20.3 – CHIP AND PITCH GREEN

PRO SHOP / STARTERS SHACK

This is the traffic control point for the golf course. All golf rounds start at the pro shop (normally for private course) or starters shack (sometimes used in public courses). It is necessary to have participant vehicular access to this point to drop off the golf clubs.

Golf bag drop-off
– Naples, Florida. Photo by Wayne Hook

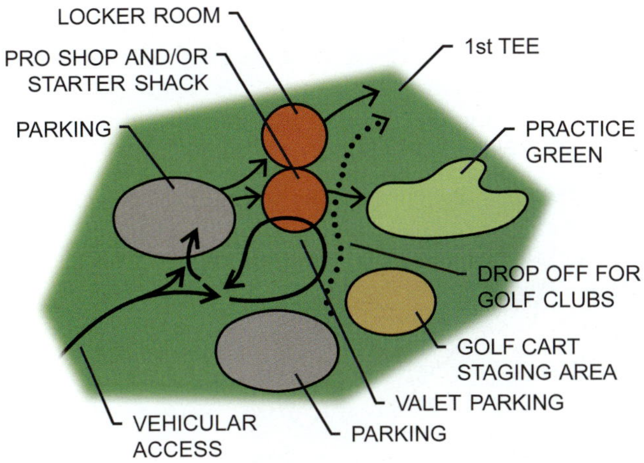

FIG. 20.4 – LOCATION OF PRO SHOP, STARTER SHACK/LOCKER ROOM

A smooth, easy flow of pedestrian traffic should be the result of a well laid out start to the golf round. The pro shop will, in addition to providing a convenient starting place, provide the normal golf supplies, equipment and repair service, and, of course, golf lessons.

PRACTICE FACILITY

A multipurpose practice and teaching area, including a driving range, practice green, and a chip and pitch area is a desirable "extra" feature. Space permitting, it can be a valuable addition to any golf course. The minimum space needed is 350 feet x 1000 feet (100 m x 305± m), and lighted. The layout should be on a north/south axis if at all possible.

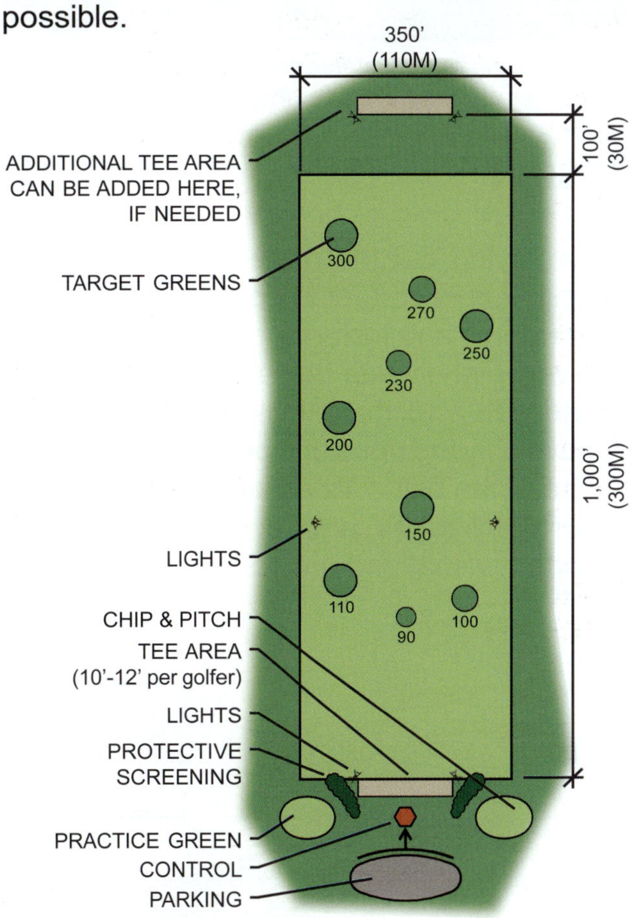

FIG. 20.5 – DRIVING RANGE

• A portion of the practice green should be available for private instruction

• Greens and fairways should be representative of the golf course.

• A water driving range can be substituted for the grass range. The targets would then need to be floating.

Golf driving range located on and over large water feature – Naples, Florida. Photo by Wayne Hook

DESIGN

When laying out the route plan for the golf course, it is important to consider the natural golf features and hazards, but they should not be overweighed with respect to the character of the soil and the site location. Plan to remove only the trees and other obstacles that will be in the way. Trees are one of the best natural hazards and are an extremely important visual and natural resource.

Most golfers are right-handed, and up to 90 percent slice the ball to the right. This factor must be taken into consideration in design, especially when the course is surrounded by housing and/or other developments. Proper hole design, screening (plants or manmade features) and locations of hazards can minimize this problem.

If at all possible, no golf hole should be laid out in an east-to-west direction because of the evening sun. If unavoidable, plan the first several golf holes in that direction. The northwest direction is extremely bad in northern states.

The distance between the green and the next tee should not exceed 75 yards (70 m); the ideal distance is approximately 30 yards (27 m) and should be visually screened. The first hole should be relatively easy, a par 4 and about 360 to 380 yards (330 to 350 m) in length.

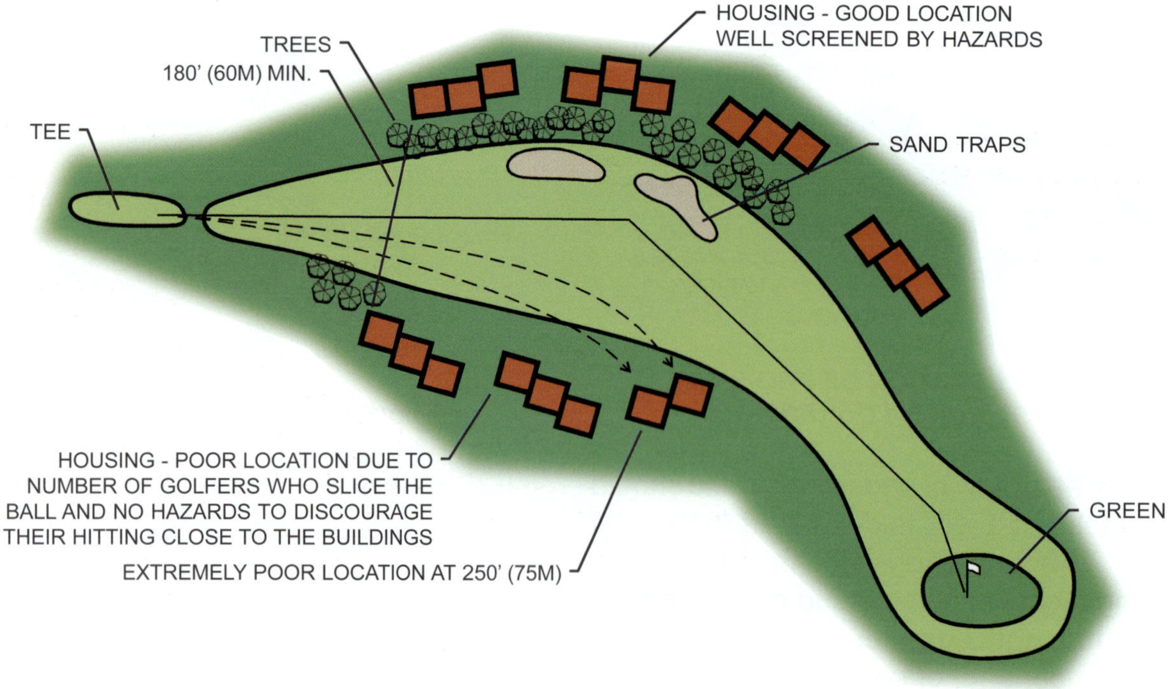

FIG. 20.6 – LOCATION OF BUILDINGS ADJACENT TO GOLF COURSE

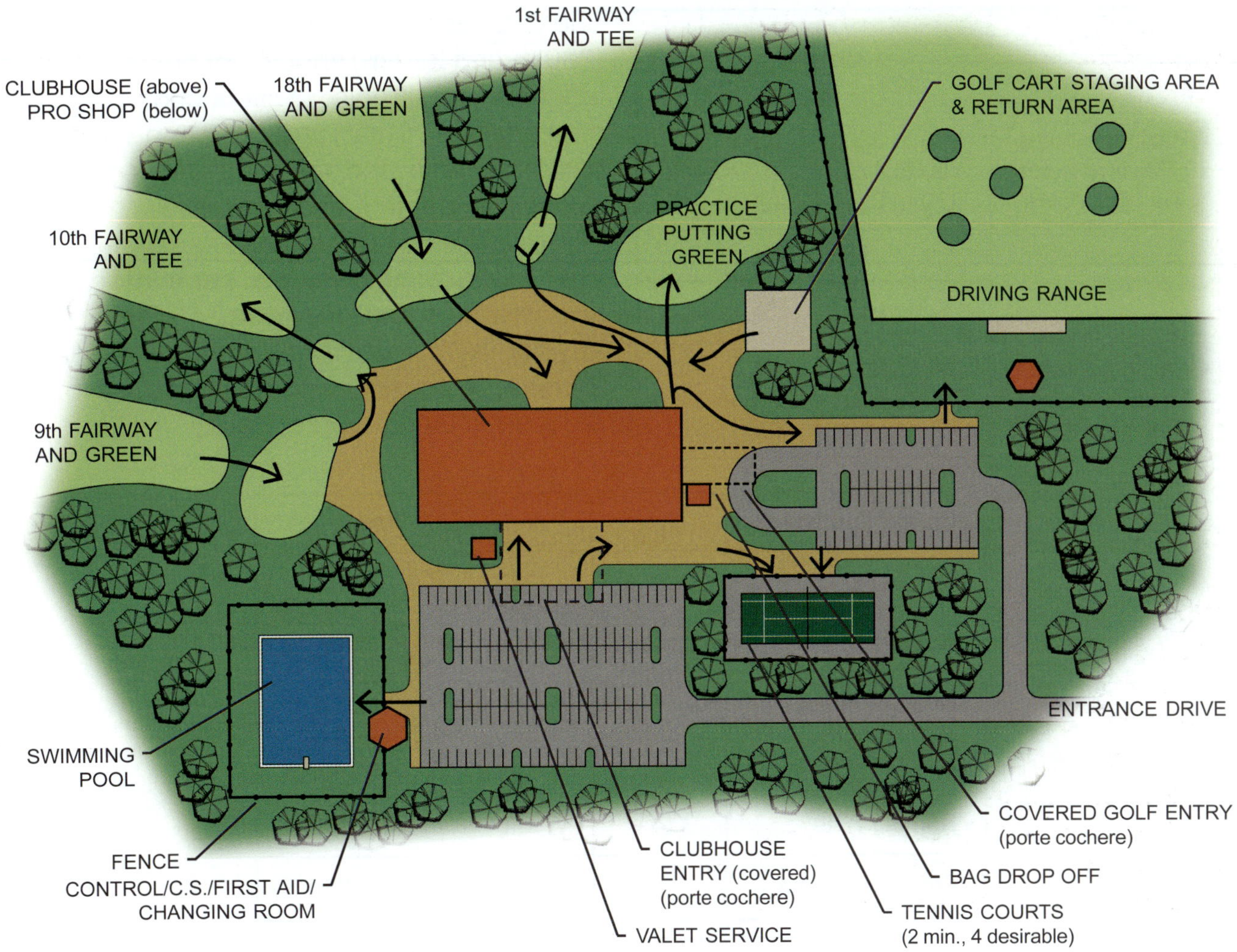

FIG. 20.7 – CLUBHOUSE COMPLEX

It should be comparatively free of hazards and of heavy rough where the ball may be lost. The first hole should have no features that will delay players. Holes should grow increasingly difficult to play as the round proceeds because of the golfers warming up.

Each nine on a regulation course should also have two par three holes, two par five holes, and five par four holes. Par for each nine should be 35, 36, or 37. Total par for the golf course should be 71, 72, or 73 (an executive course would be reduced accordingly). Par six holes should be avoided. Consideration should be given to par three holes first. The first one should be about 130 to 160 yards (120 to 150 m) long. The second one should be between 180 to 240 yards (165 to 210 m) long. Par five holes should also vary in length. The first one being on the short side, about 480 yards (430 m) long. The others range from 520 to 600 yards (475 to 550 m) long. The length of the hole determines the par for that hole.

HOLES	YARDS	
	Men	**Women**
4 Par three holes 10 Par four holes 4 Par five holes	100 to 250 350 to 470 470 to 625	Up to 210 210 to 400 400 to 575
	METERS	
	Men	**Women**
4 Par three holes 10 Par four holes 4 Par five holes	90 to 230 320 to 430 430 to 570	Up to 190 290 to 390 390 to 520

The yardage between 250 yards and 350 yards (230 m and 320 m) should not be used for the length of a golf hole. This is considered "no man's land." This yardage is too long for a par three hole and too short for a par four; **avoid** this length if at all possible.

The mixture of pars on each nine is an important consideration. One good arrangement for a regulation course is as follows, with an executive course being reduced in length appropriately.

Front Nine Holes	Par	Yards	(Meters±)
Number one*	4	380	(350)
Number two	5	485	(445)
Number three	4	400	(365)
Number four	3	260	(240)
Number five	4	410	(375)
Number six	5	580	(530)
Number seven	4	420	(385)
Number eight	3	180	(165)
Number nine*	4	440	(400)
Front Nine Total	36	3,555	(3,255)

Back Nine Holes	Par	Yards	(Meters±)
Number ten*	4	390	(360)
Number eleven	5	550	(500)
Number twelve	4	370	(340)
Number thirteen	3	200	(180)
Number fourteen	4	430	(395)
Number fifteen	5	520	(475)
Number sixteen	4	370	(340)
Number seventeen	3	220	(200)
Number eighteen	4	450	(410)
Back Nine Total	36	3,500	(3,200)
TOTAL 18 HOLES	72	7,055	(6,455)

*Holes number 1, 9, 10, and 18 should have the minimum number of features that would slow play, while being most aesthetically pleasing of all the holes. The design must be consistent with the remainder of the course design.

FIG. 20.8 – SUGGESTED TYPICAL HOLE LENGTHS AND PAR VALUE OF THE FRONT AND BACK NINES

Variety in length of each hole provides different golf shots and the use of each club in the golf bag.

Maintained fairway width generally is approximately 30 to 40 yards (27 to 36 m). Additional space is desirable on the fairway to accommodate inaccurate shots and spectators during competitions. Approximate distance between areas to be built (housing or other built uses) should be a minimum of 60 yards (55 m) width, with 70 to 75 yards (65 to 70 m) desirable. By keeping the heavily maintained fairways to a minimum width, the amount of land under intensive maintenance can be reduced to approximately 70 acres (28 hectares) substantially reducing lawn maintenance costs.

There should be no feeling of repetition throughout the round; that is, different types, lengths, and characters should be incorporated into the design of each golf hole, creating interest and challenge for the golfer.

Whenever practical, greens should be plainly visible. Sand traps and other hazards should be obviously apparent from the approach area. Generally speaking, fairways sloping directly up or down a hillside are unacceptable for several reasons.

1. Steep, sloping fairways make the playing of the golf shot by the majority of players a matter of luck rather than skill.

2. The up/down climb is fatiguing to the walking golfer.

3. Turf is difficult to maintain on such an area.

It is desirable to mark clearly the distance to the green on the fairway edge to enable the player who cannot correctly judge distances to better choose his shot and requisite club.

In golf course architecture, there are three types of golf holes: (1) Penal, (2) Strategic, and (3) Heroic.

PENAL

The sand traps guard in bottleneck or island fashion. The average golfer must either hit an accurate shot to the green or play short of the green in order to avoid trouble. One or two such holes are usually sufficient in an eighteen-hole golf course.

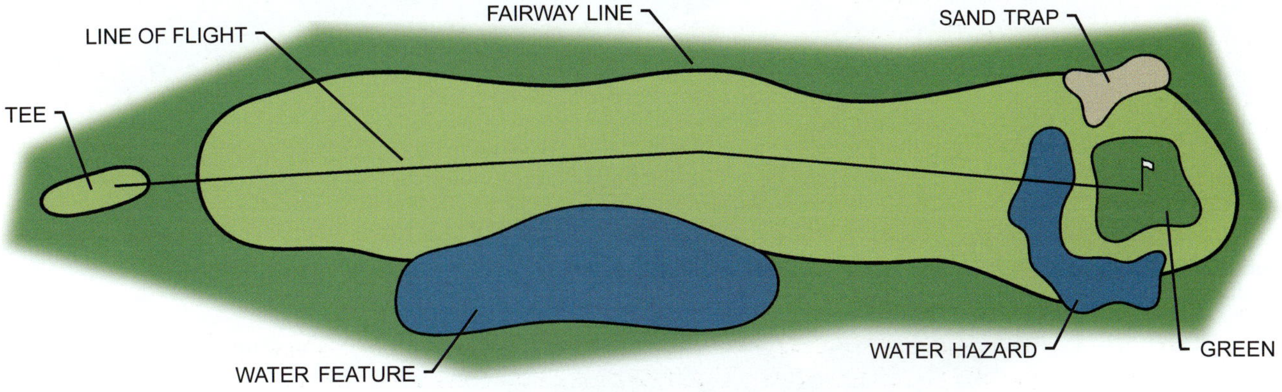

FIG. 20.9 – PENAL – APPROACH SHOT TO GREEN REQUIRES ACCURACY TO AVOID HAZARDS

STRATEGIC

This type of golf hole uses hazards in designated places so that the golfer must place his shots in a particular location to obtain the best results. About 50 percent of golf holes are of this type. These are usually the longer par four or five holes.

HEROIC

This type of golf hole is a combination of penal and strategic design. The use of natural hazards and sand traps placed on the diagonal set the stage for the golfer to gamble and bite off as much as he can chew. The more hazards he can clear, the easier his next shot will be. Thirty to fifty percent of the golf holes are of this type.

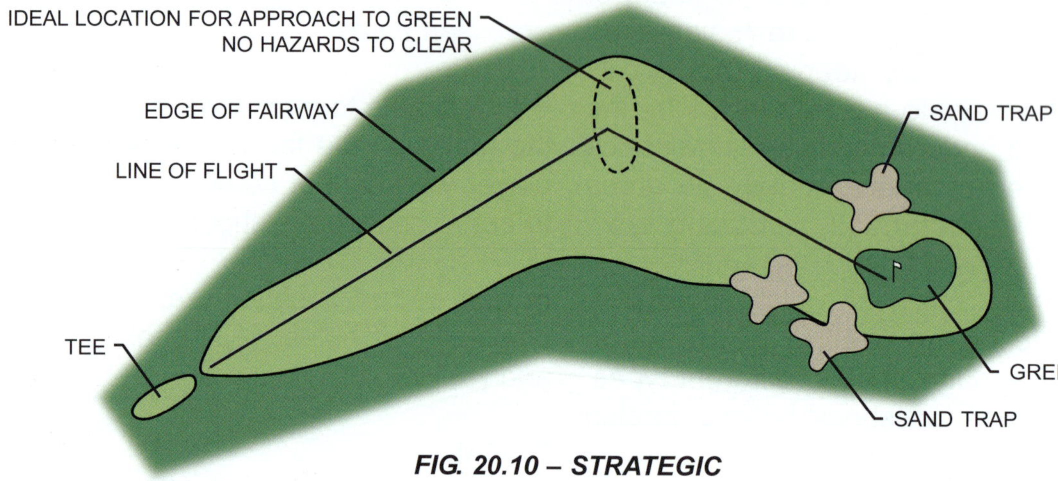

FIG. 20.10 – STRATEGIC

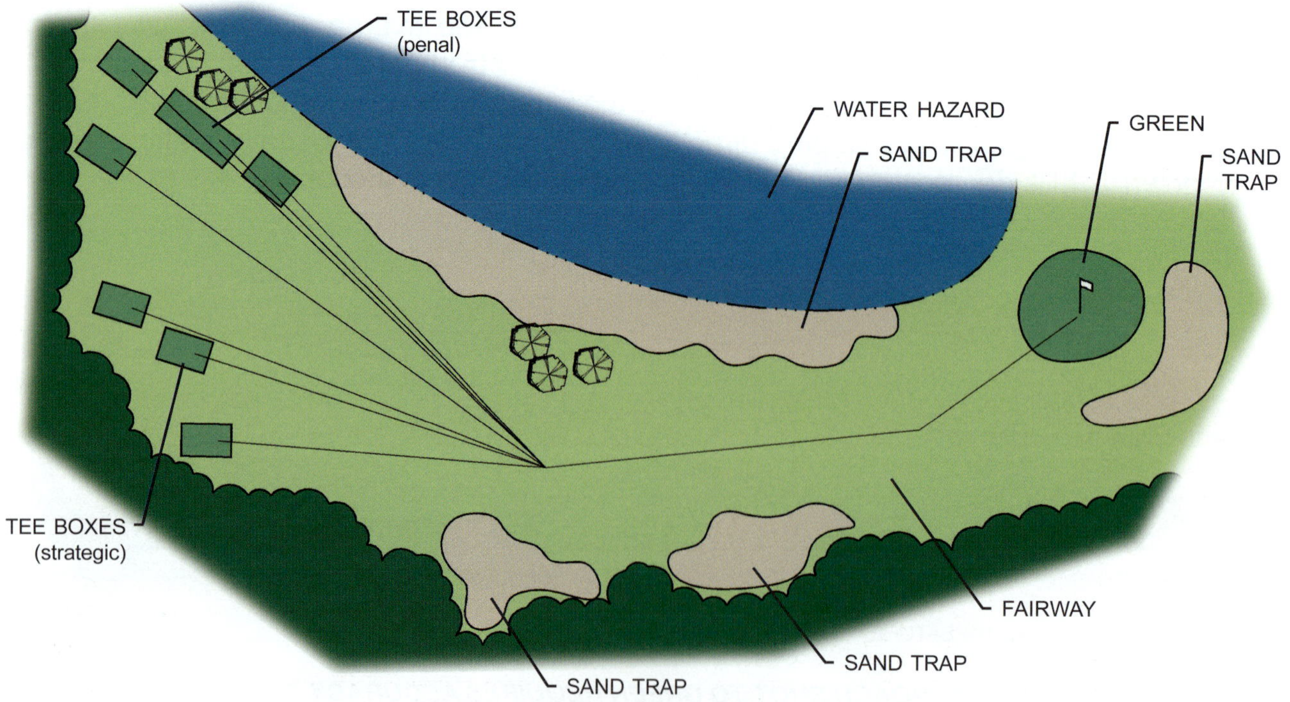

FIG. 20.11 – EXAMPLE OF A GOLF HOLE ILLUSTRATING THE DIFFERENCE BETWEEN STRATEGIC AND PENAL LAYOUT

GREENS AND TEES

Before starting the routing of the golf course, all areas that could naturally accommodate greens and tees on the site should be examined. Green sizes will vary from 5000 square feet to 8000 square feet (465 sq. m to 745 sq. m), depending on the length of the hole; tees should be 2500 square feet to 5000 square feet (220 sq. m to 465 sq. m) in size and designed to accommodate the various golfing capabilities of the expected users. This will make most tees long and relatively narrow, and sometimes result in more than one tee.

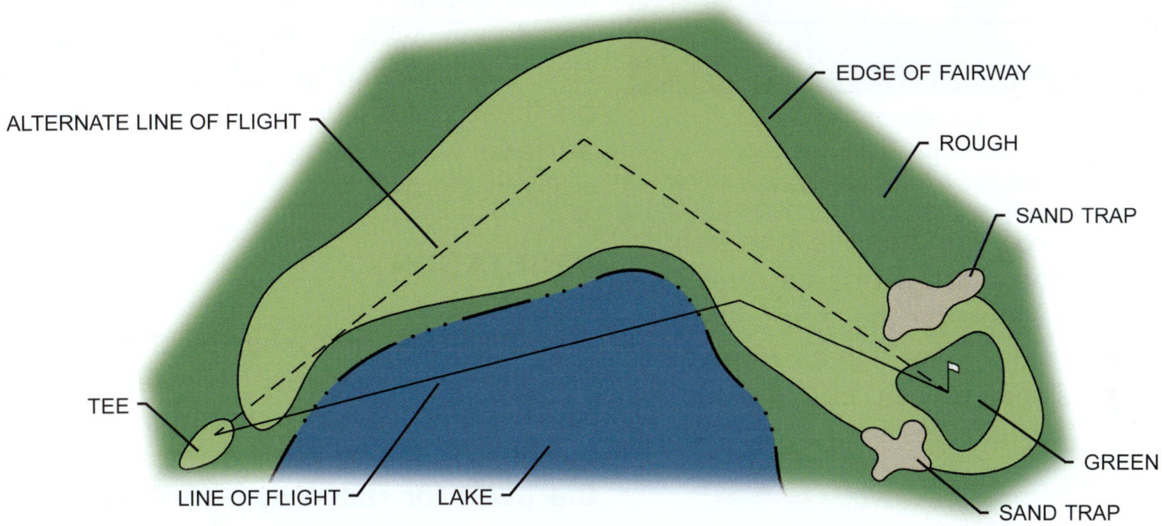

FIG. 20.12 – HEROIC – GAMBLING BY CUTTING ACROSS EDGE OF LAKE RESULTS IN SHORTER APPROACH SHOT TO GREEN

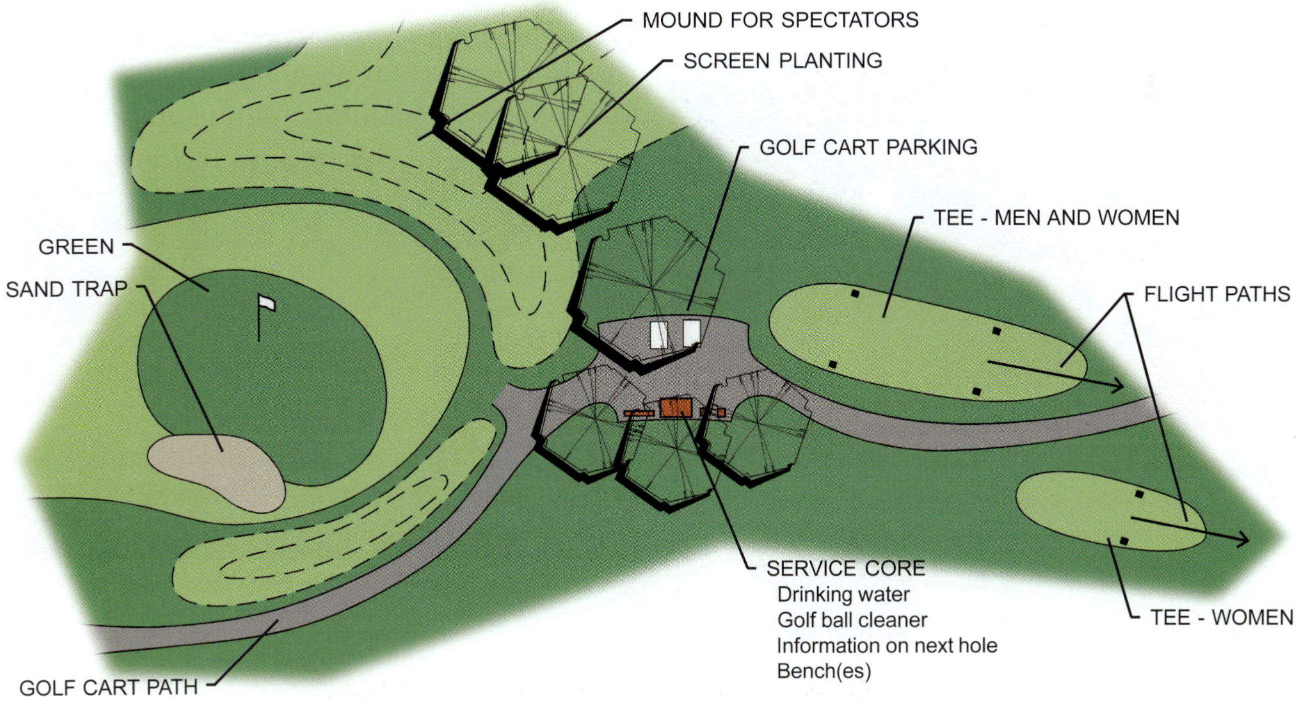

FIG. 20.13 – PLAYER SERVICE CORE AT GREENS/TEES

Multiple tees, golf cart pathway, hole information, and ball cleaning – The Links of Naples. Photo by Wayne Hook

Where the pitch of the green is from front to back, the slope should not be over five percent. The slope on the approach of a plateau green can run as high as 20 percent. Mounds and slopes running from the surface of the greens to the sides or back can run up to 20 percent.

A golf player service area should be included in the vicinity of each green/tee pair and should include information on the hole, a golf ball cleaner (every second hole)...

Extra toilet facilities at holes four and five and thirteen and fourteen – Quail Run Golf Course, Naples, Florida

...and drinking water a minimum of every third hole.

Two toilet facilities are necessary on most courses. Locate one on each nine - best between four and five and between thirteen and fourteen. This is particularly critical for golf courses that serve older people.

HAZARDS

There are three basic types of hazards - vegetation, water, and sand. The number, size, location, and type of each is dependent on the availability of existing vegetation, surface water supply, and the technical difficulty desired.

VEGETATION

Trees, shrubs, and other plant material can be formidable hazards. The retention of or the planting of plant material in strategic locations is very desirable. Because of costs, the need for reducing heavily maintained areas is expanding this type of hazard.

WATER

These features normally occur on coastal golf courses like Pebble Beach in California, and in areas with plentiful rainfall and/or high

Water hazard – Quail Run Golf Course Naples, Florida

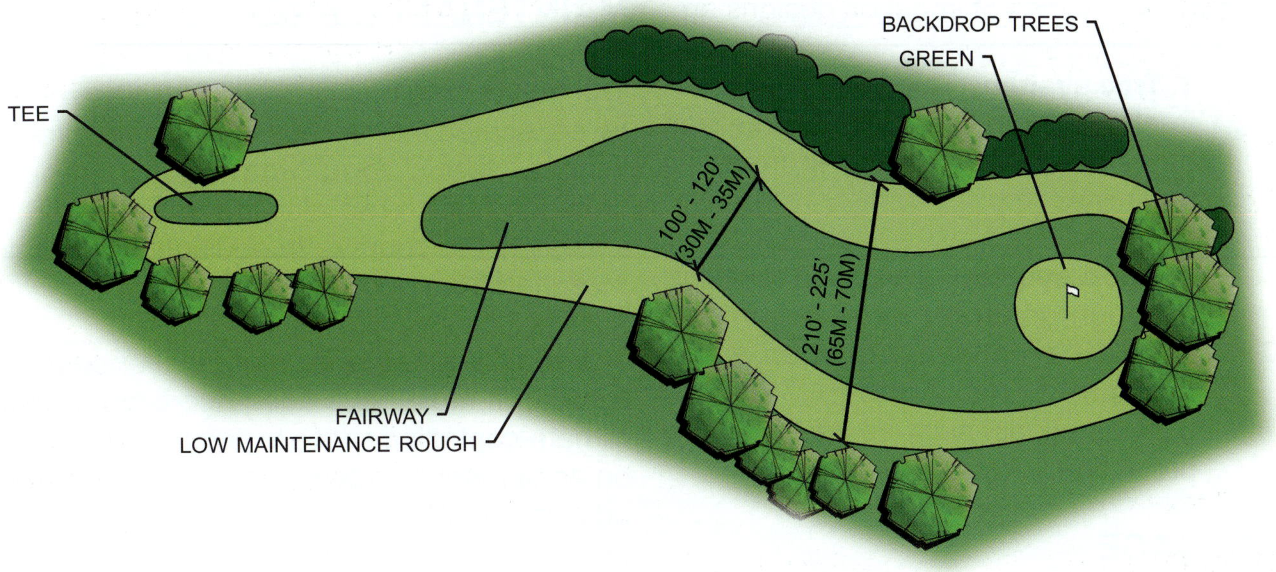

FIG. 20.14 – VEGETATION AS HAZARDS

water tables, such as in many of the Florida courses. Where water is available, it should be utilized for hazards as well as for its inherent aesthetic values.

SAND

The slope of the traps in front of or on the side playing toward the green will run from 30 to 40 percent. At the entrance of traps, the slope should not be over 25 percent so that the golfer's backswing can be taken with a full, clean stroke.

IRRIGATION

In planning a golf course, it is important to include a good irrigation system. Golf is dependent on the use of turf and, without water, it is very likely there will not be thick and healthy turf year round.

The intent of an irrigation system is to provide the needed amount of water (approximately one inch of water per week, including natural precipitation) on the main playing areas. A watering system for an eighteen-hole golf course must cover a minimum of approximately 45 acres (18 ha) of fairway, generally 90± acres (36 ha) where the roughs are irrigated, and about 5 acres (2 ha) for the greens and tees. A properly planned and designed watering system utilizes the most economical pipe sizes and produces an irrigated course, with a minimum of labor for operation and maintenance.

Tees and greens have special water requirements and should be zoned separately from the fairways. Irrigation in roughs should be minimized and, where possible, eliminated. All irrigation systems must be designed to complete watering during slow or non use periods on the course. They are almost always clock-controlled, automatic systems and should be capable of being easily reprogrammed to conserve water. Moisture sensors tied into the irrigation controls are frequently required by the local governing agencies. They should be seriously considered to reduce unnecessary watering even when not required.

The two major types of irrigation designs are:

> **1. Tree system**: This system utilizes a trunk line from the water source and has smaller lines branching from this trunk line.
>
> **2. Loop system**: The "loop" system, although generally more expensive, should be considered when water pressure or other design considerations, such as adequate fire protection, dictate.

DRAINAGE

All playing areas on the golf course must have adequate drainage to permit play soon after the rain stops falling. Very special care must be taken to ensure excellent drainage on the greens.

MAINTENANCE AREA

The golf course maintenance facilities should be so located that access is available directly from a public road/highway for vendor deliveries. It must also have easy, direct access to the course. In addition, it **must** be screened from public view.

The maintenance area must be fenced and lighted. It must have adequate covered and climate-controlled space to permit staff to work on equipment maintenance and repair during adverse weather conditions. Car parking spaces for the anticipated number of employees is needed. Indoor or, at least, under-roof equipment storage space is required to protect lawn mowers, front-end loaders, trimmers, maintenance carts, and other equipment. In addition, adequate storage space, both open and undercover, is needed for extra materials.

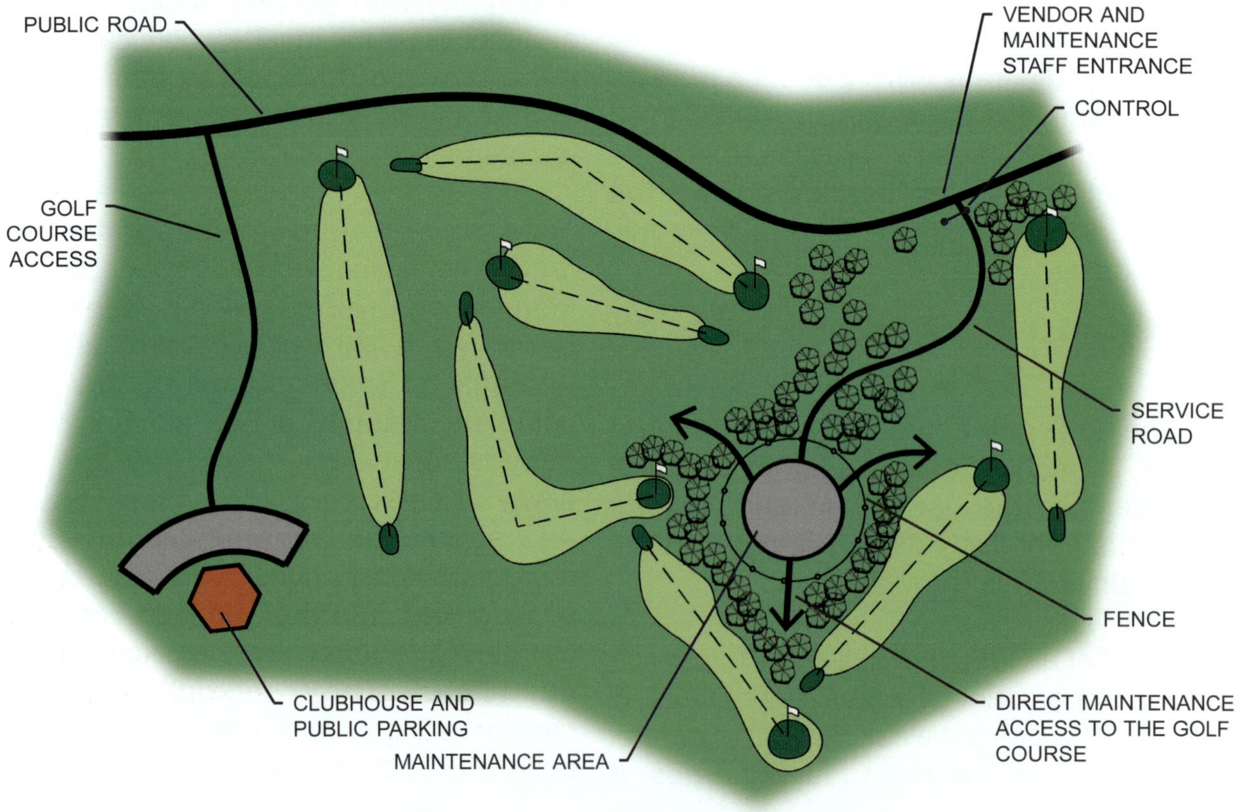

FIG. 20.15 – LOCATION OF GOLF COURSE MAINTENANCE AREA

Chapter 21

WINTER-USE AREAS

All parks in cold weather areas should be studied for possible winter-use activities. Sledding, tobogganing, ice skating, and ice fishing should be considered for all sites of almost any size. For larger sites of 100+ acres (40.5+ ha), look at the possibility of adding cross-country skiing and snowshoeing. Still larger sites should be looked at for adding snowmobiling. For resources with steep, north facing hills and mountains, consider possible downhill skiing.

GENERAL

Factors to consider in locating winter-use facilities include:

- Snow season (number of days of usable snow without the use of snowmaking equipment).

- Ice season (number of days ice is usable, 4 inches (10 cm) or thicker is needed).

- Suitable slopes for skiing, coasting and tobogganing.

- Access during winter for maintenance, snow removal, and cindering. No steep road grades are possible.

- Parking – level area needed with space for snow disposal.

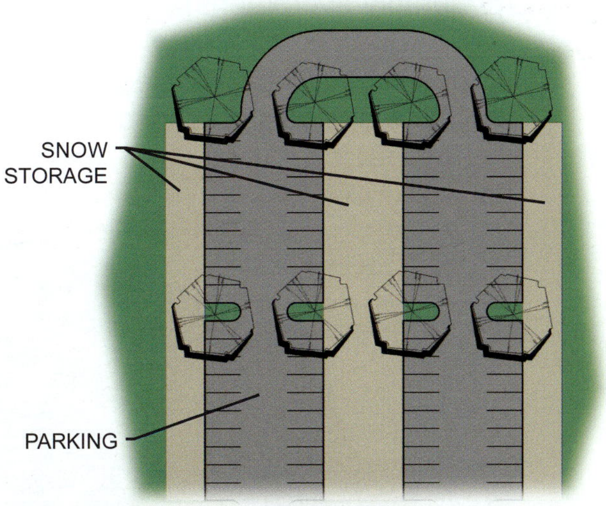

FIG. 21.1 – PARKING WITH SPACE FOR SNOW REMOVAL

- Buildings needed - warming hut, hot food service, rental of supplies and equipment, heated sanitary facilities, ticket sales, ski instruction, ski patrol, lodges, housing, etc. – all heated sufficiently to keep all utilities from freezing.

• Summer use of winter sports areas is desirable. It can expand the use season and maximize the return on investment, e.g., install a long water slide to utilize the lifts during the summer, hiking trails on the cross-country trails, fishing on winter-use lakes, etc.

• Urban areas – possibly include night activities (outside lighting will be needed).

• Utilities – all must be winterized.

• Slope orientation – north to northeast with tree cover (preferably evergreens) to provide shade. If tree cover is not existing, it should be established (preferably evergreens).

• Slopes used for skiing, sledding, etc., should be graded and seeded for safety, better performance, and ease of maintenance.

Sledding in Pennsylvania. Photo by Michael Fogg

• Snowmaking weather (number of days snow can be made) needs to be determined for all ski areas.

• If snowmaking is included in project, then an adequate winter water supply will be required, i.e., non frozen stream, reservoir or underground source. In many cases, snowmaking can make or break a commercial winter-use project.

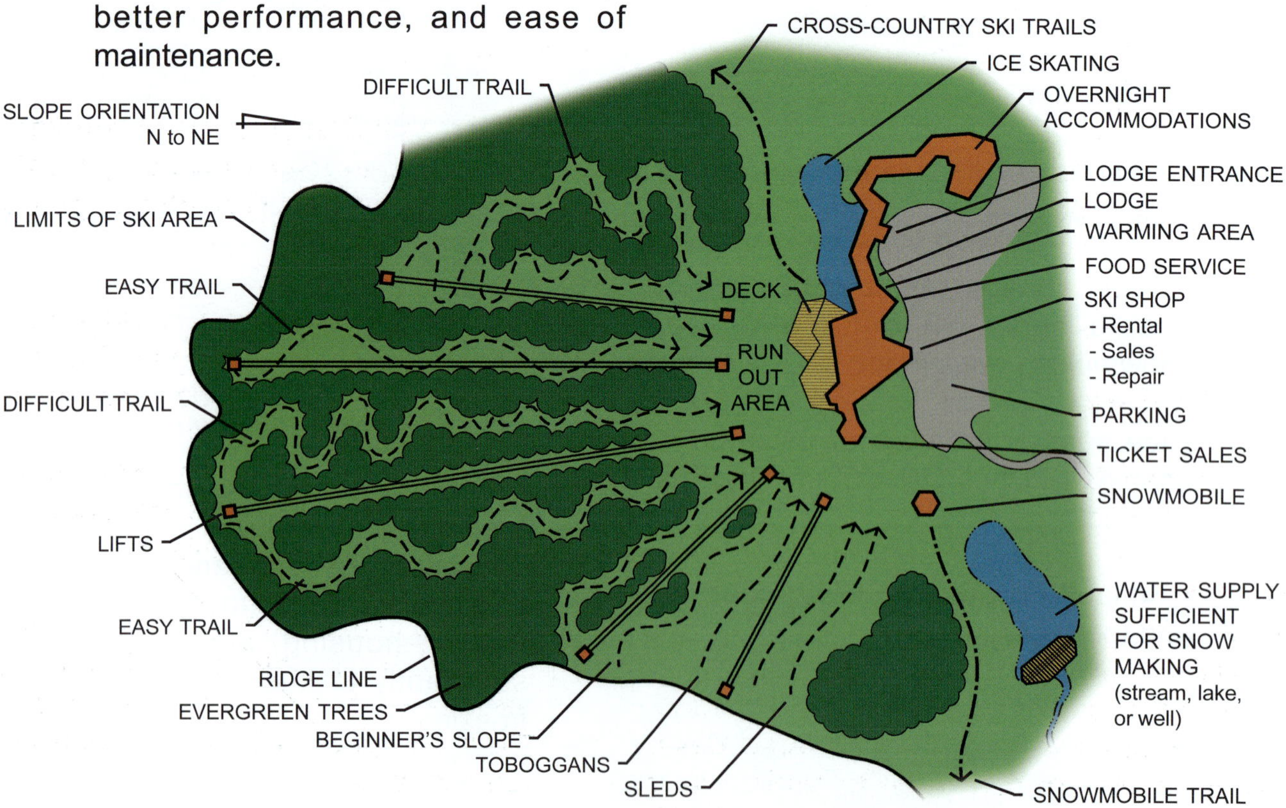

FIG. 21.2 – WINTER-USE COMPLEX

DOWNHILL SKIING AND SNOWBOARDING

The traditional type of skiing continues to have strong support. Twenty percent of the skiers account for 60 percent of the total participation, skiing 20 days or more per year. Snowboarding has become a major component of downhill slopes, especially with younger skiers. Up to 30 percent of all ski slope use is now snowboarding. Infrequent skiers account for 12 percent of the use and amount to 45 percent of the skiers. The remaining, moderate skiers, 35 percent, ski between 5 and 20 days and account for 28 percent of the use.

Snowboarding in Pennsylvania.
Photo by Michael Fogg

USER CHARACTERISTICS

Skiers are young, under thirty, 60 percent male, and 40 percent female; they tend to have high incomes, be well educated, and the average skier has skied for over six years. Recent trends are for people to continue their skiing habits into their maturity. Downhill skiers travel an average of 200 miles to get to the slopes, and frequently will stay two or three days. Older people are continuing to ski into their 50s and 60s, and some even into their 70s. [37]

ATTITUDES

Single-day skiers prefer:

- ski areas close to their residence.
- good physical quality of slope.
- low price of tow and lift tickets.
- the presence of good lift facilities.

Weekend or vacation skiers prefer:

- good physical quality of slopes.
- presence of good lift facilities with short wait times.
- good reputation with skiers.
- no crowds, especially during the week days.

Requirements:

- One hundred inches of snowfall (without snowmaking equipment), which would result in 80-85 skiing days, N-NE exposure.
- Areas within one hour's drive from major centers of population. Facilities for night skiing should be considered.
- With 3000 people on 1500 acres (600 hectares) of slopes, trails are in a relatively crowded condition.
- Ski slope trail width – 40 feet (12 m) - minimum; larger area should be developed at the top of steep slopes. Single purpose trail developments are on natural snow.

• There should always be for the beginners and inexperienced skiers an easy way to ski from the top of any slope to the run-out at the bottom.

• Rope tow – 1300 lineal feet (400 m) – maximum; 25 percent slope.

• Chair lift should be considered in all areas with vertical drop of 200 feet (60 m) or more.

• Gondolas are also available to major ski areas and can be used in summer for sightseeing rides.

• Waiting space must be provided at the base of the ski lifts for those wishing to ride to the top of slopes.

• Vertical drop should be a minimum of 180 feet (55 m); the desirable minimum – 350 feet (110 m).

• Percent of steepness of slopes needed:

Beginners	5% to 20%
Intermediates	20% to 35%
Experts	35% and up

• Avoid large open areas at the top of the mountain. Screen planting may solve the problem.

• Avoid large open areas exposed to the prevailing wind direction. Screen planting will probably solve the problem.

• Snowmaking equipment is almost a necessity for profitable ski operations, and requires a substantial supply of water during the winter months.

• Ticket sales booths should be located between the parking lot and the slopes, preferably outside of the main ski building.

• Support facilities are a necessity for an effective ski operation.

Food service
Liquor (bar)
Entertainment area
Lodging
Equipment rental
Teaching

} 20% or more of all skiing money is spent on these activities

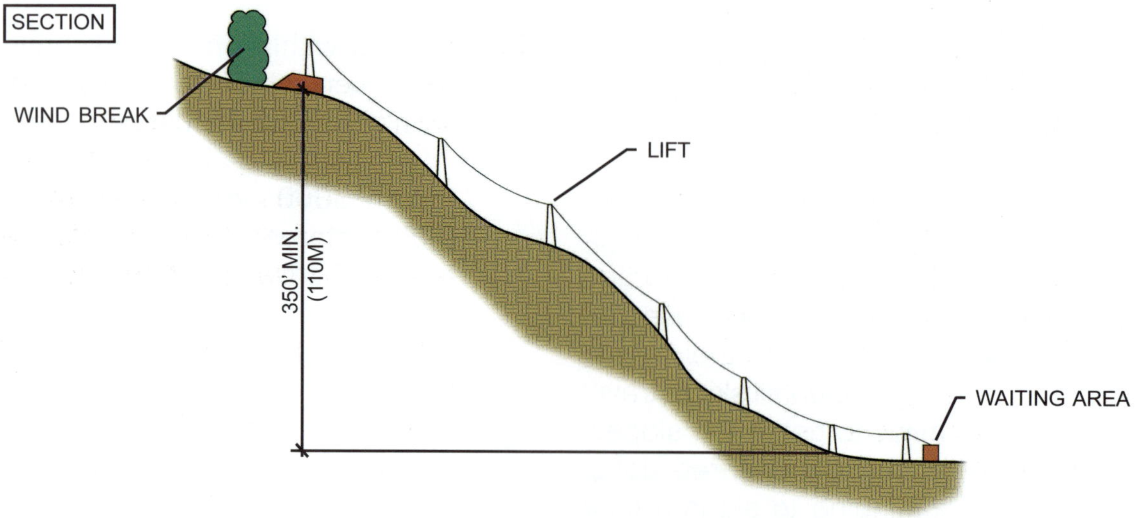

FIG. 21.3 – MINIMUM SKI SLOPE HEIGHT

Other winter activities, such as skating, snowmobiling (see Chapter 10, Off Highway Vehicles), cross-country skiing, and snowshoeing should also be considered.

CROSS-COUNTRY SKIING (NORDIC)

This type of skiing has become very popular, and its popularity continues to increase.

USER CHARACTERISTICS

Usually cross-country skiers have had some downhill skiing experience. They are looking for solitude, are frequently summer joggers, and have had approximately three years of experience. They love the out-of-doors and seek natural settings. A short afternoon or evening trip nearby is preferred to the weekend outing. Many older people are participating in cross-country skiing.

Requirements:

- Location – in close proximity (30-minute drive) to the users.

Cross-country skiing
– McCall, Idaho
Photo courtesy of the Fethke family

- Access – ideally accessible without use of cars; however, parking that can be easily plowed is normally a necessity. The parking can be combined with that needed for other winter activities.

TRAILS

- **General:**

Provide solitude with scenic diversity, varied terrain, and vegetative cover. Cross-country skiing and snowmobiling are **NOT** compatible – not even in the same sound basin. Use existing summer trails where possible. Bicycle, hiking, and equestrian trails are generally well suited for cross-country skiing during the winter. Please note, however, that back-country hiking trails frequently have much narrower clearing widths than that needed for ski trails. Like all winter activities, trails should be located, wherever possible, to the north side of hills and in shaded areas. This is particularly important in marginal snow areas, will prolong the snow cover, and, subsequently, that trail's usability. Loop trails are strongly recommended, with side trails adequately signed and of varying degrees of difficulty offered for the more advanced skiers.

- **Length:**

1 to 2 hours	for beginning trails
½ day	3 miles (5 km) – Intermediate 6 miles (10 km) – Advanced
All day	6 miles (10 km) – Intermediate 10 miles (15 km) – Advanced

• **Layout:**

Essentially the same as all trails, except that short, quick turns should be avoided. Out runs at the base of slopes must be provided before encountering obstacles (bridges, drop-offs, roads). There should be a variety of grades, with approximately one-third up hill, one-third downhill, and one-third flat.

• **Gradients:**

Beginners	As level as possible (under 8%), with some downhill slopes.
Intermediate	8%, with some slopes to 10%.
Advanced	17%, with some slopes to 20%.

Most of the trail should be much less grade-wise than noted, and the steeper slopes should be downhill as often as possible.

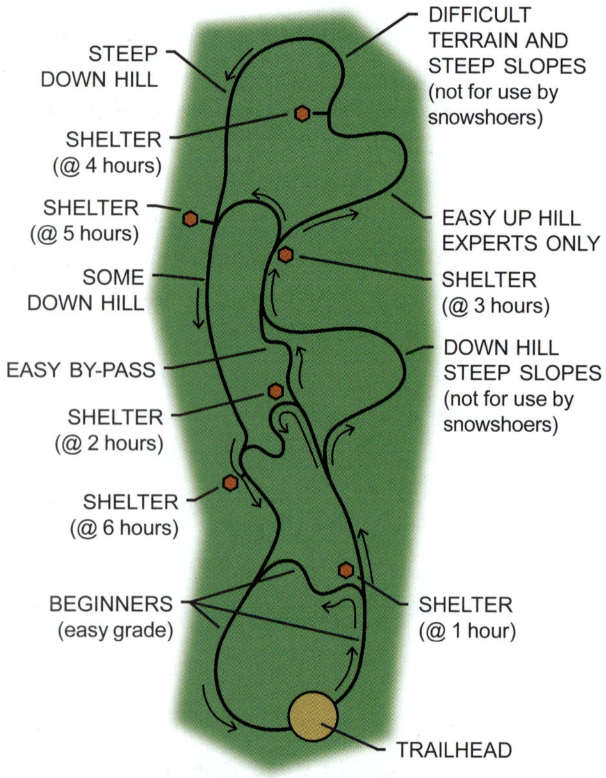

FIG. 21.4 – CROSS-COUNTRY (NORDIC) SKIING AND SNOWSHOEING

Cross-country skiing – Northern Wisconsin Photo courtesy of the Fethke family

• **Clearing Width:**

Intermediate	8 feet (2.5 m) on grades under 8%; 13 feet (4.1 m) on downhill grades over 8%.
Advanced	6 feet (1.8 m) on grades under 10%; 13 feet (4.1 m) on downhill grades over 10%.
Vertical clearing	8 feet (2.5 m) above average snow depth. Be sure to consider the cleared height under tree branches when they are covered in snow.

The increased clearing width is to allow for downhill maneuvering and various uphill steps.

• **Surfacing:**

Under the snow cover, ski trails should be free of obstructions, especially rocks. If the trail is not used during summer for other activities, it should be seeded with grass.

• **Signing:**

Adequate signs and trail markers above the snow line are important for all ski facilities from parking to all ski areas. Trail markers are especially needed on longer trails in more remote areas. Interpretive signs should be added for the trail user's enjoyment.

• **Shelter Areas:**

At all trailheads and winter-use roads, it is desirable to have a shelter(s) for warming and ski waxing. On longer trails, over 1 ½ hours, it is desirable to have shelters at approximately one-hour intervals for resting and re-waxing skis, and possibly enjoying a warming fire.

SNOWSHOEING

This recreation activity is the hottest new thing in winter sports.

• **General:**

Snowshoeing can generally use any prepared pedestrian trails. Preferably, these trails should be on the north and east sides of hills and mountains and, more specifically, in areas with evergreen trees. Do not include the most demanding trail segments.

• **Length:**

A loop system length variable with cutoffs at various intermediate distances. Figure one to two miles for beginners and one-half day for experienced snowshoers. Longer trails are not recommended.

• **Gradients:**

Standard trail gradients (see Chapter 8, Trails and Pathways).

• **Clearing Width:**

Same as in standard trails (see Chapter 8, Trails and Pathways).

• **Clearing Height:**

As per standard trails height plus the expected extra height of maximum average snow depth. (See Chapter 8, Trails and Pathways.)

ICE SKATING

Ice skating should be considered wherever water is available and safe ice conditions can be expected with reasonable regularity.

Requirements:

• Lighting for night activities is desirable in urban areas and major winter-use complexes only.

• Area for warming fires with shelter from wind desirable. Benches for resting and/or skate changing and a firewood supply are needed.

• Shaded areas directly north of evergreens or a hill or mountain are most desirable, but not required.

• Toilet facilities – winterized and, preferably, heated.

• Artificial ice skating rinks can be considered.

• Four-inch (10 cm) depth of smooth ice is required.

• Adequate level parking that can be easily plowed for snow removal.

• Use shallow water areas, 3 feet (90 cm) or less deep, if possible, for safety reasons. Where the water is deeper, accessible safety equipment must be provided (minimum of a flotation ring and a light-weight wooden ladder).

• Designate skating area limits, and keep skaters separated from ice fishing.

• Parking lots and level fields can be designed for flooding and can make a very desirable skating area. If asphalt (black) parking lots are used, they should be treated with some type of surfacing to minimize the heat absorption, i.e., painted, covered with sand, or with brushed in cement during construction.

ICE BOATING

Large water bodies, 250± acres (100± ha), in areas with good, smooth ice coverage are sometimes used for ice boating. This is not a major activity.

Requirements:

• Vehicular access and a plowable parking area near the ice.

• Toilet facility – winterized.

• Ice depth – minimum 4 inches (10 cm) for several days each year.

• Consider using existing boating facilities for this off-season function.

• Combine support facilities, if possible, with other winter activities, such as skating, coasting, and ice fishing.

• Provide area for warming fires, with a fire ring being minimum, and a warming shelter much more desirable.

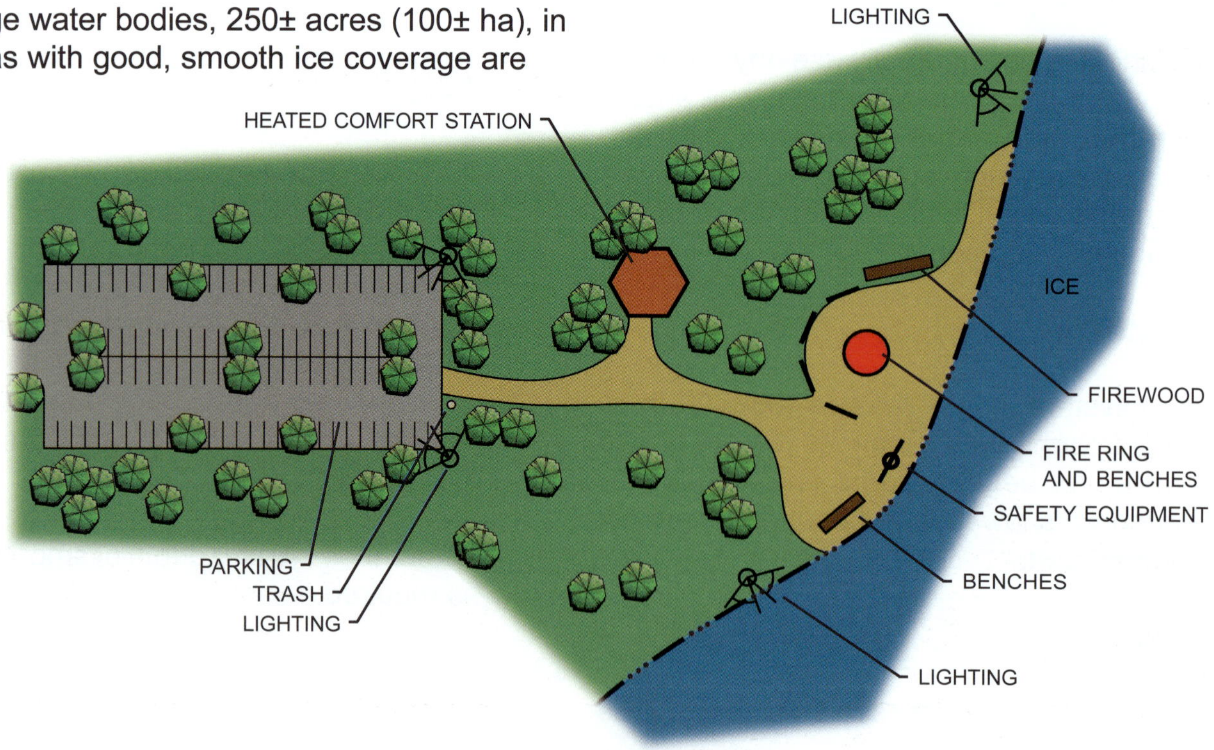

FIG. 21.5 – ICE SKATING AREA

TOBOGGANING

Requirements:

- Slope free of obstacles, especially rocks; 10 percent to 45 percent grade and 30 percent recommended. Needs a level run-out space at the bottom.
- North – northeast exposure.
- Evergreen planting on the sides of run to provide shade to slow the snow melt.
- Vault toilets acceptable. Flush toilets must be winterized and heated.
- Warming area is desirable.
- Level, plowable parking.
- A walkable path in winter, while pulling a toboggan, is necessary from the bottom of slope to top of the run.

COASTING

Should be included in all parks within one hour's drive of urban areas and population concentrations.

Sledding with one of the many new plastic sleds – Pennsylvania. Photo by Michael Fogg

Requirements:

- North – northeast exposure.
- Five percent to 40 percent slope with level run-out space.
- Multiple starting points.
- Planting – evergreen shade on sides of slope to slow the snow melt.
- Vault toilets acceptable. Flush toilets must be winterized and heated.
- Warming area desirable – fire ring/ sitting.
- Night lighting in heavily used areas, especially urban areas.
- A winter-usable walkway from the bottom of the slope to the starting point(s).

SNOWMOBILING

See Chapter 10, Off-Highway Vehicle Facilities – Snowmobiling.

Snowmobiling – Photo courtesy of NOHVCC

ICE FISHING

Should be included for all resource areas (especially parks) with good fishing and where ice conditions permit.

Musky fishing during the winter – Wisconsin. Photo courtesy of the Fethke family

Requirements:

- Four-inch (10 cm) depth of ice.
- Separate from other ice-use activities, especially skating.
- Parking – level and plowable.
- Safety equipment. As a minimum, a life preserver ring/rope and light-weight wooden ladder located at the parking area.
- Heated sanitary facilities. Flush toilets desirable; vault toilets acceptable.

Desired:

- Fire facilities as per ice skating.
- Shelter – fishermen frequently bring their own.
- It is desirable, where possible, to combine parking, safety, sanitary facilities, shelter, and warming fire with other winter-use facilities.

Ice fishing through a drilled hole – Wisconsin. Photo courtesy of the Fethke family

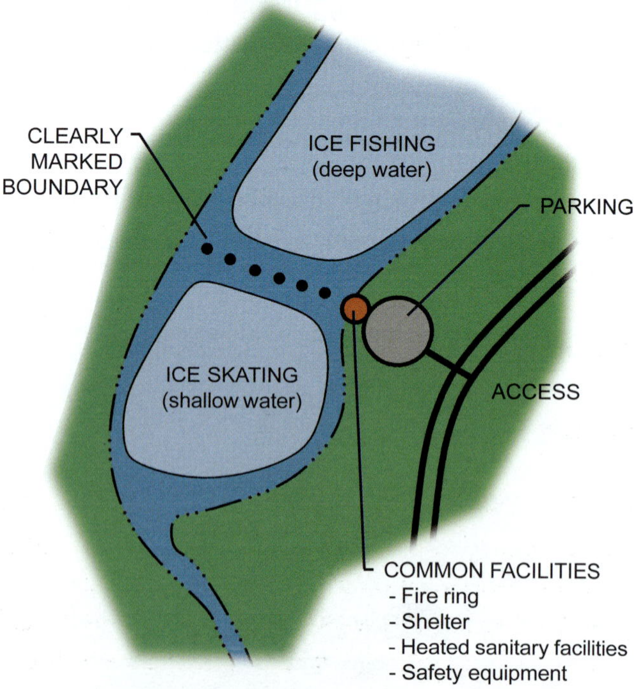

FIG. 21.6 – SEPARATION OF ICE SKATING AND ICE FISHING

Chapter 22

FISHING

Stream fishing – Wisconsin
Photo courtesy of the Fethke family

All resource facilities with relatively unpolluted water can support some type of fishing, many on a year-round basis. There are several types of possibilities for this desirable activity.

USER CHARACTERISTICS (8, 21, 38)

In 2001, 34 million people over the age of 16 went fishing a total of over 557 million days for an average of over 10 days per person per year where fishing was the primary activity. Of these, 10 million fishermen went saltwater fishing, while almost all went freshwater fishing. Fishing is done more days by men than women. Age is not a significant factor until the 65-and-older group, who participate only one-half that of the other age groups.

Fishing is income-sensitive (2.5:1) and very little educationally-sensitive. Many more Caucasians fish than others.

The percentage of people fishing is stable at this time.

ACTIVITIES

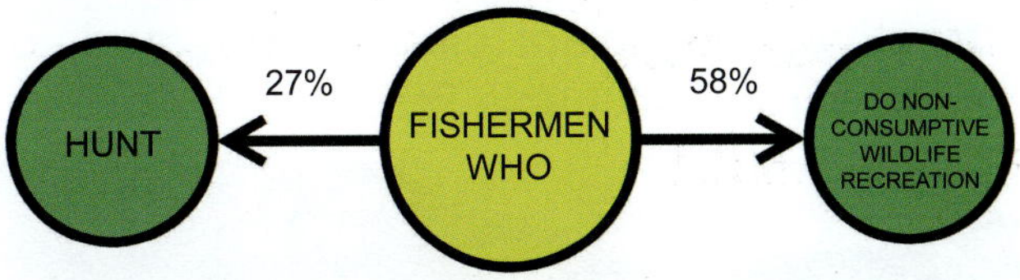

FIG. 22.1 – PERCENTAGE OF FISHERMEN (ON AN ANNUAL BASIS) WHO HUNT AND ALSO PARTICIPATE IN OTHER NON-CONSUMPTIVE WILDLIFE RECREATIONAL ACTIVITIES [38]

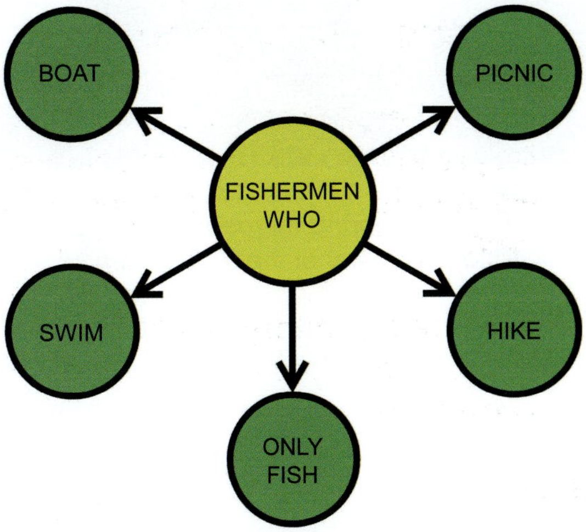

FIG. 22.2 – THE MAJOR ACTIVITIES FISHERMEN PARTICIPATE IN OTHER THAN FISHING [8]

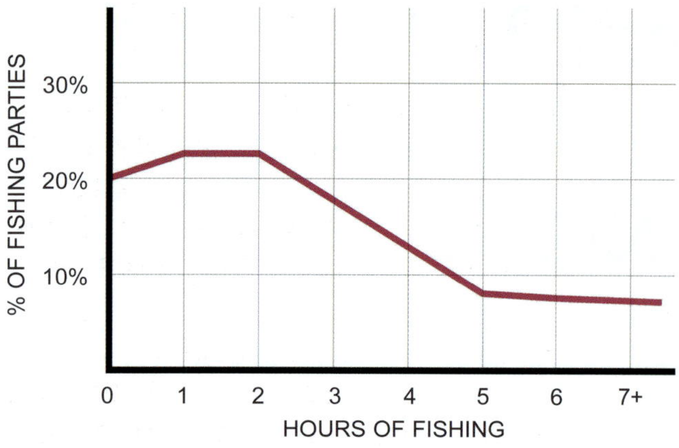

FIG. 22.3 – PERCENTAGE OF FISHERMEN WHO FISH FOR VARIOUS LENGTHS OF TIME [8]

Winter ice fishing is also popular with some fisherman. See Chapter 21 for ice fishing details.

USER ATTITUDES

Fishermen want fishing to be available and attractive, they want clear water, and, of course, large, catchable fish.

Sometimes the fish can be fairly large like this 190±-pound sturgeon in Idaho. Photo courtesy of the Fethke family

PRODUCTIVITY

Waters vary in fishing productivity, depending on physical and chemical characteristics. Productivity can be increased by a number of methods, including habitat improvement and fertilization. Both may conflict with other water uses. Supplemental stocking is effective in temporarily increasing fish populations, but increased fishing pressure and availability of food and cover will reduce the population back to the carrying capacity of the body of water within a short time.

METHODS OF FISHING

Fishing methods differ, depending on the classification of the body of water, type of fish present, time of year, and fishing pressure. [10] The following methods are commonly used:

1. Still fishing from banks or shoreline or piers.

2. Moving along banks.

3. Wading.

Wading/fly fishing – Wisconsin
Photo courtesy of the Fethke family

4. Anchored boat.

5. Moving boat.

6. Ice fishing.

ACCESS

Access is required to make an area usable for fishing. For pedestrians, trails along the shore are necessary and for vehicles, road access to appropriately placed parking.

Many fishermen prefer using facilities in early morning and late evening hours, often necessitating special-access areas in controlled-access areas.

Boat launching sites should be located within reasonable distance (depending on the type of boating permitted) of the better fishing areas.

An acceptable route for physically handicapped people must be provided, if possible, to at least some of the good fishing areas. Special fishing piers with suitable safety rails and surfaced access ways may be required. See Chapter 6, Handicapped Accessibility, for additional details.

Fishing pier at Sugden Regional Park – Collier County, Florida

GENERAL CONSIDERATIONS

• It is desirable, where possible, for some fishing areas to be developed near areas of other park activities so that the entire family (some who do not fish) can enjoy their outing together.

• Heavy fishing pressure is usually sporadic, e.g., opening day of trout season, after stocking, or during various fish runs. To make use of the needed parking areas, sanitary facilities, etc., other **non-water related** recreation facilities should be located in the area.

• Fishing may not be as successful in heavy-use portions of water bodies as in the more remote areas.

• Public sanitary facilities are required at any on-shore locations supporting areas of fishing concentrations. Ample rubbish cans must be located at parking areas in places of heavy fishing concentrations.

• Ice fishing is very popular in areas having adequate ice coverage – 4 inches (10 cm) – and fish. See Chapter 21, Winter-Use Areas.

• Provide fish cleaning facilities in major fish producing areas. Refer to fish cleaning facility. (See Chapter 19, Marinas.)

• Small streams with heavy fishing pressure - may need to prohibit wading. Wading creates a disturbance to other fishermen. [10] It also disrupts banks and stream bottoms, thus causing damage to aquatic life and fish carrying capacity.

• Fly fishing only, artificial lures only, and catch and release areas should be carefully located. They can be easily accommodated in more remote areas. The great majority who fish this way do not mind walking considerable distances. Trails to such areas could be part of a comprehensive trail system. The exception might be catch and release areas, which can also be established in certain easily-accessible and heavy-use areas.

• Set aside some easily-reached areas with reasonably good fishing water for children under 12 and which are accessible for disabled persons.

• On larger streams and rivers, float fishing is very popular. Boats are launched at an upstream location and taken out downstream at the completion of the trip. Camping facilities, areas for preparing meals, etc., may be desirable at selected points along the way.

PIERS AND DOCKS

Piers and docks should be provided in areas where the shoreline is inadequate to serve the fishing needs, e.g., shallow lakes, ocean shores, and lakes with difficult shoreline fishing access. All piers and docks should be made accessible to the disabled.

The length of pier required can be calculated by using three lineal feet (90 cm) of pier per user day of anticipated use.

Naples pier – a fishing haven and tourist focal point – Naples, Florida

Consideration must be given to the following:

PARKING

The parking required can be calculated by dividing the lineal feet of fishable pier by 1.5 and again by 2 people per car, for a factor of .75 cars/lineal feet (30 cm) of pier and sightseers' parking, which could be as much as one-half of the total fishermen parking.

Size

• Six feet (180 cm) wide minimum for a low-use area.

• Nine feet (270 cm) wide minimum for normal areas with few sightseers.

• Twelve feet to twenty feet (360 cm to 620 cm) wide for areas with large numbers of non-fishermen. This is usually the situation in coastal communities and, especially, in resort areas.

Fish cleaning area – With running water and adequate disposal facilities. At coastal piers, these necessary cleaning facilities will attract feeding birds, which can be a problem to some tourists, and a pleasant surprise to others. See Chapter 19, Marinas.

Bait sales – Major use areas only. Usually concession-operated where there is sufficient business to make it profitable.

Fishing supplies – Bait, lures, fishing line and fishing tackle are desirable sales items on larger, heavily used piers. Also, usually concession-operated.

Enclosed areas – In some lakes in cold weather areas, floating, enclosed, all-weather fishing areas are built.

Lighting – For night use – usually in urban/ suburban areas.

Food sales – Desirable on larger piers with heavy use, especially on piers with heavy non-fishing use. Again, usually concession-operated.

Sightseers – Can account for the majority of the total number of users on a pier if they are permitted access. At any given time, except at night, they may be at least equivalent to the number of fishermen, and frequently, in tourist areas, two times or more people than the fishermen. Over a day's time, they could amount to several times the number of fishermen.

Toilets – These facilities are needed where there are no other public toilets within 400 feet (120 m) of the pier. They can be unisex if desired.

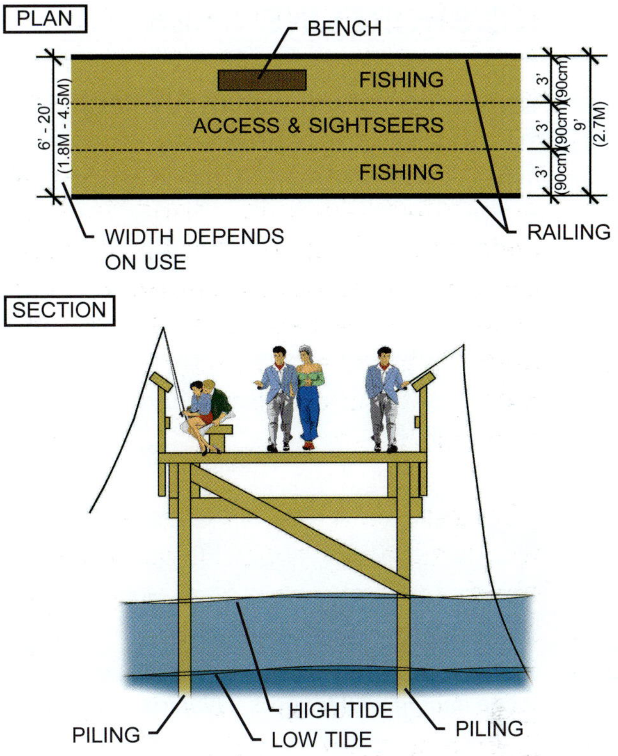

FIG. 22.4 – PIER FOR TOURISTS AND FISHING

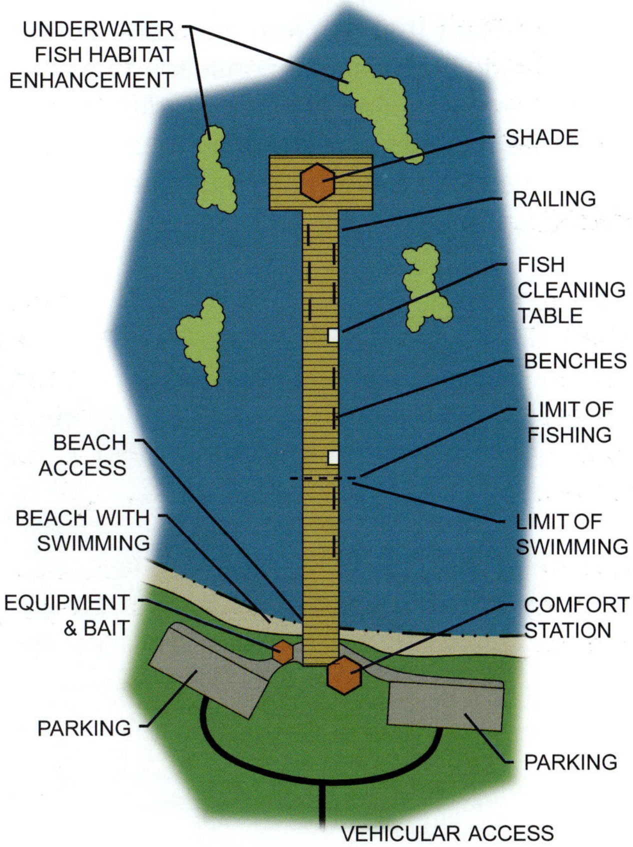

FIG. 22.5 – PUBLIC FISHING PIER

FISHING/SHORELINE USES

There can be no fishing within 300 lineal feet (100 m) of any shoreline use, such as swimming, snorkeling, beachcombing, walking, etc.

Shoreline fishing with helpers – Naples, Florida

HABITAT MANAGEMENT

It is important that fish management experts and aquatic biologists be consulted to assure proper use of fishing waters. Modification of shoreline habitats for swimming, boating, and other uses can have major adverse impacts on the fisheries.

A careful assessment of fishing as opposed to other water-based recreation is essential to prevent conflicts among users. Stumps, sunken brush, and other desirable fish cover may conflict with boating or scuba diving, for example. Aquatic growth necessary for fish cover and to sustain the aquatic food chain can conflict with boating and swimming.

Underwater habitat improvement should be considered wherever heavy use is likely to occur. Properly designed and placed underwater improvements can significantly enhance fishing success in both freshwater and saltwater habitats.

Construction of artificial reefs and other fish hiding places is frequently desirable in areas with sandy bottoms and little fish habitat.

In many areas, the underwater environment can be modified by placing clean, void-producing material on the ocean floor. Such things as old ships, junk cars, large boulders, and clean, large-sized construction debris can be utilized.

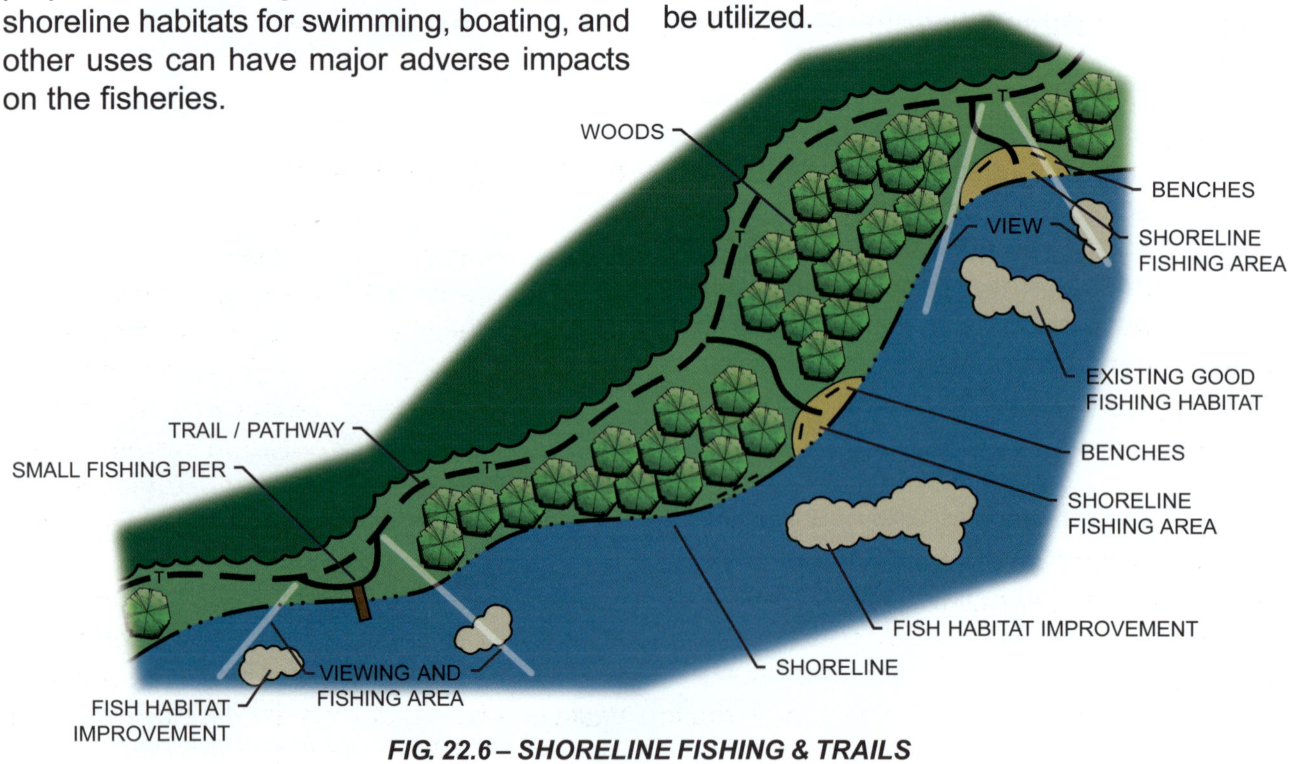

FIG. 22.6 – SHORELINE FISHING & TRAILS

PARKING

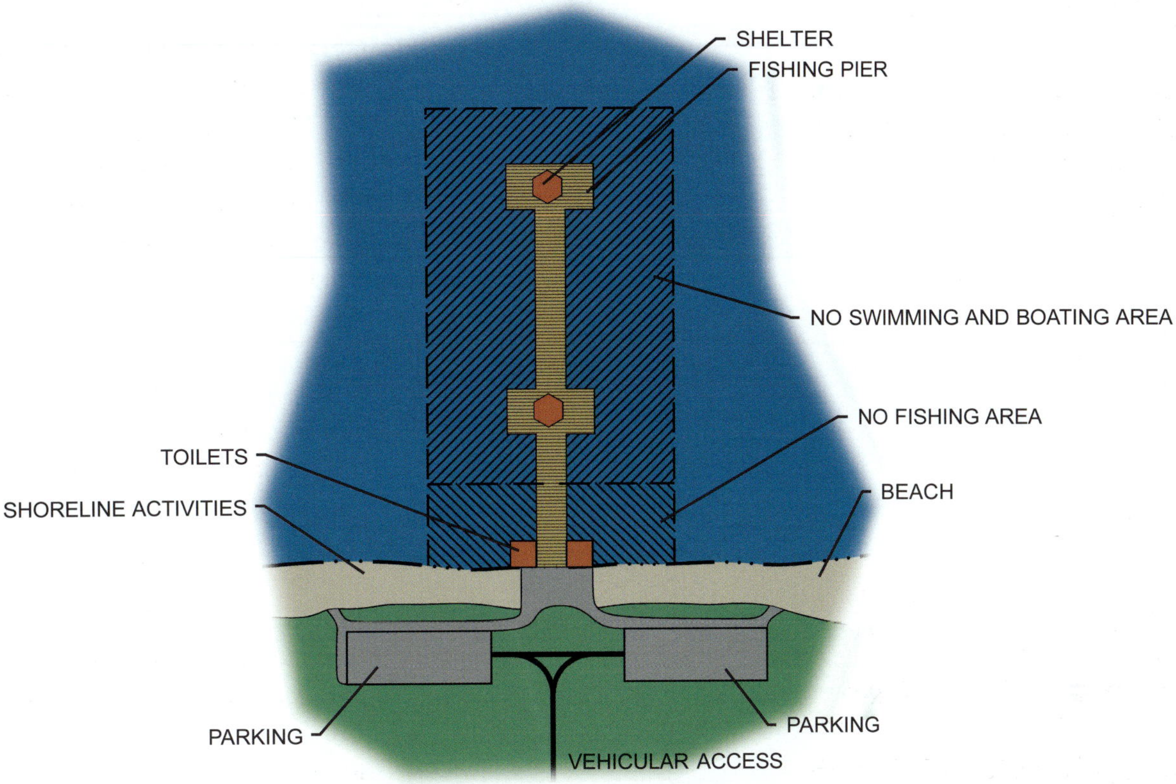

FIG. 22.7 – RESTRICTED ZONING FOR FISHING PIER

STREAM-RIVER FISHING

The support facilities shown for other types of fishing should be provided as appropriate, considering the waterway's size, productivity, and location.

Consider installation of stream-improvement devices if justified by the waterway's present or potential ability to sustain natural fish populations. Care must be exercised to ensure that the improvements do not degrade the visual environment, especially in park and tourism areas.

It may be desirable to establish specific waterway segments for fly fishing or artificial lures only. It is important, however, to recognize that a proper balance must be achieved or young or infrequent fishermen and the underprivileged may be inhibited as these groups usually use natural bait. Fish for fun projects with a one-fish per creel limit daily, permitting either bait or lure and requiring barbless hooks, may be appropriate in some areas.

CONFLICTS/FISHING

Fishing is not compatible with most other recreation activities. Fish need their special habitats, which are frequently not compatible with people needs. Fishing can be dangerous (hooking people instead of fish). This is especially true between swimmers and shoreline trails and fishermen. Zoning and/or special design considerations may be required.

In confined water areas, zoning may be necessary if unlimited-horsepower motor boating is to be permitted, since the resulting wake can be dangerous and, at the very least, disrupt the fishing experience.

Chapter 23

HUNTING AND WILDLIFE MANAGEMENT

HUNTING

Resource facilities with 400 acres (160 hectares) or more of undeveloped land, and/or water areas that are presently or potentially capable of sustaining hunting within their boundaries, should be considered for hunting. It should be noted that this is a very controversial area and one that should be thoroughly explored with conservationists, sportsmen, and local citizens before making a decision.

Hunting requires extensive acreage free of or with minimal conflicting activities. The average desirable density of hunters-per-acre is extremely variable and depends on game species and the game capability of the natural resources involved. It is important to work closely with game experts to develop properly this particular activity.

Consider the types and volumes of day or overnight uses occurring or anticipated in the resource site during hunting season(s) in relationship to the area's hunting opportunities, game species, and weapons to be used. It probably will not be desirable in densely populated areas to permit hunting at all, and especially not in heavy-use recreation seasons.

HUNTING USER CHARACTERISTICS

In 2001, 13.8 million people went hunting as their primary activity – down 3 million since 1985. They spent an average of 18 days in the field, for a total of 228 million days of hunting – down from 334 million in 1985. Generally, hunting is down significantly, and the trend may be continuing. See also Chapter 27, Non-Consumptive Wildlife Recreation. The activity can be further broken down into:

Big Game	10.8 Million hunters	Down 14% from 1985
	153.1 Million days	Up 44% from 1985
Small Game	5.4 Million hunters	Down 50% from 1985
	60.1 Million days	Down 52% from 1985

Hunting in a forested area
Photo by Mark Anderson

Migratory Birds	2.9 Million hunters	Down 42% from 1985
	29 Million days	Down 18% from 1985

Bird hunting
Photo by Mark Anderson

Other	1.1 Million hunters	Down 61% from 1985
	20.2 Million days	Down 89% from 1985
	Total hunters	Down 74% from 1985
	Total days	Down 17% from 1985

The percentage of hunting population by age who hunted in 2001 was ages 16-17, 4% (down 10 from 1985); 17-24, 10% (down 1 percent from 1985); 25-34, 19%; 35-44, 27%; 45-64, 8%; 65 and over, 3%. Over 90% of hunters are Caucasian, and over three-quarters are from non-metropolitan areas. The rate of participation was not significantly affected by education or income.

The male/female ratio is 10:1.

Hunting is either decreasing or stable in popularity, depending on the survey consulted, with a 16% decrease in the percentage of people hunting from 10% of the population in 1955 to 8.4% of the population in 1985.

Most types of hunting have the hunters on site ready to hunt at dawn before the sun rises, with a turnover of close to 0%. Vehicular access and parking must be designed for basically all of the hunter population. Calculate at 1.2 people per vehicle.

FIG. 23.1 – PERCENTAGE OF HUNTERS (ON AN ANNUAL BASIS) WHO ALSO MAY FISH OR PARTICIPATE IN NON-CONSUMPTIVE WILDLIFE RECREATION

REQUIREMENTS

LAND REQUIREMENTS

An extensive acreage of land, wetlands, and/or water that by reason of its established or establishable habitat and game populations is conducive to hunting.

FACILITIES

- Access (gravel and dirt roads acceptable) – must be identifiable and easily negotiated at night.

- Parking – small (3 to 10 cars) dispersed parking with gravel or stabilized turf. Hard paving not needed or necessarily desirable. Parking must be identifiable at night during the hunting season. These areas could also be used by non-hunters during the non-hunting season as starting points for wildlife observation and hiking. See Chapter 27 for non-hunting activities.

- Game cleaning area – shade with tables for cutting up game, and garbage disposal for getting rid of unwanted carcasses.

Game cleaning/dressing shelter
– South Florida Water Management District

- Refuse disposal.

- The need for picnic or overnight use is contingent on hunter origins and local customs. Hunting is generally permitted only during the low-use park seasons, and park facilities can frequently be used, especially the campgrounds, which would normally be in no-hunting zones.

- Sanitary facilities, if any are provided, should be located in areas of concentrated hunting, i.e., on game preserves. They must be findable at night. Lighting is not a necessity, and pit and portable toilets are acceptable. Unisex toilets are suitable since most hunting is by men.

MANAGEMENT

Clearly visible and well-defined and well-marked boundaries between hunting and non-hunting activities must be established. Adequate safety zones (buffer space) must be provided. The type of game, terrain, and weapons used must, of course, be considered in establishing the extent of the buffer zone.

ALTERNATIVES TO HUNTING

Analysis of the site may determine that game harvesting is not practical. As an alternative means of accommodating the hunting public, the following should be considered for development:

- Skeet, trap, rifle, or archery ranges (see Chapter 26, Firearm Ranges and Chapter 25, Archery).

- Hunting dog training and/or dog field trial events can be permitted and promoted.

GAME MANAGEMENT

Manipulation of a site's natural resources to improve game habitat may be desirable or even necessary. This may include:

- Management of existing vegetative cover.

- Planting of trees and shrubs suitable for game food, and may include crops, such as domesticated grains.

- Establishment of additional impoundments or wetlands.

- Opening habitat and feeding spaces in woods, e.g., removing some trees.

Resource improvements to sustain game animal and bird wildlife population are of equal importance to improving the non-hunting visitors' wildlife observation opportunities. Again, see Chapter 27. In addition to the cultural practices noted for hunting, it is desirable to consider closing certain habitat areas to public use during breeding or other sensitive biological seasons. Keep in mind that healthy game habitat is generally good for the overall wildlife population. Managing areas for hunting will also likely increase the number of non-game birds and animals that are of interest to many resource users.

Non-consumptive wildlife and nature observation facilities such as trails, photography, and observation blinds should be considered in hunting areas with significant wildlife concentrations. They should be designed to keep man's intrusion into the wildlife habitat at an absolute minimum, while permitting observation and/or photography of the birds and animals during non-hunting seasons. (See Chapter 27, Non-Consumptive Wildlife Recreation.)

Chapter 24

EQUESTRIAN FACILITIES

Horses/foals – jump horses being shown to tourists at a private farm in rural Finland

USER CHARACTERISTICS

Riding is heavily skewed to females, probably in the seventy percent to thirty percent ratio. All sex-related support facilities must, therefore, be heavily skewed to women. Toilets must reflect this fact and should probably be designed as unisex facilities or skewed at about a three female to one male ratio.

Riding is normally a short-time activity. Most riding is done close to home. A few available hours account for about half of all rides, while slightly over one-quarter of all rides are one-day outings. Sometimes, equestrian activities are related to overnight campground and/or trail camping. (See Chapter 8, Trails and Pathways, and Chapter 14, Overnight Use.)

For any equestrian facility to be truly successful, it must be associated with an equestrian trail system. The more comprehensive and varied the trails, the better the opportunity for an equestrian center success.

Most successful stables depend on boarding horses as their main source of income. This activity can be combined with a rental (hack) operation. Rental of horses is difficult to make financially self-sustaining due to high insurance costs.

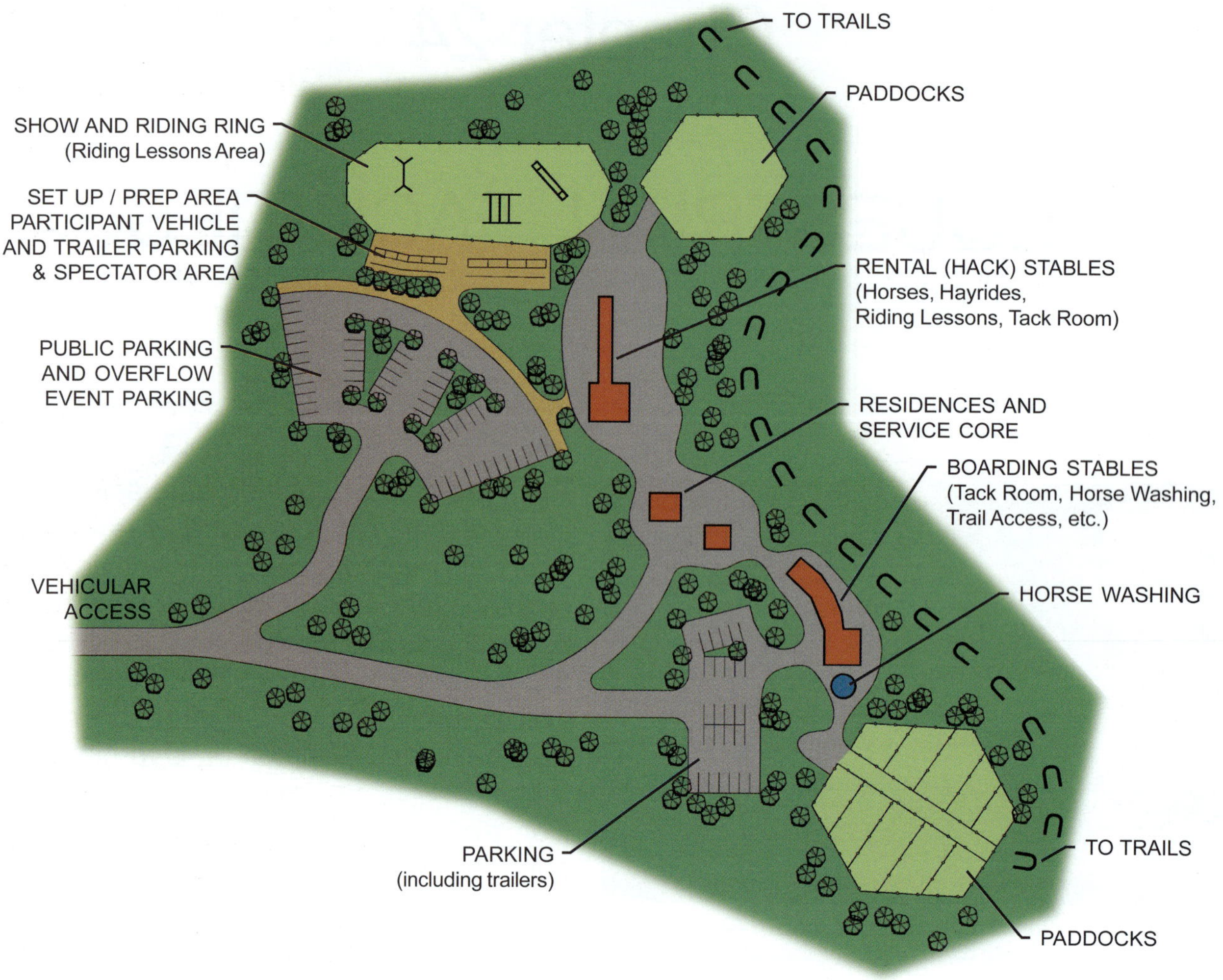

FIG. 24.1 – LAYOUT – EQUESTRIAN COMPLEX

Items to be considered:

1. Is there a need and, if so, how big should the facility be, and what should it contain?

2. Kind of stable(s).

- Boarding (thirty horses minimum or multiples thereof).*

- Rental (thirty horses minimum or multiples thereof).*

*The approximate number of horses one person can care for is thirty.

Paddocks
Photo by the Rowland family

3. Types of activities at the center.

- Show
- Rodeo
- Hunting (not normally done in most of the U.S.)*
- Cross-country*

Jumping ring
Photo by the Rowland family

- Show jumping*
- Equestrian riding lessons
- Dressage*
- Hayrides
- Trails and/or trail access (see Chapter 8, Trails and Pathways)
- Equestrian assembly area for trail rides (see Chapter 8, Trails and Pathways)

*See Equestrian Sports [24] for additional details on the design of these elements.

4. Parking (including horse trailers).

- Boarding – one car/two horses
- Rental – one car/one horse
- Spectators - if equestrian events are planned
- Staff

Concession trail ride (mules) into the canyon at Grand Canyon National Park, Arizona

5. Availability of trails or land for trail development. Without trails an equestrian center is likely to fail.

6. Corrals/paddocks.

7. Sanitary facilities.

8. Picnic area(s).

9. Food service.

10. Employee housing – a necessity for safety purposes.

11. Overnight housing accommodations for users – not normally provided.

12. Utilities – water, sewage, electrical and communications.

13. Indoor riding ring – a necessity in areas with many days of inclement weather (rain, snow, or heat).

14. Equestrian camping. (See Chapter 14 – Overnight Use.)

15. A place to wash and groom horses (locate between stables or, better, at the boarding stables).

16. Removal of manure.

17. Storage of feed (grain and hay - needs access for large trucks, including semis).

18. Tack room.

19. Meeting, lounge, and office space.

20. Special wagon rides. Should be easily transportable to take horse(s) and wagon(s) to events and celebrations.

Wagon ride in a tourist area in Europe

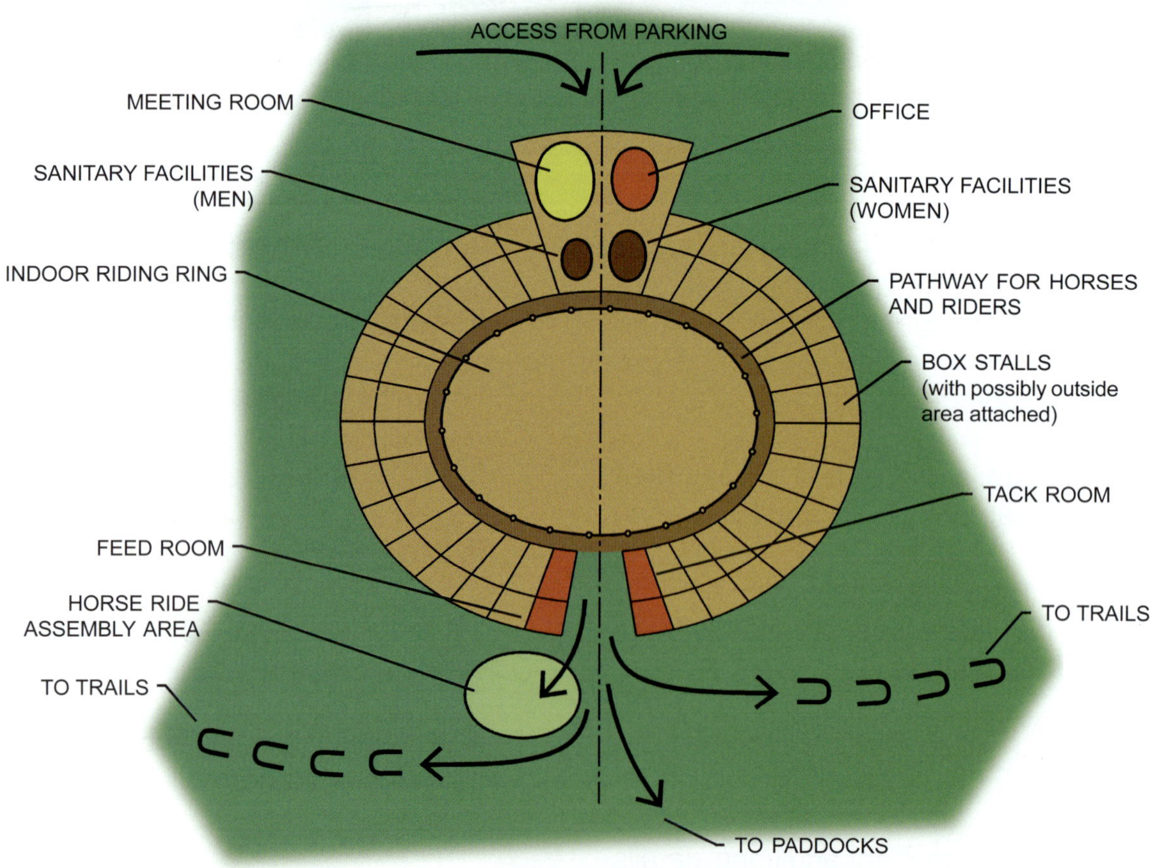

FIG. 24.2 – INDOOR RIDING RING SURROUNDED BY STABLES

Chapter 25

ARCHERY

There are three types of archery – target ranges (open fields), field courses, and hunting archery. All three can be used for competitive shooting. Field courses are frequently used for skill sharpening by bow hunters. Bows, crossbows, and similar equipment were originally designed for and are still used for killing. Safety is, therefore, a primary requisite of any archery range facility. This is especially true with the new "fast bows" with their greater range and velocity. (39)

3D Archery is for all ages and both sexes. One-third of the participants are women and children. 3D courses run from twenty to forty targets. (40)

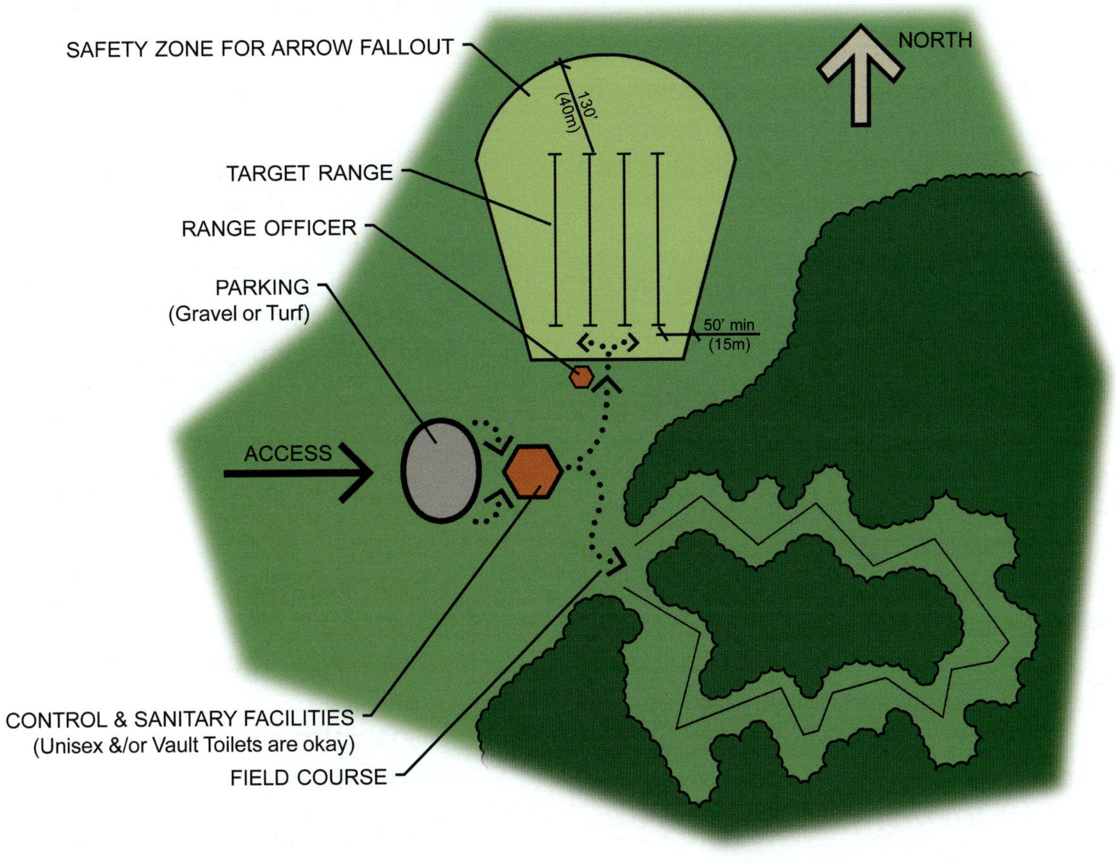

FIG. 25.1 – CONCEPTUAL LAYOUT FOR AN ARCHERY COMPLEX

TARGET RANGE

Minimum Requirements:

- An open field and surrounding buffer area of approximately 1.5 acres (1 ha) for 10 shooting stations, and 5 acres (2 ha) for 25 shooting stations are needed.

- Turf field around targets with good, non-stony soil to protect arrows is needed.

- As an absolute minimum, a safety fence located a minimum of 80 feet (25 m) is needed.

- A marked/signed, fenced safety fan of 300 yards (250 m) is needed from any shooting station/position.

- Safety embankments and/or arrow stops may be desirable, especially in multiuse park areas where space is limited and possible conflicts could occur with other park uses.

- Align ranges as close to north/south as possible.

- Targets should be placed at various distances.

- Communications – A minimum of one accessible land line is necessary. Cell phone use may be suitable if reception is adequate at the site.

- Electrical supply is desirable, except at night-use ranges where it becomes necessary. Solar panels or other alternative power sources will normally be adequate.

- Sanitary facilities – unisex vault compost-type toilets are acceptable.

- Parking – minimum of one space per shooting station is needed; more space, usually gravel or grass, will be required if there are many spectators anticipated.

- Accessibility – primarily for the mobility impaired.

- Adequate information and directional signs must be provided.

- Ten feet (3 meters) per shooting lane is required.

- Trash receptacles.

Desirable: (41)

- Clubhouse.

- Spectator area(s).

- Wind direction indicator.

- A support structure, which should have, as a minimum, a meeting room/ registration room, equipment storage, and sanitary facilities.

- Maintenance/storage building.

- Flush toilets.

- Potable water supply.

- Bow racks (portable).

- Spectator parking (could be overflow turfed area equal to 100 percent of required parking).

- Larger facilities can support a food service operation.

- Night lighting.

- Shaded registration area.

- If frequent competition is planned, a permanent scoreboard would be useful.

- Practice shooting area.

- Picnic facilities.

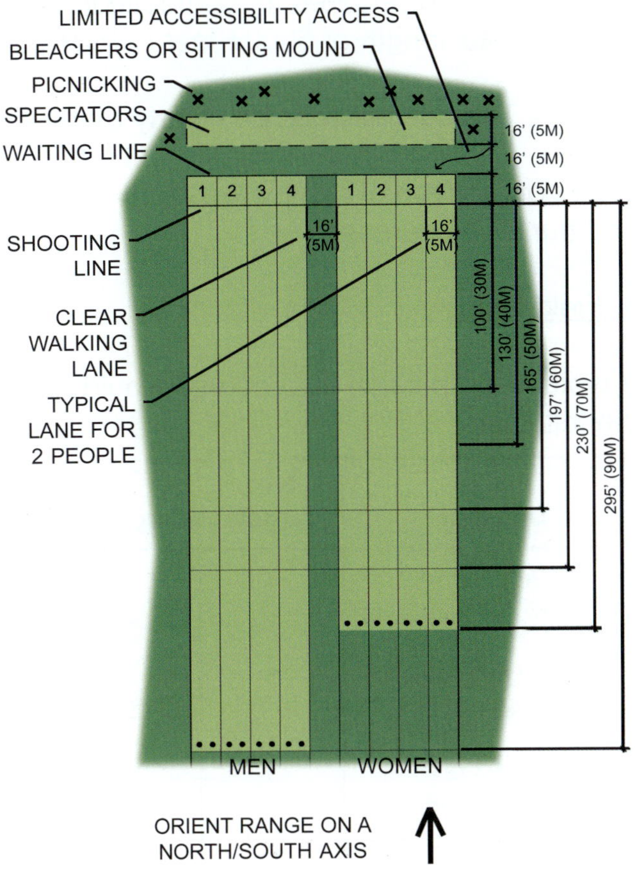

FIG. 25.2 – TARGET RANGE

RANGE DETAILS

- Open grass field to be approximately 400 feet (120 m) long oriented on a north/south axis.

- Men - maximum 295 feet (90 m) shooting distance plus overflight 82 feet (25 m).

- Women - maximum 230 feet (70 m) shooting distance plus overflight of 82 feet (25 m).

- If space is critical, a backstop can be installed. Size varies, depending on target size. Use 3-butt widths wide x two-butt widths high – 12 feet x 8 feet (3.65 m x 2.4 m).

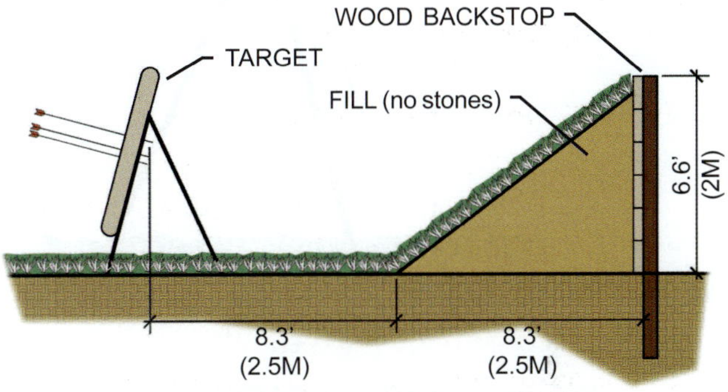

FIG. 25.3 – ARCHERY BACKSTOP

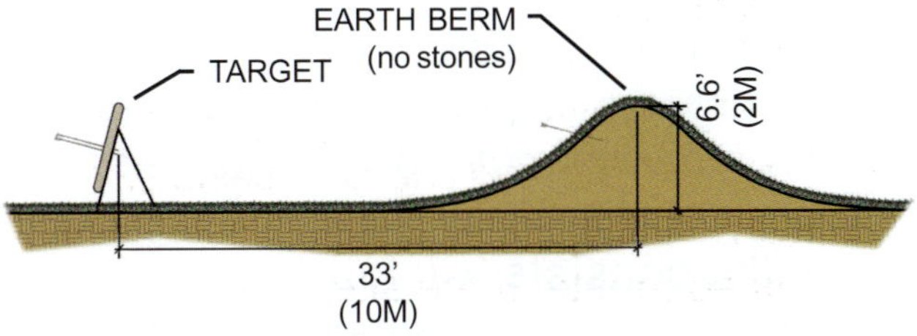

FIG. 25.4 – ALTERNATE ARCHERY BACKSTOP

• Sixteen foot (5 m) lane width is normally sufficient for two shooters at one time; however, major competitions may restrict the lane to one shooter only at ten feet (3 m).

• Either targets or shooting lines can be moved to accommodate the varying target distances.

Target butts are of four normal sizes, depending on the shooting distance. They vary from 30 inches x 30 inches (76 cm x 76 cm) to 42 inches x 42 inches (106 cm x 106 cm).

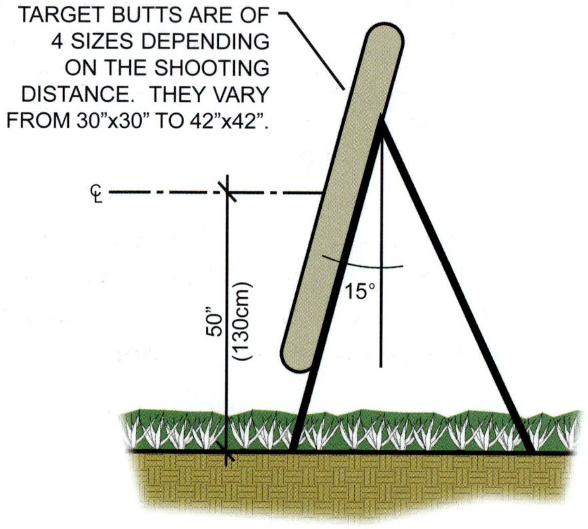

FIG. 25.5 – TYPICAL TARGET (17, 41)

FIELD COURSE

A field course consists of a roving archery game where an archer moves to successive targets of varying lengths and difficulties similar to a golf course. A competition field course normally consists of fourteen targets. Generally, they are constructed in a manner that will keep an area looking as natural as possible.

Minimum Space Requirements:

• Approximately 40 acres (16 ha) are required. The absolute minimum with lots of walk-backs and good terrain is 20 acres (8+ ha); about one target per acre. (41)

• Field archery trails are frequently of compacted gravel or crushed stone. They can be made of wood chips, especially in wooded areas.

• Targets have a minimum of 48 positions required for competition, with a total length of 5000± feet (1480± m).

• The course must be clearly marked.

Field courses are of two types – field courses and hunter's courses.

1. Field Course

A typical competition field course would have the following: (17, 41)

Distance	# of Targets	Ø of Target Faces
50'/65'/82'/98' (15 m/20 m/25 m/30 m)	4	14" 35 cm
130'/148'/165' (40 m/45 m/50 m)	3	20" 50 cm
180'/197'/213' (55 m/60 m/65 m)	3	25" 65 cm
65'/82'/98'/115' (20 m/ 25 m/30 m/35 m)	1	8" 20 cm
98'/115'/130'/148' (30 m/35 m/40 m/45 m)	1	20" 50 cm
165'/197'/230'/263' (50 m/ 60 m/70 m/80 m)	1	25" 65 cm

FIG. 25.6 – TYPICAL FIELD COURSE TARGET SIZES

Distance	# of Targets	Total Distance Of Arrow Flight	Ø of TargetFaces	# of Arrows
Single position walk up	4	260'/80m	Vary	8
4 Position walk up	4	1050'/320m		16
2 Position walk up	3	1970'/600m		20
4 Position walk up	3	1600'/480m		12
		Total 4880±'/1480m		

FIG. 25.7 – FIELD AND HUNTER COURSE TYPICAL TARGET DISTANCES

2. Hunter's Course

A typical competition hunter's course would have the following: (41, 17)

- 14 Targets (seldom shot in the same sequence).
- Uses animal silhouette targets.
- A hunter's course takes much more space than a competition field course.

Required Features:

- Safety barrier(s) are absolutely necessary, especially in wooded areas. They are to protect park users and others who are unaware of the range and its safety hazards. Fencing off the safety zone is a must.
- Communications for emergency purposes. At least one land line or an in-place, secured cell phone may be adequate if reception is good.

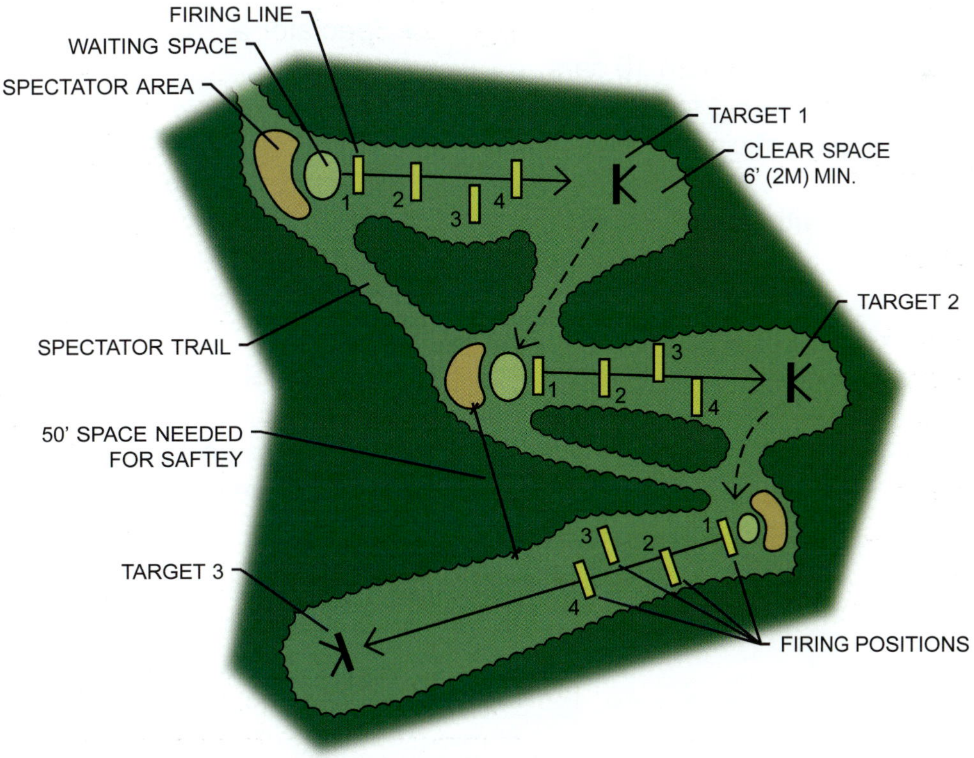

FIG. 25.8 – PREFERRED HUNTER'S COURSE LAYOUT (17, 41)

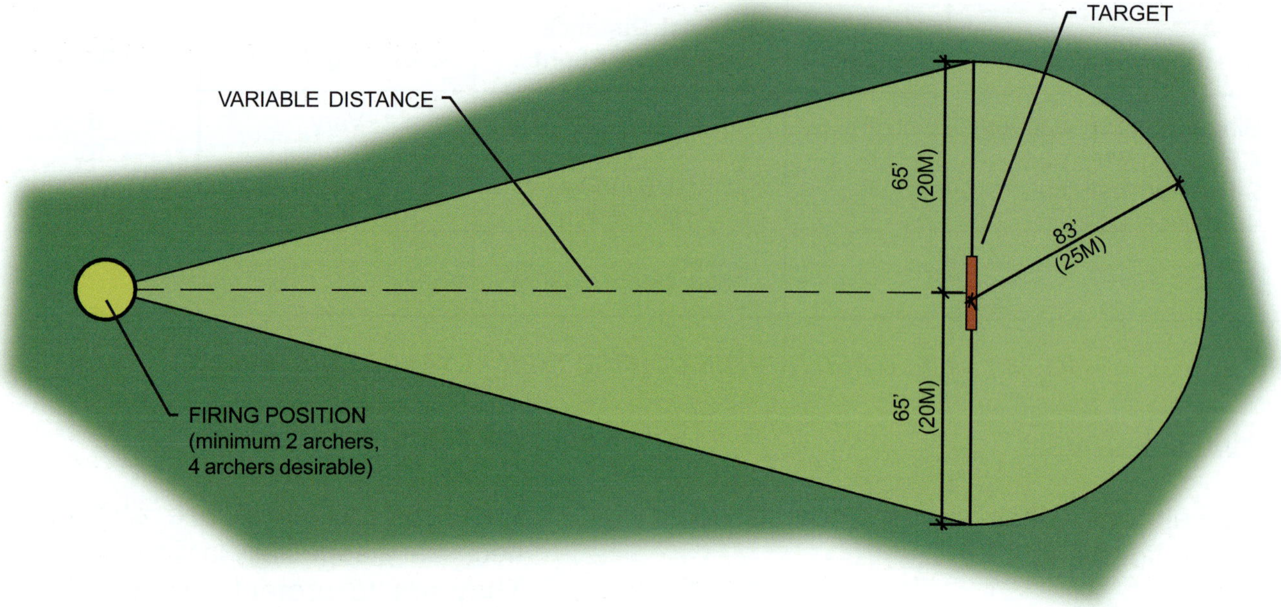

FIG. 25.9 – SAFETY ZONE FOR A TARGET

• Sanitary facilities – vault or composting type are probably sufficient.* The number of toilets is dependent on the anticipated amount of use.

• Parking for users – minimum 10 cars or at least enough parking for one car for each 1.5 people anticipated.

*Can be shared facilities with Target Range.

Desirable additional Field and Hunter Course Features:

(See Target Range)

• Spectator areas.

• Permanent bow rack.

• Spectator parking.*

• Benches 15 feet (4.5+ m) behind shooting stake.

• Directional signs.

• Practice area (one or more butts at up to 180 feet (55 m).

*Can be shared facilities with Target Range.

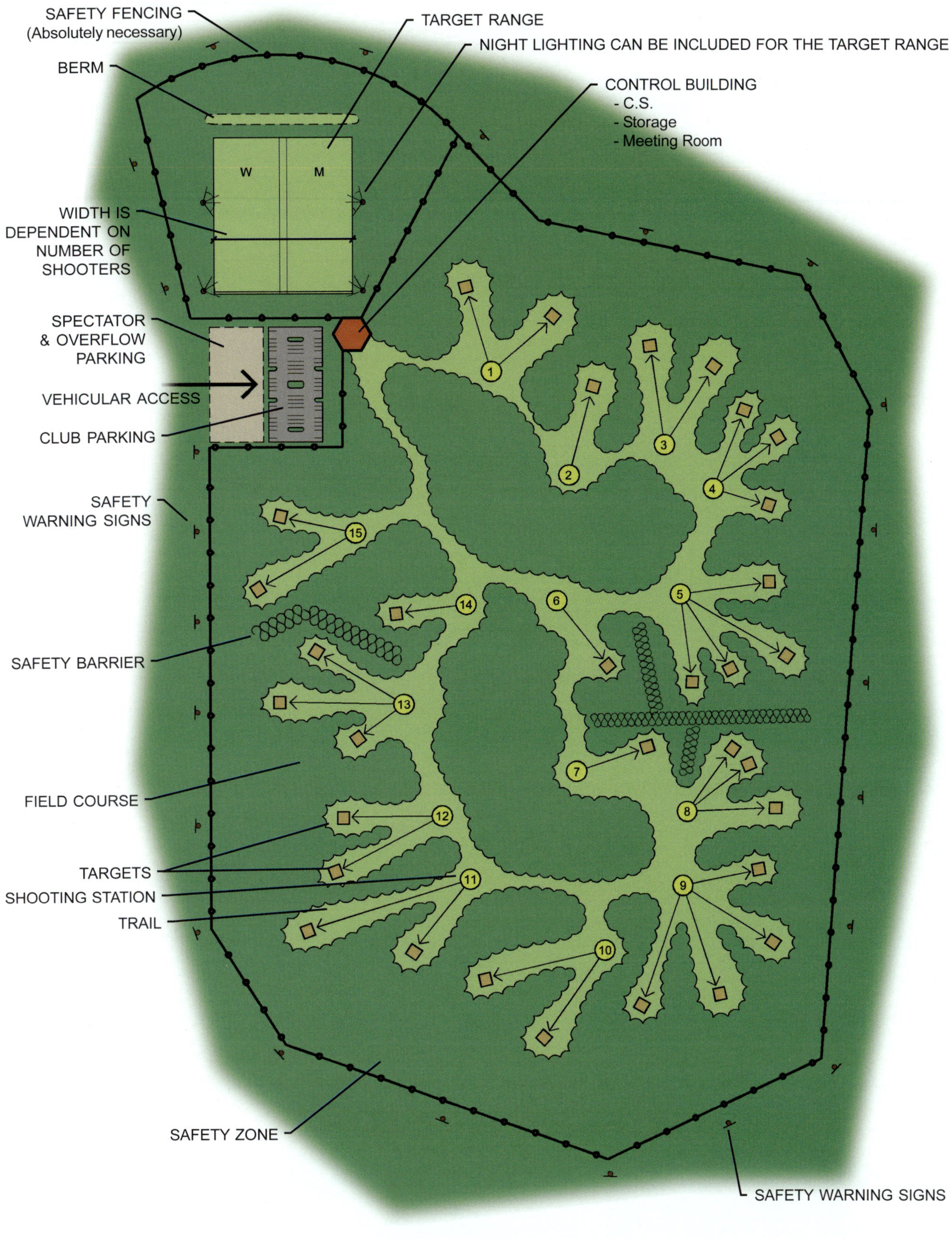

FIG. 25.10 – COMBINED TARGET RANGE AND FIELD COURSE ARCHERY FACILITY

Chapter 26

FIREARM RANGES

The number of hunters has remained fairly constant over the last several years, but has decreased as a percentage of the total population. [21, 38] It is assumed that the number of target shooters is directly related to the number of hunters. If this assumption is true, it would indicate that the need for new rifle ranges will be minimal, and that they will probably be needed only in areas of increasing population. Older, established ranges will, however, need renovations, additions, and, possibly, they will need to be relocated. The National Rifle Association has extensive detailed information on the development and operations of all types of firearm ranges and should be contacted for additional information and advice in this area of recreation facility development. [19]

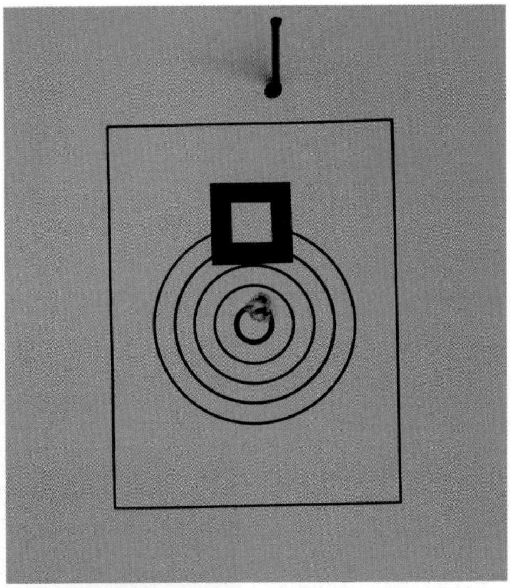

Target – Poulsbo, Washington
Photo by John Parrish

Some statistics regarding users of firearms:

- The male/female ratio is about 10:1.
- The use of firearms is very race-sensitive, with participation at about ten Caucasians to one of all other races.
- Use of firearms is more focused on rural and, possibly, suburban areas at a ratio of three or more to one.
- Educational level is not a significant factor in relationship to the use of firearms. (See Chapter 23 for information regarding hunting.)

Firearm ranges can be used for a variety of shooting activities utilizing a wide range of equipment.

Activities	Equipment
	Pistols – still and rapid fire Rifles Bench rest target guns Air rifles Big bore rifles
Target shooting	Muzzle loading rifles Shotguns Bows Crossbows } (See Chapter 25, Archery)
Trap and skeet shooting	Shotguns
Practical shooting (hunting, simulation combat situations, etc.)	Pistols Rifles Shotguns Assault guns [72, 73]

All of these activities can be done for (1) learning, (2) skill enhancement, or (3) competition. The ranges can be for a single activity or for the entire list as noted above. They can include archery and dog training areas as well (outside of the rifle/pistol range itself), but this is quite unusual. They may be indoor and/or outdoor and vary from 10± firing points to a hundred or more.

Many, if not most, ranges are operated by a sportsmen's club or a law enforcement agency. These clubs provide the opportunity for fellowship, which is a major aspect of shooting activities.

Many sportsmen's clubs have their own facilities while others cooperate with and/or lease land from governmental agencies. This chapter will cover only larger-scale facilities requiring open air range(s) for both public and private developments.

LOCATION CRITERIA

Pistol range/backstop and multiple firing lines – Collier County, Florida. Photo by Thomas Brooks

SOUND

Ranges must be separated from other outdoor land use activities due to safety needs and noise from the firearms – ½ mile for rifle noise; ¾ mile for shotgun noise. The sound distance (unless baffled) can often cause the location of the clubhouse and ranges to be quite distant from the nearest public access. Range isolation will cause problems of long utility line runs to any available utility tie-ins. It will also increase the normal access road costs to the activity nodes.

SAFETY ZONES

Rifle, up to three miles (5 km); shotgun, up to 2000 feet (600 m±); pistols, 1.5 miles (2.2 km).

SIZE

Approximate acreage needed without barriers:

Rifle and pistol	Large bore – 1260 acres (510 ha) Small bore – 660 acres (270 ha) and pistol
Shotgun	370 acres (150 ha)

The needed acreage can be drastically reduced for all ranges by constructing berms and baffles.

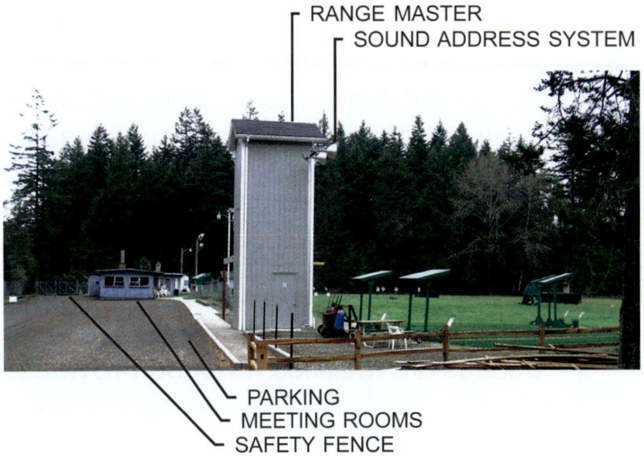

Rifle range – Poulsbo, Washington
Photo by John Parrish

DESIGN

Required:

- Range safety is the most important aspect of all shooting areas. See the Safety Factors section of this chapter.

- Orientation of all ranges (safety permitting) should be on a N/S axis.

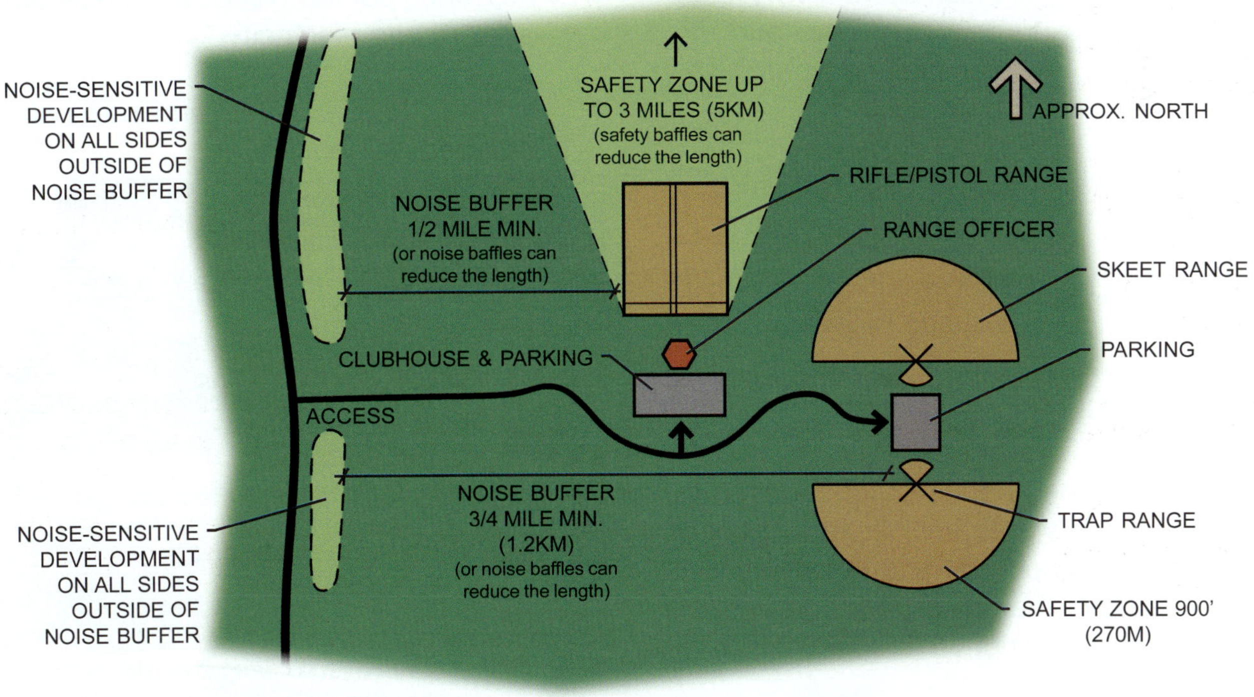

FIG. 26.1 – RIFLE RANGE COMPLEX

• Parking – 1.2 spaces per firing point plus parking for anticipated spectators; paved for normal use, although well-drained gravel lots are acceptable; gravel and/or stabilized turf is adequate for competitions and spectators. All parking must be located outside of the safety fan. Handicapped parking facilities and an accessible route to accessible facilities must be provided.

• Clubhouse

- Storage { Targets; Ammunition must be tightly secured; Tables and chairs }

- Meeting room
- Sanitary facilities — Unisex is best – the numbers of facilities would be heavily skewed to men – probably 5:1 ratio will normally be adequate.

  Flush system very desirable; vault and composting types acceptable.

- Table(s) space for target scoring

• Electricity { Clubhouse; Range towers }

- Solar power may be acceptable if cost effective.

• Land line phone service required for emergency calls, and helpful for general use. If good cell phone reception is available, then emergency ground line service may not be needed.

• Water – potable

- Municipal service is most desirable where economical connection can be made.

- Well water satisfactory if quality is alright.

- Can get by with bottled water. It may be the only source available if municipal and well water are not feasible.

• Sewage – can be septic system or composting and, if truly necessary, vault toilets can be used.

• Vending machines for beverages and snacks. They also provide a good income source.

• Access road must be controlled by lockable gate(s) for security purposes.

• Range tower – must be able to see ALL firing points. Needs a loudspeaker system and electricity.

• Firing line – paved and preferably covered and baffled.

Paved, baffled, and covered firing line with benches for bench shooting – Poulsbo, Washington
Photo by John Parrish

• Gun racks – space for two guns per firing point and benches for pistol ranges of 3 feet (90 cm) per firing point.

• Bench rests for bench rest firing competition.

Bench rest rifle shooting
– Poulsbo, Washington. Photo by John Parrish

• Targets – frequently have pulley systems for shorter distances – up to 150 feet (50 meters).

• Pits for people manning targets for high-powered rifles seldom needed and then only for ranges of 600 feet (180 m) or longer.

• Backstops – height is dependent on firing point baffling and size of safety zone. Must be able to collect and recycle shots.

Pistol range with backstop
– Collier County, Florida. Photo by Thomas Brooks

• Side berms – where unlimited space is not available.

• Safety baffles – usually needed at or near firing line.

• Maintenance building/storage building – only on large complexes, and then only where other project maintenance facilities are not available.

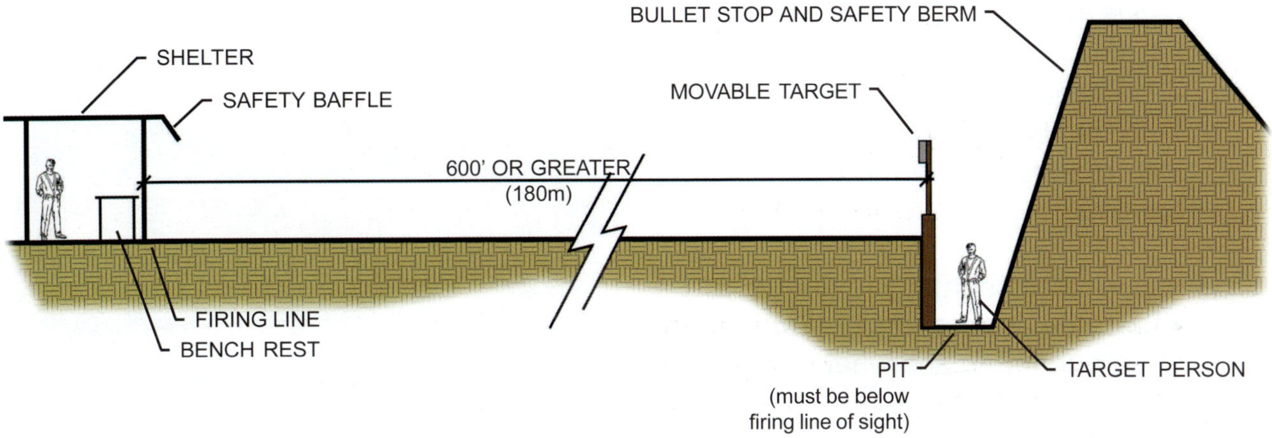

FIG. 26.2 – PITS (ONLY ON VERY LONG RANGES)

• Solid waste disposal system – usually a combination of dumpsters and trash cans. Usually government-run, but could be facility staff responsibility.

• Walks – constructed for light service vehicle access to pick up trash and for facility security patrol and maintenance purposes.

• Internal communication – required for all large complexes and for those with target pits [600 feet (180 m) range distances or greater]. Could be cell or land line.

• Topography – must be such that the firing line and targets are at the same elevation. Very desirable if steep hill is located behind targets.

Desirable:

• Work room for loading, etc.

• Water line tie-in to a municipal system.

• Sewage tie-in to a municipal system.

• Night lighting on ranges where night use is likely.

• Covered firing line – usually needs artificial lighting. May be constructed in a manner to permit cold weather heating.

• Spectator seating – needs to be separated from participants, but still close enough to see what is going on; shading desirable.

SAFETY FACTORS

There are three zones to be considered: direct fire, safety, and ricochet.

DIRECT FIRE ZONE

Distance that a bullet will travel from the firing line. The distance can be in miles (kilometers) for high-powered rifles unless baffled by hills and/or constructed barriers.

• High powered rifles –
16,500 feet (5,000 m) - approximately 3 miles (5 kilometers)

• Small bore rifles –
9,000 feet (2,700 m) - approximately 1.7 miles (2.7 kilometers)

• Pistol –
Maximum 9,000 feet (2,700 m) - approximately 1.7 miles (2.7 km) - normally about 7,200 feet (2.2 km)

• Shotgun –
2,000 feet (600 m) or less, depending on the shell selection permitted on the range.

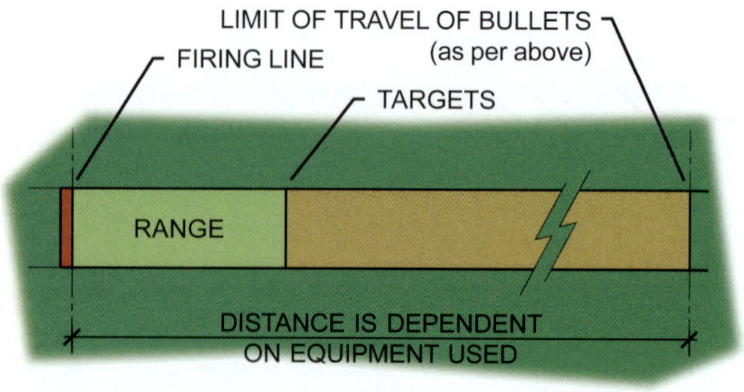

FIG. 26.3 – DIRECT FIRE ZONE

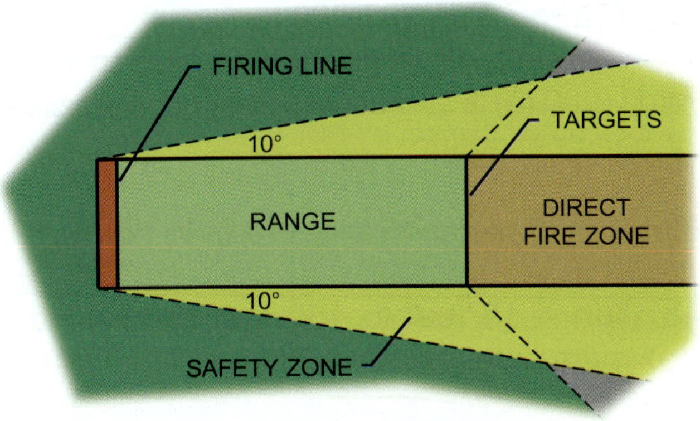

FIG. 26.4 – SAFETY ZONE

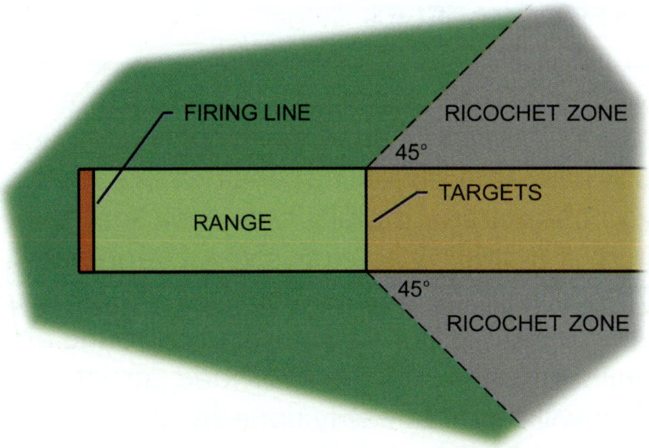

FIG. 26.5 – RICOCHET ZONE

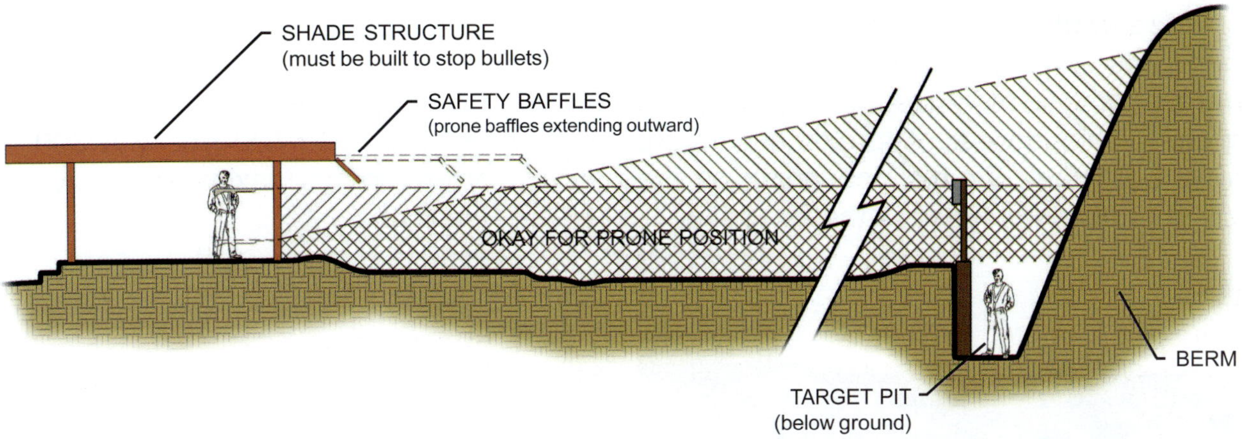

FIG. 26.6 – SAFETY FEATURES

SAFETY ZONE

An area ten degree or more angle from either end of the firing line.

RICOCHET ZONE

An area of approximately a 45 degree angle from the targets and extending.

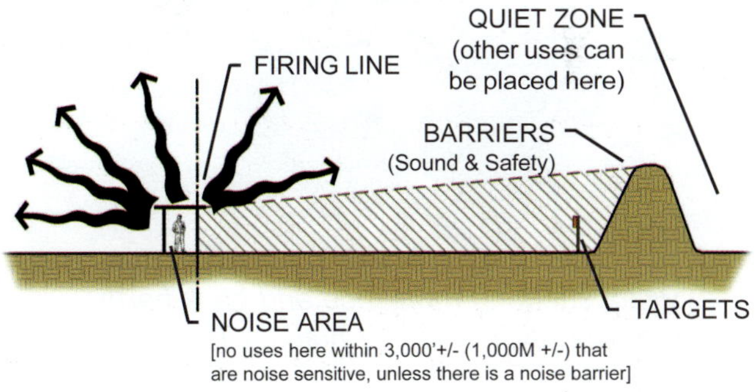

FIG. 26.7 – THE EFFECTS OF FIREARM NOISES

BARRIERS

Because of the vast amount of land that would be required for ranges without baffles and/or barriers, it is imperative to either locate them in areas with hilly terrain or to install baffles and barriers. These barriers will also help in reducing noise problems. Basically, sound travels in line of sight; therefore, if the area of noise concern cannot be seen from the firing line (excluding vegetation), there will be little noise. (See Chapter 3, Parkscape).

SAFETY BAFFLES

A structure or series of structures that will restrict the bullets/arrows to a confined space. Basically, they should be constructed such that you cannot see the sky or see off the range from the firing line (exclusive of vegetation). They should be maintenance free if possible, i.e., vegetated earth berms on the ground and bullet-proof wood for overhead structures. This will be most easily done by constructing an overhead shelter at the firing line with tall side berms and a backstop. The backstop could be a natural hill. Side baffles of mounded vegetated earth are recommended, although other types of construction are possible and, where space is at a premium, should be seriously considered. Approximate height should be 8 feet (2.4 m), depending on the baffling protection offered at the firing line.

Pistol shooting (note side and back berms) – Collier County, Florida. Photo by Thomas Brooks

RANGE LENGTHS

Distance on ranges from firing line to targets is variable.

Small Bore – 25 feet to 300 feet (7.5 m up to 100 m).

Rifle Range – up to 1,000 feet (200 m to 300 m); in long-range target shooting up to 1,000 yards (900 m) is sometimes desired, especially for bench shooting.

Pistol – 25 feet to150 feet (8 m to 50 m).

Air Gun – 15 feet to 150 feet (5 to 40 m - maximum safety zone 1,000 feet (300 m)).

Muzzle Loading Pistol – to 150 feet (to 50 m - maximum safety zone 1.5 miles (2.4 km)).

Muzzle Loading Round Ball - to 300 feet (to 100 m).

Muzzle Loading Mini Ball – 50 feet/80 feet to 300 feet (25 m to 100 m), with 300 feet (100 m) or less normal maximum - safety same as large bore rifle.

SKEET AND TRAP

Skeet and trap shooting were originally started to improve hunter skills and, like many sports activities, quickly became competitive events in their own right. Trap shooting is one of the most active parts of the shooting sports and must be seriously considered in any firearms range complex. It is strictly an outdoor event and, other than the problem of noise, takes relatively little space. Approximately 2 ½ acres (1,000 feet x 1,000 feet) or one hectare (300 m x 300 m) for skeet, and somewhat less for trap.

Trap houses for both trap and skeet competition are required to meet certain specifications. See the most recent NRA Range Manual for specifics.

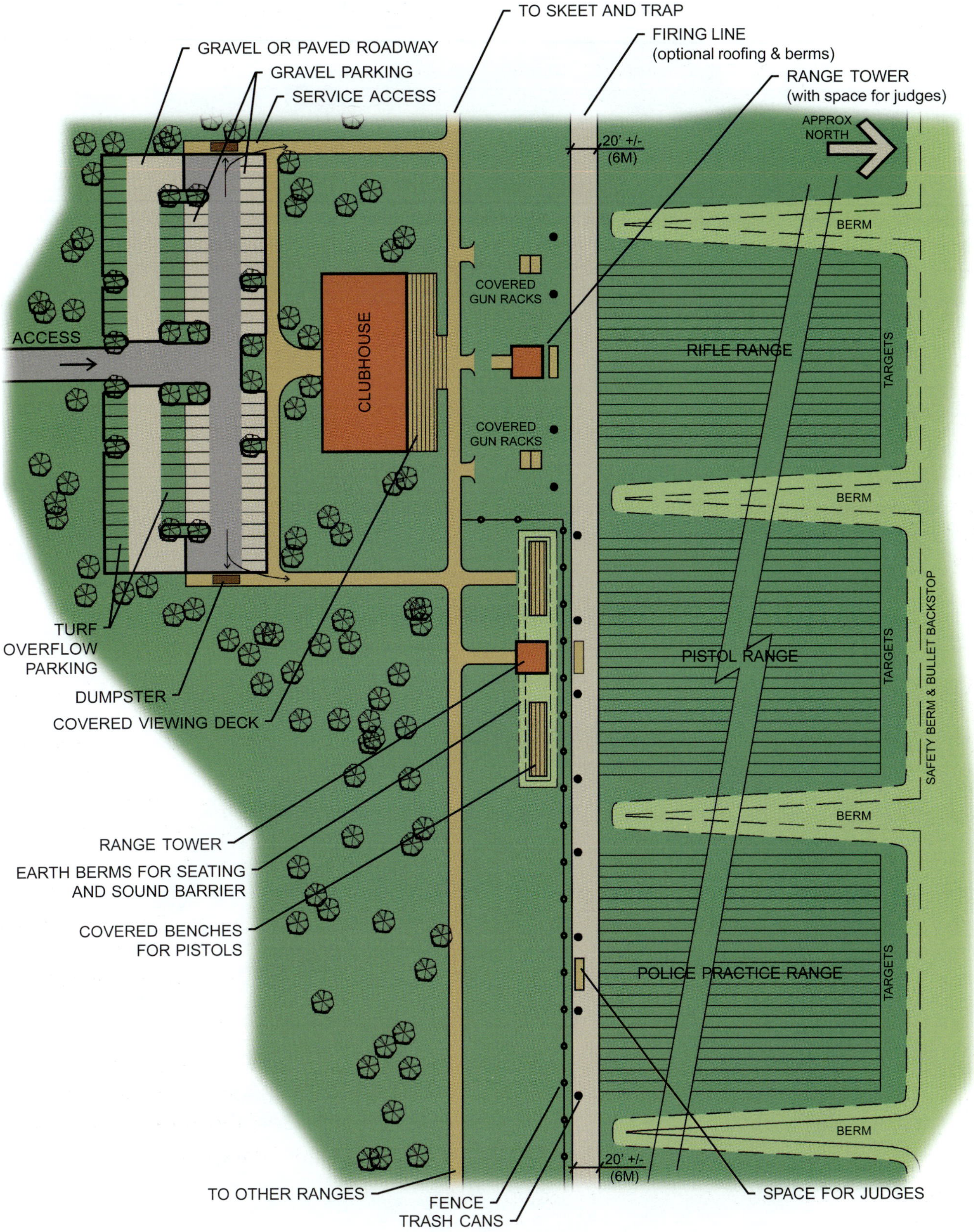

FIG. 26.8 – FIREARMS RANGE – MULTIPLE FIRING AREAS

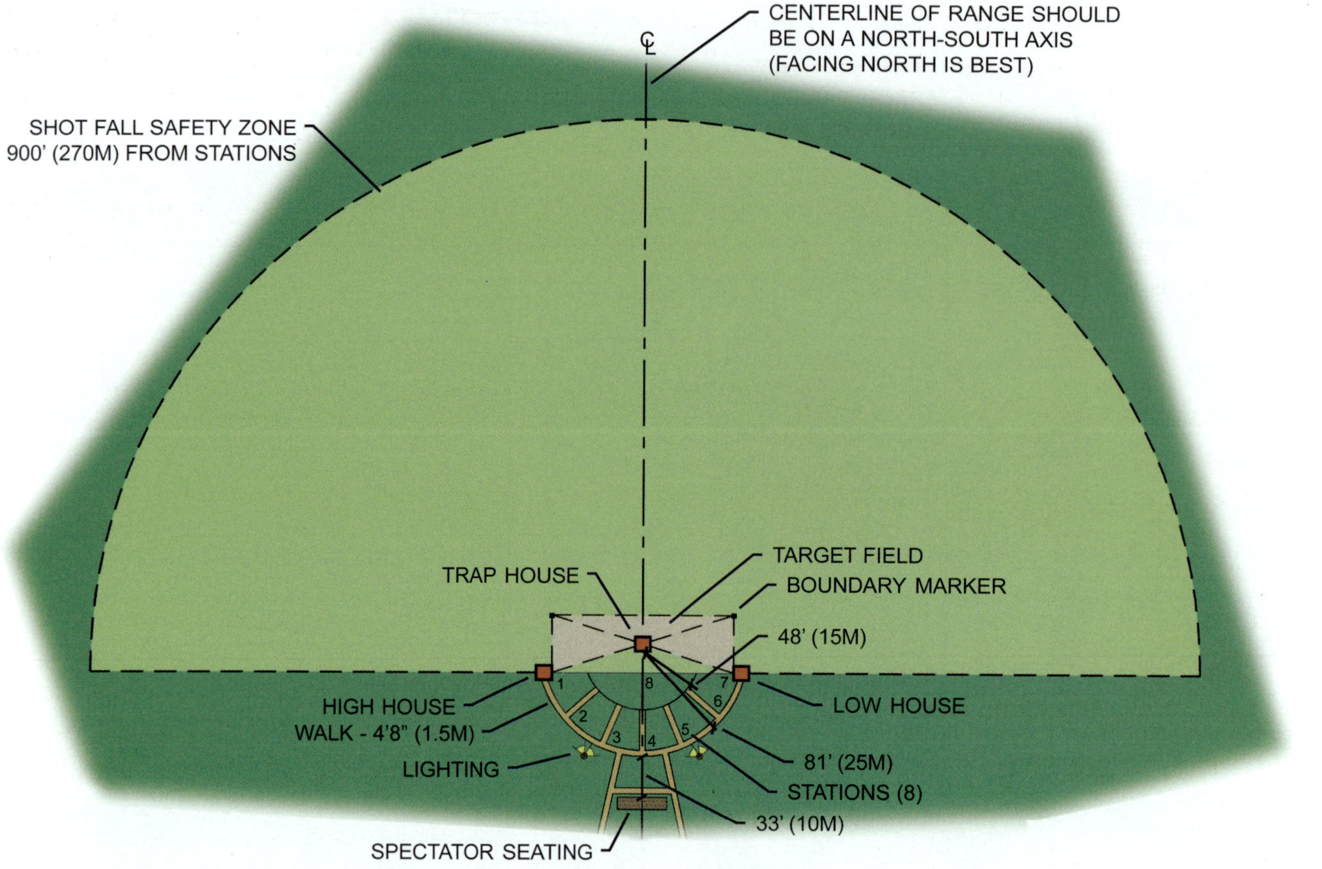

FIG. 26.9 – SKEET RANGE [19]

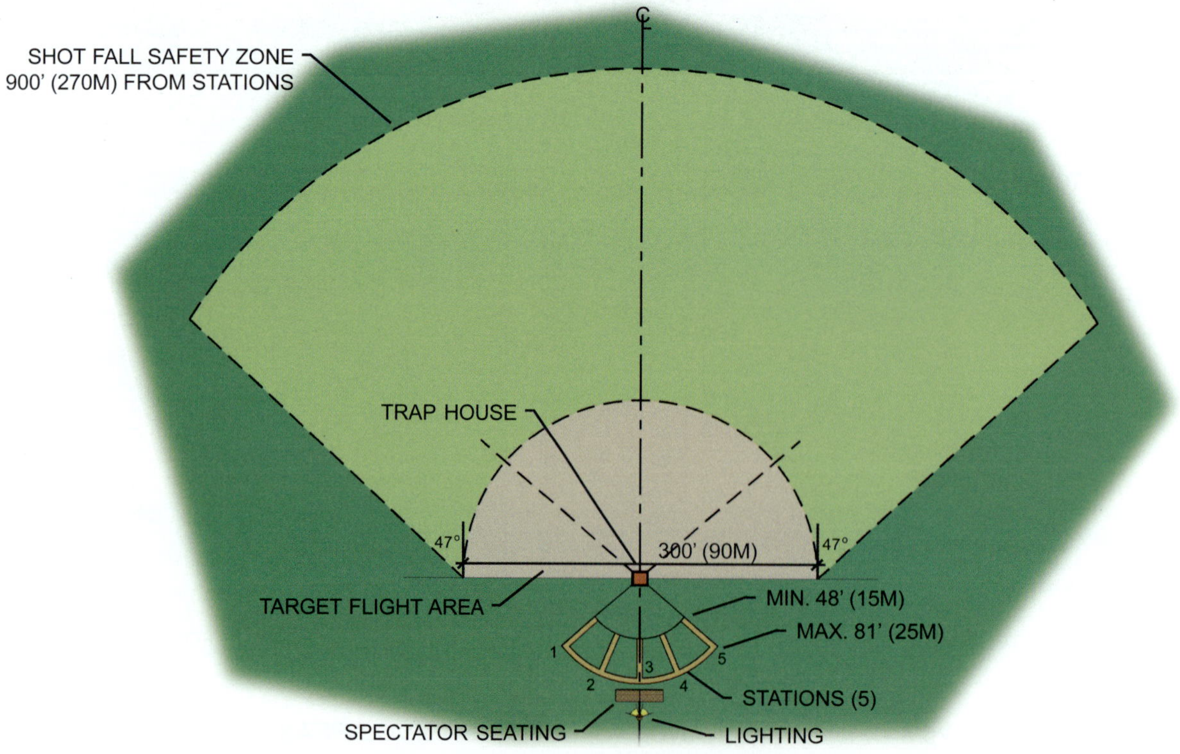

FIG. 26.10 – TRAP RANGE [19]

The Olympic and international competition ranges may vary slightly from the configuration shown. [26] If the ranges are to be used for international competition or for practice for these competitions, they should be made to conform to the latest standards by the governing body under which the competition is to be held. There are a variety of other types of ranges and competitions that are practiced in various places, such as turkey shoots, crazy quail, running deer, etc. This guide will not attempt to provide information on these and other local variations. For further assistance, please contact the National Rifle Association.

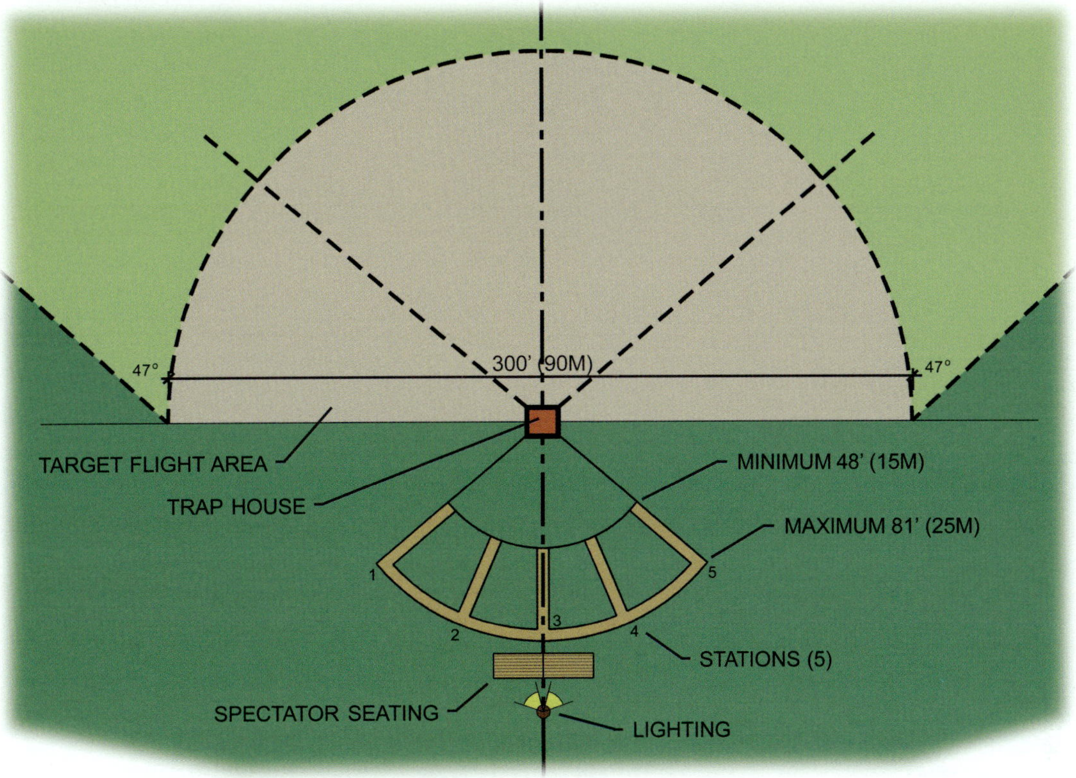

FIG. 26.11 – TRAP RANGE DETAILS

Chapter 27

NON-CONSUMPTIVE WILDLIFE RECREATION

USER CHARACTERISTICS

Many people in the United States participate in some form of non-consumptive wildlife recreation, such as feeding wildlife (especially birds), maintaining plantings, observing wildlife, or nature photography, as a primary activity. In 2001, 22 percent of the population participated. Approximately 25 percent of these activity days were away from home, while the remaining 75 percent of the activity was done around the home. Such a primary activity as going swimming might be combined with a secondary activity of going shelling, or a family might primarily be going for a typical park outing, and also do bird watching while at the park or while in transit to the park. [21]

A significant number, perhaps as much as 33 percent, of non-consumptive wildlife users are also hunters and/or or fishermen.

The participation in wildlife watching as a primary activity in 2001 was mostly Caucasians. It was slightly weighted to more women than men. More family income generally means greater participation (1:2). More education, likewise, means more users in the same 1:2 ratio.

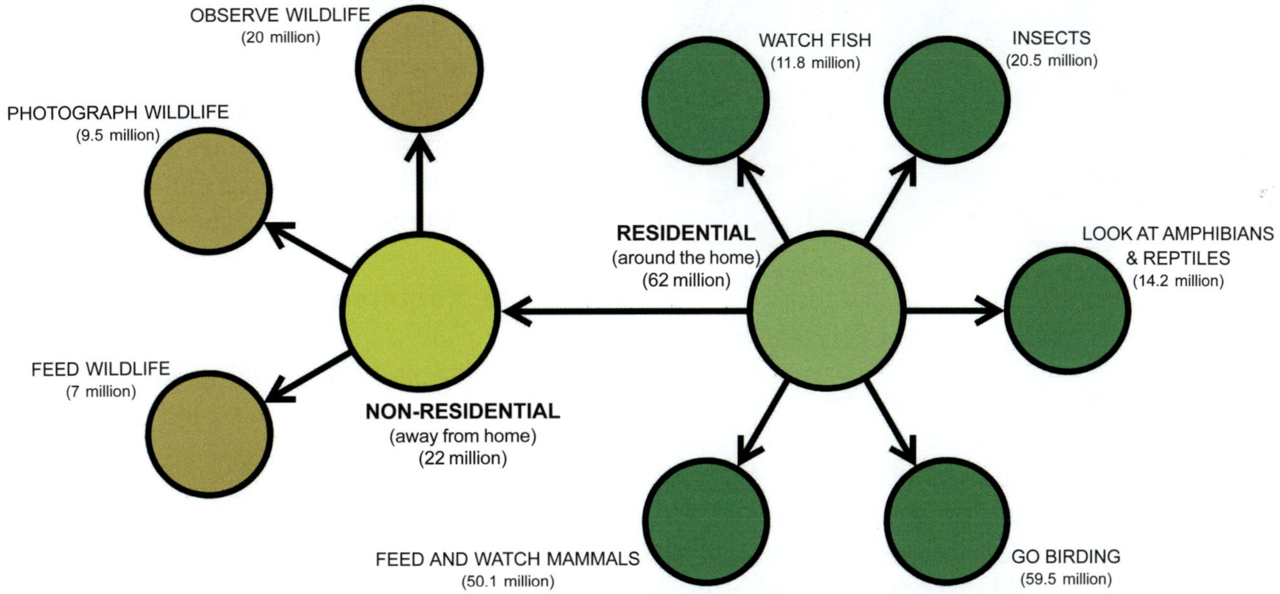

FIG. 27.1 – NON-CONSUMPTIVE WILDLIFE WATCHERS ARE LIKELY TO DO VARIOUS KINDS OF ACTIVITIES AT ANY ACCESSIBLE AND AVAILABLE SITE. [38]

Reindeer – a spectacular sight for the lucky non-resident, non-consumptive wildlife watchers – The North Cape, Norway

GENERAL

All existing park, recreation, conservation and preservation areas, and those types of areas being considered for some form of leisure activity or preservation status, should be inventoried for possible areas to observe and photograph wildlife and plant life.

Gopher tortoise – an endangered species seen from the beach access walk at Clam Pass County Park in Naples, Florida.

Look for areas where human use is limited or can be controlled, such as varied habitats and where foraging birds can be seen, but not disturbed. Consideration should also be given to establishing and/or enhancing habitats that will encourage wildlife to come to and/or stay in or near the people areas.

All areas to be utilized for nature/wildlife viewing should provide interpretive information about what is at the site. See Chapter 7, Interpretive Facilities, for details on this planning aspect, and Chapter 31, Management Planning, on a practical approach to providing ongoing quality services and facilities.

BIRDING

Ibis – Southwest Florida

Controlled access and trails should be established that will go through a variety of habitats that are likely to have bird life. In general, the edge or interface between fields and woods, swamp and woods and shoreline areas (especially coastal and estuarine areas) are the most productive locations for birding.

Minimum Required:

- Suitable habitat, either natural and/or manmade.

Storks are a perfect sight for residential birdwatchers - Eastern Europe

• In shorebird areas, up to 300 feet (100 m) buffer exclusion zones are sometimes required to protect the birds. Check species and determine their needs for these zones and the extent of these protected areas.

Habitat for bird watching site at a sanctuary in Eastern England

• Access to the vicinity of the site, either by foot, boat, or vehicle of some type.

• Parking – carefully designed to fit into the natural surroundings.

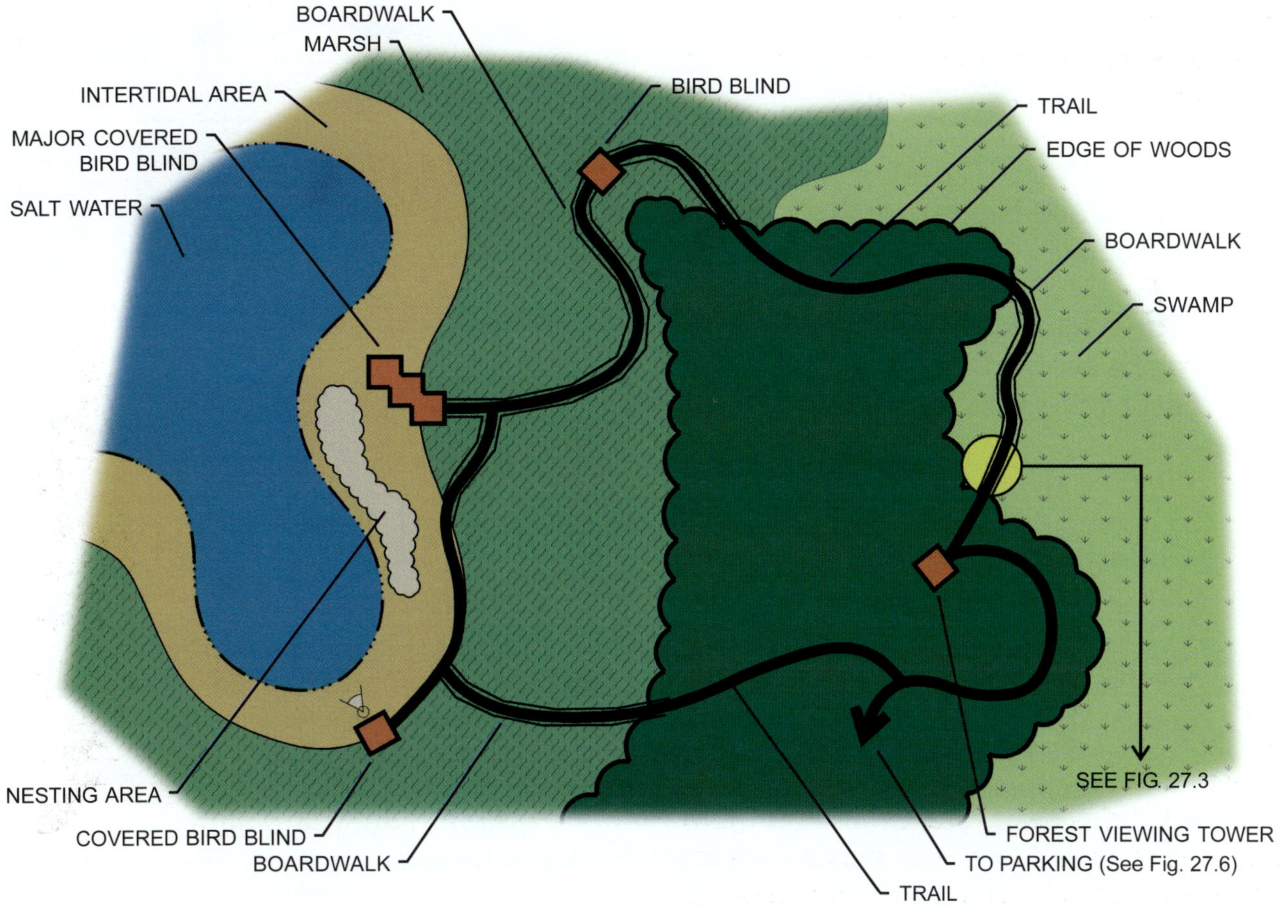

FIG. 27.2 – VARIETY OF HABITAT AND VIEWING EXPERIENCES ARE DESIRABLE

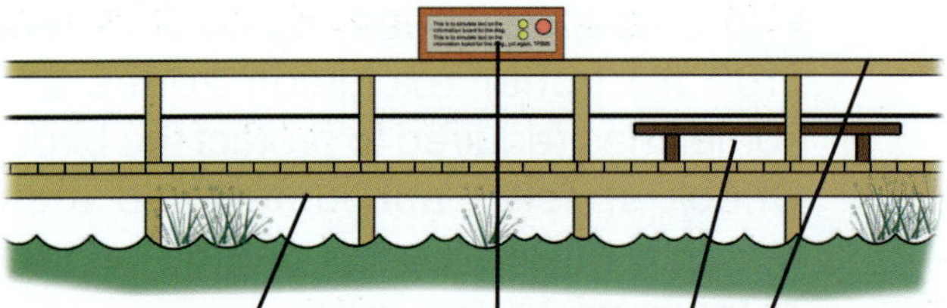

FIG. 27.3 – BOARDWALK

- Maps and interpretive information showing the site and best birding areas.
- Trails.
- Trailside information.
- Solid waste collection and disposal system.
- Toilet facilities.

Desirable:

- Maps and bird lists of likely birds to be sighted.
- Information at the parking lot on what can be seen on the site and where the best birding is located.
- Bird blinds.
- Interpretive exhibits – possibly changing with the seasons.
- Sanitary facilities.
  - Composting and unisex toilets acceptable.

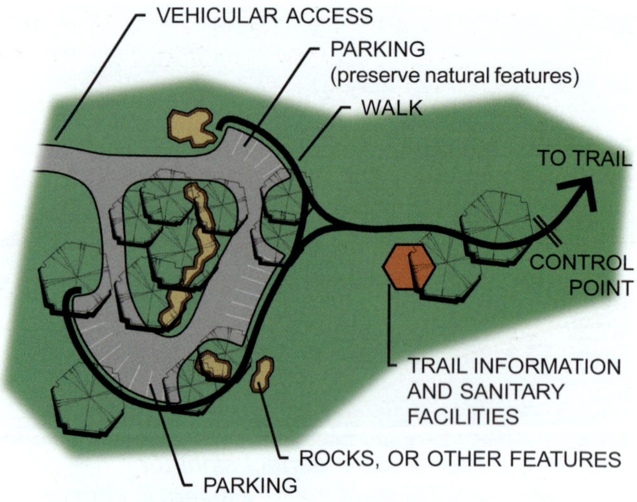

FIG. 27.4 – PARKING AND TRAILHEAD FACILITIES

Elaborate bird blind at an Eastern England birding preserve

Interior of a large sophisticated bird blind area is frequently used for teaching purposes – Eastern England

- Night lighting (early morning and late evening). Viewers need lighting to get to and from the parking area.

- Potable water.

- Observation platform(s), preferably with some type of screening from the birds.

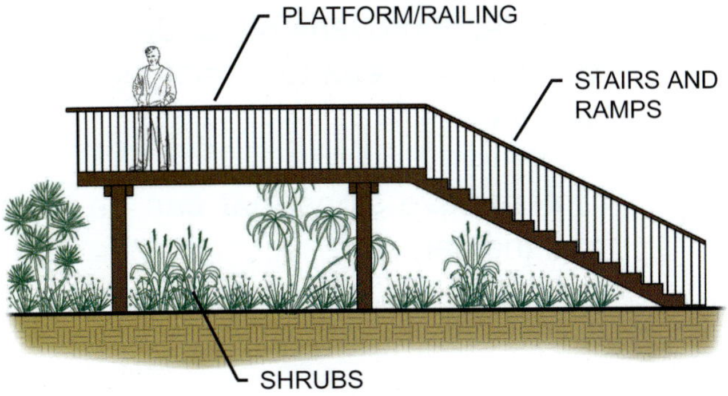

FIG. 27.5 – MINIMUM BIRDING AND OBSERVATION PLATFORM ESPECIALLY GOOD IN WET AND MARSHY AREAS

- Photography and observation blinds.

- Interpretive signs along trails.

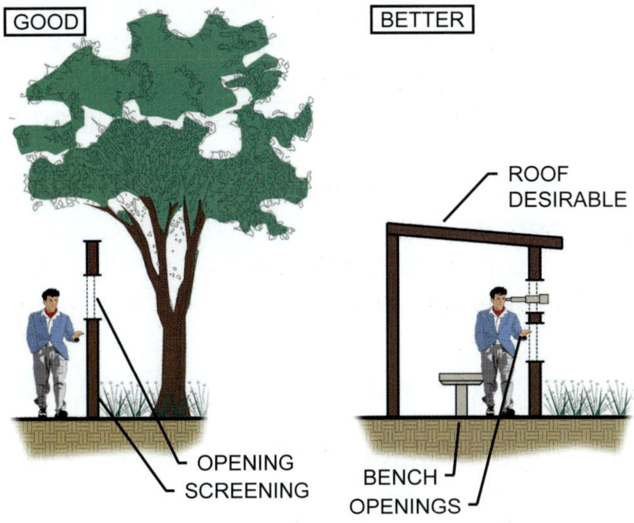

FIG. 27.7 – BLINDS

Natural bird blinds and backdrops in an Eastern England bird preserve.

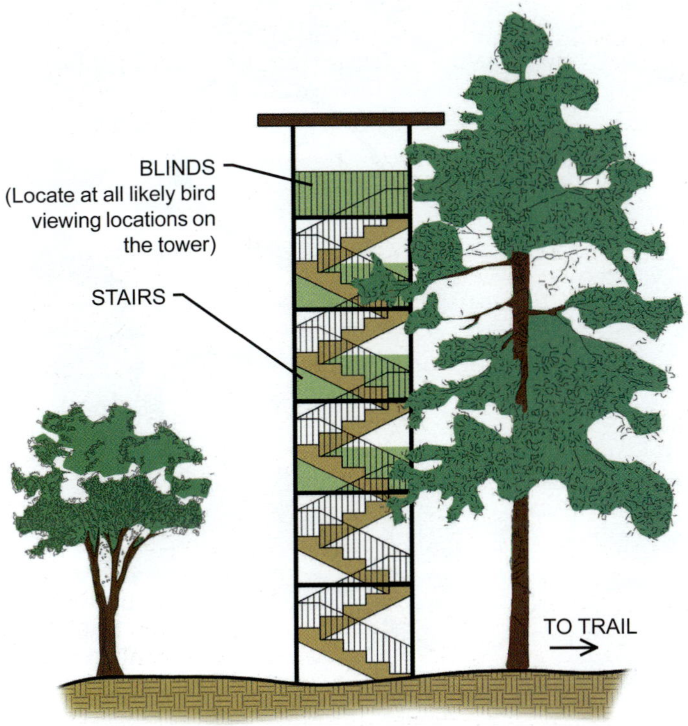

FIG. 27.6 – HIGH TOWERS – ESPECIALLY USEFUL IN FORESTED AREAS ENABLING THE VIEWER TO OBSERVE LIFE AT DIFFERENT LEVELS FROM FLOOR TO CANOPY. PROVIDING ACCESSIBLE ACCESS WILL BE A CHALLENGE, BUT CAN OFFER EXCITING POSSIBILITIES

In some situations, special conditions are present that lend themselves to boat trails, boardwalks, and one-way, low-speed car trails. It is interesting to note that wildlife does not seem to be adversely affected by slow moving vehicles and, in fact, wildlife observers who stay in their vehicles can observe much more at closer range than can those walking on a trail.

DRIVING TRAIL

Required:

- One-way road - 12 feet (3.6 m) wide to minimize their aesthetic and environmental impact and to make travel safer for the drivers looking at birds and other wildlife.
- Numerous pull-offs (preferably visually screened) at likely wildlife observation areas.
- Road to be inconspicuous visually and hidden, where possible, from people viewing wildlife.

Desirable:

- Habitat improvements at designated observation areas to attract the target species.
- Interpretive signs that can be read from the cars.

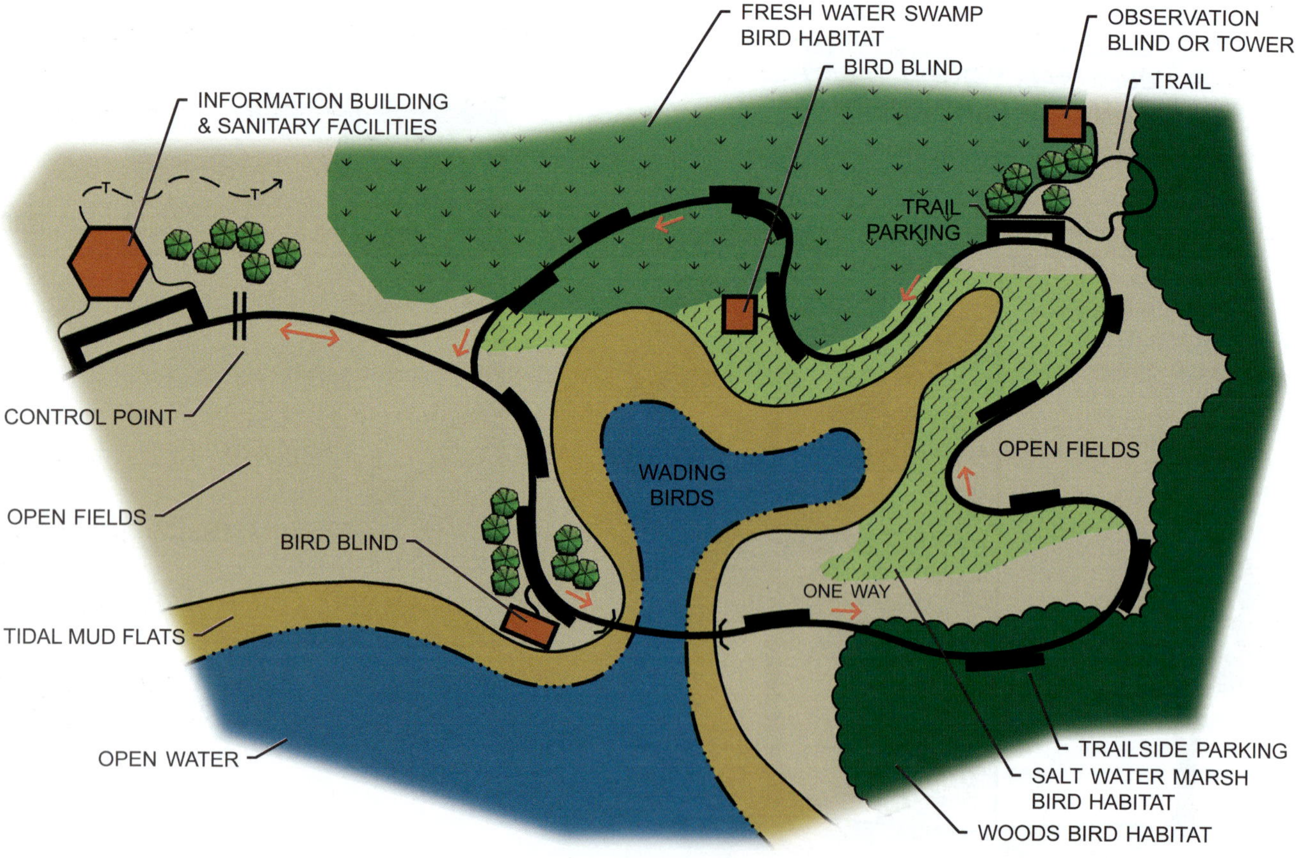

FIG. 27.8 – DRIVING TRAIL – ONE-WAY ONLY FOR SAFETY PURPOSES

OTHER NON-CONSUMPTIVE WILDLIFE RECREATION ACTIVITIES

Alligator watching – South Florida

WILDLIFE VIEWING (other than birding)

The requirements are the same as for birding, except where special habitats require modifications, i.e., underwater viewing or protection from animals such as alligators.

On land, this is best done from vehicles, either on a self-guiding basis like Assateague National Preserve in Virginia or Ding Darling Preserve in Florida; or on mini-buses, with guides such as is done on wildlife safaris in Africa or the larger school buses in Denali National Park in Alaska. Birds and other animals do not seem to consider slow-moving vehicles a threat, and usually ignore them. These extensive vehicle tour areas are almost always supplemented with vehicle stops at special viewing locations. Underwater viewing can be spectacular, especially at coral reefs and manmade habitats. (See the information on fish viewing in this chapter.)

Required:

- On vehicular touring, it is almost always desirable to have one-way traffic. (See Fig. 27.8 in this chapter.)
- Surfaced road (asphalt, gravel, etc.) to keep down dust.
- Informational signs and interpretive displays.
- Pull-off spaces along road, where possible, and screened from views as you are driving. Screening is especially important when you are at special viewing areas.
- Parking at special viewing areas.
- Accessibility to views required.
- Toilets – unisex and composting-type are acceptable.
- Protective barriers from dangerous animals, heights, and plants.

Desired:

- Detailed information about the species (bird, plant, animal) being viewed.
- Drinking water at major stop areas.
- Shade at special interest points.
- Manmade or natural screening to keep the viewed species from being frightened.

FISH AND UNDERWATER INVERTEBRATE VIEWING

Glass bottom boats with a knowledgeable guide in acceptable prime fish habitat areas are usually available in tourist locations for a fee. Tours of this type are currently done at many natural underwater features such as John Kennekamp State Park in the Florida Keys, Green Island at the Great Barrier Reef in Australia, and at cruise ship stops in the Caribbean.

Many tourist areas are constructing manmade underwater reefs and fish and invertebrate habitats.

Underwater observatories are another option. These types of spaces and their exhibits are extremely popular. They resemble an aquarium, only with the people in the container, and the fish swimming free. These live exhibits come without the normal habitat maintenance requirements.

Required:

- Ticket sales.
- Must be accessible (ramps or elevator).
- Space for parking (cars and/or boats).
- Toilets.
- Drinking water.
- Interpretive signs and displays.

Desirable:

- Shaded waiting area.
- Benches in waiting area.
- Food and drink at the site, either at parking or at the ticket sales area.

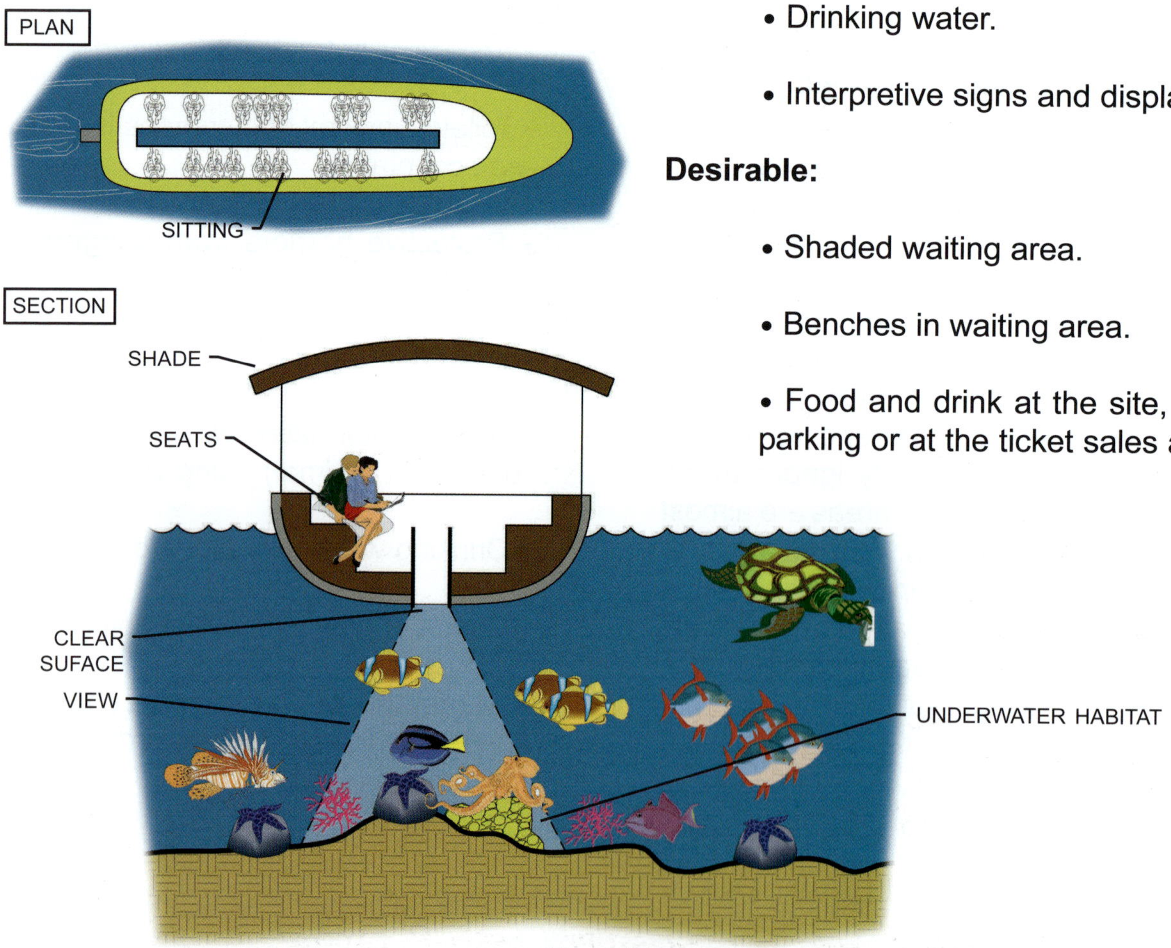

FIG. 27.9 – GLASS BOTTOM BOATS ARE AN EXCELLENT WAY TO VIEW FISH

SNORKELING AND SCUBA DIVING FOR NATURE STUDY

Snorkeling continues to enjoy growth. It is inexpensive and can take place any where there is water. It is also possible for people of almost any age and swimming level to at least participate. Snorkeling trails can be installed underwater with information markers.

Required:

- Viewing features, such as sunken ship wrecks, fish concentrations, interesting invertebrate material, and varied and interesting plant material are needed.
- Water access, either from boat or shore.
- Site access by vehicle or boat, and for the disabled.
- Parking.
- Sanitary facilities – composting and unisex facilities acceptable.

Desirable:

- Drinking water.
- On-shore shade in any waiting areas.

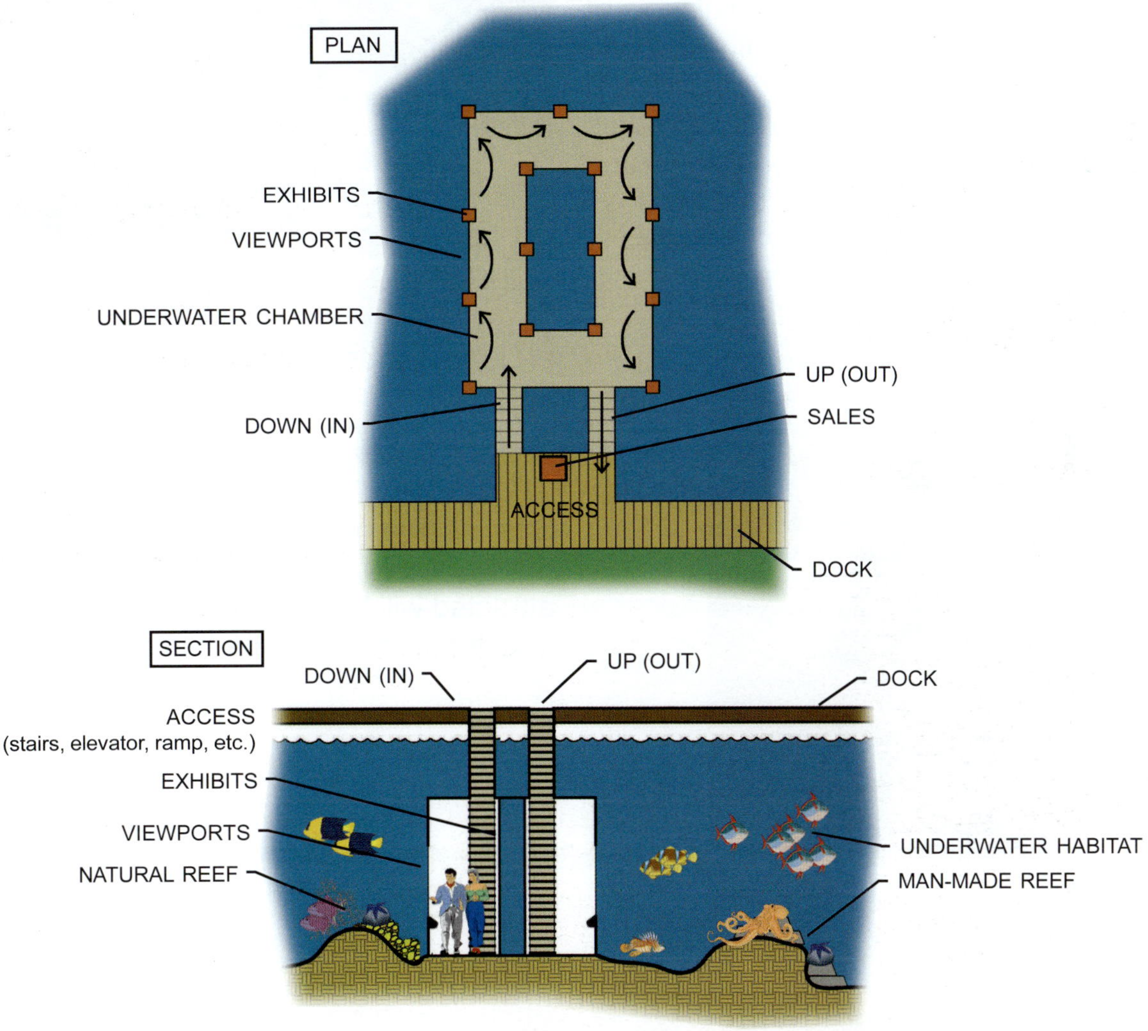

FIG. 27.10 – UNDERWATER OBSERVATORIES ARE VERY EXCITING WAYS TO VIEW FISH AND THEIR HABITATS. THEY MUST BE ACCESSIBLE

- Concession services.
  - Equipment rental.
  - Fish food.
  - Food service.
  - Souvenirs.

- Flush toilets.

- Showers, especially in saltwater areas.

- Interpretive information about the site.

PHOTOGRAPHY

Wildlife and plant photography have the same basic requirements as birding, wildlife, and nature viewing. The only modification to these requirements would be to provide additional space for the photographer (who usually takes considerable time setting up his equipment and waiting for the right picture) so that he does not interfere with the normal flow of traffic.

Photographing wildlife – Spitzbergen, Norway

WILDLIFE FEEDING

This activity is usually done only to increase the number and type of animals in a given area. Feeding stations are very popular with the viewing public. Many wildlife specialists consider this an undesirable activity because the wild animals' normal habitats are distorted, and if the feedings were to be interrupted for any extended time period, the birds and animals would find it very difficult, and frequently impossible, to adjust to "natural" conditions. Feeding can also attract unwanted and or non-native species.

Feeding stations enhance a preserve's numbers and types of animals – Asa Wright Nature Preserve, Trinidad in the Southern Caribbean

Special care needs to be taken to ensure that the type of feed provided to the animals attracted will be what is needed by them, and that the food will not be harmful.

HABITAT ENHANCEMENT OR MODIFICATIONS

This work is also done to increase the number and types of animals (or plants) in a given area.

- Feeders placed at good viewing spots (group windows, etc.) are very useful in attracting birds. They are especially appreciated in residences where there are older people and those with mobility problems.

- The installation of salt licks is very useful in bringing wild animals to areas where people can view them. This is extensively done in game parks in some regions of Africa.

- Artificial reefs and underwater habitats previously discussed are commonly built in many coastal areas, especially in southern states.

- Site-specific wildlife friendly plantings for such things as butterflies and birds can greatly enhance the "wild" insect, bird, and terrestrial bird populations.

- Water holes in dry areas as another type of habitat improvement that is very useful in concentrating all type of wildlife in dry climates.

- Creating edge-type environments can greatly enhance the number and variety of wildlife and, for that matter, plant life.

- Proper management of grazing lands can help increase the number and variety of wildflowers.

- Grain and other forage crops can be planted to encourage local and migrating birds.

- Management agreements with surrounding farms (where present) can be prepared that will enhance their wildlife carrying capacity.

The last two items are especially useful in migratory bird stopping areas such as is done at Pymatuning State Park and Game Preserve in Pennsylvania and in many other state and national game preserves.

Visitor control guidelines and an ongoing habitat management plan will be necessary to ensure a long-term success of any wildlife or plant viewing area.

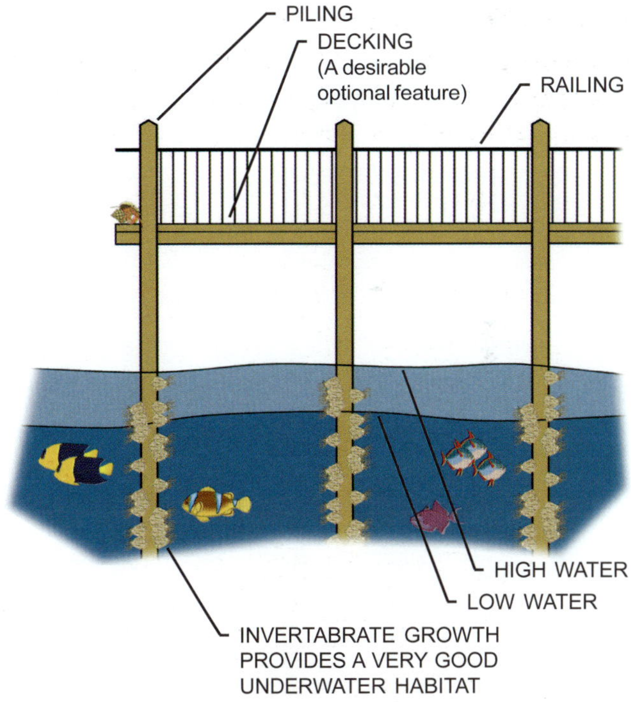

FIG. 27.11 – PILINGS ARE EFFECTIVE BREEDING AND LIVING AREAS FOR FISH

Chapter 28

MINOR TOURISM FACILITIES

Tourism is a major leisure activity and has spawned an entire leisure industry throughout much of the world. The facility itself, the support facilities, and the souvenir tourist facilities serve all segments of the world's population. Many of the facilities are, however, geared to those who have disposable income and available leisure time. This makes those facilities that serve significant older populations (those over 55) the principal users/participants on many tourist ventures. It is important to understand that younger people can and frequently are the primary tourists. It is strongly urged that a careful market analysis be done prior to establishing any tourist facility(ies) to determine who the users will be.

Farm in Finland that is used as a tourist stop on trips through the countryside

Tourism facilities typically are either for small groups, usually arriving by car or small buses; or large groups, usually arriving by bus(es) or other mass means of transportation, such as boats, trains or planes. This book has provided a chapter for each – Minor Tourism and Major Tourism (Chapter 29). These two chapters are concerned with providing guidance on what facilities are needed for each, and how they can most effectively be arranged.

NEEDED FACILITIES

First and foremost, there must be a reason for the tourists to come. The fountain off to the side of the Mall in Washington, D.C., a lighthouse, such as the one at Cape Cod

Tourists at one of the many fountains at the Mall in Washington, D.C.

National Seashore in Massachusetts, the monastery at a village in newly open Eastern Europe, or a small national park.

Lighthouse
– Cape Cod National Seashore, Massachusetts

Hopewell Furnace National Historic Site
– Pennsylvania

REQUIRED FACILITIES

Having established that there is a reason for tourists to come, it is next necessary to determine how many visitors will come, who they are (this determines many of the facilities needed), how they will get there (access and parking requirements), and what they will do at the site. Consideration must also be given to what happens adjacent to the tourist destination, which can directly affect what support amenities to provide on site.

This will likely require careful coordination with local governing authorities and to be truly effective with the neighboring property owners.

From the information gathered above, a facility resource development program can be prepared and a conceptual site master plan created. The book, *A Site Design and Management Process*, published by NRPA, gives a detailed description of the process and how to prepare programs and master plans. As a minimum, such a plan must consider access, parking, internal circulation, emergency access, toilets, trash disposal, and sales of various types. Additional facilities that might be desirable or even needed are a maintenance area, guided tours, food service, and visitor amenities, such as picnicking, benches, shade, drinking fountains, etc.

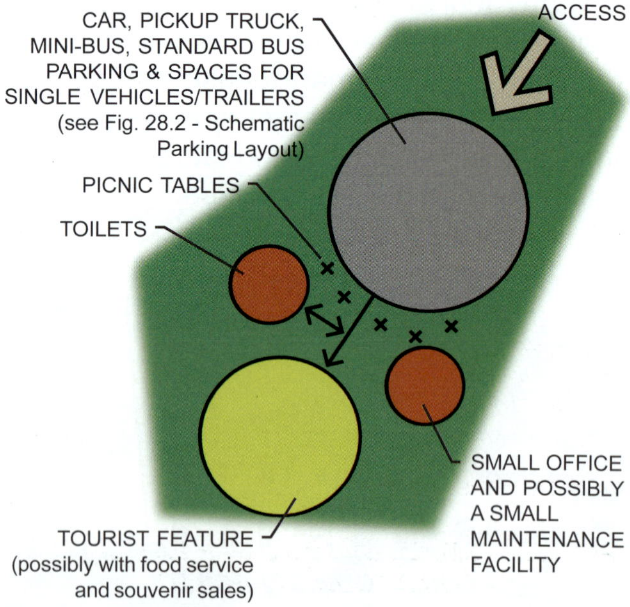

FIG. 28.1 – CONCEPTUAL LAYOUT FOR A MINOR TOURIST FACILITY

Site amenities, such as benches and shade, add a great deal to any tourist attraction. – London, England

ACCESS TO SITE

Most small tourist sites are accessed only by motor vehicles (cars, pickups - including those that are pulling trailers and buses), small and large. Access roads must be able to accommodate these vehicles in section and profile. Lower standard existing roads may need to be upgraded to enable the larger vehicles access to the site.

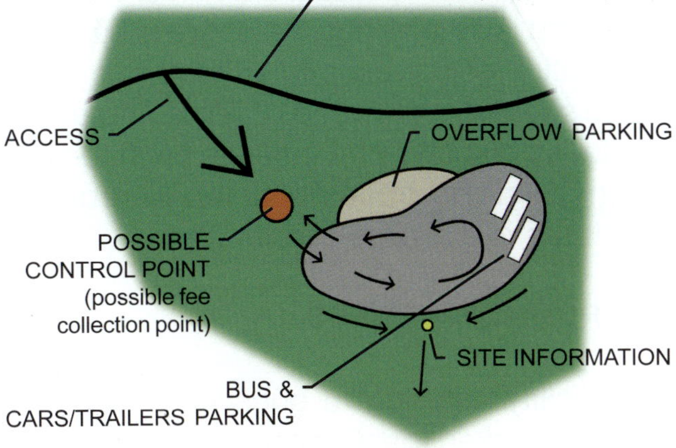

FIG. 28.2 – SMALL BUS AND CAR PARKING LOT FOR A TOURIST FACILITY

Some tourist sites are on navigable waterways, and might be accessed by ferry boats and small tour boats. If access to the site is in part or totally by watercraft, then the pedestrian access would be from the water's edge. A landing dock will normally be needed.

Riverboat (100± passengers) on the Danube River – Eastern Europe

PARKING

Shown in Fig. 28.2 is a schematic layout of a parking lot that will serve most types of tourist vehicles. It is necessary to provide space for the number and types of vehicles expected. All too frequently, circulation and parking do not effectively consider buses or cars and pickups pulling trailers. If not properly planned for these larger vehicles, each can utilize four or five standard parking spaces.

Accessible parking must, of course, be provided, and it must have easy access to the site's accessible way(s).

Bus and car parking for a vineyard for a winery near the Black Sea in Romania

Bus loading and unloading areas are needed. It is desirable to have these spaces shaded and with benches 6 feet to eight feet (1.8 m to 2.4 m). If the tourist facility is fairly extensive, it would also be desirable to have a shaded waiting area with benches for the regular parking lot. Many tourist areas have peak use days.

Royal Family Church – Sandringham, England

Please note that most tourist facilities will need additional staff parking space. This should be so located as not to utilize needed visitor spaces or obscure the view of the tourist feature or features.

ADDITIONAL FACILITIES MAY BE DESIRED AND SOMETIMES NEEDED

SITE INFORMATION

Many, if not most, minor tourism sites can benefit from informational signs and/or displays. These are best located on the pedestrian main entrance to the site. See Figs. 28.1 and 28.2 and the tourist information photo. The tourist information sign shown in the next column is an outstanding example of what can be effectively depicted in such a display. It is desirable to light display sites that are used during dusk and nighttime hours.

Tourist information significantly improves the enjoyment of a site for most people. – Cathedral in Peterborough, England

Another frequently desirable feature is the use of interpretive pathways and/or trails. (See Chapter 8, Trails and Pathways).

In some situations, a small museum can be a useful addition. It is not normally recommended due to its high initial costs and very high annual operations and maintenance costs. If it is determined that there is sufficient information of interest and artifacts to display, space should be provided. It is recommended that these displays and artifacts be made part of any historic building or new, required structures in the development.

EMERGENCY ACCESS

Any facility catering to guests/tourists must have unblocked, easily accessed, and usable emergency vehicle access for police, fire, and medical. These vehicles could be coming from different directions and, therefore, may require different access roads. The fire access is particularly sensitive to access road requirements, i.e., no parking or stopping in front of any buildings, and access for fire trucks must be provided around all of the buildings.

Contact the local fire department for its requirements. It might also be desirable, if the site is remotely located in relationship to a medical facility, to have an emergency helicopter landing location. This is especially true for larger facilities or places that have infrequent but major attendance events.

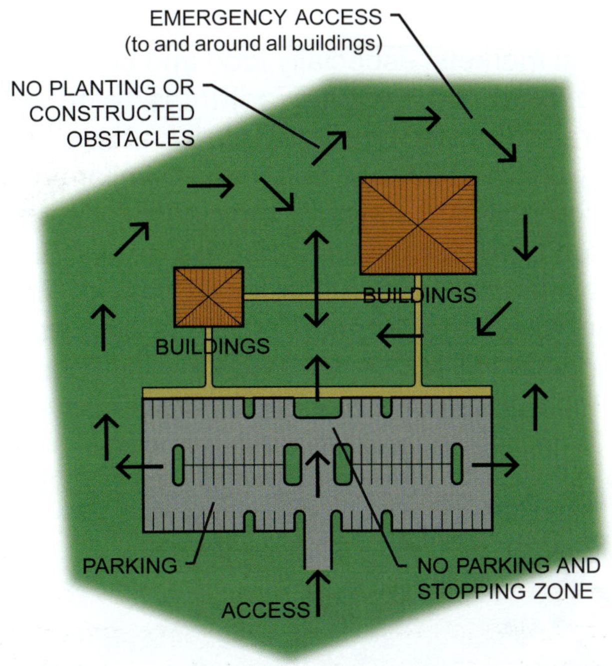

FIG. 28.3 – EMERGENCY VEHICULAR ACCESS

TOILETS

This is a critical aspect of any tourist/leisure facility. The number of locations and size of each toilet facility is dependent on two things: (1) how long people have likely been traveling to reach the site, and (2) how many people of what sex mix will be at the site. If the visitors have been traveling more than one hour (or sometimes slightly less), the toilets should be located as near to the parking /bus area as possible. This is especially true if the visitors are primarily women or older people. If the facility is small and/or has relatively few visitors, a single toilet building or toilet room in the building may be sufficient.

Toilets at a cathedral in central England

If the site is a spread out area, the toilets should be broken into separate facilities located no more than 1000 feet (300 m) apart.

FOOD SERVICE AND/OR SALES AREA

Most tourist facilities normally must be self-supporting. This can be accomplished through user fees (usually an entrance fee), parking fees, and sales (food and/or souvenirs). Provision must be made for space for these critical functions.

Entrance fees are usually collected at the actual entrance to the tourist feature. Parking fees are collected via an entrance booth along the entrance road before the parking lot, by parking ticket dispensers located at the parking entrance, or other strategic, easily- identified locations throughout the parking area(s). Parking meters are not normally used but could be considered, especially in urban or even suburban areas.

Souvenirs and food sales must be located at the greatest activity area and have access for service (usually from the rear of the building(s).

TRASH PICKUP

All leisure use projects must have adequate, easily picked up trash disposal facilities. This will frequently be of two and, possibly, three types: (1) for the tourist, attractive and, sometimes themed, trash receptacles strategically placed along all walks (8 feet to10 feet (2.4 m to 3 m) for service truck access), at the parking lots, and at any sales or food service area(s); (2) within the site's delivery or service area, if any, a dumpster site(s) must be provided. It must be screened with appropriate material from view of any visitors. Plants or compatible-style walls and gates may be used. This screening is especially important if the site is a historic facility. In larger sites, it might be desirable to have more than one screened dumpster, including at the parking lot(s).

UTILITIES (See Chapter 12.)

Water, sewage, electrical, and communications are almost always needed. Special accommodations must be made for drinking water. These fountains are best located at or near parking lots, feature buildings, and toilets. In addition, tourist areas are frequently more highly landscaped and maintained, and normally require an irrigation system.

Communications are often extremely important to the ongoing success of a tourist facility. A fax line, internet connection, and good phone connection, either land line and/or cell, are needed. An emergency phone line that is reliable and available to the public is a necessity.

SHADED WALKS AND RESTING AREAS

Desirable additions to most tourist facilities are well-shaded walkways and benches. This is especially necessary if older people are expected.

OTHER FACILITIES AND FEATURES

Local markets, especially food and crafts, can and often do become adjuncts to tourist attractions, or become tourist attractions themselves. If these markets or similar types of vendors are present, their addition to the main site facilities must be taken into consideration in the tourist facility design. They can affect the location of toilets and other support facilities. A close working relationship to local governing authorities will be necessary to work effectively with these vendors.

Local farmer's market in the Caribbean

Small town crafts sales – Eastern Europe

Chapter 29

MAJOR TOURISM

Major tourism sites are a step up in scale and complexity from minor tourist facilities. They sometimes are so significant that they drive the economy of an entire geographic area, e.g., Disney World in Orlando and vicinity in Florida, or the Grand Canyon in Arizona and surrounding private lands. This chapter will deal with some of the planning and design considerations of many mid- to large-sized tourist developments. It will introduce you to the items that need to be considered and offer some suggested directions that should be taken to make these tourist projects and surrounding developments as successful as possible.

Major tourist developments have at least one major primary facility and very likely a number of secondary features. They are usually large in size - few tens of acres (hectares) to sometimes thousands of acres (hundreds of hectares). All of the features discussed in the chapter on Minor Tourism are valid for major tourist facilities, only in a larger context.

Figure 29.1 – Conceptual Layout for a Major Tourism Site – is an indication of the complexity of such a development.

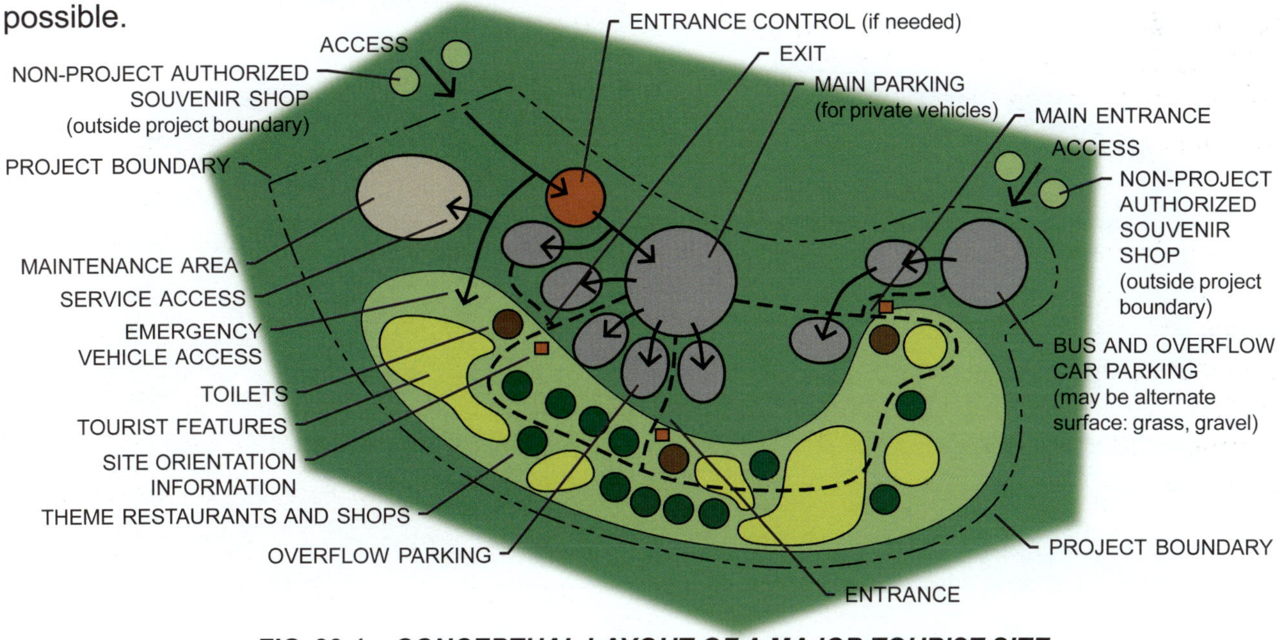

FIG. 29.1 – CONCEPTUAL LAYOUT OF A MAJOR TOURIST SITE (A VILLAGE IS USED IN THIS EXAMPLE)

Roman ruins adjacent to the Coliseum in Rome, Italy (a multiplicity of archaeologically important features)

Historic Creek Street in Ketchikan, Alaska The entire downtown is the tourist attraction. Access is almost exclusively by cruise ships.

Summer Palace in St. Petersburg, Russia

Cruise ship crew making phone calls when in port – Key West, Florida

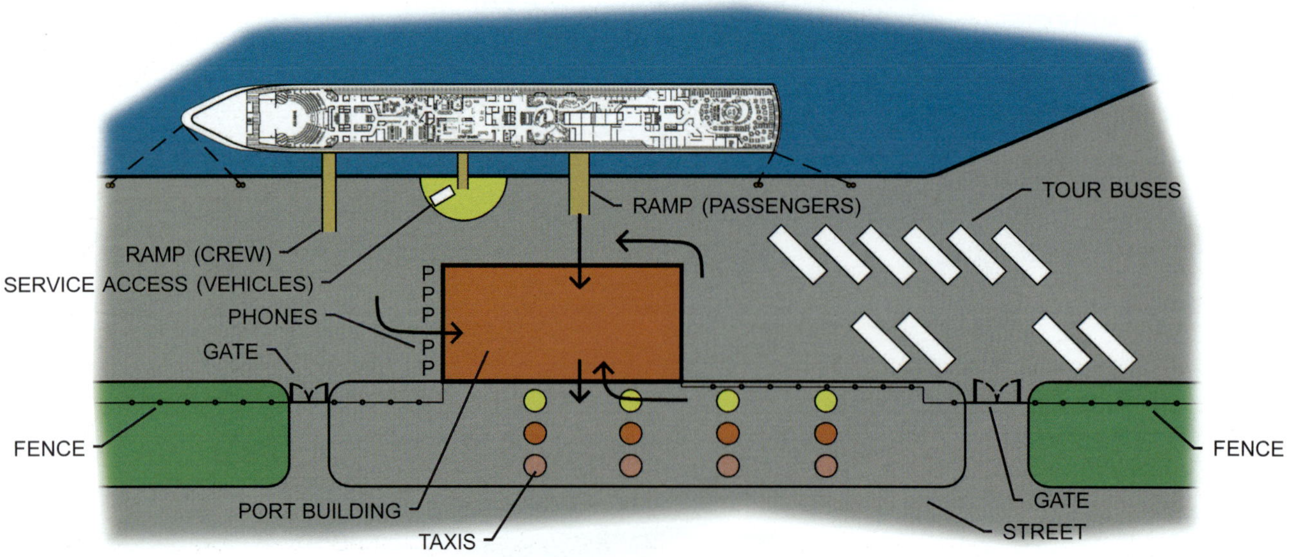

FIG. 29.2 – CRUISE SHIP ON TOUR ROUTE AT A DOCK

NEEDED FACILITIES

Major tourist facilities normally have more than one reason for their existence. People usually come from a multiplicity of places. They may arrive by any means of mass transportation, from trains, buses, tour boats, cruise ships, private vehicles, or planes.

A large cruise ship can dominate the area in which it docks. – The Azores (1,200 to 3,000 or more passengers can disembark from a single ship for the day in a waterside tourist area.)

ACCESS

Docking space for cruise boats needs adequate room for tour buses and other tour vehicles to pick up and return their passengers. These tours may include, in addition to buses, party/tour boats of all types, both chartered

Musicians of various sized groups frequently welcome the cruise passengers.

Dockside hub for transfer of cruise ship passengers to on-shore excursion buses to tourist sites – St. John's in the Virgin Islands

and private, private taxi service, and small, private tour buses and vans.

In addition, space should be available for re-provisioning the ship and for pedestrian access direct to shore facilities. Long distance pay phone service for crew members to talk to their families is almost a necessity.

Most cruise terminals have sales booths or areas available for vendors within the terminal building, where it exists, or immediately outside the end of the passenger ramp(s).

Weaver at port facilities demonstrating her craft and selling her work – West coast of Guatemala

Almost all ports also have numerous vendors located immediately outside of the port property.

Typical vendors outside of any major tourist attraction, including cruise ship terminals and bus parking areas – Eastern Europe

PARKING

Tourists can and usually do arrive by vehicles from hotels and other starting points in addition to coastal sites, cruise ships, and tour boats. These usually are by tour buses and cars (pickup trucks). Tour buses deposit large numbers of people in a short period of time and require special loading and unloading areas, preferably shaded.

Tour bus parking – Eastern Europe

SITE INFORMATION

Site information on large sites is best disseminated by tour guides and docents (usually costumed providers of site information, especially in historic areas). This information would be in addition to interpretive displays and trails as discussed in Chapter 7, Interpretive Facilities and Chapter 28, Minor Tourism.

Most tourist areas need to have some type of information about the site. Without it, these usually paying visitors do not know what they are experiencing and can become unhappy visitors.

Tour guide and group in historic district of downtown – Vienna, Austria

Costumed in period attire, tourist facility staff providing authentic local music in Norway.

ON-SITE CIRCULATION

Moving large numbers of people through a major tourist site requires careful planning, adequate space, and sufficient support facilities (walk/service roadways, fire lanes, shade, and sitting spaces). See also Fig. 28.3 for emergency vehicle concepts. In-site tourist circulation is primarily by foot; however, it is frequently supplemented by open buses of all sizes, rubber tired trains/trams, horse and buggy rides (especially in older historic building areas), etc.

TOILETS

These required facilities come in all sizes, sophistification, and aesthetic considerations. They must be located as needed throughout the complex. Because this is a major tourism site and tourist patrons have frequently been traveling for quite some time, it is necessary to have toilets located near the parking areas.

Flush toilets are expected.

Toilets within the site should be within 800 feet (240 m) of each other - 1000 feet (300 m) maximum. Toilets are needed adjacent to any.

Toilet building at historic government building and event complex in Eastern Europe. The facility reflects the style of the surrounding buildings.

eating areas and can also serve general site needs

FOOD SERVICE AND SALES AREA

Eating out for pleasure is one of the primary leisure activities of many people. This is especially true of the more affluent who also are more likely to be tourists. Providing good restaurants, both indoor and outdoor, can enhance the tourists' experience and significantly help a major tourist facility defray its operations and maintenance costs.

One of many eating areas in historic downtown – Vienna, Austria

Major tourists enjoy purchasing souvenirs, and sites can significantly benefit from a portion of the profit from these sales. Care should be taken by management to ensure that the quality and type of products being sold fits the character or theme of the tourist attraction. Lavenham, in eastern England, is a good example of how the unique, out-of-plumb building construction in this historic village was made into a publicized feature that drove the development of a thriving tourist industry. All of the shops and restaurants tie into these unique historic buildings. The whole village benefits and makes a living from the tourists.

Village street in Lavenham, England

In addition, many tourist areas have both small-scale vendors selling usually homemade products to the visitors. Some tourist areas like Dracula's Castle in Romania are the community's only major industry and support many souvenir vendors and their backup product manufacturing.

Dracula's Castle
– Romania
(Dracula's Castle is not the true site as depicted in the novel, but it is successfully promoted as such for tourist purposes. The castle itself, however, is authentic and old.)

Major tourist sales area at the entrance to Dracula's Castle in Romania supports many vendors.

SERVICE AND TRASH PICKUP

Major tourist facilities are similar in many aspects to villages and even small towns. They need effective municipal utilities for water supply, sewage disposal, electricity, communications (should be all underground for aesthetic purposes), and trash pickup.

Care must be taken to ensure that none of the utility lines and water and sewage treatment plants adversely affects the aesthetics of the tourist features. That means all utilities must be underground or screened in such a manner that they become essentially invisible to the visitors. Please note that no utility lines mar the landscapes or are significantly visible in any of the photographs in both this and the Minor Tourism chapters.

Major tourist facilities require major operations and maintenance staff and supporting facilities. (See Chapter 30, Administrative and Service Areas.) These facilities, like utility lines and plants, must be kept out of site of the tourists. The use of modern equipment to do the maintenance is usually alright as long as it is normally not seen.

Maintaining a historic vegetable garden using modern equipment
– Hopewell Forge National Historic Site, Pennsylvania

ADDITIONAL SUPPORT FACILITIES

Unique events like the cliff divers at Acapulco, Mexico, can in themselves create a major tourist attraction. Much of the development of this corner of Acapulco is based on this event. Several restaurants and souvenir shops exist solely because of these divers.

Cliff diving at Acapulco, Mexico.

Two examples have been included to show what can happen. Both are sculptures. The first is the Raising of the Flag at Iwo Jima in Arlington, Virginia. It has required bus and

Raising the Flag at Iwo Jima Memorial
– Arlington, Virginia

car parking, toilet facilities, and interpretive signs and displays. The second is the Little Mermaid at the harbor in Copenhagen, Denmark. It, too, has become famous and is a stop on most tours of this old, historic city. Unfortunately, the support for tour buses and cars has not kept pace with its popularity.

The famous "Little Mermaid" statue at the harbor in Copenhagen, Denmark

Chapter 30

ADMINISTRATIVE AND SERVICE AREA

SERVICE AREA

All major leisure facilities need some type of service area(s). The size and complexity and number of service areas increases as the size and complexity of the site increases. Before locating or designing a service area, it is necessary to have a preliminary site master plan and, at least, a conceptual site management plan. A study of the service needs should be completed in cooperation with the site operator(s).

Service area
– French Creek State Park, Pennsylvania
(This is a typical large-scale facility; however, it is missing security fencing and screening from the public road system.)

Some factors to consider:

- Access from a good, all-season road to most areas of the site. If the facility being served has controlled access(es), it is desirable to have a separate entrance to the service area from a public road. This will permit material deliveries to the maintenance area when the site is closed, and may reduce circulation conflicts between maintenance functions and facility users.

- Adequate power, water, sewage disposal, and good communications.

- Storage space, both inside buildings and outside. Exterior storage space should be much larger than most site programmers and designers believe necessary. All types of items are stored – tables, trash cans, gravel, ball field clay, old equipment, salvaged lumber, trash, plant material prunings, etc.

- Screening from roads and winter-use areas. This can be any aesthetic type, from walls, berms, plant material, etc.

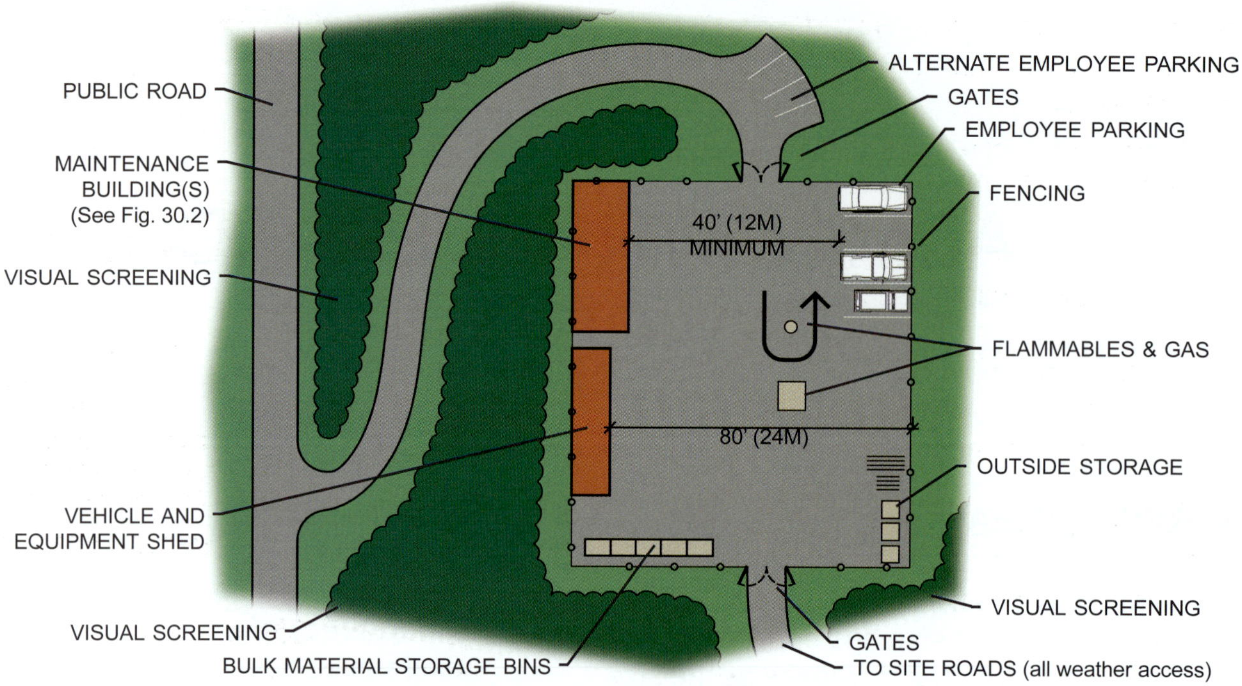

FIG. 30.1 – SERVICE AREA

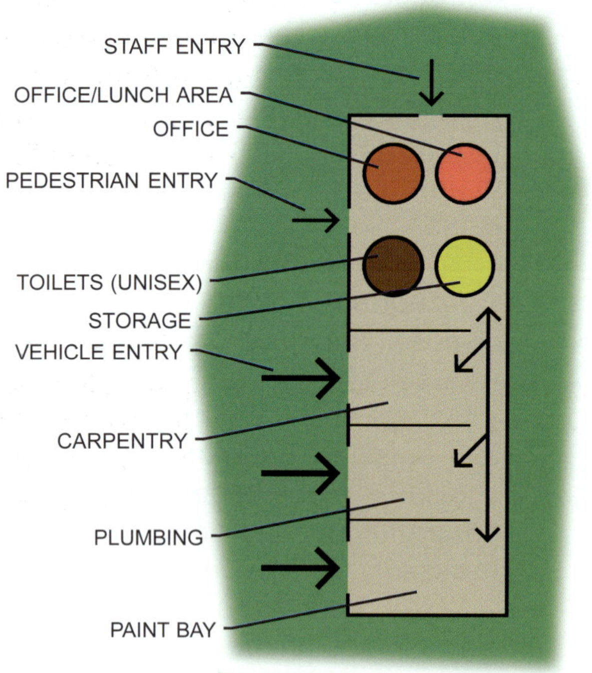

FIG. 30.2 – TYPICAL MULTIPURPOSE MAINTENANCE BUILDING

• Security fencing around service areas is a necessity as these facilities are frequently the target of thieves and vandals.

• Space to load and unload heavy maintenance equipment.

• Indoor and outdoor work and repair space(s).

• Park vehicle storage space.

• Fuel pumps – away from all buildings and flammable material.

• Flammable materials storage structure – must meet local fire and safety codes.

• Office space.

• Night lighting for entire fenced area.

• Employee lunch area.

• Employee locker space and shower(s).

• Employee parking spaces, either within or outside of fenced enclosure.

Large facilities and isolated small sites frequently require sub-maintenance areas for efficient operation. The function and design of these facilities are much simpler than a standard maintenance area. At a minimum, they need:

- Equipment storage.
- Perimeter fencing.
- Vehicular access.
- Toilet or good access to a toilet.
- Night lighting.
- Screening from site and neighboring users.

Eagle Lake County Park – Collier County, Florida (This sub-maintenance area was added by maintenance staff. Note lack of screen planting.)

They may also need the following:

- Employee parking.
- Frequently, bulk storage (requires easy delivery truck access).

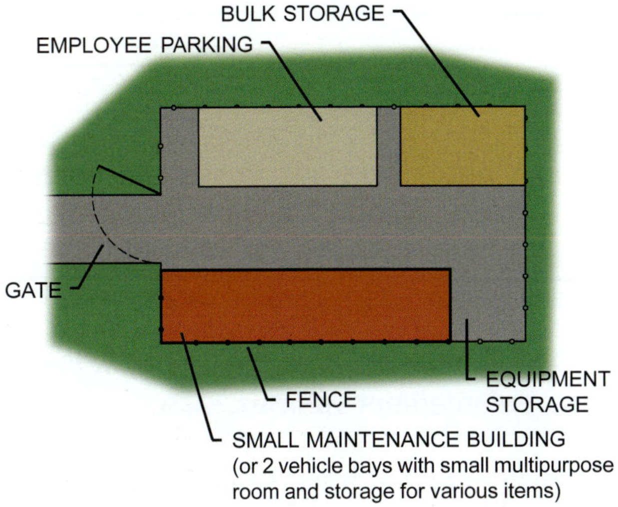

FIG. 30.3 – TYPICAL SUB-MAINTENANCE AREA

ADMINISTRATION

Facilities with heavy attendance, or major sites that are located at a considerable distance from the resource system's headquarters, will normally need secondary administrative facilities. These facilities can serve a dual function of public contact and site operations and maintenance.

LOCATION

Administrative buildings should be located adjacent to a public road and, generally, before any visitor entrance station to the facility. This will permit the resource's/site's business to be handled easily without conflicts with users.

PARKING

- Employee.

- Visitor cars and buses – If boating and/or camping are permitted in the facility, provide for car and trailer parking.

- Staff vehicles, especially patrol/legal enforcement vehicles.

Administration and maintenance facilities are frequently located within a short walking distance – 300 feet (100 m) - of each other. Screen from maintenance area.

RESIDENCE

There are four, possibly five, reasons for on-site employee housing: (1) remoteness, (2) reduction of vandalism, (3) protection of historic buildings and settings, and (4) security for overnight users. A fifth reason – enhanced recruiting – might also be a valid reason for on-site employee housing. Please be aware that government-built housing is frequently twice the construction cost of privately built homes.

REMOTENESS

Where facilities are located in areas remote from sources of housing for employees, provision must be made for their needs in the park.

Requirements:

- Privacy – locate away from public-use area.

- Access, if possible, is needed to public roads outside of any project control point(s).

- It is desirable to have easy access to the site area(s) where the employees are working – usually the office and/or maintenance area.

- Size and design character need to fit the intended resident and can vary from dormitory to apartments to single-family residences.

- Sites with overnight accommodations need 24-hour access to the facility's personnel, which may require some on-site housing.

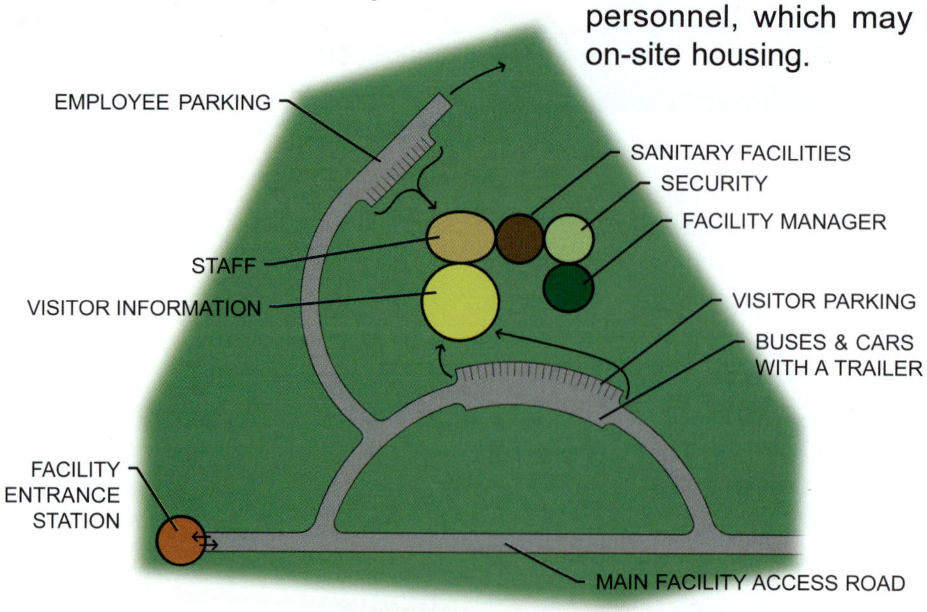

FIG. 30.4 – ADMINISTRATION – PUBLIC CONTACT

REDUCTION OF VANDALISM

Some resource sites subject to vandalism may need housing as a protective measure. One solution may be to use mobile or manufactured homes to house local law enforcement personnel.

Manufactured home for security personnel – Sugden Regional Park, Collier County, Florida

Requirements:

- Must have visual control of site access.
- Provide residence some degree of privacy.

RECRUITING

Provision of housing for various staff members can be useful as a recruiting tool. This is especially true for remote sites and for very desirable resort or destination areas. Care must be taken to analyze the housing needs/ desires of the perspective employees to ensure that the suitable type of accommodation is built in the right location.

PROTECTION OF HISTORIC BUILDINGS AND SETTINGS

Where buildings of historic or visual significance are to be preserved in a site, it is necessary to keep them occupied to prevent vandalism. This can be done by putting the employees in the buildings or by leasing them to private parties.

Requirements:

- Unobtrusive parking.
- Some privacy from site visitors.
- The buildings must be maintained at the appropriate level and kept in the correct character or style.

Chapter 31

SITE MANAGEMENT PLANNING

A management plan is the last step in the site design process described in the Introduction of this book, and much more completely covered in Chapter 11 of *A Site Design and Management Process*, published by NRPA. It is the necessary follow-up to any site plan and resulting development. Without a well thought out and implemented operations and maintenance plan, the best conceived project can soon become less than satisfactory and can, in fact, quickly become a major disaster.

Lack of maintenance in a major Caribbean island park

If there was a management plan that was enforced, this would not happen because the park would have been regularly checked and these obvious maintenance deficiencies taken care of.

INTRODUCTION

Comprehensive site management planning is not a new idea, but it is, however, still new to many resource managers. A comprehensive management plan combines several different functional areas: planning, operations, maintenance, and activity programming, where appropriate, into one integrated document. Some agencies, especially most federal and state land management agencies, have been preparing site management plans of varying degrees of completeness and sophistication for many years. [27]

All aspects of preparing a site management plan are discussed in detail in Chapter 11 of *A Site Design and Management Process*. Some facilities will require most, if not all, of the steps shown there. Some will require only a few. As in design, use only that much of the process that is necessary to manage the site under consideration effectively . Keep it as simple as possible so that the people for whom it is prepared (the planners, managers – especially the site manager and his staff – and in some instances, the public) will understand and use the management guide.

UNDERSTANDABILITY AND EASE FOR USE IS MOST IMPORTANT FOR THE SITE MANAGER AND, IN PARTICULAR, HIS STAFF. (27) Many agencies and companies employ operations and maintenance people who do not speak English fluently. Because of this, the portion of the management plan that they must implement might need to be translated into their native language.

Docent explaining the building activities and their affect on the surrounding gardens at one of the many buildings at Cambridge University, England

The plan must:

1. provide an adequate **DATABASE** for effective decision-making.

2. establish **DIRECTION** and **LIMITATIONS** for resource management, maintenance, and, to some extent, operations, programming, and, frequently, resource preservation.

3. ideally provide **BACKUP INFORMATION** on the facility, such as a record of the location of significant facts, maps, agreements, permits, and other pertinent information.

The amount of data required for small areas, e.g., neighborhood playgrounds, small tourist sites, and single-purpose areas, such as a tennis complex, would, of course, be much less than that needed for major multipurpose facilities.

WHERE TO START

Before starting the preparation of a management plan, there are a number of points that need to be resolved.

WHO IS THE PLAN FOR? WHAT SHOULD IT INCLUDE? (27)

WHO	WHAT
Management	Overall direction and control. Budgeting.
Staff	Continuity – especially useful when staff changes occur. This is particularly true for contracted operations and maintenance. Direction for establishing day-to-day operations and maintenance procedures.
Public	If it is a public project, the public has a right to know who the facility is intended to serve, what facilities and programs are to be provided, what is going to be available initially (or it has now), and what will be available in the future.

PUBLIC INVOLVEMENT – SHOULD THERE BE ANY?

The public should be involved:

1. only if you are truly interested in what they have to say.

2. if the facilities, especially public facilities, are to accurately reflect the affected users' needs.

3. if a good rapport with the users and neighbors is desired.

4. if you are going to use the public input, which may be different than the desires of the owners and/or managers.

If the decision is made to go "public," then do it openly and fairly.

WHO IS GOING TO DO THE WORK IN PREPARING THE MANAGEMENT PLAN – STAFF OR CONSULTANTS?

Be sure that whoever is chosen to do the management plan knows how to do such a plan. Most staff and consultants have previously not done so.

DATABASE

All management decisions are based on the information that is made available to the decision-maker(s). It is imperative that **NECESSARY** data be collected and presented in a clear, concise manner that can be understood by those who are going to use the document. Existing company and agency files – field and/or central office – should be checked first before looking to other sources. All information gathered from any source should be verified, where possible.

A reminder and a strong word of caution – collect **ONLY** the information that is **NECESSARY**. All too frequently, planners and, especially, scientists will collect data that is "nice" to have or that is useful, but not really needed, and seldom utilized in the decision-making process. Do not succumb to this temptation. **GET ONLY WHAT INFORMATION YOU NEED,** and then get on with the management planning process.

INTRODUCTION TO THE PROJECT / FACILITY SITE

ORIGIN OF THE PROJECT / FACILITY

What:

Prepare a complete, clear, and concisely written history of the project/facility; a chronology of events from its inception up to the present time. Include any significant staff and/or public meetings; legislative acts, i.e., city council, county commission, and state legislature. Record land acquisition information, including when started/finished, previous owners, maps, etc. Detail the project's construction history, if any. List all of the facilities in general, e.g., 500-car parking; 100-seat restaurant; ski area with four lifts, including graded and seeded slopes, snow-making equipment, and 150-room lodge. Note when construction started/finished, when first opened, and when additional developments were started, finished, and first opened, etc. Where possible, include names of people involved, such as the owner (present and past), citizen groups and their leadership, key individuals, etc. Whether the project is a private development or a government facility, people like to know about its origins.

How:

This is a classic research effort. Check the files first, both central office and field. Talk with those people who were around during the time the facility was established. If necessary, check local court deeds and records. These are usually located at the county seat.

LOCATION

What:

Maps and supporting text showing: (1) regional identity, (2) service area of the project (where the people come from), (3) access routes (how the people get there), and (4) governmental boundaries.

Why:

A must for those not familiar with the facility/ project and its surroundings. Necessary for administrators and site staff for identifying (1) governmental jurisdictions with whom they will be dealing, i.e., fire district, police district, sanitary district, etc., and (2) identifying from where the people using the site are coming, etc., and consequently, how they will arrive at the site.

SERVICE AREA

What:

The population area from which the project/ facilities will draw its patrons. The service area boundary should be determined by travel time and method of travel, not distance.

How:

People will only travel a limited distance (time) to get to any facility. The travel time/distance is dependent on the type(s) of activities and scale of the project. The extent of the service area may also be affected by population concentrations, uniqueness of the project features, availability of similar facilities at other sites within the service area, activities, promotion efforts, publicity, and, of course, accessibility.

Normally people will not drive over one and one-half hours, and usually less than one hour, to a day-use activity, such as a major shopping mall, the beach, etc. For an overnight-use area, such as Disney World, Six Flags, ski resorts, large national parks, etc., the distance is increased to two and one-half hours' travel time, and more if the features are unique. (See Fig. 1.1, Chapter 1, Methods for Determining Visitor Demand.)

PROJECT PURPOSE

What:

Describe briefly what the facility's (or administrative unit's) dominant or major identity or theme is, together with any other significant characteristics, if any. Why was the facility established? How is it supposed to be used? How is it actually used?

Why:

The reason(s) for the facility's development, be it commercial, governmental, residential, natural or historic preservation, park or recreational use, or other special purposes, strongly affects many of the facility's operating and management decisions.

Please note that in larger projects and resources systems, some way for the patrons to identify the type of park, recreation, or tourist area is necessary for marketing and management purposes. Although it is not necessary to label the resources by type for staff purposes, it is useful in setting each site's management approach. For public purposes, it is, in many situations, helpful in establishing public expectations. Hopewell Furnace National Historic Site in Pennsylvania would lead the user to believe it to be a historic site, not a place for swimming, picnicking, and camping. Their expectations would be met, if they found historical features and did not find a park with typical "park" features. Also, the government level or name is helpful for public identification and use level expectations.

A suggested system for designating parks and recreation and leisure facilities would include:

1. Natural resource-type area/facilities – and might be called "Parks" or "Natural Areas."

2. Historic/cultural resource areas facilities – and might be called "Historic Parks" or "Historic Districts."

3. Recreation activity-oriented parks – and might be called "Recreation Areas."

4. Preserves – areas (usually resource based) that are established for a specific "preservation"-type purpose, i.e., game or botanical preserve or perhaps archaeological preserve.

5. Special use parks – zoo, stadium complex, golf center, environmental education, etc.

A park may, of course, have more than one purpose. These other or secondary purposes should be listed and described in the same manner as the primary park purpose.

Secondary purposes or other functions, such as flood control, water supply, harbor protection, etc., must be included, where appropriate, as enhancements to or encumbrances upon the leisure facility's primary functions.

This same approach would also be helpful in understanding how a large tourist facility would be planned. Each function/activity brings certain expectations to mind and would be described in a similar manner as in the preceding example.

RELATIONSHIP WITH OTHER AGENCIES, GROUPS, BUSINESSES AND INDIVIDUALS

What:

In addition to governmental jurisdictional boundaries, ALL organizations and individuals that affect the project area should be identified.

Name of Facility	Type of Facility	Outstanding Features
Sheldon Waterfront Recreatoin Area	Recreation Secondary Purposes: • Natural system preservation • Historic interpretation of a major battle.	7 Miles of waterfront Unique sand spit formation with an endangered shorebird species nesting area. Major battleground events interpreted through dioramas and audiovisual displays.

FIG. 31.1 – EXAMPLE OF A MULTIPURPOSE PARK AND RECREATION FACILITY

Include full name, address, telephone number(s), and, if possible, the name of a contact person. Include here any special relationship that might exist, e.g., information or understood agreement with the seller of a large parcel of land that a portion of the land will be used for conservation purposes only. Although this informal agreement may have no legal standing, it would, however, be a major factor in how the facility would be developed and managed.

Why:

Necessary primarily for operation staff and management to know who to contact.

LEGISLATIVE AND ADMINISTRATIVE CONSTRAINTS

LEGISLATIVE CONSTRAINTS

What:

A list with an adequate description of any legislative or legal constraints that affect the site, e.g., designation of the river passing through the site as a state scenic river, thereby, precluding any buildings along the riverbank; project approval by the permitting agency or agencies states that the project must have 4-car parking per 1,000 square feet of sales area in a particular commercial development; existing rights-of-way through the site, such as subsurface mineral ownership retained by a previous owner, sewer pipeline easement through the back of the site that has not yet been utilized, etc.

Why:

These constraints can directly affect what can be done on and to the site.

ADMINISTRATIVE CONSTRAINTS

What:

List with an adequate description any using agency or owner policies that affect the site under study, e.g., policy to minimize the use of energy consumption, close the facility from 9:00 p.m. to 6:00 a.m., or a promise to a major supporter that the site will have some special facility.

USERS – EXISTING AND POTENTIAL

EXISTING USERS

Know your users.

What:

Information on the current users is needed and should include as a minimum:

1. Who the users are or will likely be.

2. Where they come from.

3. Number of users and what they do at the facility.

4. What they would like to do at the facility. This is often difficult to impossible to secure simply because people do not necessarily do what they say they will or want to do.

5. The degree of user satisfaction with existing facilities and programs.

This information will probably not exist and will be difficult and/or expensive to secure. If the facility or a similar facility is available, it may be possible to get user information from these facilities' operators. If not, a survey could be conducted. This is usually time consuming and can be expensive.

People will make their own walks if not properly provided for in the development.
– Municipal park in Copenhagen, Denmark

Why:

Development projects exist because of people. It is imperative to know which people use the facilities and what they expect from the area and facilities. The degree to which the facilities meet the users' expectations will determine their success.

POTENTIAL USERS

What:

A projection of who the future users will be, where they will come from, and what their interests and expectations will be is absolutely necessary. This will tell you how and at what level the facilities are to be maintained.

SITE AND ACTIVITIES INVENTORY

Most people who are actually responsible for on-site facilities and programs are usually concerned with what they must do on a day-to-day basis to keep the facilities and programs operational.

To assist in establishing the best direction for those day-to-day functions, it is necessary to know the current and proposed physical and program components of the site/project. Three major areas must be studied: (1) the natural resource base, (2) manmade facilities, current and proposed, and (3) program activities. The information must be recorded and analyzed clearly and concisely in both graphics and writing.

A reminder: **COLLECT ONLY THAT INFORMATION THAT WILL ACTUALLY BE NEEDED IN THE DECISION-MAKING PROCESS**.

NATURAL RESOURCE BASE

What:

Inventory all significant natural features of the site. The object is to know the site and its resources in sufficient detail to be able to manage those resources so that they will remain in the desired condition.

Tree graffiti – Europe

Why:

The base for all projects is the land and the facilities built thereon. It is necessary to know what is there and its sensitivity to use to be able to make effective decisions on how to manage the area. This is true for all levels and degrees of development, from the most primitive natural areas to intensive-use, urban, commercial facilities.

If you are not careful, this part of the management plan will get to be much too detailed and time consuming and, therefore, too expensive.

MANMADE FACILITIES

What:

Inventory and record information on all manmade features within the site area boundaries. Any major manmade features outside the site area that might significantly affect it should also be included.

Heavily used urban park and pathway – London, England

Why:

Most project areas have incomplete or inaccurate information on their physical facilities. For established projects, this information is vital for effective site operation, maintenance, and, especially, budgetary purposes. New projects require information on existing manmade features and facilities, including their condition and potential for park or recreation use.

Graffiti-decorated concert stage at an outdoor amphitheater – Norway

PROGRAMS AND ACTIVITIES

What:

A complete listing of all of the programs and activities occurring in the project area is needed. Current facility user figures should be included, if known, and estimated, if not known.

Why:

PROJECTS ARE NORMALLY BUILT FOR PEOPLE. How many people and how they use the resources and facilities is the major method or tool of determining the success of the development.

DIRECTIONS

The directions established in this portion of the management plan are the key to the project's success and its successful site operation and maintenance. All of the previous work only provides the necessary background for effective management planning decision-making.

There are two levels of decisions: (1) establishing first the overall direction for the entire project area (for small sites this may be all that is necessary), and (2) developing directions for the various components (management zones) of the overall project.

OVERALL DIRECTION

What:

Establish the primary and all secondary purposes for which the project is/will be managed. These purposes may be different from the original purposes previously described under "Database" - "Project Purpose" in this chapter. Include here only proposed project changes, including expanding the site.

Why:

A thorough review of the existing/proposed project, its surroundings, and its clientele has been completed. This review should have identified, if they exist, any discrepancies between the current purpose(s) and the site's resources and program capabilities to carry out these functions. In many projects, some or all of the original purposes may be in need of revisions and, possibly, complete change, e.g., a resort used for long-term stay has had an interstate highway built nearby and is found in the "Database" to be better suited for short-term business guests, or an area that was originally established as a "rural drive-to" park has become a "suburban" park surrounded by new industrial developments.

The **OVERALL DIRECTION** portion of the management plan is the heart of the plan. All subsequent directions, down to and including day-to-day operating of such things as pruning shrubs or planting flowers, take their cues from the overall direction.

Planting flowers – Eastern Europe

MANAGEMENT ZONE DIRECTIONS

What:

Establish management direction. Many project sites have areas or zones that have similar types of functions. These areas should be identified and shown on the map(s).

Why:

To enable the site manager to implement the overall project's direction(s).

How:

Establish management zones and, if necessary, sub-zones. Each zone and sub-zone identified must be listed and defined in sufficient detail so that there is no question as to what each is. The following five-zone functional grouping, in spite of its bureaucratic appearance, has been used successfully by the author in preparing a limited number of park management plans.

(1) Concentrated Use Zone(s):

All areas that serve concentrations of people should be considered in this zone, including land and water activities, and both day-use and overnight use. It does not include things such as pedestrian/bike/rollerblade paths, hiking trails, and dispersed activities like wildlife viewing, fishing, hunting, etc., which would be included in the Natural Zone (Land and Water).

Seasonal beach use
– Clam Pass County Park, Collier County, Florida

Larger sites – 100 acres (50 hectares) – may require several sub-zones. For example:

- Main Beach Use Area – give name to area, if possible, for ease of identification, e.g., "North Shore Area." Include all visitor services in each unit.
- Kobs Marina
- Big Cypress Resort
- Kingfisher Bay Visitor Center
- Winter Use Complex

(2) Support Zone/Administration:

This zone consists of the facilities that aid in the operations and maintenance of the facility and its surrounding area, including maintenance and administrative facilities. It will also include the necessary vehicular access and utilities (water, sewer, electrical, and telephone), and any staff housing. Plant nurseries, cutting-flower gardens, vehicular storage areas, etc., found in the site would be included under this heading.

Waiting area gazebo
– Clam Pass County Park, Collier County, Florida

(3) Historical and Cultural Use Zone:

All buildings and grounds that are historic or have historic qualities should be included in this zone. In addition, areas managed to demonstrate period agricultural fields and practices, historic or old formal gardens, and visually or culturally significant buildings and landscapes, should be considered. The National Park Service has done considerable research in this area of park management.

Historic buildings – this one with a sod roof
– Norway

(4) Controlled Limitation Zone:

This consists of any situation that occurs within a facility where complete owner control is lacking or limited. This might include such items as dangerous animals, non-owner utilities, public and private rights-of-way (roads, railroads), in-holdings, government-required landscape buffers, wetlands preserves, subsurface minerals (especially oil, gas, and coal), or water bodies (non-owner controlled, e.g., stormwater management areas, storage considerations). A brief but clear description should be prepared on what the nature and the extent of any limitations are.

Alligator protection zone - basically signs are used to keep people and alligators separated and NOT FRIENDLY.
Eagle Lakes County Park, Collier County, Florida

(5) Natural Zone (Land and Water)

This zone consists of the various types of natural ecological or natural-appearing areas that exist in the site, with the major emphasis being on the perpetuation of this natural condition. Some of the area may be jurisdictional (basically, do not disturb space for environmental or required mitigation or stormwater retention). Some dispersed types of activities, such as non-motorized trails, bird watching, nature study, cross-country skiing, and possibly hunting and fishing, may be included in this zone where the type of activity is compatible with the natural environment.

<u>Land</u> (may include some of all of the following):

- Bird watching.

- Grasslands, deserts, rock outcroppings.

- Original growth woodlands (low density recreation, e.g., trails, hunting, or no hunting, etc.).

- Environmental education/interpretive program areas (nature trail area, teaching stations).

- Natural feature(s) (scenic, geologic, etc.), unique areas specially set aside for preservation and interpretation.

- Natural area (limits must be clearly defined).

- Habitat zone (restricted entry by the public, e.g., bald eagle nest, red cockaded woodpecker, trout stream, etc.) – may be subject to controlled burns.

Controlled burn – used to maintain appropriate vegetative mix and growth – South Florida

Water (may include some or all of the following):

- Natural lakes and their shorelines.

- Natural-looking impoundments, streams, and swamps.

- Fishing.

- Stormwater retention areas (There may be vegetative restrictions on these areas.)

- Bird watching.

- Nature study.

Each management zone and any sub-zones included in the project site must be described and shown graphically. The description should include a brief but complete statement of the existing resource character, manmade facilities, and any identified problems. A map delineating the extent of the zone(s) and physical features is required.

The available material must be analyzed by the planner and/or the site manager to:

1. determine the extent the existing or proposed facilities and management practices aid in carrying out the established overall management directions.

2. identify deficiencies or problems.

3. develop solutions for the deficiencies or problems.

4. prepare management, planning, program and operational directions in sufficient detail to guide the carrying out of day-to-day working-level decisions.

IMPLEMENTATION

A management plan is only worth preparing if it is implemented. Implementation must be conducted at and reinforced by all levels of the agency managing the site from the decision-makers to the middle management, technical, and supervisory staff to, most importantly, the field staff.

WHO DOES WHAT

Decision-makers

The involvement (function) of the decision-makers(s) does not stop with the approval of the management plan. The staff must believe that all levels of the agency managing the site support the on-site staff's efforts to implement its provisions. This is particularly true during budget approval. Available monies should be channeled in such a way that they assist and support the staff in carrying out the management plan directives.

Technical, Supervisory, and Management Staff

Without the support of technical, supervisory, and management staff, the management plan will not, in the long run, be implemented. This is especially true on larger projects. These people must be available to provide both technical and morale assistance when needed. Through their allocating of resources to approved management plan efforts and discouraging and withholding assistance in non-approved directions, they can materially aid in carrying out the plan.

One specific activity that will go a long way in assuring field compliance in carrying out the management plan is for the appropriate management personnel to conduct at least an annual and, where needed, more frequent review of the site to determine how well the facilities are being maintained and operated.

Incorporated in the annual review would be a complete evaluation of the effectiveness of the management plan. During the site review, any adjustments needed in the plan should be discussed and necessary changes initiated.

Field Supervisor and His/Her Lead Workers

The project's management plan is the field supervisor's approved guide for the management, operations, activities, and programs in this area of jurisdiction. Within this framework, the manager should have the necessary freedom and authority to implement the plan.

Some tools toward effective implementation include the preparation, by the field staff, of a yearly work schedule and chart.

Task	Number and/or Positions Needed	Number Man Days Needed	Notes
Paint signs	2 Laborers	60	Install by March 1
Check boundary lines	1 Security	2	Check boundary encroachment
Overhaul lawn mowers	1 Maintenance	60	4 Power, 2 Tractor
Set up seasonal program and notify participants	Project Manager Program Specialist	2 20	Check for additional volunteers
Start request for seasonal help	Project Manager	2	Personnel Form X-22
Order supplies	Supervisor	20	Form 3.7-2 Estimates
Service all cars and trucks	1 Maintenance	20	Contract out major repairs
Cut 60 cords of firewood	4 Laborers	80	60 Full cords needed
De-winterize irrigation system	Etc.	Etc.	See details at golf maintenance building and pro shop
Re-start golfing			
Fertilize lawn			
Pick up all winter debris			
Drain and clean pool			
Paint and touch up pool complex			
Mow lawn in pool and concession			

FIG. 31.2 – YEARLY WORK SCHEDULE FORM FOR A NORTHERN U.S. PARK

WORKING LEVEL IMPLEMENTATION LIST

Open play field mowing at Paris Mountain State Park in South Carolina

The following is only an outline of items that should be covered in preparing **"working-level"** detailed implementation tasks. It is imperative that this portion of the management plan be prepared by the field staff and, where available, technical assistance should be provided by headquarters staff. It may need to be translated into the native language of the worker. A typical list would include Natural Resources, Operations and Program Activities, Maintenance, and Security. Each category would be broken down into its component parts.

NATURAL RESOURCES

Botanical – check for problem plants on the site and immediate surroundings, especially prohibited and/or nuisance exotics.

Melaleuca - Lee County, FL

Zoological – check insect and/or animal damage.

- Feral animals, especially non-native animals that may cause damage to the site – generally in relationship to natural areas, e.g., wild pigs, cats, dogs.

- Insects and animals that cause human problems and disease, e.g., fire ants, mosquitoes, rabid raccoons, poisonous snakes, etc.

Water Management

- Water quality control.

- Aquatic weed control.

Natural systems management plans – make sure the plans are current and that necessary action is being taken.

OPERATIONS AND PROGRAM ACTIVITIES

- Review current activities schedule and adjust for two new programs.

Cleaning the urban circulation system – Stockholm, Sweden

MAINTENANCE

- Check all buildings for any needed repairs.
- Check for termites and treat as necessary.
- Check for any carpenter ant infestation and treat.
- Install newly delivered boat docks.

SECURITY

- Verify that all patrol roads are usable.

When a project is planned and built and in use, its continued success will depend on the people who operate and maintain the facilities.

METRIC CONVERSION TABLES FOR COMMONLY USED PLANNING/DESIGN UNITS

ABBREVIATIONS

ac = acre
°C = degrees celsius
cm = centimeter
cu = cubic
ft = foot
ft^2 or SF = square foot
g = gram
gal = gallon
ha = hectare
in = inch
kg = kilogram
km = kilometer
l = liter
lb = pound
m = meter
m^2 or SM = square meter
Mg = megagram
mi = mile
mm = millimeter
sq 0^2 or S = square
yd = yard
yd^2 or SY = square yard

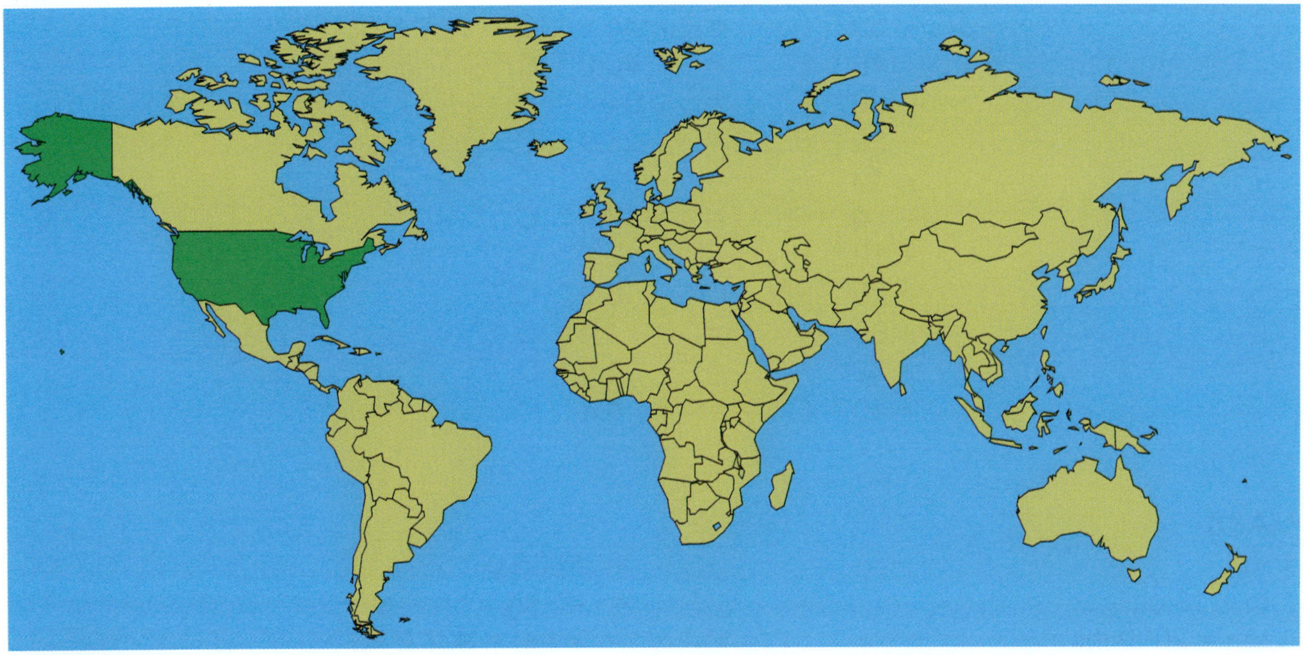

U.S. CUSTOMARY SYSTEM: The United States of America, Puerto Rico, and U.S. Protectorates

METRIC SYSTEM: The rest of the world

U.S. TO METRIC *

U.S. UNIT	METRIC EQUIVALENT
LENGTH	
1 mi = 1760 yds = 5280 ft	= 1609.3 m = 1.6093 km
1 yd = 3 ft	= 0.9144 m
1 ft = 12"	= 0.3048 m = 30.48 cm = 3048 mm
1 in =	= 2.54 cm = 25.4 mm
AREA	
1 sq mi = 640 ac = 1 section	= 2.59 km^2
1 ac = 43,560 ft^2 = 4840 yd^2	= 4046.7 m^2 = 0.40 ht
1 yd^2 = 9 sq ft	= 0.8361 m^2
1 ft^2 = 144 in^2	= 0.0929 m^2 = 92.9 cm^2
VOLUME	
1 qt	= 0.95 l
1 gal	= 3.79 l

TEMPERATURE

Degrees Fahrenheit **Degrees Celsius**

= 5/9 after subtracting 32
or (Temp in F. –32 x 1.8)

- 50 ° F.	=	- 45.5 ° C.
- 40 ° F.	=	- 40.0 ° C.
- 30 ° F.	=	- 34.4 ° C.
- 20 ° F.	=	- 28.9 ° C.
- 10 ° F.	=	- 23.2 ° C.
- 0 ° F.	=	- 17.8 ° C.
+ 10 ° F.	=	- 12.2 ° C.
+ 20 ° F.	=	- 6.7 ° C.
+ 30 ° F.	=	- 1.1 ° C.
+ 32 ° F.	=	0.0 ° C.
+ 40 ° F.	=	+ 4.4 ° C.

MASS	
1 oz	= 28.35 g
1 lb = 16 oz	= .45 kg
1 ton = 2000 lbs	= .9 mg = 907.2 kg

NOTE

2" = 5 cm so a 2" x 4" = 5 x 10 cm

METRIC TO U.S.*

METRIC EQUIVALENT	U.S. UNIT
LENGTH	
1 km = 1000 m	= .6214 mi = 3281 ft
1 m ** = 1000 cm	= 1.094 yd = 3.281 ft
1 cm = 10 mm	= .3937 in
1 mm	= .03937 in
AREA	
1 sq km = 100 ht	= 247.1 ac
1 ht = 10,000 sq mi (100m x 100m)	= 2.471 ac
1 sq m = 10,000 sq cm	= 1.196 sq yd = 10.76 sq ft
VOLUME	
1 cu m = 1,000,000 cu cm	= 1.308 cu yd = 35.31 cu ft
1 liter ***	= 0.26 gal = 1.057 qt

TEMPERATURE

Degrees Celsius		Degrees Fahrenheit
- 40 ° C.	=	- 40 ° F.
- 30 ° C.	=	- 22 ° F.
- 20 ° C.	=	- 4 ° F.
- 10 ° C.	=	+ 14 ° F.
- 0 ° C.	=	+ 32 ° F.
+ 10 ° C.	=	+ 50 ° F.
+ 20 ° C.	=	+ 68 ° F.
+ 30 ° C.	=	+ 86 ° F.
+ 40 ° C.	=	+104° F.
+ 50 ° C.	=	+122° F.
+ 60 ° C.	=	+140° F.
+ 100° C.	=	+212° F.

MASS	
1 g	= .035 oz
1 kg ****	= 2.2 lbs
I Mg	= 1.1 tons
I ton (t) = 1000 kg	= 0.9842 ton

NOTES

*   Calculations done with Metric Conversion Calculator by Radio Shack.
**   The easiest unit to use – 1 m is approximately 1 yard.
*** Essentially 1 liter = 1 quart or 4 liters to the gallon.
**** In lbs to kilos, 2.2 is it. There is no easy way.

BIBLIOGRAPHY

1. Ratios and Distances Between People, Land, and Facilities on Recreation Areas, U.S. Bureau of Reclamation (a summary from other "reliable sources").

2. Standards for Particular Recreational Activities and Facilities, U.S. Department of the Interior, Bureau of Outdoor Recreation, Northeast Region.

3. Snowmobile Manual, Commonwealth of Pennsylvania, Department of Forests and Waters, Bureau of State Parks, Ralph A. Romeo.

4. Analysis of Water Used in Camp Areas in Pennsylvania, Division of Outdoor Recreation, Department of Environmental Resources, Commonwealth of Pennsylvania.

5. Sanitary Fixture Requirements for Pennsylvania Park Facilities-Day Use, Engineering Report, Division of Outdoor Recreation, Department of Environmental Resources, 1973.

6. Concept Design Standard for Culvert Underpass, Larry Sharer, 1973, an unpublished report.

7. Sailing Facilities, Larry Sharer, October 1973, an unpublished report.

8. Commonwealth of Pennsylvania, Bureau of Resources Programming, unpublished research papers, Cyrus A. Yoakam, assisted by Pamela J. Werner, Division of Outdoor Recreation, based on 1971, 1972, and 1973 summer recreation surveys and other Pennsylvania state park user information.

9. Beach Capacities, Brij Garg, Pennsylvania Department of Environmental Resources, Division of Outdoor Recreation, 1973, an unpublished report.

10. Conversations with Kenneth Okorn, biologist, fisherman, and hunter.

11. 1975-1977 Summer Recreation Survey of Pennsylvania State Parks, June 1979, Division of Outdoor Recreation, Commonwealth of Pennsylvania.

12. 1977 and 1980 Summer Recreation Survey, questions on the effect of increased gas prices on visits to state parks, analysis by George Fogg.

13. The Recreation Trailbike Planner, Vol. II, No. 1.

14. "Off Road Vehicle Trends," Proceedings – 1980 National Outdoor Trend Symposium, Vol. II, U.S. Department of Agriculture, Forest Service, Garrett E. Nicholas.

15. Recap of International Travel To and From the United States in 1987, U.S. Department of Commerce, Washington, DC, July 1988.

16. Recreation Standards for Comprehensive Planning in Florida, Stephen M. Holland, Department of Recreation and Parks, University of Florida, Gainesville, FL, December 1988.

17. Rules of the Game (The Complete Illustrated Encyclopedia of All Sports of the World), Bantam Books, New York, NY, 1980.

18. The Sports Fan's Ultimate Book of Sports Comparisons, The Diagram Group, St. Martin's Press, New York, NY, 1982.

19. The Range Manual, National Rifle Association, Washington, DC, 1988.

20. National Golf Foundation, North Palm Beach, FL, 1987 data.

21. 1985 Survey of Fishing, Hunting, and Wildlife Associated Recreation, U.S. Department of the Interior, Fish and Wildlife Service web page.

22. Uniform Federal Accessibility Standards, General Services Administration, Department of Defense, Department of Housing and Urban Development, and U.S. Postal Service, as printed in the Federal Register, Vol. 49, No. 153, August 7, 1984.

23. Highway Noise, prepared for U.S. Department of Transportation, 1974.

24. Equestrian Sports, Sally Gordon, et. al., Pelham Books. London, UK, 1982.

25. "Trends in Private and Public Campgrounds 1978 to 1987," Trends, Vol. 26, No. 2, 1989, U.S. Department of the Interior, National Park Service/National Recreation and Park Association, Washington, DC, McEwen & Profaizer.

26. Design for Sport, Gerald A. Perrin, Butterworths, London, UK, 1981.

27. A Site Design and Management Process, George E. Fogg, National Recreation and Park Association, Ashburn, VA, 2000.

28. Park Guidelines for Off-Highway Vehicles, George E. Fogg in association with the National Off-Highway Vehicle Conservation Council, National Recreation and Park Association, Ashburn, VA, 2002.

29. Leisure-Time Physical Activity Among Adults: United States 1997-98, Advance Data, Charlotte A. Schoenborn and Patricia M. Barnes, Department of Health and Human Services, April 7, 2002.

30. National Forest Survey, 1999.

31. **Outdoor Recreation in America**, 2001.

32. **NSRE Survey**, 2000.

33. **National Bicycle Dealers Association**, Website data.

34. **National Sporting Goods Association**, Website data, 2003.

35. **National Golf Foundation Figures**, www.iseekgolf.com, 10/0/04.

36. **"Golf: An Update on the Movement Toward Full Inclusion of People with Disabilities,"** Jennifer K. Skulski, Access Today, 2003.

37. **Associated Press**, April 3, 2004.

38. **Quick Facts – National Survey of Fishing, Hunting, and Wildlife Associated Recreation**, U.S. Fish and Wildlife Survey.

39. **3-D Archery – A Guide to Course Design**, Michael O'Leary, The Regimental Rogue, 2004.

40. **What's New in 3-D Archery Range Design**, Jay Scholes, 1996.

41. **NFAA and IFAA Archery and Bowhunter Range Guidelines**, Paul H. Davidson, 2000.

42. **Walking and Biking Survey**, U.S. Department of Transportation, 2002.

43. **Anybody Want to Play Frisbee???**, Charles Witherspoon and Steven Liddle, July 18, 2003.

44. **So, You Want to Design a Disc Golf Course**, Disc Golf Association, www.discgolfassoc.com.

45. **Disc Golf Course Installation: Course Design**, www.innovadisc.com/coursedesign/course5.htm, 9/6/04.

GLOSSARY OF COMMONLY USED PARK & RECREATION PLANNING TERMS

4 x 4: A self-powered four-wheeled passenger vehicle, or light truck, having motive power available to all wheel positions.

4 X 4 EVENTS: Organized fun activities that test a four-wheel drive vehicle, the skill of the driver, and, at times, the passenger(s).

4 X 4 OBSTACLE COURSE: A designed course to provide training and practice for driving over terrain and obstacles a four-wheel vehicle driver may encounter while driving off of a highway surface.

4WD: A 4 x 4 vehicle.

ACCESS AISLE: An accessible pedestrian space between elements, such as parking spaces, that provides clearances appropriate for use by the disabled.

ACCESS ROAD: The road serving as the route of vehicular travel between an existing public thoroughfare and the park, recreation, or leisure area.

ACCESSIBLE: A site, building, facility, or portion thereof that meets the Federal Accessibility Standards and that can be approached, entered, and used by disabled people with physical limitations.

ACCESSIBLE RAMP: A walking surface to an accessible space that has a slope greater than 5 percent (1:20) and less than 8 percent.

ACCESSIBLE ROUTE: A continuous, unobstructed surfaced way connecting all accessible routes in a facility, and may include parking access, aisles, curb ramps, walks, ramps, and lifts.

ACTIVITY DAY: A measure of recreation use by one person in one facility or area for one day or part of a day. One person may exert more than one activity day per day. The activity day is probably most useful for apportioning total use to single uses and for sizing various parts of a given development.

ACTIVITY MIX: The term used to define the group of activities that a person or group participates in during a visit to a leisure facility.

ACTUAL OR PRACTICAL CAPACITY: The number of people that can use the area, considering the requirement of dual usage, traffic, vacant units, and the capacity of the land to support the people without deterioration of the resource.

ADA: Americans With Disabilities Act, i.e., the Federal act that requires that all new public built and remodeled facilities must have at least some of every type of facility accessible to the disabled.

ADAAG: Abbreviation for Americans With Disabilities Act Accessibility Guidelines for Building and Facilities.

ADMINISTRATIVE AREA: An area set aside for facilities used by an operating agency in administering a park, recreation, or leisure facility; may include office building, kiosks or visitor centers.

ALIGNMENT: The layout of a road or trail in horizontal and vertical planes; its bends, curves, and ups and downs.

AMENITIES: Any element used to enhance the visitor's experience and comfort during a park, recreation, or leisure facility visit.

AMERICAN COUNCIL OF SNOWMOBILE ASSOCIATIONS (ACSA): A national nonprofit association dedicated to providing leadership and advancing the efforts of all snowmobile-affiliated organizations to promote the expansion and education of responsible snowmobiling in the United States.

AMERICAN MOTORCYCLIST ASSOCIATION (AMA): A national membership organization comprised primarily of road, off-highway, and dual-sport motorcycle and all-terrain vehicle riding enthusiasts. Membership and association board representatives also include promoters and vehicle and after-market product manufacturers.

ANNUAL CAPACITY: The total capacity for use in a given year, considering the daily, weekly, and seasonal variations in density of use.

ARMORING: Reinforcement of a surface with rock, brick, stone, concrete, or other surface-hardening material.

ATV (ALL-TERRAIN VEHICLE): A three- or four-wheel vehicle, 50 inches or less in width, intended for off-highway use, which receives power transmission to the drive wheels from one motorcycle-type engine. The vehicle is controlled by the use of handlebars and is equipped with a seat that requires the rider to straddle the vehicle. ATVs are manufactured in four categories: general, sport, utility, and youth.

ATV RIDERCOURSE: A nationwide program developed and managed by the ATV Safety Institute to provide hands-on rider training with an emphasis on safety and skill development.

BACKCOUNTRY: An area where there are no maintained roads or permanent, modern buildings – just primitive roads and trails.

BACKSTOP (when used in conjunction with rifle and archery ranges): A device (usually a barrier) to stop or redirect bullets or arrows fired on a range.

BAFFLES (when used in conjunction with rifle ranges): Barriers to contain bullets and arrows and to reduce/redirect sound waves.

BATHHOUSE: A toilet building with showers.

BEACH: An area of shoreline, which is developed and/or designated for swimming use.

BERM (when used in conjunction with rifle ranges): An earth embankment used for restricting bullets or arrows to a given area or as a divider between ranges.

BERM: A mound of earth and/or stone used in many types of developments for visual effect and/or sound abatement.

BMX (BICYCLE MOTOCROSS) COURSES: Bicycle racing on a dirt track by same age groups. Vary in length from 1,000 to 1,500 LF (300 to 460 m).

BOAT DOCK: A facility located in or adjacent to the water, which is designed and constructed to provide for the mooring and/or in-water storage of boats.

BOAT LAUNCHING AREA: An area for boat launching and removal. Area could include a launching ramp, maneuvering and rigging area, and/or other launching facilities, such as a crane, tramway, etc.

BOAT LAUNCHING RAMP: A graded and surface-stabilized facility designed and constructed to allow for the launching and removal of boats from the waterway by means of boat trailers.

BUBBLE DIAGRAM: A schematic layout of a project or project component made up of "bubbles" of various sizes. These "bubbles" are shown in either their physical or functional relationships and are usually connected by lines showing circulation or relationships.

BUFFER AREA: An area set aside to preserve the integrity of an adjacent park, recreation, or leisure facility, and to prevent physical or aesthetic encroachment on that area.

BUNKER: See "Sand Trap."

"C" CURVE: Maximum flood level. This is a much greater height than that typically known as the flood plain for one-hundred-year floods.

CAD: Computer-aided design.

CAMPGROUND: A portion of land surface within a recreation area or recreation site, which is designated and at least partially developed for camp use. Includes camp units and/or campsite, roads, parking, sanitary facilities, water supply, etc. **Note:** Camp areas, campgrounds, campsites, camp units, and camp facilities are usually planned for family use. In general, the unmodified term "camp" implies family use (or use by other than a large group). Consequently, the modifier "group" should be used if group use is planned.

CAMPING: Overnight recreation use, which involves sleeping one or more nights in the out-of-doors. In this definition, "out-of-doors" implies outside of an established dwelling.

CAMPSITE: An area, which is constructed to accommodate camping use, e.g., a table, a camp stove, a fire ring, a tent site, a trailer space, etc.

CAPITAL BUDGET: The budget or a portion of a budget that is related to new construction and not to operations and maintenance.

CAREGIVER: That person responsible for the care and safety of another individual – usually an older person caring for one younger, but is becoming common for younger people being responsible for the elderly.

CARRYING CAPACITY: The amount of use that land can support over a long period without damage to the resource. It is measured in terms of recreation use per time unit (usually a day or a year), and varies with the conditions of rain, topography, soil, climate, and vegetative cover. It can be increased by protective measures, which do not in themselves harm the resources. The harmful effects of use greater than the sustainable carrying capacity can/will probably decrease the amount of use.

CC: The size displacement of an engine in cubic centimeters.

CIRCULATION ROAD: A road for vehicular traffic within the park, recreation, or leisure facility.

CLASSIC/VINTAGE: Motorcycles or events that feature motorcycles that are non-current models, typically of 1974 and earlier, or equivalent.

CLIMBING TURN: A turn that is constructed on a grade of 20 percent or less when measured between the exterior boundaries of the turn and follows the grade as it changes the direction of the trail 120 to 180 degrees. Climbing turns are encouraged, in place of switchbacks, on motorized trails.

COASTAL CONTROL SETBACK LINE (CCSL): The limit beyond which generally no hardscape construction can take place.

COMFORT STATION: Another term for toilet building that is commonly used by park and recreation professionals. (See "Restroom.")

CONCESSION AREA: That portion of the recreation area or facilities, which is to be operated by private parties and may include ski areas, food service, marina, motels, etc.

CONCESSIONAIRE: A person or business that contracts with a park, recreation, or leisure facility-operating agency (public or private) to run an operation.

CONSULTANT: An individual or organization hired to perform professional advisory or design services. Usually refers to architects, engineers, landscape architects, planners, etc.

CONTOUR INTERVAL: The vertical separation between contour lines – usually 1 foot, 2 feet or 5 feet (30 cm, 1m or 2m).

CONTOUR LINE: A line on a map connecting points of equal elevation.

CONTROLLED BURNS: Burning areas to manage the buildup of combustible material. Used to lessen the number and severity of wildfires. (See "Prescribed Burns.")

CORRAL: A fenced area for holding horses.

COURTESY DOCK: A facility located on the water adjacent to a boat launching facility and provided for the convenience of those using the launching and retrieving facilities.

C.S.: Comfort station – a toilet building.

CURB RAMP: A short ramp cutting through a curb or built up to it.

DAILY CAPACITY: The number of people who can use an area in a day, considering the rate of turnover.

DAY USE: Recreation use of an area for one day or less. Day use may include participation in a number of recreation activities, e.g., picnicking, play, water sports, sightseeing, etc., but excludes overnight use.

DAY-USE AREA: A portion of a park, recreation, or leisure area, which is designated for use by recreationists remaining in the area for one day or less. Does not include overnight use. Commonly a day-use area will be developed to accommodate a number of recreation activities, e.g., picnicking, sightseeing, water sports, etc.

DECIBEL LEVEL (dB): A level of sound; usually referred to in governmental ordinances.

DESIGN LOAD OR INSTANTANEOUS CAPACITY: The theoretical number of people the area can accommodate at a given moment.

DEVELOPED AREA PLAN: A drawing showing the existing and proposed development of a unit within a park, generally at a scale of 1 inch = 200 or 400 feet (1:2000 or 1:4000).

DEVELOPMENT PLAN: A plan showing development proposals for a given leisure facility or portion thereof.

DIRT TRACK (DXT): A prepared flat or banked oval dirt track between 2,250 feet (685 m) and 2,640 feet (805 m) in circumference designed for competitive motorcycle racing. (See "Short Track.")

DISC GOLF: A skilled recreation activity using a disc (a special Frisbee) to play "golf" on a 15- to 18-acre (6 to 7.3 ha) course

DISTANCE ZONE: Also known as "service area zone" or "travel zone." Areas are delineated around a recreation resource, measured by units of distance or travel time. The distance zone is used for defining populations from which users of a recreating resource come or will come. A better designation method is actual travel time and becomes freeform shapes.

DOG PARK: An enclosed space – usually a 3- to 4-acre (0.5 to 1.6 ha) site – where dogs can be let off of their restraints to run freely and interact with other dogs and people.

DRAG RACE: A time trial or a final race between two contestants from a standing start to a finish line over a measured distance.

DRAG STRIP: A prepared course of a given length, perfectly straight, with a hard, smooth surface, and sufficient distance beyond the finish line to allow a safe stop.

DUAL SPORT MOTORCYCLE (DSM): A four-stroke motorcycle originally manufactured and sold legal for street usage, and that is specifically designed for both on- and off-road riding. Depending on state requirements, some two-stroke and four-stroke motorcycles manufactured for off-highway trail use can be converted to street legal, dual sport motorcycles.

DUAL SPORT RIDE: A noncompetitive, long-distance, organized ride using street legal off-highway motorcycles. The ride is primarily on back roads, dirt roads, and trails, and is carried out on a designated route.

DUNE BUGGY or RAIL: A custom-built passenger vehicle specifically designed or modified for use off of paved roads, with four wheels, operated by a driver seated within the vehicle. Modification for use on beaches or in dunes may include extra wide or paddle tires.

ENDURO: A meet in which speed is not the determining factor, and a time schedule must be maintained. Enduros take place on a variety of terrain and on little-used roads and trails.

ENVIRONMENTAL ASSESSMENT: An assessment of a site to determine if it has any features of environmental significance, and usually required on all Federal projects.

ENVIRONMENTAL IMPACT STATEMENT/ REPORT: A report on the development of any project regarding its impact on the environment with alternative courses of action compared and a recommended direction established. Required on most Federally-funded projects.

EQUESTRIAN CAMPGROUND: An overnight facility designed for campers with their horses.

FIRING DISTANCE: The distance between the firing line and targets.

FIRING LINE: A line parallel to the targets from which firearms or arrows are discharged.

FISH CLEANING FACILITY: A structure designated and constructed to provide for the cleaning of fish and for the sanitary disposal of the unwanted fish parts.

FISHING PRESSURE: The amount of fishing that occurs.

FLAT TRACKS: A groomed dirt oval track one-quarter to one mile in length.

FLOOD PLAIN: Those areas subject to periodic flooding, usually defined as the "100-year flood."

FOOTPRINT: As in building footprint – the actual ground floor plan of a structure.

FORCE ACCOUNT WORK: Construction work done by in-house staff. Usually small scale, and frequently labor intensive. (See "In-House Construction.")

GARBAGE DISPOSAL SYSTEM: Those sanitary facilities, which are normally necessary to receive and dispose of garbage and refuse; also known as solid waste disposal.

GENERAL DEVELOPMENT PLAN: A drawing showing the existing and proposed development of a unit of the park system, generally at a scale of 1 inch = 500 feet (1:5000) or larger. (See "Site Plan.")

GIS (Graphical Information System): A computer program that integrates CAD with various graphic and statistical databases. It is useful for developing base maps and regional studies.

GO KARTS: Small, four-wheeled engine-driven vehicles with no suspension, a maximum length of 74 inches (188 cm), and a maximum width of 50 inches (127 cm).

GPS (Global Positioning Satellite): Used in accurate location of planimetric features, primarily on larger-scale projects.

GREEN: In golf, it is the place where each hole ends; sometimes called a putting green.

HABITAT ZONE: An area designated to be managed for the perpetuation of specific plants or animals.

HANDICAPPED ACCESS AISLE: Now referred to as accessible aisle. (See "Access Aisle.")

HANDICAPPED ACCESSIBLE ROUTE: (See "Accessible Route.")

HANG GLIDING: A recreation activity that uses non-powered, fixed-wing types of crafts, e.g., mini gliders.

HARDSCAPE: The term normally used for the built facilities portion of the landscape, e.g., walks, benches, fountains, walls, signs, trashcans, lights, play areas, etc.

HILLCLIMB: A series of trials against time or distance, or a series of match races against time or distance, on a specially prepared hill.

HOLE: In golf, it has two definitions; first, it is the entire combination of a tee, a fairway, roughs, hazards, and a green, which make up one unit of play. There are 18 holes on a normal golf course. The second definition is the hole in the ground located on the green, which is the ultimate target of each "hole" played.

ICE RACING: Meets conducted on short tracks and half-mile ovals marked on frozen lakes and ponds. A variety of motorcycles are used, with minor modifications made to the steering geometry, and the insertion of hundreds of sheet- metal screws placed through the tires.

IN-HOUSE CONSTRUCTION: Various projects that are carried out with company or governmental entity employees. (See "Force Account Work.")

INITIAL STAGE DEVELOPMENT: That portion of the total park, recreation, or leisure facility development that is constructed first. Ideally, the initial stage should be planned and constructed to accommodate a predicted level of visitation, e.g., an initial stage recreation development that will accommodate the predicted visitation in the tenth year of park operation.

INTERNET: A worldwide network of computer networks that use the TCP/IP network protocols to facilitate data transmission and exchange.

INTER-TIDAL ZONE: The coastal shore area between high tide and low tide.

JURISDICTIONAL: A term used to indicate that some governmental agency has an interest in and the legal authority to have some level of control over what can be done on a site. It has come to primarily refer to environmental matters.

JURISDICTIONAL AREAS: Those waters and wetland areas that a governmental agency can claim by law to have authority over its development. The Corps of Engineers is the agency at the Federal level that oversees wetlands.

KIOSK: A building or shelter so located in reference to the recreation area that it might be operated for the collection of fees, as a checkpoint for control of use, and/or for the dissemination of information.

LAND USE MAP: A map showing, in a diagrammatic fashion, the existing and/or proposed land uses.

LAND USE PLAN: A plan showing, in a diagrammatic fashion, the proposed facility uses.

LEISURE FACILITY: A development constructed for people to use during their leisure time.

LEISURE TIME: A person's time not required for the necessities of life in which activities, such as watching TV, playing football, going to a concert, playing cards, etc., may be done.

LIFE CYCLE: The expected useful life of any constructed facility.

LIFE CYCLE COST: (See "Lifetime Cost.")

LIFE EXPECTANCY: Like human life expectancy, all projects have a definitive length of time that they can survive and be utilized for their expected functions, usually figured at 20 to possibly 30 years. Major repairs are normally needed to extend the life expectancy of most projects.

LIFETIME COST: The cost of a project over its useful lifetime. Includes initial construction plus operations and maintenance costs.

LOOP TRAIL: A trail that returns the user to the original beginning point.

MAINTENANCE: The upkeep of the physical facility and grounds of a park, recreation, or leisure facility project.

MANAGEMENT PLAN: The controlling document that establishes direction for development, operation, programming, and maintenance of a park, recreation, or leisure facility.

MANAGEMENT ZONE/AREA: Area(s) within a site with similar functions, e.g., Customer or Visitor Use Zone, Natural Zone, Service Zone.

MARINA: A combination of facilities, which might include a boat launching area, boat launching facilities, boat dock, boat rentals, and boat service facilities (gas, oil, repairs, snack bar, etc.). The connotation is a general boat-associated facility that may be operated by a concessionaire.

MASTER PLAN: The document in written and graphic form that is proposed to guide the development of a park, recreation, or leisure facility.

MEET: A competitive activity during which one or more sports events and related practices for such events are conducted.

MGD: Millions of gallons per day.

MICROCLIMATE: The climate in a small area, e.g., a shaded, windy area between buildings or an exposed hillside.

MITIGATION: Usually refers to the repair or replacement in kind, either on site or off site, of environmentally- sensitive lands.

MOORING RAIL: A device to secure boats located along the edge of a body of boating water; basically, a boat bicycle rack.

MOTOCROSS (MX): A meet conducted on a closed course that includes left and right turns, hills, jumps, and irregular terrain.

MOTORCYCLE: A two-wheeled vehicle receiving power only to the rear wheel from a single motorcycle engine.

MOTORCYCLE INDUSTRY COUNCIL: A not-for-profit trade association representing manufacturers and distributors of motorcycles, parts and accessories, and other allied trades.

MOUNTAIN BIKE: A two-wheeled bicycle specifically designed to be ridden on rough terrain with multiple gears, straight handlebars, and a strong braking system.

MUD or SAND DRAGS: A timed, competition event over a specified distance through a designed mud or sand course.

NATIONAL OFF-HIGHWAY VEHICLE CONSERVATION COUNCIL (NOHVCC): A national, not-for-profit, educational foundation that promotes off-highway vehicle enthusiast club and association development, and provides educational materials and programs to improve OHV recreation management, opportunity, and resource protection.

NATURAL AREA: An area, sometimes within a park, which is left generally undeveloped for passive recreation use, and usually serves the function of enhancing the aesthetic quality of the overall development.

NON-RECURRING MAINTENANCE: Usually major, costly items that must be carried out to keep the facility functional.

NRPA: National Recreation and Park Association.

O & M: A commonly used term among property managers for operations and maintenance, i.e., the O & M budget.

OBSTACLE COURSE: A course designed to test riding or driving skills through, around, and over natural or built obstacles.

OFF-HIGHWAY VEHICLE (OHV): Any motorized vehicle specifically designed for travel off of paved highways. OHVs generally include off-highway motorcycles (OHMs), dune buggies, four-wheel drive vehicles (4WDs), snowmobiles (OSVs), and all-terrain vehicles (ATVs).

OFF-HIGHWAY VEHICLE PARK: A park designed, developed, and operated to primarily serve the needs and desires of OHV enthusiasts.

OFF-ROAD BICYCLES: (See “Mountain Bike.”)

OHM: An off-highway motorcycle.

ON-SHORE RECREATION FACILITY: A recreation facility that is provided in relation to a water-associated recreation area.

OPERATIONS: The day-to-day operating of a park, including security, clean-up, trail grooming, interpretation, etc.

OPERATIONS MANUAL: A document usually prepared by staff and/or suppliers describing how a facility or piece of equipment is to be operated and maintained.

ORV: An off-road vehicle – a former term for what is now more commonly referred to as off-highway vehicle (OHV).

OSV: An over-snow vehicle, most commonly a snowmobile. (See “Snowmobile.”)

OUTSOURCING: The process by which a private or governmental entity contracts work for various tasks outside of the agency or company.

OVERLOOK: A sightseeing and/or observation area so located and constructed that visitors can view a dam, reservoir, lake, surrounding countryside, and/or other objects or areas of interest.

OVERNIGHT USE: A portion of a development that is designated for recreational use that includes an overnight stay. An overnight use area may include a campground, motels, hotels, cabins, lodges, etc., and may include other facilities primarily for use by the overnight guests, e.g., boat ramp, trails, etc.

PAINTBALL: A sport where the participants are tagged by a paintball marker. Requires a restricted use area and natural or manmade cover.

PARAGLIDING: Very similar to hang gliding, except it uses an inflatable canopy. It is lightweight and can be taken almost anywhere.

PARKING AREA: An area designated and constructed for the parking of vehicles. Implies parking developed for a number of automobiles, pickup trucks, etc., e.g., a parking lot. A specialized type of parking area is needed for buses and in connection with boat-launching areas, equestrian areas, and off-highway vehicle areas.

PARKING SPUR: An area designated and constructed for the parking of a vehicle. In a campground, it implies a parking area for one or two small vehicles or a trailer and one or two small vehicles.

PARTICIPATION RATE: The percentage of the population that participates in any given activity.

PASSIVE USE: That type of use that involves limited physical activity, e.g., bird watching, picnicking, etc. This is in contrast to active use, e.g. sports activities, rock climbing, etc.

PEAK LOAD DAY: The day of maximum use, usually the Fourth of July or some other major holiday.

PEEWEE TRACK: A track designed and restricted to OHMs and ATVs of 80 cc or less. Peewee tracks, also referred to as children's or beginner tracks or loops, are generally for young riders just learning to ride.

PERCENT (%) GRADE: A figure used in determining the rise or fall of the ground. Vertical change (distance) divided by horizontal distance = % grade.

Ph: Soil acidity or alkalinity; a Ph of 7 is neutral, less than 7 is acid, and over 7, alkaline.

PHASING (PHASED DEVELOPMENT): The construction of recreation facilities in stages. The basis for phasing or phased development may be recreation demand (for types and/or numbers of facilities), availability of funds, etc.

PHYSICALLY LIMITED (formerly referred to as handicapped): An individual who has limitations, including mobility, sensory, manual, or speaking abilities, which result in a functional limitation in access to and use of a facility.

PICKET LINE: A line of stakes or posts temporarily connected with a rope to act as a holding area for overnighting horses.

PICNIC: A type of day-use recreation that includes at least one meal in the open air. **Note:** Picnic areas, picnic grounds, picnic sites, picnic units, and picnic facilities are usually planned for either family use or group use. In general, the unmodified term "picnic" implies family use (or use by other than a large group). Consequently, the modifier "group" should be used if group use is planned.

PICNIC AREA: That portion of land surface within a recreation area or recreation site designated or zoned for picnic use.

PICNIC FACILITY: A device that is constructed to accommodate picnic use, e.g., a table, a stove.

PICNIC UNIT: A group of facilities developed to accommodate picnic use.

PIT AREA: The location where participants set up their equipment for practice and/or events.

PLANT ASSOCIATIONS: A group of plants that is normally found together, usually in similar conditions, e.g., alders, willows, and cattails, are usually found together in wet areas.

PLAY AREA: A space, usually with play apparatus, and generally for young children ages 3 to 12.

PLAY FIELD: Open play space for activities such as Frisbee, softball, volleyball, football, etc.

POST CONSTRUCTION EVALUATION: Review of a project after it has been in operation to determine how it is being used and whether the built facilities are physically working as planned.

POTABLE WATER: Water that can be used for drinking.

PRESCRIBED BURNS: Areas of a project designated for undergrowth management through controlled burning. Used to control types of vegetation and limit the effects of wildfires.

PRIMARY USE SEASON: The time of year when the heaviest park, recreation, or leisure facility use occurs. Usually the summer season in northern areas, but may be winter for ski areas, and for some southern areas it may be all year round or primarily during the winter.

QUASI-PUBLIC: Agencies that are open to the public and are owned and/or operated by a nonprofit organization such as the "Y," religious groups, Elks, etc.

RECREATION: An activity beyond that required for personal or family maintenance or for material gain; that is, for enjoyment rather than for survival.

RECREATION AREA: That portion of land and water surface that is designated for recreation use.

RECREATION DEMAND: The measured, implied, or predicted ability and desire of the people in a designated recreation service area to expend (exert) recreation in a designated recreating resource. It may be latent, as in an undeveloped area that would be used if it were developed. It may be expressed or measured in units of use plus units turned away.

RECREATION FACILITY: A specific device provided to accommodate recreation use, e.g., a table, stove, road, marina, or museum, etc.

RECREATION SITE: A parcel of land within a recreation area that has recreation potential and is designated for recreation development and use. Does not imply specific development for the type of designated recreation use.

RECREATION UNIT: A grouping of recreation facilities that is constructed to provide a type of recreation accommodation, e.g., a camp unit is a type of recreation unit and is developed with the following facilities: a table, camp stove, parking spur, tent or trailer space, etc.

RECREATION USE: The occupation, utilization, consumption, or enjoyment of a recreation resource, or of a particular part of a recreation resource.

REMOTE-CONTROLLED MODELS: Any type of model (planes, cars, boats, trucks, farm equipment, etc.) with a power source that can be controlled with electronic signals from a nearby (remote) station.

RESTRICTED USE ZONE: A portion of a park, recreation, or leisure facility that is designated to serve a specified recreation function or functions to the exclusion of other activities.

RESTROOM: A building designed and constructed as a portion of the sewage system that contains toilet facilities.

RETENTION AREA: An area constructed to hold stormwater run-off.

RIPARIAN: Relates to the shore of a watercourse or body of water.

ROCK RUN: A short trail section for off-highway vehicles that is made up of large rocks placed to test the driver's skill and equipment capability.

ROUGH: In golf, it is an area outside the fairway that is still within the course playing area and which can be rough and have little care.

SAFETY ZONE: The area needed to ensure the safety of shooters, spectators, and other people. This is the zone where bullets, arrows or vehicles and other objects will impact, taking into consideration the installed protective berms, baffles, etc.

SAND BUGGY: A dune buggy or rail with rear paddle tires and smooth front tires specifically designed or modified for driving in sand

SAND TRAP: In golf, it is an area void of vegetation and filled with sand. They are strategically placed around a golf course to make the game more challenging; sometimes called bunkers.

SANITARY FACILITIES: Developments of services that are necessary for the disposal of human wastes in a manner that will protect the public health and environment.

SCRAMBLES: A meet for motorcycles or ATVs designed more to test rider skill rather than the speed of the vehicles. Scrambles are conducted on an unpaved, prepared course between one-quarter mile and two miles long, and include left and right turns, hills, and other natural terrain.

SEASONAL USE: The numbers of people using a facility during various seasons. Most facilities experience variations in the numbers of users during different times of the year, e.g., skiing, Christmas shopping, and summer tourism are seasonal activities.

SERVICE AREA: An area set aside for facilities used in routine operation for maintaining a park or recreation area; may include equipment yards, shops, and dwellings. A second definition is the area served by the park, recreation, or leisure facility.

SERVICE ROAD: Vehicular road within a park, recreation, or leisure area used primarily for maintenance vehicles. This road may also serve as a public pedestrian path or fire trail.

SEWAGE DUMPING STATION: A facility for the disposal of human wastes from camp trailers.

SEWAGE SYSTEM: Sanitary facilities that are normally necessary to dispose of waste products of the human body, food preparation, showers, and laundry facilities.

SHARED-USE or MULTIPLE-USE TRAIL: A trail utilized by two or more trail interest groups, which may or may not include both motorized and non-motorized use.

SHOOTING RANGE: Places where people may participate in recreation, competition, skill development, training with firearms, archery equipment, and/or air guns.

SHORELINE MOORING: An area designated for boat tie-up along the shore of a body of water. Frequently requires grading and a mooring rail and/or boat storage rack.

SHORT TRACK: A prepared flat or banked oval dirt track less than 2,250 feet (685 m) in circumference designed for competitive motorcycle racing. (Also see "Dirt Track.")

SITE PLAN: A plan drawn to scale on a topographic base map showing all of the features of the proposed development. Elements included are building locations, parking, roads, walks, bicycleways, play areas and/or facilities, plant masses, lawns, various management areas, major grading, and other appropriate features. All of these are shown from the point of view of a ground floor plan.

SIZING: The level capacity, volume, magnitude of development within a stage of development, e.g., a given facility may be sized for a larger capacity than is needed in initial stage development. Initial stage development sizing is primarily a function of economic considerations.

SKATEBOARD: An over-sized roller skate similar to a surfboard or ski board.

SNOWMOBILE: An engine-driven vehicle manufactured solely for travel over snow that has an endless belt tread and sled-type runners or skis, and that a rider sits astride to operate. In some parts of the country, particularly Alaska, snowmobiles may be referred to as snowmachines or snowgos.

SOLID WASTE: Rubbish, trash, etc. (See "Garbage Disposal System.")

SOUND BASIN: An area where sounds can be heard; usually the line of site, excluding vegetation, from the source of the sound.

SPEEDWAY: A prepared flat, oval track less than 2,250 feet (685 m) in circumference designed for competitive racing with lightweight, four-stroke motorcycles equipped with no brakes, and designed specifically for power sliding.

SPRAYGROUNDS: Spaces similar to traditional playgrounds, only the primary feature is water play – zero depth.

SPREADSHEET: A chart showing a number of pieces of information. It is usually computer-generated and used for such things as estimating, plant lists, color schedules, etc.

STABILIZED TURF: An area that has been constructed for occasional use for parking or vehicular access. Usually requires grading, improved drainage, and generally a gravel surface or manufactured reinforcing material, choked with fines and seeded/sodded.

STAGING AREA: A designated area where park visitors gather prior to riding or driving in dispersed recreation experiences.

STATIONARY SOUND TEST: A test procedure, approved by the Society of Automotive Engineers (SAEJ1287 JUL98), to readily test vehicle sound levels in the field.

SUPPORT FACILITIES: As used in this text, it refers to the facilities necessary to support the planned development. They are usually utilities, such as water (including fire), sewage, electrical, and communications systems. They also may include signage and maintenance facilities.

SUSTAINABLE DESIGN: A design that results in a completed facility that is easily maintained with a limited use of resources.

SUV (SPORT UTILITY VEHICLE): A street legal, high clearance vehicle used primarily on-highway, but designed to be capable of off-highway travel.

SWIMMING: A general term that includes actual swimming, water play, wading, etc.

SWIMMING AREA: That portion of a body of water designated specifically for swimming use.

SWIMMING IMPOUNDMENT: A portion of a reservoir, lake, or stream that is specifically constructed for swimming and/or swimming use, e.g., an arm of a reservoir that may be diked to form a sub-impoundment for swimming.

SWITCHBACK: A sharp turn in a trail that reverses the direction of travel in order to reduce grade while still allowing gain in elevation on slopes generally 15 percent or steeper. The turning portion of the switchback is the "landing;" the approaches to the landing are the "upgrade" and "downgrade."

TEE: In golf, it is the place from which each hole begins. It is frequently different for men and women.

TIME TRIAL: An event in which a participant competes against a clock.

TOPO: Topographical information for a site.

TRAIL: A pathway or roadway designed and constructed to carry other than normal vehicular traffic. Use of a trail may be as restricted as is desired by the recreation operator. For example: Hikers, hikers and cyclists, or motorized vehicles, etc. may use a trail.

TRAIL GROOMING: Refers to the care of trail surfaces, including snow surface on winter-use trails, for both snowmobiles and cross-country ski trails.

TRAILBED: The finished surface on which base course or surfacing may be constructed. For trails without surfacing, the trailbed is the tread.

TRAILHEAD: A developed area that serves as the beginning point of a trail and includes at least parking, trail information, rubbish containers, and usually water and sanitary facilities.

TRANSIENT CAMPER: A camper who is staying in an area overnight only while en route to his ultimate destination.

TREAD SURFACE: Wearing surface of a trail.

TREAD WIDTH: The width of the actual travel way.

TRIALS MOTORCYCLE: A motorcycle manufactured specifically for observed trials competition. The bikes are extremely quiet and operated at low speed on very technical and difficult course terrain.

TRICK BIKE: A specially equipped bicycle used for stunts; usually in a skate/bike park.

TURNOVER RATE: The number of times a given facility is used during a given period of time, usually a day.

UFAS: Abbreviation for Uniform Federal Accessibility Standards.

UNIVERSAL ACCESSIBILITY: The design of a facility so that basically all of the site and its activities are accessible to people with all levels of ability.

UNIVERSAL DESIGN: Designing facilities to be usable to all people, to the greatest extent possible, regardless of age, size, or abilities.

USER DAY or VISITOR DAY: A measure of recreation use by one person for one day or part of a day. It may be brief or it may be as long as 24 hours. Brief views, as from a highway, are not visits in this sense nor are brief stops at such places as overlooks. So far as accuracy of data permits, one person will log only one visitor day at a given recreation resource during any 24-hour day. The visitor day is probably the most convenient unit for purposes of economic analysis; it is probably less convenient when used for sizing recreation facilities and apportioning total use to various activities.

USER DEMAND: The number of users that would use a facility if it were available.

USGS: The United States Geological Survey.

USGS QUAD SHEET: Maps covering the United States prepared by the U.S. Geological Survey; usually at a scale of 1:24000 or 1inch = 2000 feet (2.5 cm = 610 m).

VAULT TOILET: A "primitive" bathroom without running water where human wastes are stored in a waterproof vault, and are periodically pumped out by a special "honey wagon" tank truck for disposal into an approved system.

VECTOR MANAGEMENT: Utilization of site maintenance procedures that will minimize the presence of dangerous animal/insect populations.

VECTORS: Nuisance and/or dangerous animal/insect populations that can endanger the health of the visitors.

VENUE: An area designed to support specific organized recreation activities, e.g., motocross, equestrian facilities, downhill skiing, etc.

VISITOR or USER PROFILE: Information on the people who use or will use a facility. The data is gathered from all available sources, but may frequently require user surveys.

VISUAL RESOURCE SURVEY: A graphic report of the key visual points in a facility, both good and bad.

WATER-ASSOCIATED RECREATION: Recreation that is carried on at, near, in, under, or because of the presence of standing or running water.

WATER HAZARD: In reference to a golf course, it is a watercourse (even when containing no water) or any other areas of water, i.e., ponds, lakes, reservoirs, rivers, streams, and even drainage ditches.

WATER SYSTEM: Facilities, including developments for supply, treatment, storage and distribution that supply water to the recreation area and/or recreation sites.

WC (Water Closet): A term used in much of the world to describe a toilet or a toilet building.

WH (Washhouse): A building containing laundry facilities and showers in addition to toilets.

WINTERIZATION AND DE-WINTERIZATION: Preparing a project site and/or building for the winter or non-seasonal use and then readying them again for the use season. Normally refers to buildings and water and sewer systems in seasonally-used facilities or portions of facilities in the sections of the country where freezing occurs.

X SPORTS (EXTREME SPORTS): Consists of non-traditional recreation activities, such as trick biking, skateboarding, snowboarding, bouldering/climbing walls, etc.

XERISCAPE: The design of a project for effective conservation of water. Includes such things as minimizing plantings requiring irrigation, grouping plants of like water needs, and water conserving irrigation design.